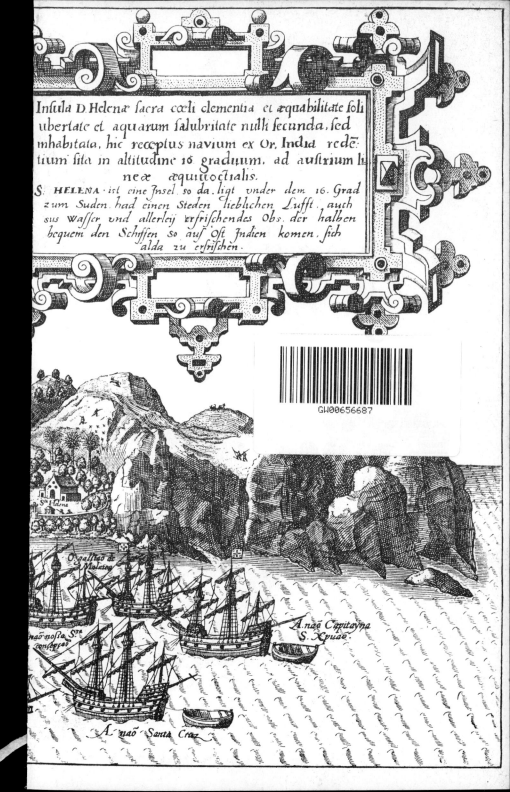

Infula D. Helenæ facra cœli clementia et æquabilitate foli
ubertate et aquarum falubritate nulli fecunda, fed
inhabitata, hic receptus navium ex Or. India redē-
tium fita in altitudine 16 graduum, ad auftrium li-
neæ æquinoctialis.

S. HELENA · ift eine Infel. fo da. ligt vnder dem 16. Grad
zum Suden. had einen Steden lieblichen Lufft, auch
sus Waffer vnd allerleij erfrifchendes Obs. der halben
bequem den Schiffen fo auß Oft Indien komen, fich
alda zu erfrifchen.

Sᵗᵃ Helena

Os galleao de
Malaca

naõ noffa Sⁿᵃ
conceyçaõ

A. naõ Cappitayna
S. Xpuaᵒ.

A. naõ Santa Craz

ST. HELENA
1502–1938

St Helena

1502-1938

*

Philip Gosse

Introduction by Trevor Hearl

Anthony Nelson

© Jennifer Gosse
Introduction © Anthony Nelson Ltd

This new edition published 1990 by Anthony Nelson Ltd,
PO Box 9, Oswestry, Shropshire SY11 1BY, England
First published by Cassell & Co, London, England 1938

ISBN 0 904614 39 5

Printed by The Bath Press, Avon

THE ENDPAPERS
The endpapers are taken from the earliest published view
of St Helena, sketched 400 years ago, in 1589, by Jan
Huyghen van Linschoten (c.1563–1611), Dutch
navigator of a Portuguese fleet returning from Goa.
  It was engraved at Amsterdam that year by Baptista
van Deutecum for Linschoten's *Itinerario* (1596).

TO
GEOFFREY CHARLES KITCHING
ST. HELENA

PREFACE

PROBABLY no spot in the whole world has become more closely associated with the name of one man or with one historical event than St. Helena. It is little exaggeration to state that to ninety-nine people out of every hundred the name St. Helena conveys the place of incarceration of the great Napoleon and nothing else. Surprisingly few seem to know, or to be quite certain if the Island is even a British possession.

Yet this little, and now almost forgotten tropical isle, lying remote and isolated in the vast expanse of the South Atlantic Ocean, has a vivid history of four hundred and thirty-six years, and has been in unbroken possession of Great Britain for two hundred and fifty-five, and therefore can boast of being one of her oldest colonies. Though to-day one of the least important and most impoverished members of the British Empire, St. Helena once was, for her size, the most important and vital possession of them all.

Sic transit gloria S. Helenae.

In the pages which follow, an attempt has been made to shew that without St. Helena there would be no British possessions in the far East to-day. She has had her ups and her downs; at present she is in a bad way, but there are good reasons for believing that better days for her are in sight, and if this book should prove to be an instrument, however humble, towards her return to prosperity, then it will not have been written in vain.

A vast quantity of ink has been spilled over the captivity of

Napoleon. Having nothing new to say or offer about this much over-written period, I have endeavoured to treat those few if important years with a just sense of their relative value to the rest of the Island's history. Yet in spite of the fine combing of all available material which has gone on for more than a century in the endeavour to find anything new about the Captivity, I have had the good fortune to discover in the files of an old St. Helena newspaper a long and curious piece of rhyming doggerel concerning Napoleon's life and death at St. Helena which appears to have escaped the notice of all the historians of the Captivity. I have been unable to resist the temptation to print it at full length, not only for the benefit of those who make a closer study of that epoch, but also to gratify my own vanity in having unearthed it.

In the compilation of a work such as this, the author must of necessity be under an obligation to the researches, the knowledge and also the kindness and generosity of others. It is not possible to thank, in this preface, every one of my benefactors, but only to name a few to whom I am most indebted.

First and foremost there is Mr. G. C. Kitching, O.B.E., Government Secretary at St. Helena. His knowledge of the Island and its history is profound, and this, with his writings on the subject, he has most generously put at my disposal. Other friends at St. Helena to whom I offer my thanks are the Reverend Canon L. C. Walcott, Dr. Paul Wilkinson, Mr. E. J. Warren, J.P., Mr. G. E. Moss, and Mr. Kenneth Toms. I also take this opportunity to thank Mr. W. C. Palmer, M.A., for the invaluable help derived from his thesis: *The History of St. Helena and the Route to the East Indies, 1659–1702,* which is in the keeping of the Institute of Historical Research, London, where I was kindly allowed to examine it; and the London University Library for the loan of a copy of the same thesis. My thanks are offered to Dr. Arnold Chaplin, the authority on the

Captivity and author of *The St. Helena Who's Who*, from which he, and the publishers, Messrs. Hatchards of Piccadilly, have permitted me to quote several passages; to Mr. N. B. Kinnear, Mr. F. C. Fraser, D.Sc., and Mr. H. W. Parker of the British Museum (Natural History), to Mr. G. E. Manwaring, F.R.Hist.S., of the London Library, and to Sir William Foster. At the Colonial Office I received every assistance, particularly from Mr. A. J. Dawe, O.B.E., and Mr. O. G. R. Williams, C.M.G., as well as from Miss Bromley and other members of the library staff. I am under a deep obligation also to the staff of the India Office library, where I was rendered much assistance by Mr. W. T. Ottewill, O.B.E., Superintendent of Records, and Mr. S. C. Sutton, B.Sc.

Captain C. R. Boxer, the authority on early Portuguese Naval history, gave me valuable help, and needless to say I have made copious use of the publications of the Hakluyt Society.

Mr. R. Bylsma, Rijksarchivaris, The Hague, has given me permission to reproduce a photograph of a rare Dutch document, and I thank, as well, Mr. L. C. Vrijman for bringing it to my notice.

Sir Geoffrey Callender has been more than kind in shewing me various treasures, particularly early maps of St. Helena, which are in his keeping at the National Maritime Museum at Greenwich, and he has obtained permission of the Trustees for photographs of some of them to be reproduced.

The Hon. Ben Bathurst has allowed two interesting photographs of portraits of Sir Hudson Lowe to be used for illustration.

Many descendants of Governors of St. Helena in the days of the East India Company, and of other distinguished St. Helenians have lent me letters and other unique family records, and owing to their generosity and kindness I have been able to reproduce several interesting portraits.

Amongst these benefactors I particularly wish to express my deep gratitude to Mrs. J. R. B. Atkinson, Mrs. E. B. C. Boddam, *née* Olivia Walker, Admiral C. F. Dampier, Mrs. F. S. Gray, Mrs. H. J. Hands, *née* D. Bennett, Lt.-Col. C. St. L. Hawkes, Miss E. Hyde-Gardner [Janisch], Mr. Basil H. Johnson, Mrs. Frederick Lonsdale [Brooke], Mr. A. C. Marshall, Mr. Digby Marshall, Mr. John B. Murray, Dr. J. A. Nixon, Mrs. David E. Norton, *née* Maud Bazett, Miss E. H. Patton, Mr. Philip C. Patton, Lt.-Col. H. E. Pritchard, Mr. Reginald M. Tuke and Mr. Dundas Walker.

Messrs. Ellis and Smith, of Grafton Street, brought to my notice a superb portrait in their galleries of Governor John Skottowe and kindly had a photograph taken of it for reproduction.

Miss G. Matthews has once again typed my almost undecipherable MS. and has made many corrections in the text.

Last, but not least, I thank my wife for reading through the proofs, for several translations, and for giving me much useful help and encouragement.

P. G.

WEPPONS
January 1st, 1938

CONTENTS

APPENDICES

xi

ST. HELENA

LIST OF ILLUSTRATIONS

ST. HELENA

INTRODUCTION

PHILIP GOSSE AND ST. HELENA

"A WELL documented, enthusiastic and easily read book, permanently valuable. With Dr. Gosse as guide, St. Helena has taken its place upon the map, has become an island to visit, and a name to remember." Thus in 1938 *The Sunday Times* greeted *St. Helena 1502–1938*. Of its qualities, critics were agreed. "Mr. Gosse writes like a romantic, a humorist and a scholar", pronounced Sir John Squire in *The Illustrated London News*. Time has vindicated their opinion for it has remained the most sought-after study of Britain's isolated outpost in the South Atlantic. Of its optimism, perhaps time has judged more harshly.

Since the Falklands War, however, times have changed for Britain's South Atlantic communities. Thrust into the limelight, they have become visible to the outside world. For St. Helena, and its Dependencies of Ascension Island and Tristan da Cunha, recognition has generated an unaccustomed interest and investment. New associations have sprung up in support of these traditionally British communities, while learned societies fund rescue operations to save threatened flora and fauna, and plead for conservation of their cultural heritage. Philip Gosse had appealed for such action on behalf of St. Helena half a century ago and so it is fitting that we should again turn to him as our historical guide. Gosse is not without minor errors – a flawless history has never been written; nor have Island studies stood still for the last fifty years. Specialist attention has since been given to postal and currency history, early telegraphs and photography, architecture and surveying, church history, medical and scientific topics, and aspects of its natural history, including the recent re-discovery of the "extinct" St. Helena Ebony. Facilities for research, moreover, are incomparably better than Gosse ever enjoyed, both in Britain and in Jamestown, where a valiant rescue operation has been slowly salvaging the Castle's precious archives. Yet far more grist to the historian's mill must be provided by specialist research before Dr. Gosse's vivid panorama is to be superseded. And so in 1987, faced with frequent demands but copies unobtainable, the then Governor of St. Helena, His Excellency F. E. "Dick" Baker, CBE, asked the St. Helena Link at Cheltenham to explore the possibilities of reprinting the colony's "classic" history. Thanks to the enthusiastic response of the author's daughter and literary executrix, Miss Jennifer Gosse, and the generous support of the publisher, Mr. Anthony Nelson, his request is now realised.

*   *   *

What first attracted Dr. Gosse to St. Helena remains a mystery. A youthful fascination for islands, especially "treasure islands", was kindled by Robert Louis Stevenson regaling the Gosse family with "tales of blood-curdling adventures and disaster", but St. Helena has no such buccaneering background. His earliest reference to it occurs nevertheless in *The Pirates' Who's Who* in 1924, quoting "a friend" on the Island for a local belief in Captain Dampier's hidden treasure on Ascension Island. Also in 1924, *IBIS* quoted "Captain" Philip Gosse on the birds of both Islands, but his contacts may have begun even earlier as he had a *St. Helena Almanac for 1913* from Harry Cordeaux, Governor 1912–1920. Certainly by the time of his visit in 1937, he had long been an ardent collector of all to do with St. Helena with arguably the finest St. Helena library in private hands. It is still privately owned in London.

For freedom to pursue his boyhood ambitions as naturalist

and author, Gosse had retired at fifty in 1930 as Medical Superintendent of the London Radium Institute. He had always sought to exploit talents inherited from his famous forebears, his father Sir Edmund Gosse, poet and man of letters, and his grandfather Philip Henry Gosse, the naturalist. Ironically, failure at school (Haileybury) brought him a brief, youthful career of exploration. He went at 15 in his grandfather's footsteps to Newfoundland; at 17, as naturalist with the pioneering FitzGerald expedition to the Andes; and at 20, on publication of his *Notes on the Natural History of the Aconcagua Valley* in 1899, to join an expedition to Kashmir. But his father, even then pondering the theme of his own *Father and Son*, would hear no more of it. This Philip Henry Gosse must have a "proper" profession. After a fruitless term at Farm School and a disastrous interview with Field-Marshal Wolseley for the Army, it had to be medicine. Trained at "Bart's" and as houseman at Colchester (legendary birthplace of St. Helena), Dr. Gosse entered general practice at Beaulieu, saw war service in Flanders and India, followed, after a brief term with the Ministry of Pensions, by ten years at the London Radium Institute, finally as Medical Superintendant. Although he later used it as a source of humourous reminiscence, he found it an uncongenial career, burdened by medicine's inevitable failures.

Truanting to distant islands helped release the frustrations of medical training and practice; recounting dastardly deeds of piracy relieved the tensions of an uneasy first marriage. To his surprise he had started a literary vogue with *The Pirates' Who's Who* (1924) and *My Pirate Library* (1926), later rewarded by Fellowship of the Royal Society of Literature, and although his "pirate period" virtually ended in 1932 with *A History of Piracy*, he remained "Brother Buccaneer" to certain literary friends for the rest of his life. His hobby as a naturalist resulted in contributions both to the Natural History Museum (444 bird specimens alone from Europe and India), and to journals of learned societies, including articles on *Bird-Marking* (1912), *Birds of the Balearic Islands* (1914), and *The Mammals of Flanders* (1916). In the 1920's, apart from a rare professional paper, "Tubercolosis Adentis treated by Radium", Gosse compiled with his first daughter Helen a modest vocabulary, *Gathered Together*, and some wartime anecdotes, *Rest Billets*, illustrated by his talented sister Sylvia, yet faintly forlorn booklets which seem to reflect years of stress as Gosse faced a watershed in his life. In 1928 his father died and his marriage finally collapsed; by 1930, he had retired, remarried and removed from Kensington to an idyllic Sussex retreat, "Weppons", at Steyning.

There, during a decade of domestic contentment he produced not only his history of St. Helena and two biographies (of Sir John Hawkins and the naturalist Charles Waterton), but a series of popular light-hearted memoirs. In these – *Memoirs of a Camp Follower* (or *A Naturalist goes to War*), *Go to the Country* and *Travellers' Rest* – Gosse wielded his skill as a raconteur, exploiting his somewhat capricious career in a "companionable treasury of counsel, confidence and confession," as Arthur Waugh wrote in 1935. Critics admired his style, combining "learning with modesty and both with humour", causing *The Times Literary Supplement*, when reviewing his breezy medical memoir *An Apple a Day* in 1948, to conclude: "The author has not wasted a moment of life nor failed to extract from it some residue of wisdom or of laughter."

By then he had launched himself into a third career following a sudden family crisis in 1940/41, to become, unusually at 62, a Research Student and Fellow Commoner at Trinity College, Cambridge. Ever youthful in spirit, his life unexpectedly enriched by a happy marriage, he enlivened the proceedings of many a learned society and, in 1952, published his last book, *Dr. Viper: the Querulous Life of Philip Thicknesse*. A critic once computed that he had upheld "one of the longest and most prolific family traditions in English literature" by which, since 1840 "father, son and grandson have averaged well over a book a year." He died at eighty on 3rd October 1959 from salmonella poisoning. In an unusually jaunty tribute in *The Times*, the broadcaster S. P. B. Mais spoke for a wide circle of friends when he concluded, "No one ever came away from meeting Philip Gosse without feeling immensely exhilarated and (temporarily at any rate) filled with the milk of human kindness."

*   *   *

Thus it was as naturalist, historian, physician, photographer, popular author, and inveterate collector of St. Heleniana, that Philip Gosse set sail for the South Atlantic in January 1937. Few writers could have been better qualified by knowledge, talent or personality to present the story of St. Helena than this island-loving countryman. To a correspondent at the Natural History Museum he seemed to "know the history of St. Helena backwards". But Gosse set out more modestly as "a sympathetic listener ... to gather first-hand information about the Island, to examine buildings and the records in the Castle", and explore a habitat "of surpassing interest" to naturalists.

His six-week sojourn on St. Helena proved a bitter-sweet experience, however. On the one hand he was enchanted by the Island and its people; on the other, he was angered by the apparent indifference of the government and influential settlers towards social distress and environmental decay. Gosse rented a fine bungalow in the country, "Kingshurst", ideal for exploration. He hiked the length and breadth of the rugged interior, collected flora and fauna from the heights of Actaeon to the shores of Rupert's Bay, studied birdlife from Deadwood Plain to the slippery summit of Egg Island, a daring exploit recounted by Police-Sergeant Dillon in 1953 to South African author Lawrence Green. Gosse swam and fished and circumnavigated the Island; he skilfully recorded places and people in scores of striking photographs; he had an essay, "A Visit from George Moore", printed by William C. Benjamin in Jamestown and he joined the Ancient Order of Foresters. "So much of the pleasure of a visit to a country depends on its inhabitants," he wrote in *The Field*, recommending St. Helena as "one of the loveliest and happiest spots in the world [for] a peaceful holiday ... The St. Helenians are the most polite, friendly people I ever had the good fortune to find myself among." But he also found them desperately poor, while the Island's historic buildings, its unique flora, its priceless colonial and East Indian Company records, each told a tale of shameful neglect. His notebooks betray his sense of outrage. The contrast, for example, between the immaculate French enclave at Longwood, Napoleon's last home (1815–21), given to France in 1858, and its "disgraceful surroundings", provoked him to comment acidly: "Govt. should have given more land (and garden) opposite. Farm filthy – litter, tin sheds, scrap iron, boiler – fine Thorn trees hacked, starving cattle ..." On tapping all shades of Island opinion, he found the country folk philosophical, the settlers cynical, and colonial officials disheartened. But as a genial guest he gained the confidence and retained the friendship of several Island families, his host, the chemist E. J. Warren, the Government Secretary, Geoffrey Kitching, the Medical officer, Dr. Paul Wilkinson and others named in his Preface. Sir Steuart Spencer Davis was less forthcoming however, and although he cajoled the corpulent governor to view St. Helena's threatened flora from its mountainous central Ridges, his concern met only cold resentment, a rebuff that determined Gosse to champion the St. Helena cause.

Returning laden to his Sussex home, flora, fauna and photographs first demanded attention. There were Island lilies and a rare St. Helena Redwood for "Weppons"; collections of "Reptiles, Molluscs and Insects" for the Natural History Museum, where over a hundred of his specimens (though no molluscs) can still be seen; and photographs and lantern slides for book, articles and lectures. The lonely task of writing *St. Helena 1502–*

1938 he recorded tersely in a notebook, "Begun May 7, 1937; finished 12 Jan. 1938". By now the work had assumed a new and unexpected significance: "... if this book should prove to be an instrument, however humble, towards [St. Helena's] return to prosperity, then it will not have been written in vain ..." Yet as he wrote, still garnering material through appeals in the press to descendants of East India Company governors, Gosse felt driven to take more direct action. But what? While each monthly mail from the Island added fuel to his resolve, the Governor's rebuff had made him cautious and he discreetly asked friends how "a complete stranger" could best challenge the authorities about "the sad state of affairs in St. Helena". A distant relative, John Wedgwood, suggested a frank report to the Colonial Secretary followed, if necessary, by "some nasty questions" in the House and so, on 23rd June, "in the hope of bettering the condition of these charming, long suffering British subjects", Gosse despatched a courteous 3,500-word statement to the Rt. Hon. W. G. A. Ormsby-Gore.

His report, though outspoken in comparison with the studied discretion of his book's closing chapters, avoided the vehemence of his notebook jottings. He cited conditions of work which "would in England have brought about immediate prosecution", quoting women's farm wages at 4s. 6d. [22½p.] for a 54-hour week (with overtime paid in potatoes), and high indirect taxation which, with chronic unemployment and low wages caused malnutrition and ill-health. As a doctor he was appalled at the poor medical facilities, staffed by one or two over-worked doctors (neither surgeon nor dentist) with one qualified nurse, and to find that Beri-Beri was prevalent which could be eradicated by the Government selling unpolished rice at cost. As a naturalist, concerned at the continuing destruction of Island flora, he pleaded for laws to protect "the last surviving trace of the wonderful indigenous forest from the flax-growing Barons ... Could not something be done now to save the Ridges ... I beg you".

At the root of the Island's social problems, believed Gosse, lay the economic and political power exercised by three major employers, as members of Council and monopoly landowners. Thus the people, who "ought to be a race of peasant proprietors", were land-hungry, but had "no means whatever of stating their views." Gosse carefully supported his complaints with facts and photographs, such as that of Governor Janisch's neglected memorial [between p. 324/25], needing £30 to rescue it for future generations. Referring to the "unseen hermit in the leafy boscage of Plantation", he suggested that the Governor of St. Helena should be a young man of promise, married and a good walker, who knows the people, not from a motor car, but by living in Jamestown. Plantation House should be converted into a much-needed hotel! Not all his proposals were quite so radical. More typical were suggestions that talented pupils should be able to continue their education in England (having admired Miss Evans' work at Country School), and that essential plant oils be produced to make high-quality drugs in short supply, such as Ephedrine. Others were based on existing ideas, developing high-class tourism, a health centre, bulb-growing, handicrafts, and domestic service overseas. Why, he wondered, was so little done to capitalise on the Island's advantages, strategically and economically, and on the extraordinary talents of the people?

But St. Helena's settlers and officials were inured to criticism from casual visitors, and if pressed could have countered even Gosse's carefully considered complaints. For example, the Longwood farmer could justly claim to be leading the fight against destitution by producing more work, wages and food than the farm had ever achieved hitherto, while the Governor would point to his success in turning a £7,219 deficit into a £25,265 surplus within five years. But Gosse was no casual visitor, nor a tyro in the study of islands in general or of St. Helena in particular. He knew the arguments but could not see glaring and soluble problems being ignored, such as the 200-year-old scourge of free-ranging goats, providing meat rarely, milk never, consuming rare endemic flora and crops at will. "Destroy every goat which is not enclosed," he insisted. Yet what colonial governor dare risk discontent today to prevent a desert tomorrow!

Gosse's report evoked a predictable response from Whitehall. The Colonial Secretary thanked him for his "interesting survey" and referred him to the relevant official, A. J. Dawe. Gosse promptly called with an updated copy of his report, after which a further meeting was arranged with Governor-Designate Garry Pilling, but unfortunately no record has been found of either occasion. On St. Helena, meanwhile, Gosse's influence may perhaps be seen in some pertinent Government Ordinances, in May *For the Preservation of Forests*, and in July for *The Supervision of Factories*. In October, Geoffrey Kitching became Acting-Governor and, in correspondence with Gosse, prepared a 28-page Memorandum for Governor Pilling "on all aspects of the Island situation and life", which explains the dedication of this book and the optimism of its final chapter. Among other improvements, Governor Janisch's memorial was repaired, Longwood garden was extended, and in 1941 St. Helena took its first step towards popular secondary education by transforming Country School, significantly, into "The Gosse Central School".

The exigencies of war were now dictating Island affairs, raising its income, making good its most glaring deficiencies and slowly generating a momentum of reform and development later to be accelerated by the Falklands conflict. Yet despite the amenities and affluence bought by public funds, Gosse's words are echoed still: "One cannot come away from St. Helena without shaking one's head and muttering that something must be done", declared Simon Winchester in 1985, describing it in *Outposts* (Hodder & Stoughton 1985) as "a tragedy of decay and isolation, poverty and ruin, and all played by a principal cast of proud and enchanting islanders, in their home of magical beauty." Was Gosse's optimism so badly misplaced? It would surely be more to his taste to note, as today's auguries for the future, that the re-publication of his book coincides with the marketing of St. Helena's fine coffee, the long-awaited provision of its splendid community High School and the launch of its new Royal Mail Ship.

Today's revival of interest in the Island's heritage, partly stimulated among St. Helenians by their bewildering loss of British citizenship after 300 years, is evident in Jamestown at the New Museum set up by the St. Helena Heritage Society. To mark the 50th anniversary of Philip Gosse's visit in 1987 the Society mounted an exhibition of his photographs which, incidentally, revived memories for his housekeeper, Mrs. Eva Fowler, of his collecting frogs in bottles for the Natural History Museum! But already attention is being focussed realistically on 2002 A.D. in preparation for the 500th anniversary of the Island's discovery. By then the people of St. Helena may well have welcomed another Gosse to chronicle the Colony's recent past. Meanwhile, adapting the author's own words, if this book should prove to be an instrument towards nurturing a love and understanding of 'our Island story', then it will not have been published in vain.

19 July 1989   Trevor W. Hearl.

EDITOR'S ACKNOWLEDGEMENTS

This new issue of Philip Gosse's *St. Helena 1502–1938* has only been made possible by the practical help and encouragement of many benefactors.

Foremost among those to whom I am indebted is Miss Jennifer Gosse whose generous gift of her father's St. Helena correspondence, lecture slides and massive St. Helena Scrapbook put this unique material at my disposal and secured it ultimately for the St. Helena U.K. archive, at Rhodes House Library, Oxford.

For invaluable assistance with particular aspects of the work my grateful thanks are tendered to Mrs. Ann Thwaite, author of *Edmund Gosse, A Literary Landscape*; Mr. and Mrs. Raymond Lister, Cambridge friends of Philip Gosse; Mrs. K. S. Martin, Deputy Librarian, Miss J. Harvey, Dept. of Entomology, and Mr. Michael P. Walters, Dept. of Ornithology, of the British Museum (Natural History); Mr. John Lawson of Didcot and Mr. E. M. Dring of Bernard Quaritch Ltd., for essential bibliographical information; Mr. Roger B. West of Bracknell for details of St. Helena letters addressed to Gosse; Mr. Alan Cooper of Huntly for providing elusive Gosse titles; Miss Clarice Chapman of Colchester and Dr. John B. Penfold, author of *The History of the Essex County Hospital*, Colchester; and to Mrs. Jane MacDonald and Mr. Nick Thorpe for information from St. Helena.

The enthusiasm and advice of Mr. Anthony Nelson must finally be acknowledged, not only for translating the original request into reality but for imaginatively launching the *South Atlantic Library* focussing, as Philip Gosse would have welcomed, on this fascinating but formerly forgotten quarter of the globe.

19 July 1989   Trevor W. Hearl.

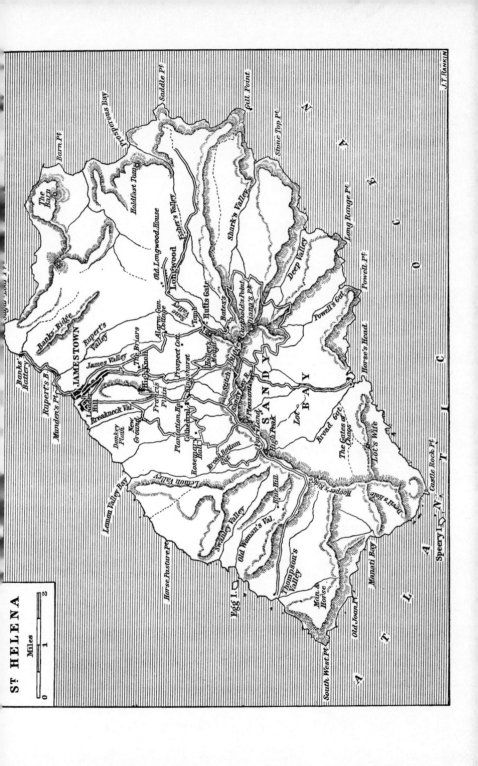

ST HELENA

Miles

0   1   2

J.T. RANKIN

CHAPTER I

1502–1629

ALTHOUGH it did not take place until fifteen years later, the discovery of St. Helena became inevitable when the Portuguese navigator, Bartholomew de Diaz, rounded the Cape of Good Hope in 1487.

For many years the Portuguese, the greatest race of sailors who ever ventured into uncharted seas, excluded from the Mediterranean, had gradually explored farther and farther along the mysterious unmapped western coast of Africa.

Ten years after the epoch-making discovery of Diaz and after Columbus and Cabot had opened up the Atlantic to the races of the West and North of Europe, the King of Portugal, Emmanuel the Fortunate, sent out a fleet under the command of Vasco da Gama with orders to sail beyond the Cape of Good Hope in search of a direct sea route to India and thus tap the wealth of the East.

Hitherto for centuries all trade between Europe and the East had been carried overland across Arabia, and by ship along the Mediterranean, and had been in the hands of the Italian cities of Venice and Genoa.

Da Gama achieved his ambition, and arrived at Calicut, on the west coast of the Indian Peninsula, and from that day the Mediterranean, which for centuries had been the centre of civilization, began to decline.

The Portuguese lost no time in building forts and setting up trading posts along the west coast of India, but their principal one was at Calicut.

It is not to be wondered at that the "Moors" or Arabs who for centuries had held the monopoly of the trade between India and the Mediterranean began to take active measures to turn out these dangerous interlopers from Europe.

The intrigues and the perfidy of the Zamorin or ruler of Calicut soon brought about a state of open warfare between the Portuguese and the King of Calicut, which led King Emmanuel to send out reinforcements, consisting of a powerful fleet, again under the command of da Gama. But as it took time to equip so large a fleet, and, as the plight of the Portuguese at Calicut was acute, three ships were sent on ahead under the Admiral, João da Nova Castella, to reinforce de Cabral, the Portuguese commander in India.

In due time da Nova arrived at his destination, met, attacked and defeated a fleet belonging to the Zamorin, and was appointed commodore of the returning ships to Europe. When at last he rounded the tempestuous Cape of Good Hope, da Nova ran his ships before the steady south-east trade wind, and it was on 21st May, 1502, the anniversary of Saint Helena, mother of the Emperor Constantine, that the sailor at the mast-head cried out, "Land ho!" and on the horizon could be made out a lofty island. In honour of the saint, da Nova at once christened the unknown island and new possession of the King of Portugal, Santa Helena.

Da Nova anchored opposite a deep valley on the leeward and sheltered side of the island, where Jamestown, the little capital, now stands.

He found there a stream of fresh water and set out to explore the island. No inhabitants were seen, but sea-birds, sea-lions, seals and turtle abounded. No other animals are said to have been found. The interior of the island was covered by dense forest, and even some of the precipices overhanging the sea, now bare rock, were covered by gum-wood trees. The only land bird was the wire bird—*Aegialitis sanctæ-helenæ*—which, by some strange fluke of fortune, is still existing and to be found in considerable numbers.

According to several early legends a large carrack, one of the fleet, was either wrecked or else became so unseaworthy that the Portuguese broke her up and "drew on shore her weather-beaten sides and all the armory and tackling, building with the timber a chappell in this valley, from thence is called Chappell Valley".[1] Although this chapel and a stone one built afterwards by the Portuguese have long since disappeared, the valley in which Jamestown stands still goes locally by the name of Chapel Valley.

It did not take the Portuguese long to appreciate the vital importance of the island upon which they had stumbled. Lying, as it does, in the direct route between the Cape of Good Hope and Cape Verde, the most westerly point of Africa, and in the track of the almost constant south-east trade wind, it was the very place which was needed as a calling-station for replenishment of their ships sailing home from the East. The harbour at what is now Cape Town was not a good nor a safe one, in fact in certain winds it was a very dangerous one. So that once a ship had successfully battled her way around the Cape all that had to be done was to set every sail and run before the trade for some seventeen hundred miles until reaching St. Helena, where a safe anchorage was always to be found opposite Chapel Valley, snug and sheltered under the lee of the high cliffs.

Concerning the eleven years immediately following the discovery of St. Helena we know nothing. No doubt the clumsy carracks as they lumbered along, laden deep with Eastern merchandise, with their crews sick of tropical fevers or decimated by scurvy, their casks running short of the stinking water, used the island to water at, to refit and to rest

[1] Osorio, *Narrative of the Voyage of João Da Nova in 1502.* Translated by J. Gibbs. 1752.

their men. Probably they did what the Portuguese always did when they discovered an uninhabited island, and introduced goats, to supply future ships with fresh meat. But history records not one word about St. Helena during those eleven years. For many more years the island and its whereabouts remained a secret known only to its discoverers. But in the year 1513 a visitor arrived there who became its first resident; some might describe him as the first governor of St. Helena. This was Dom Fernando Lopez, a Portuguese gentleman and an officer, but his arrival was neither honourable nor glorious, for he came there a prisoner in disgrace.

As St. Helena was destined to be the place of captivity of many broken men, some famous, some infamous, no apology need be made for recounting at some length the narrative of this Portuguese prisoner, Fernando Lopez. By great good fortune his story was recorded by the Portuguese historian Correa,[1] and in far more detail than was all too often the case in his day.

During the fighting in 1512 between the Portuguese at Goa under Afonso Albuquerque and the Indian commander Rasul Khan, the latter surrendered, and according to the terms of capitulation delivered up several Portuguese deserters, renegade Christians, but only on the promise that their lives should be spared.

The great Afonso, the *Commentaries* tell us,[2] "could not break his word", but for all that he went as near to doing so as he well could.

He commanded to bring up before him Fernando Lopez and the other renegades. These men fearing he would not keep his promise of sparing their lives, threw themselves at his feet, and with many tears besought him to have mercy

[1] *The Earliest Exile of St. Helena.* Hugh Clifford. *Blackwood's Magazine*, vol. 173.
[2] *The Commentaries of the Great Afonso Dalboquerque.* Hakluyt Society.

upon them. This he did, but ordered that their right hands, and the thumbs of their left hands, and their ears and noses should be cut off in memory and as a terrible example of the punishment meted out to them for the treason and wickedness which they had committed against God and their King.

For three days these and other atrocities were inflicted on the wretched prisoners, from which more than half of them died.

The leader of the renegades, Fernando Lopez, after his mutilation and during the remainder of the life of the great Afonso, continued to drag out a miserable existence, an object of contempt and derision to his countrymen, shunned and despised by the natives. In 1515, however, Afonso Albuquerque died, and in the following spring this poor victim of his wrath contrived to stow himself away on board a vessel homeward bound.

According to Correa he had left a wife and child behind him in Lisbon, and he thought, in the depths of his ignominy, to seek comfort from the woman who had once loved him.

As the slow ship lumbered up the west coast of Africa, drawing each day nearer to her destination, Lopez began to have doubts as to the sort of reception he was likely to encounter in Portugal, a mangled and ignominious prisoner and traitor, so when the ship put in to water at the uninhabited island of St. Helena, he escaped into the woods and hid himself. In vain his companions searched for him, and they soon set sail for home leaving behind for his use "a barrel of biscuit and some pieces of hung beef, and dried fish, and salt, and a fire, and some old clothes, which each one contributed". They also left a letter for him to say that "in the case of any ship putting in there he was to make signs to show whether he were alive or dead, and show himself in order that they might supply him with whatever he required."

From now onwards a new life began for Fernando Lopez, the outcast, which was to continue, with a single interruption, for the remainder of his days.

Here on this lonely island he was to find solace and peace, both of which would be denied him either in India or Portugal. The delight which the sense of his complete isolation brought to him was natural, for he was weary of exciting the disgust, the contempt and the pity of his kind, and here there were no men to be startled by his deformities, to point the finger of scorn at him for the deeds which had earned so heavy a punishment, or to make a mock of his calamities.

First of all, with the four fingers that remained to him and with the stump of his right arm, he scooped out a sort of cave in the side of a soft bank of earth, in which to make his home. Into this he carried the provisions which had been left behind for him, while much of his time was spent tending his precious fire lest by accident it should become extinguished. Such was his haunting fear of this happening that, according to Correa, "he set to work to find stones, which he beat one against the other, and he saw that they struck fire and he kept them."

After this discovery he was able to explore his kingdom and could wander through the forests which clothed the high hills in the interior of the island. In them he found "many tender herbs which were savoury to eat" and these he boiled in salt, living on them and upon such fish as he had the luck to catch.

For a whole year Fernando Lopez lived his solitary but not unhappy life, wandering over the hills by day and sleeping at night in his burrow, the mouth of which he guarded with "prickly bushes".

But one day his heart stood still with fear, for far away towards the horizon he could make out a ship under full sail bearing down upon his island, a ship, too, which he soon recognized to be Portuguese.

The thought flashed through his mind, what if they should capture him and carry him back to slavery in India, that hell of evil memory?

All that day and the next he hid in the kindly woods, and then gaining courage, ventured down in the valley where he entered his cave to find gifts of biscuits, cheeses—new cheeses of Portugal—and many other things to eat, and a letter "bidding him not hide himself, but when any ship should touch there he should speak with it, for no one would harm him".

Then, creeping round a promontory to the east he lay down and watched the ship getting under weigh, and as she spread her sails to the wind and began to edge away from the shore, something fell fluttering into the water.

The canvas filled and the vessel swept majestically away, but Fernando Lopez had no eyes for her.

His gaze was riveted upon that struggling object which the tide was bearing nearer and nearer to him each moment, and at last he made it out to be a cock, with draggled feathers, floating helplessly on the surface of the sea.

Here was another outcast like himself, a victim of the callousness of man and the cruelty of fate.

Plunging into the sea, he managed with some difficulty, owing to his maimed condition, to catch the half-drowned creature and bring it safe to land and carried it to his cave, where he dried it at his fire and fed it with some rice which was among the stores that the ship had left him.

In a very short while the cock and the man became the closest friends. "The cock," Correa says, "became on such loving terms with him that it followed him wherever he went, would come at his call, and at night it roosted with him in the hole."

And thus love of a sort came into the life of this lonely man, and with it companionship.

7

For ten years Lopez continued to live on the island, hiding whenever a ship appeared, never trusting himself to his fellow-men.

His cave became one of the stock sights to the Portuguese mariners who landed, and although the owner never suffered himself to be seen while men were abroad in his kingdom, his fame spread far and wide and came at last to the ears of King John III, who sent a letter to Fernando promising him safe conduct if he would return to Portugal.

It was while Lopez was still considering the invitation of the king that a new inhabitant arrived on what he had now come to consider his own exclusive property. This was a Javanese slave-boy, who made his escape from a calling ship and hid in the woods until the vessel left.

Apparently Lopez did not at all appreciate this new comer to his lonely isle, which he preferred to share with his tame cock.

More than probably the Javanese had a somewhat sorry time of it and often wished he was back on board the ship he had run away from, for when the very next vessel called at St. Helena he gave himself up and offered to shew where the white man was hiding.

Led by the slave, Pero Gomez Teixeira, the captain of the ship, went with his crew and captured Fernando who, "when he found that he was taken made loud outcries, thinking that they were going to take him on board, but Pero Gomez consoled him and talked for a long time with him, and assured him that he would not carry him away, and gave him many things, although Lopez did not care for them, but very earnestly besought the captain to take the youth with him in the ship. Pero Gomez, therefore, took him, on receiving a promise from Lopez that he would not hide himself from other crews. And when this had been agreed to, Pero Gomez left with him a paper, signed and sealed, wherein he desired all captains who might touch there of their kindness not to use any force in desiring to carry him to Portugal against his will, for it was from fear of this that Fernando Lopez used in bygone times to hide himself. Therefore he gave him a safeguard in the king's name, and swore to it, that no one should carry him away from the island against his will."

From this time onwards, Lopez was less shy with the crews of passing ships, though he was always glad when they left him alone again on his island.

Gradually his conscience and his early faith in religion overcame his distaste for the company of his fellow-men and he decided he would go to Portugal and confess his sins and make his peace with God, and he was taken on board a homeward-bound vessel and sailed to Portugal.

When he reached Lisbon, the outcast of the island found the noise and bustle of the busy port frightened him who was used only to the murmuring silence of his island. To escape the hurrying crowd and the strenuous life around him he disembarked by stealth and lay hidden from the sight of prying eyes in the house of the captain of his ship, and afterwards "went by night to converse with the King and Queen, who gave him a hermitage, and a house of friars wherein he might remain; but he would not accept aught of this, but obtained permission of the King and went to Rome."

"A hermitage and a house of frairs", indeed, were things little suited to the taste of one who had found even the company of a single Javanese slave-boy too much for him. As Sir Hugh Clifford so happily suggests, the very thought of the holy friars welcoming him as a guest whose coming made a delightful break in the monotony of their lives, plying him perhaps with questions of eager curiosity, was enough in itself to drive him mad.

He would have none of it, for his one desire was to return to his island as soon as ever the business which had brought him from it was done.

This was the confession of his sins, and he felt that his sins were so grave that no ordinary priest or bishop had the authority to grant absolution. His sins came under the category of "reserved cases" and had to be delegated by the Pope to one or other of his cardinals, although in the sixteenth century the Pope himself frequently heard such confessions in person.

So to Rome Lopez went and there at the foot of the Vicar of Christ the mutilated exile sobbed out the story of his transgressions, the double crime of apostasy and the taking up arms for the infidels against a Christian people, and there he received absolution.

Afterwards the Pope gave him audience and asked him to name the boon he most desired, but Lopez had but a single wish in life. He longed to return to St. Helena and solitude, but he feared the King of Portugal might detain him in Europe.

This he told the Pope, who "gave him letters to the king that he would send him back again to the island. This, likewise, the king performed."

So back at last he arrived at St. Helena, a different man to the one who left there in constant fear of his fellow-men.

"As time went on," Correa tells us, "he would shew himself and converse with the people of the ships which passed by, and all gave him things to plant and to sow, so that he cultivated a great many gourds, pomegranates and palm-trees, and kept ducks, hens, sows and she-goats with young, all of which increased largely, and all became wild in the woods."

And there in the steep gulley which runs down to the sea, Lopez continued to live happily, tending his orange trees, his pomegranates and his poultry, or sitting basking in the sunshine in peaceful solitude, alone except for the rare visits of the ships from India, until he died in the year 1545, after living on St. Helena for nearly thirty years.

From this time onwards we hear no more news of St. Helena nor of any further settlers in the island until—the exact date is not known, but it must have been before the year 1557— two kaffirs from Mozambique and a Javanese man and two women slaves swam ashore from a ship and hid themselves in the woods until the vessel had sailed. They soon multiplied to twenty. There was by then plenty of food for them, half-wild cattle, goats and swine, as well as the plantations of vegetables and fruit which were grown for the provision of calling Portuguese ships by sailors left on shore by previous vessels. For a long while the blacks defied all attempts to capture or destroy them. The upper part of the island was almost covered by dense jungle, and the runaway slaves knew of every cave and other hiding place. At the first appearance of an approaching ship they would hide, and remain hidden until the danger was past.

After this the island was again without any permanent inhabitants, the only men there being convalescent Portuguese sailors who, while waiting for a ship to call and take them home, tended the crops and fruit trees, and hunted goats, whose flesh they sun-dried for the use of passing ships.

Had Edward Fenton, Elizabethan sailor, pirate, explorer and adventurer, had his own way, St. Helena might have become an English possession in the year 1582.[1] In May of that year he sailed in command of four ships, nominally to discover a North-West passage, but actually to trade in the Moluccas and China. His orders were to proceed there by way of the Cape of Good Hope, but instead they sailed to Sierra Leone on the West Coast of Africa to trade.

In any case the expedition was foredoomed to failure by the constant quarrels between Fenton and his second-in-command, William Hawkins, of whom he was intensely jealous, and with Captain Carlyle, the commander of the

[1] *Col. State Papers, 1513–1616.* Col. East Indies, No. 231.

soldiers. On the 25th of September Fenton astonished his colleagues by informing them of his intention to seize the island of St. Helena, "to possess the same, and there to be proclaimed Kyng". After carrying out this bold stroke, the enterprising Fenton intended to surprise the Portuguese fleet when it arrived there from the East Indies, and after plundering it, to send the spoils in one of his ships, the *Edward Bonaventura*, to England. In the end nothing came of this romantic scheme, which might well have altered the whole history of St. Helena.

The next visitor to the island whose name is recorded was Bermudez, the Patriarch of Abyssinia, head of the Christian Church of that remote kingdom. He is known to have been a truculent and tiresome character, and little better than an adventurer. He landed on St. Helena in April, 1557, on his way back to Portugal "where I remained much against his (the ship's commander's) will, I being obstinate. I remained one year, suffering some corporal discomfort from hunger and other needs, for the island is so cut off from human society that no one touches save by good luck at a year's interval.

"Still, as to the spirit, I was consoled by thinking that I was here away from the disorders of the world, and that I would stay here all my life, but that enemy of the peace of souls— Satan—had detained in that refuge certain fugitive slaves from some ships that called there, it was said they had killed another chaplain; they began to seduce my slaves, who would not work for me.

"Despairing of any human help in my old age and sickness, I was compelled to return the next year to Portugal in the ship *St. Paul.*"[1]

Although the early records are so reticent about St. Helena and its visitors, travellers are known to have landed there in 1583. These were, surprising as it must seem, three Japanese ambassadors on an embassy to the Pope. Considering that

---

[1] *The Portuguese Expedition to Abyssinia in 1541-1543.* Hakluyt Society, 1902.

Japan was a closed country to Europeans until the middle of the last century, it is extraordinary that three Japanese should have left their native country to sail all the way to Europe, three hundred and fifty years ago.

The story of these three travellers is not without interest and is to be found in the Diary of Jan Huyghen van Linschoten which he kept during his five years' service with the Portuguese in India.

About this time (December, 1583) there came certain Jesuits to Goa, from the island of Japan; and with them three Princes (being the children of Kings of that country) wholly apparelled like Jesuits: not one of them was above sixteen years of age. They were minded, by the persuasions of the Jesuits, to travel to Portugal; and from thence to Rome, to see the Pope: thereby to procure great benefits, privileges and liberties from him for the Jesuits, which was their intent.

They continued in Goa till the year 1583, and then set sail for Portugal. From thence, they travelled into Spain, where, by the King and all the Spanish nobility, they were received with great honour and presented with many gifts, which the Jesuits kept for themselves.

Out of Spain, they went to see the Pope; from whom they obtained great privileges and liberties. That done, they travelled throughout Italy, as to Venice, Mantua, Florence; and all places and dominions of Italy; where they were presented with many rich presents, and much honoured by means of the great report the Jesuits made of them.

To conclude. They returned again to Madrid; where, with great honour, they took their leave of the King; with letters of commendation, on their behalf, unto the Viceroy and all the Captains and Governors of India. So they went to Lisbon, and there took shipping, anno 1586, and came in the ship called *San Felipe* (which, on her return, was taken by Captain Drake); and after a long and troublesome voyage, arrived at Mozambique, where the ship received her lading (homeward) out of another ship, called the *San Lorenzo* (laden in India, and bound for Portugal) that, having lost her masts, had to put in there. And, because the time was far spent to get into into India, the said *San Felipe* took in the lading of the *San Lorenzo*; and was taken, in her way returning home, by the Englishmen: and was the first ship that was taken coming out of the East Indies; which the Portuguese took for an evil sign, because the ship bore the King's own name.

But returning to our matter. The Princes and Jesuits of Japan, the next year after (1587), arrived at Goa, amidst great rejoicings and gladness; for that it was verily thought they had all been dead. When they came thither, they were all three apparelled in Cloth of Gold, and of Silver, after the Italian manner; which was the apparel that the Italian Princes and Noblemen had given them. They came thither very lively; and the Jesuits very proudly, for, by them, their voyage had been performed.

In Goa, they stayed till the monsoon or time of the winds came to sail for China; at which time, they went from thence, and so to China, and from thence to Japan; where, with great triumph and wondering of all the people, they were received and welcomed home, to the furtherance and credit of the Jesuits.

The safe return of the three princes appears to have prompted other Japanese to undertake the dangerous and tedious voyage to Europe, for in November in the same year, two embarked on the great Spanish ship, the *Santa Anna*, for Panama, on their way to Spain. All went well until the Pacific was crossed and the ship almost in sight of the Californian coast, when she was so unfortunate as to fall in with the *Desire*, commanded by the Englishman, Captain Thomas Cavendish, who attacked and eventually captured her. Out of her he took a vast treasure. Before burning the galleon Cavendish landed all the 190 prisoners, men and women, except the pilot and the two young Japanese, whom he carried away with him. The latter were well educated and could both read and write Japanese. The eldest, aged about twenty, they named Christopher; the other, a lad of seventeen, Cosmus. These two, no doubt, like their more fortunate fellow-countrymen, visited St. Helena when Cavendish called there on the last stage of his famous voyage round the world in 1588; and it was his foresight in detaining the pilot of the *Santa Anna* that made it possible for him to find the way to that small and isolated South Atlantic island, and in doing so to reveal to the world what had been a close secret of the Portuguese for eighty-six years.

Cavendish stayed at St. Helena for twelve days and wrote a lucid description of the island. As almost any account of it in these early days is both valuable and interesting, it is here quoted at some length.

The eighth day of June (1588) at break of day we fell in sight of the island of St. Helena, seven or eight leagues short of it, having but a small gale of wind, or almost none at all; insomuch as we could not get into it that day, but stood off and on all that night.

The next day having a pretty easy gale of wind we stood in with the shore, and about one of the clock in the afternoon we came unto an anchor in twelve fathoms of water in a very fair and smooth bay under the north-west side of the island.

The same day, in the afternoon, we went on shore, where we found a marvellous fair and pleasant valley, wherein divers handsome buildings and houses were set up, and especially one which was a church, which was tiled, and whitened on the outside very fair, and made with a porch, and within the church at the upper end was set an altar, whereon stood a very large table set in a frame having in it the picture of our Saviour Christ upon the Cross and the image of our Lady praying, with divers other histories curiously painted in the same. The sides of the church were all hanged with stained cloths having many devices drawn on them.

There are two houses adjoining the church, one on each side, which serve for kitchens to dress meat in, with necessary rooms and houses of office: the roofs of the said houses are made flat, whereon is planted a very fair vine, and through both the said houses runneth a very good and wholesome stream of fresh water.

There is also right over against the said church a fair causeway made up with stones reaching unto a valley by the seaside, wherein grow great store of pumpkins and melons: and upon the said causeway is a frame erected whereon hang two bells wherewith they ring to Mass; and hard unto it is a Cross set up, which is squared, framed and made very artificially of free-stone, whereon is carved in ciphers what time it was builded, which was in the year of our Lord 1571.

This valley is the fairest and largest low plot in all the island, and it is marvellous sweet and pleasant, and planted in every place with fruit trees or with herbs. There are fig trees, which bear fruit continually, and marvellous plentifully: for on every tree you shall have blossoms, green figs, and ripe figs, all at once: and it is so all the year long: the reason is that the island standeth so near the sun. There is also great store of lemon trees, orange trees, pomegranate trees, citron trees, date trees, which bear fruit as the fig trees do, and are planted carefully and very artificially with very pleasant walks under and between them, and the said walks be overshadowed with the leaves of the trees: and in every voide place is planted parsley, sorell, basil, fenell, annis seed, mustard seed, radishes and many special good herbs; and the fresh-water brook runneth through divers places of this orchard, and may with very small pains be made to water any tree in the valley.

The island is altogether high mountains and steep valleys, and down below in some of the valleys, marvellous store of all these kinds of fruit before spoken of do grow: there is greater store (of trees) growing in the tops of the mountains than below in the valleys: but it is wonderful laboursome and also dangerous travelling up unto them and down again, by reason of the height and steepness of the hills.

There is also upon this island great store of partridges,[1] which are very tame, not making any great haste to fly away though one come very near them, but only to run away and get up into the steep cliffs. We killed some of them with a fowling-piece. They differ very much from our partridges which are in England both in bigness and also in colour. For they be within a little as big as a hen, and are an ash colour, and live in coveys twelve, sixteen and twenty together. You cannot go ten or twelve score (paces) but you shall see or spring one or two coveys at the least.

There are likewise no less store of pheasants[2] in the island, which are also marvellous big and fat, surpassing those which are in our country in bigness and in numbers of a company. They differ not very much in colour from the partridges before spoken of.

[1] *Caccabis chukar*, from the Persian Gulf.
[2] *Phasianus torquatus*, Chinese ring-necked pheasant.

We found moreover in this place great store of Guinea cocks, which we call Turkeys, of colour black and white, with red heads: they are much about the same bigness which ours be in England: their eggs be white and as big as a turkey's egg.[1]

There are in this island thousands of goats, which the Spaniards call cabritos, which are very wild: you shall see one or two hundred of them together, and sometimes you may behold them going in a flock almost a mile long. Some of them are as big as an ass, with a mane like a horse and a beard hanging down to the very ground. They will climb up the cliffs which are so steep that a man would think it a thing impossible for any living thing to go there. We took and killed many of them for all their swiftness, for there be thousands of them upon the mountains.

Here are in like manner great store of swine which be very wild and very fat, and of a marvellous bigness. They keep altogether upon the mountains, and will very seldom abide any man to come near them, except it be by mere chance when they be found asleep, or otherwise, according to their kind, be taken laid in the mire.

We found in the houses at our coming three slaves which were negroes and one which was born in the island of Jave, which told us that the East Indian fleet, which were in number five sails, the least whereof were in burthen eight or nine hundred tons, all laden with spices and Calicut cloth, with store of treasure and very rich stones and pearls, were gone from the said island of St. Helena but twenty days before we came hither.

When the Portuguese call at the island from the East Indies they find all things in plenty for their relief, by reason that they suffer none to inhabit there who might eat up the produce of the island except some very sick persons of their

[1] *Numida meleagris*, guinea fowl, lately become extinct in the island.

company, whom they suspect will not live until they come home. These they leave there to refresh themselves and take them away the year following with the other fleet, if they live so long.

On the 20 day of June having taken in wood and water and refreshed ourselves with such things as we found there, and made clean our ship, we set sail about 8 of the clock in the night toward England.

Eleven months after the departure of the *Desire*, the annual Portuguese East India fleet arrived, piloted by the Dutchman, van Linschoten. They had left Cochin on January 1, 1589, and during the long voyage of one hundred and thirty-two days had had no sight of land. So unmolested by pirates and other enemies of the type of Drake and Cavendish was the route from India to St. Helena in these days that each ship took her own course and did not even consider it necessary to run out her cannon until they all assembled for mutual security at St. Helena for the last stretch of the voyage, which was invariably begun on May 25 each year.

It was always an event for rejoicing when the towering island showed up on the horizon. "The 12th of May, in the morning, betimes, we discovered the island of St. Helena; whereat there was great joy in the ship, as if we had been in heaven."[1]

On going ashore Linschoten found a few Portuguese sailors left behind by the last ship, to recover from sickness. From them he learned of Cavendish's visit, and amongst other bits of gossip, that the English had beaten down the altar and cross that stood in the church, and left behind them a kettle and a sword. This caused a good deal of speculation amongst the Portuguese for "they could not conceive or think what

[1] *The Voyage of John Huyghen van Linschoten to the East Indies.* The Hakluyt Society.

that might mean. Some thought it was left there for a sign to some other ship of his company, but every man may think what he will thereof."

Naturally such an indefatigable traveller and observer as Jan Huyghen van Linschoten wrote down in his diary a full description of St. Helena: "a very high and hilly country, so that it commonly reacheth unto the clouds. The country itself is very ashy and dry. Also all the trees (whereof there is great store, and grow themselves in the woods) that are therein, are little worth, but only to burn. The water is excellently good, and falleth down from the mountains, and so runneth in great abundance by small channels into the sea, where the Portuguese fill their vessels full of water, and wash their clothes."

After enumerating all the animals, birds and plants which had been introduced to the island by the Portuguese, Linschoten had a good word to say in praise of the "great abundance of fish round the island, that it seemeth a wonder wrought by God, for with crooked nails, they may take as much fish as they will: so that all the ships provide themselves with fish of all sorts in that place, which is hung up and dried, and is of as good taste and savour as any fish that I ever eat, and this every man that hath been there affirmeth to be true. . . .[1]

"It is an earthly Paradise for the Portuguese ships, and seemeth to have been miraculously discovered for the refreshing and service of the same, considering the smallness and highness of the land, lying in the middle of the Ocean seas, and so far from the firm land or any other islands, that it seemeth to be a Buoy placed in the middle of the Spanish seas. For if this island were not, it were impossible for the ships to make any good or prosperous voyage. For it hath often fallen out, that some ships which have missed thereof, have

[1] And is still the case.—P.G.

endured the greatest misery in the world, and were forced to put into the coast of Guinea, there to wait the falling of the rain to get fresh water, and afterwards come, half dead and spoiled, to Portugal."

The little settlement in Chapel Valley must have been a lonely and deserted place between the annual visits of the East India fleet. Beside the chapel there were between thirty and forty well-built houses, which stood empty, until the fleet arrived. The only inhabitants at other times, if any, would be a handful of sick or convalescent sailors, with perhaps occasionally a runaway slave who ventured down into the town only when the coast was clear of ships.

"The sick men stay there till the next year, till other ships come hither, which take them with them. They are commonly soon healed in that island, it being a very sound and pleasant country, and it is very seldom that any of them die there because they have always a temperate air and cool wind, and always fruit throughout the whole year."

There was plenty of meat for those men left behind, "for when the ships are gone, then all the beasts (which, by reason of the great number of people fly into the mountains) come down again into the valleys, where they may take them with their hands and kill them as they list."

Linschoten heard also about a business-like Franciscan, for he says: "In time past there dwelt an hermit in the isle, under pretence of doing penance, and to uphold the Church. He killed many of the goats and bucks, so that every year he sold at the least 500 or 600 skins, and made a great profit thereon, which the king hearing, caused him presently to be brought from there to Portugal."

The quiet valley must have been quickly transformed when the annual fleet arrived. Then every soul on board the ships who could be spared, took the opportunity to stop on shore, and the houses would only be enough to lodge the officers and more important passengers.

> When the ships come hither, every man maketh his lodging under a tree, setting a tent about it, and the trees are so thick that it presently seemeth a little town or an army in the field. Every man provideth for himself, flesh, fish, fruit and wood, for there is enough for them all, and everyone washeth his linen.
>
> There they hold a General Fasting and Prayer, with Mass every day, which is done with great devotion, with procession and thanksgiving and other hymns, thanking God that He hath preserved them from the danger of the Cape of Good Hope, and brought them to that island in safety. They use oftentimes to carve their names and marks in the trees for a perpetual memory, whereof many hundreds are there to be found, which letters with the growing of the trees do also grow bigger and bigger.
>
> We found names that had been there since the years 1510 and 1515 and every year following, orderly, which names stood upon fig trees, every letter being of the bigness of a span, by reason of the age and growing of the trees.

On St. Helen's Day, 1589, a Whitsunday, the Portuguese fleet set sail in company, directing their course for home, leaving behind them fifteen sick men and some slaves who, escaping from the ship, had swum ashore.

Once the secret of St. Helena and its whereabouts in the South Atlantic had been revealed by Sir Thomas Cavendish, his fellow-countrymen were not long in following his example. The next English ship to call there was the *Royal Merchant*, Captain Abraham Kendall. She was one of three vessels which sailed from England in 1591, under the command of

Sir James Lancaster, to make the first voyage to India ever undertaken by English merchants. By the time the flotilla reached the Cape of Good Hope so many of the crews were down with scurvy that it was decided to send home all the invalids in the *Royal Merchant*, whilst the rest continued the voyage in the other two ships. Captain Kendall arrived safely at St. Helena where he landed his fifty sick men, all of whom, with one exception, quickly recovered, thanks to the climate, pure water and the anti-scorbutic vegetables planted there by the Portuguese. The one exception was John Segar, a tailor of Bury in Suffolk, of whom we shall hear again shortly. Before sailing, Segar's mates made for him two suits of goat-skins, with the hairy side outwards—"like unto the Savages of Canada"—an uncomfortable outfit, one would imagine, to wear in the sweltering heat of Chapel Valley.

One of the results of Cavendish's discovery of St. Helena was that English ships of war began to haunt the neigh-bouring seas, lying in wait to attack the Portuguese India carracks on their voyage home. The policy of the English was to allow them to sail unmolested to India and only to attack them when they were returning deeply laden with eastern merchandise and treasure. As St. Helena was now known to be their place of call, it was there the piratically minded heretics lay in wait for them. It was this which caused King Philip II of Spain, in 1592, to order the annual fleet returning from Goa on no account to touch at St. Helena.

In the meanwhile, Captain Lancaster sailed up and down the Indian Ocean carrying on a trading voyage in which was a strong dash of piracy, and eventually, without his consort, which was lost, returned to England with his ship full of merchandise and plunder. He, too, broke his journey at St. Helena, anchoring off Chapel Valley on April 3, 1593, "where we staid to our great comfort nineteen days; in which mean space some one man of us took thirty good congers in one day, and other rocky fish and some bonitos".[1]

And now we hear some further news of the Suffolk invalid left behind by Captain Kendall.

In the first boat to go ashore was the surgeon and a party of sailors, who, as they drew near to the chapel, heard someone within singing. Thinking it might be a Portuguese, they thrust open the door and went in to find to their astonishment their old shipmate, John Segar. Whether it was the sudden transition from acute fear to intense pleasure, or some other cause, no one will ever know; but the fact remains that from that moment Segar became demented, or "idle-headed" as the narrator described it, and this in spite of his being "fresh in colour, and in good plight of body to our seeming", and for eight days and nights he took no natural rest and died literally for want of sleep.

The English were not the only intruders into what the Portuguese considered their private preserve. No sooner had the London merchants sent out a trading expedition to India than the Dutch entered into the field as well. The happy days for Spain and Portugal, when their carracks could sail unmolested to the East, load up a precious cargo and unmolested return safely home, were over. It was Cavendish's discovery of St. Helena which had been their undoing. And now the old enemies of Spain were daring to compete, by sending their fleets from Holland to win a share of the prize. One of the Dutch expeditions, the second of its kind, consisted of the *Lion* and the *Lioness*, which sailed from Flushing in March, 1598, piloted by the famous English Arctic explorer, John Davis.[2] After many vicissitudes the two ships returned to Europe, calling on their way at St. Helena on April 13, 1601, to refresh and refit. But on the second day there, while they

[1] *The Voyages of Sir James Lancaster, Knt., to the East Indies.* Hakluyt Society.
[2] *The Voyages and Works of John Davis the Navigator.* Hakluyt Society.

were busily employed in getting on board fresh water and fruit, a large Spanish caravel appeared round the point and dropped anchor only a musket shot to windward of the Dutchmen. The *Lion* and *Lioness* immediately opened fire and kept up a steady bombardment of the caravel, to which the Spaniard could not reply because, in defiance of the King's strict orders, her guns were dismantled, and it was not until midnight that she was able to retaliate. But she now began to use her guns in good earnest, hitting the *Lion* several times and killing two men. Lefort, the French commandant of the Dutch ships, then decided it would be prudent to retreat, and they sailed away for Ascension Island with many wounded as well as sick men on board, leaving the Spaniards in possession of St. Helena.

When at last, in July, the Dutch ships arrived back at Middleburg, John Davis was able to return to England at an opportune moment, for the English East India Company, newly incorporated under the auspices of Queen Elizabeth, was then fitting out its first fleet, and the services of the illustrious pilot were needed by his own countrymen. The concern opened with a capital of £72,000, part of which was laid out in the equipment of four ships: the *Dragon, Hector, Ascension* and *Susan*, all under the command of the experienced Captain Lancaster. This first venture of the new company well justified the confidence of the shareholders, for successful negotiations were opened in India, and the *Ascension* and *Susan* were sent back to England laden with spices, to be followed later by Sir James Lancaster in the *Dragon*, accompanied by the *Hector*.

Off the Cape of Good Hope the two ships encountered a violent storm, which occasioned the loss of the *Dragon's* rudder, but after extreme difficulties and hardships the storm-tossed mariners eventually made St. Helena on June 16, 1603. Besides fresh water the English were in need of fresh meat, but although plentiful, the goats had become very wild and difficult to procure, so Lancaster appointed four of his best shots to go up into the hills of the interior, with four men to attend each gun, who at once carried the dead goats to a rendezvous. A party from the ship was sent daily to the rendezvous to bring down the previous day's shooting, and in this way a plentiful supply of fresh meat was soon obtained. The sick men all recovered, and the *Dragon's* new rudder having been carefully secured, the two vessels were refitted and sailed from St. Helena on the 5th of July.

The Portuguese and Spanish had by this time given up calling regularly at the island. It was no longer the peaceful, undisturbed retreat and haven it used to be. One early traveller reported that the Portuguese "at this day dare hardly land to oversee their seminary or own their labours; the English and Dutch, in the churlish language of a cannon, sometimes disputing the propriety". The rightful owners complained that not only had English sailors damaged their chapel and images, but that the Dutch had destroyed their live-stock, laid waste their plantations, desecrated the chapel and broken down the large cross of free-stone which had been brought to St. Helena all the way from Lisbon. That the Dutch may have had some provocation for such acts of vandalism appears probable, from their having on one occasion left behind them a billet containing the following words: "Portuguese, leave us our inscriptions and letters and we will leave you your crosses and pictures." Yet another traveller records: "Some years ago, the Hollanders ruined all that was good, only to spite the Spaniards, who afterwards did the same, that the English etc., might have no benefit of it."

Interesting confirmation of the destruction which went on at St. Helena is provided by François Pyrard who twice visited the island, first in 1601 and again in 1610; in Portuguese or Spanish vessels.[1] His second visit was on the 25th June, 1610,

[1] *The Voyage of François Pyrard, of Laval, to the East Indies.* Hakluyt Society.

the time of year when almost all ships from India arrived at the island. The travellers were relieved to meet with no Dutch ships at anchor, but found some letters in the chapel left there by three other carracks some time previously, as well as one left by a caravel sent by the King of Spain to try to discover what had become of Pyrard's ship, which was many months overdue. On landing Pyrard was astonished to observe the bad state of the chapel, for when he had seen it last, nine years before, it was in good condition, and adorned with a fair altar and several handsome images and pictures,while in front of it stood a fine cross of free-stone, "white as marble and well carved, which the Portuguese had brought from Portugal". It was now broken in pieces, done in revenge, said Pyrard, by the Dutch, because the Portuguese used to take away all the drawings, letters and writings the former were in the habit of leaving for other Dutch ships which might call there afterwards. In spite of the letter left by the Dutch appealing to the Portuguese to "leave our drawings, writings and notes, and we will leave yours," the destruction went on just the same, not only of buildings but of the fruit trees as well. The pious Portuguese during their nine days' sojourn at the island repaired the chapel door and the altar and replaced, as far as was possible, the ornaments. Like all sailors, Pyrard praised the island, its good roadstead, its healthy air and excellent water.

In his day the heights were still covered with the wild native ebony trees, now extinct, and red-wood trees, of which there are now only seven living specimens, and which will also soon become extinct if an indifferent government does not quickly take steps to save them. Such fruits as lemons, oranges, and figs were still in abundance as at his first visit, and the surrounding seas swarmed with edible fish. No wonder sailors of the sixteenth and seventeenth centuries were fond of calling St. Helena an "Earthly Paradise", or that the pious Pyrard exclaimed: "I think that God has been pleased to fix it in this place as a half-way house in the midst of the great ocean, so that we should give to all the Indian peoples a knowledge of the faith, and obtain knowledge of all the wondrous things to be seen in these far-distant lands. To this end has Providence bestowed upon it all that is best of air, earth and water; and nowhere in the world, I believe, will you find an island of its size to compare with it."

But in 1610, only nine years later, Pyrard found such a clean sweep had been made of the fruit trees, lemon, orange and fig, that they had now to be searched for, because the crews of passing Portuguese ships had taken to cutting down the fruit trees, though still in flower, on the pretext that it was better to do this than leave them for the Dutch or English.

This wanton destruction of fruit trees was confirmed by the French traveller Tavernier, when he visited St. Helena in 1649.[1] "There are quantities of lemon trees," he reported, "and a few orange trees, planted originally by the Portuguese. For these people have one thing to their credit, that wherever they go they attempt to improve the place for those that come after. The Dutch do just the reverse, and destroy everything, so that those who follow after them shall find nothing left. It is true that this is not due to their leaders, but to the sailors and soldiers, who, knowing that they are not likely to return to the place, combine together to cut down the trees, so as to get all the fruit with the least trouble."

As an historian, not too much reliance should be placed on the French traveller's tale.

There is only a little settlement near the sea, where a chapel was once built, and where a Portuguese Franciscan friar lived for fourteen years; but this chapel is now half a

---

[1] *Six Voyages.* Tavernier, J. B. Paris, 1676.

ruin. While he lived there the friar was very useful to the ships which put in there, as he provided them with fish caught and dried by himself, and was given in return rice, biscuits and Spanish wine. After having lived there in a very austere manner for some time, he fell ill, luckily just as a Portuguese ship appeared. They did all they could for him, but he died five days after the vessel dropped anchor, and was buried by his compatriots.

Since any early account of St. Helena is interesting and important, it is worth while noting what Mr. Thomas Best, the chief commander of the English East India Company's tenth voyage, had to say about the island when he visited it thirty-five years before Tavernier, in March, 1614.[1] A party was sent on shore at Chapel Valley to collect lemons, but finding none, Best ordered the boats to row to the westward where the sailors landed at Lemon Valley, where they found what he describes as the largest and finest valley in the whole island after Chapel Valley. Here they were able to gather twelve to fourteen thousand lemons and capture thirty hogs, and he adds, "but if we had laid ourselves out for the purpose, I daresay we might have got two hundred hogs besides many goats."

When Peter Mundy[2] paid his first visit to St. Helena in June, 1634, he noted down in his journal—and he was a very reliable and careful observer—that there were only about forty lemon trees on the whole island, twenty in Lemon Valley, and the rest in twos and threes at other places, a very different state of things to Captain Best's description twenty years earlier.

Mundy commented on "the abundance of Hoggs, store of

[1] *Tenth Voyage of the English East India Company, in 1612.* Written by Mr. Thomas Best, chief Commander. *Kerr's Voyages.* 1824.
[2] *The Travels of Peter Mundy in Europe and Asia, 1608–1667.* Hakluyt Society.

little speckled guiney Henns, partridges and Pigeons, also of doggs and Catts (runne away) of whome the Companie killed divers".

When he visited the island for the third time, in 1656, he found no goats but many more wild dogs, an increase to which he ascribed the extermination of the goats.

He praised the lovely woods on the high hills, and described the now extinct ebony tree, the excellent grass, the thickets of tree ferns and the many running streams.

As a Cornishman and a seaman he was greatly interested in the variety of fish they caught in the sea, and boasted how he caught and brought on board to show to his admiring fellow-sailors, a monster flying-fish—"none in the ship ever saw a bigger"—which was nineteen inches long and weighed twenty-six ounces "good". One day they landed on a small rocky island—probably Egg Island—where they knocked down with sticks nearly a hundred "sea fowle, russett-colour, almost as big as a pigeon, but tast very fishy". To this day Egg Island in the nesting season is covered by the same Noddy terns, which are so tame that they will allow you to take up their fluffy young without showing alarm or leaving their nests. In four days, Mundy says, they procured one hundred and forty goats and pigs, mostly by small shot, but some taken by hand, while the rest of the crew spent their time fishing from the shore or from boats.

Peter Mundy had visited St. Helena a second time, in 1638, but in the month of October, instead of June, which may account for the improvement he found in the trees and plants, and in the volume of water running down the valleys. He says they "never saw more store nor better water than now ran in every valley, never saw it more green and flourishing in grass and trees than now at present, (I mean aloft); never so many lemons, having now found among the woods many other trees not formerly known . . . most bending with their burthens, on whom besides the multitude of well coloured ripe ones were as many green and small, and many more blossoms. The cattle also never in better case: all this aloft as afforesaid. For from the place where we rode, which was on the northwest side, there is hardly such another ragged, steepy, stony, high, cragged, rocky, barren, desolate and comfortless coast to be seen. But above the ground is excellent mold, although for the most part in very high, round, rising, small hills, steepy ascents and descents, painful and difficult to be travelled . . . here and there thicketts of shrubs, weeds and ferns, harbours for hogs as the rocks are for the goats . . . also some mints, malloes, purcelane, a kind of camomile smelling sweet are here to be found.[1] The goats for the most part black, some white and party-coloured. The hogs grizzled or grey, with very long bristles and hair, the flesh of them savouring of fish."

He mentions amongst the land birds the only indigenous one peculiar to St. Helena, "a small land fowl, somewhat like a lark in colour, shape and flight, and but only that one kind here to be seen", the wire bird, *Aegialitis sanctae-helenae*, a small ringed plover, which is still quite plentiful in the island.

On ascending Lemon Valley, "as we were going up it, we saw a kennel of dogs of sundry sorts, about 15 or 16, all white for ought we could see, who, as soon as they had espied us, took right up against the steepy rocky hill."

Higher up the same valley, "we found a certain wall of stone by plying them one on the other, enclosing a pretty (fair sized) piece of ground, and about 22 or 23 several names of Dutchmen written and graven on the stones in Anno 1637."

This enclosure must have been built by the Portuguese in former years for the pigs they brought to the island, while the names Mundy saw inscribed on the walls were those of some Dutch ship's crew who landed in the previous year.

---

[1] *Cotula anthemoides*, a plant indigenous to St. Helena.

In Chapel Valley the sailors found more traces of the recent visit of the Dutchmen, for the Chapel had for once been repaired by them, recently, and covered with a tarpaulin of "New double canvas", and "the names of divers ships, principal men, as also of some women, were fairly written on boards and nailed up in the said chapel."

Before leaving the island the names of the commanders, and the date of their arrival and departure were carved on a board and nailed up in the chapel alongside the others.

Before the middle of the seventeenth century, whenever the Spanish or Portuguese did venture to call at the island they were liable to find an unwelcome English or Dutch ship lying at anchor off Chapel Valley, the only watering place at the island, and such meetings as often as not led to fierce engagements. This happened on 18th June, 1613, when the great ship *Nossa Senhora da Nazaré* (Our Lady of Nazareth), laden with valuable merchandise from the Indies, and towing her damaged consort, *La Conceicão*, arrived at the anchorage. Scarcely had she dropped anchor when to their annoyance and surprise five big Dutch ships of war, bristling with cannon and their decks crowded with men, appeared sailing round the point towards them, with trumpets sounding and guns firing. The *Conceicão*, already disabled, was unable to take any part in the action which followed, but the *Nazareth* put up a gallant fight, sinking the largest Dutch ship and partly putting out of action another by shattering her forecastle. The rest of the Dutch vessels were soon in such a poor plight that they were obliged to take flight, "leaving our ship," as the Portuguese narrator of the battle jubilantly recounts, "victorious, with little damage and great exultation for having fought alone and each one for himself; and all those who were on her began to clamour and praise and give thanks for such prosperous success to the Virgin of Nazareth, as principal protectress and defender, promising to go to the House with alms and offerings, and the

32

Commander-in-Chief, Dom Geronimo de Almeida, handed me forty-two Portuguese pounds of indigo as alms for India, which were sold for good works, and a large piece of frankincense for use at the altar."

This naval battle ending in so pronounced a victory for the Portuguese was an exception to the rule, for in almost all sea fights of the seventeenth century between the Portuguese and the Dutch or English, the former were defeated. The reason for this is explained by Captain C. R. Boxer[1] in the following translation of an article written in Portuguese by him for the *Boletim da Agencia Geral das Colonias*.

This naval action is almost unknown and only a few Portuguese writers refer to it lightly. The exploit from a military point of view is very extraordinary, for this reason: in the whole course of naval fighting between Portugal and Holland, in the seas round India—a war which lasted from 1508 to 1663, with very few intervals—we only know two cases in which Dutch ships were sunk by Portuguese ships, *by cannon fire*. Many Portuguese ships were sunk by the Dutch—nearly always by the powerful and well-directed artillery of their ships. Many Flemish ships were sunk by the Portuguese, nearly always by boarding them or by burning them with pot-fulls of wild-fire or hand-grenades or similar methods.

All the contemporary writers are in agreement that the Portuguese artillery and artillery soldiers were always or nearly always inferior. The Portuguese, confident of their natural bravery, which was excessive in fighting face to face with the enemy, always preferred to win victory by the gentlemanly way of boarding the ships. This was all very well when fighting against the Moors or the Turks in the

[1] *Uma Desconhecido Vitoria Naval Portuguesa* No Seculo XVII. *Boletim.* Oct. 1929.

Indian Ocean, but not effective against the English and Dutch, both accustomed to, and clever on the sea, with clear-headed and well-disciplined bombardiers.

St. Helena, once so peaceful a paradise for sailors, was fast becoming a Tom Tiddler's ground for the Portuguese and the Dutch, where forays and fights took place whenever they met off Chapel Valley, skirmishes in which the English would join when the opportunity presented itself. And yet it never occurred to any one of these maritime powers to fortify and make a permanent colony or stronghold on this important half-way house between the East Indies and Europe. In 1625 another typical affray took place between the Dutch and the Portuguese. A Spanish or Portuguese carrack—between the years 1580 and 1640 they were one and the same—was lying at anchor off Chapel Valley when a large Dutch ship hove in sight, approaching the anchorage. Immediately the captain of the carrack ordered his ship to be warped close in and her stern made fast to a hawser from the shore. Some of her guns were quickly landed and placed so as to cover the position the ship occupied. At first the Dutch commander, Bontekou,[1] thought the carrack would prove an easy prize and that all he had to do was to cut the cable and tow her out.

He was soon to learn his mistake. First of all, sudden gusts of wind blowing down the valley made it difficult for him to work his ship within musket shot of the carrack, and when he did get close up doubts began to enter his mind, and discreetly he sent a civil message to the Portuguese asking for permission to water. This civility did not have the effect he wished, for the Spaniards answered abusively, "Anda perro, anda canalla."—"Go away dogs, go away riff-raff." But the Dutch were in desperate need of fresh water, so Captain

---

[1] *Voyage de Guillaume Isbrantoz Bontekou.*

Bontekou decided to fight for it, and a sharp action commenced, in which considerable damage was sustained on both sides. The guns on shore were so well aimed that the Dutch had to beat an ignominious retreat and anchor under the point (Mundens) which covered them from the fire of the battery. There the ship lay all night while a council was held to decide whether to renew the fight or to retreat and continue their voyage on a reduced allowance of water. They decided on the latter course, but when, at dawn, a boat was proceeding to weigh their kedge-anchor, a party of Spaniards appeared at the waterside and, opening fire with their muskets, drove off the Dutch who escaped, with several casualties but no water. The carrack, however, had suffered so severely in the action that she sank at her moorings. A considerable part of the wreck was saved, including most of the guns, and these were soon mounted in a breastwork and so formed the first permanent fortification on the island, and proved its value very shortly afterwards when the Portuguese succeeded in beating off a Dutch fleet of six sail which, as in the case of Captain Bontekou, had to sail away without water.

With all the wood saved from the wreck of the carrack which was not used for the fort, the shipwrecked sailors built themselves temporary dwellings, which were referred to in 1629 by Sir Thomas Herbert[1] as "some ruins of a little town", which he stated had become "a magazine of private trade", and for that reason had been destroyed by the Spanish Government. Sir Thomas took the opportunity of his visit to explore the island, which he found "hard to be ascended—it is so precipitous. The sailors have an ironic proverb: *'The way is such as a man may choose whether he will break his heart going up or his neck coming down'*, but being once up, scarce any place can yield a more large or more delightful prospect".

He referred to the chapel as "by the Dutch of late pulled

---

[1] *New and Complete Collection of Voyages and Travels.* 1785.

down, a place once intended for God's worship, but now disposed of to common uses".

He saw the "ribs of a weather-beaten carrique and some broken pieces of great ordnance", traces no doubt of the fight with Captain Bontekou four years previously. Those great ordnances or guns were then being used to serve instead of anchors.

There were now no houses or habitations, nor any inhabitants, but the sailors with little trouble procured plenty of "pheasants, powts, quails, hens and partridges", and what was described as being no less acceptable, such anti-scorbutic herbs as "basil, parsley, mint, spinage, fennel, annis, mustard-seed" etc., "which by a willing hand, directed by an ingenious eye, may soon be gathered".

These health-restoring plants, Sir Thomas informs us, were sown by Fernandus Lupises, "a Portugal", in the year of our Lord 1509, for the good of his countrymen.

CHAPTER II

1629–1673

W ITH the beginning of the seventeenth century the claims of Portugal to St. Helena came to an end. For this there were two principal reasons. Having secured an East India Empire, with such African ports of call as Sofola, Mombassa, Mozambique, Melinda and Madisha, the Portuguese began to think less of their little island in the South Atlantic as an essential port of call for their carracks returning from India. This neglect increased as St. Helena became a more-and-more frequented place of call for the ships of their enemies, the Dutch and the English, who now had begun to use it as a regular place of "refreshment" on their own voyages from the East. The Portuguese and Spanish found that the risk of a hostile reception to their vessels made it not worth their calling except under the most pressing circumstances. Thus the island came to belong to no one; those who called there took what they would or could, water, fruit, vegetables and fresh meat, and sailed away. It was uninhabited; it was nobody's business to plant fresh vegetables or to tend the fruit trees, or repair the ruined buildings in Chapel Valley.

The history of St. Helena during the first half of the seventeenth century is obscure.[1] All we have are the brief accounts written by occasional visitors and the descriptions of periodic sea-fights off Chapel Valley.

Sometimes a passing sailor would carve his name and that

[1] The author offers full acknowlegment for information about this period to Sir William Foster, for his learned article which appeared in the *Historical Review*, 1919.

of his ship, with the date of his visit, and some of these stones still exist. Only lately such a stone was discovered and placed beside the entrance of the castle, which bears the following inscription, recording the arrival and departure of the *Dolphin*.

SHP DOLPHIN
WILL FREMLEN COMr.
JOHN PROWD   MASTER
(? landed)   NED HERE Mo CH Ye 21
(departed)   RTD HENCE MAY Ye 18
STLO NOVO
1645

According to Anderson's *History of Commerce* and Bruce's *Annals of the East India Company*, the Dutch took possession of St. Helena about the year 1645 and held it for five or six years, when they abandoned it preparatory to settling at the Cape of Good Hope, whereupon the English at once seized the island. But there is no sort of authority for this belief, which is unsupported by any of the various travellers who touched at St. Helena during or immediately after this period.

Tavernier, who was aboard a Dutch fleet which called at the island in 1649, says nothing about a Dutch occupation, nor of there being any regular inhabitants, while the Sieur de Flacourt, in 1655, found the island deserted.

The veil which hid this obscure period of St. Helena's history was partly raised by an Icelander, Jon Olafsson, a gunner on board the Danish ship *Pearl*, which called at the island on her return voyage from India in 1625.

The following is his description of his visit to St. Helena.[1]

It is like a bluff standing very high up out of the ocean, and difficult to climb up. In former times some Portuguese lived there for a while and kept swine and goats and other domestic animals. They sowed crops of tobacco and had

[1] *The Life of the Icelander Jon Olafsson, Traveller to India.* Hakluyt Society.

planted splendid fruit trees in many places down by the shore, and right up on the fair smooth pleasant plateau every tree bore the most delicious and sweetest fruit. It is very difficult to reach from below, for when a man thinks he sees the highest point there proves to be another, and yet a third peak, and it is believed that no other land exists like it, or with such a formation. A landing can only be made at one place, which is called Church Harbour, where the Portuguese had their church. At the time we were there, Anno 1625, it was still standing in good repair.[1] But when the Spaniards (Portuguese) and Dutch were at war, their people were at enmity with each other wherever they met, and hence these islanders did not venture to remain there on account of the raids and attacks of the Flemings which they continually had to encounter, especially towards the last, so that they were obliged to flee both land and possessions in great fear and terror.[2] For this reason there are great herds of swine on the uplands, and in the valleys of the islands, left behind by the fugitives, and these have become wild and cannot be caught save by the chase, many persons joining in it. They have weapons to attack them, which they call cross-lances, and it is seaman's custom that any who use them (of those who land) should leave their weapons behind on the path where it first rises towards the mountain, and anyone may use them who has need of them. Our men caught nine large swine, but with great trouble. I also clambered up these lofty heights and lay there with my companions in a large tent. We made a great bonfire, and sat around it, having both wine and provisions, and a goat which they had just killed was roasted on the aforesaid lances and afterwards eaten. And while we were sitting over our meal, as snugly as possible, a huge wild boar came

[1] Mads Rasmussen preached in the chapel at St. Helena on 6 February 1625 "to our sick" and said, "this church or chapel had been built by the Portuguese."
[2] This is inaccurate.—P. G.

trailing past us to the fire. Those appointed for the purpose (in case aught should befall) instantly flung aside their knives and meat, and pursued him till they killed him. Then we all slept till morning, save only the watchman.

We caught four swine on this expedition, and by midday we went out to our great ship. Towards evening men who had climbed to the mast-top saw a large sail towards the island. We were not afraid of the Spaniards, because the Kings (Philip IV of Spain and Christian IV of Denmark) were friendly at that time; nevertheless telescopes were snatched up and their flag at the top-mast examined, and it was seen that they were Flemish, a Company-vessel (Dutch E. I. Coy.) plying between the East Indies and Amsterdam. The vessel was called the *Fair Falcon*, captain Johan Cather. They were in need of bread and other provisions. . . . And when we had lain there five days we sailed away in company out to sea under excellent fair winds.

It was only after this chapter had been written that an extremely interesting and important piece of information came to hand through Mr. L. C. Vrijman, of the Hague.

This was the exciting news that he had discovered in the State Archives an old parchment on which was written in Dutch, the formal claim on the part of Holland to the possession of St. Helena in the year 1633. In the parchment can be seen the perforations made by the nails when it was originally nailed up to a pillar or post in Chapel Valley over three hundred years ago. This appears beyond all question to prove that the Dutch did actually take possession of the island in that year, not, be it noted, for the Dutch East India Company but for the United Provinces.

This proclamation has been translated for me by Mr. Vrijman and runs as follows:

On the 15th day of April 1633 the noble sire Jacques Specx, late Governor General of the State of the United Provinces of the Netherlands in India, together with the Council-in-pleno of the Dutch fleet which has just arrived here, consisting of the ships, the *Prins Willem*, the *Princesse Emilia*, *Hollandia*, *Zutphen*, *Rotterdam* and *Hoorn*, have accepted the possession and proprietorship of the island, named of yore *St. Helena*, with all its grounds, hills, cliffs and rocks belonging to it, for the State of the United Provinces, in order to the benefit and advantage of the said Netherland State, as soon as the circumstances shall allow, to fortify, occupy, populate and defend it against the invasion of enemies, in the way as their Highnesses the High and Mighty States General of the said United Provinces shall deem advisable.

As is shown clearly by the solemn deed, made out in due form, of the aforesaid possession and proprietorship.

To certify this and confirming the truth, that nobody may pretend ignorance thereof has been erected this pillar, as well as this notification, duly sealed and signed and nailed thereonto in the above mentioned year and on the date mentioned.

Lieve Douwis
Cornelius Theunissen Drent
on command of the said Hon.
General and Council-in-pleno
J. Van Vossele
as secretary.

From the above it is clear that St. Helena was taken possession of, in all due legal form, by the Dutch. What is far from clear is whether having taken the island they ever occupied, colonized or fortified it.

All the evidence—and most of it is negative—points to the

fact that St. Helena was not occupied for another thirty-six years and then by the English East India Company, and that until then it continued to be a no-man's-land and house-of-call for ships of the five maritime nations.

In an article written by Dr. F. W. Stapel[1] he attempts, but I think without success, to claim that after Jacques Specx took formal possession of the island in 1633 the Dutch fortified and occupied it. This would appear to be the obvious inference, but there is no scrap of evidence that the Dutch ever did make any attempt permanently to hold the island. Dr. Stapel puts forward as his principal witness "the good ship *de Molen*" which sailed from Holland on the 1st of July, 1656, for Batavia. Her cargo had been badly stowed, the ship was top-heavy and consequently the captain dared not carry much sail. She made little headway, and it was not until the 9th November she dropped anchor off Chapel Valley.

Here the captain decided to clean ship, re-stow his cargo and take into the hold a quantity of stones for ballast. While engaged on this work a small English ship from Plymouth to Bantam came in and anchored in the roads. The English were badly in need of provisions and asked the Dutch to be allowed to obtain some meat. This the Dutch commander politely refused, because, he said, he wanted what meat there was for his own use, but he gave the English captain permission to fish.

It will be noted that nothing is said about a Dutch governor or garrison on the island. The refusal of meat and the permission to fish was given by the commander of the big Dutch ship which was already there, to the captain of the small English one which arrived later.

It appears that Dr. Stapel overlooked the evidence of Peter Mundy,[2] the Cornish sailor who visited St. Helena for the

[1] "The Netherlanders on St. Helena." *Koloniale Wiehblad.* March 24, 1927.
[2] *Travels of Peter Mundy.* Vol. V, p. 79. Hakluyt Society.

third time in the same year as the *de Molen*, from the 25th to the 31st of May.

During his stay of six days this indefatigable traveller and sightseer explored the island and described all he saw, and yet made no mention of one single inhabitant, nor is it likely there were any inhabitants since he and his shipmates "looked for letters, and found none".

The only mention he made of the Dutch was when he spoke of four horses he saw in Chapel Valley, "doubtless left here by the Hollanders to encrease for provision".

This last sentence with the mention of the pig pound on page 31 are the only hints we have of any occupation of St. Helena by the Dutch, and if such occupation did take place, it must have been for a very short period and a long while before 1656.

Neither did Mundy mention having seen any survivors of the two Portuguese ships which were wrecked in 1643 and are known to have replenished the island with cattle, hogs and goats.

Between the years 1633 and 1669, many sailors landed at St. Helena, and of those who left written accounts of their visit, not one is known to the present writer to have alluded to any inhabitant on St. Helena.

For facts concerning the first permanent occupation of St. Helena we are indebted to the existing records of the English East India Company. From these we learn that the decision to take possession of the island was arrived at a year after Cromwell granted a charter to the Company, in 1657, and then only because their previous plan to fortify and colonize the small island of Polu Run in the Malay Archipelago had been dropped, owing to the opposition of the Dutch who were all-powerful in the far East.

In October, 1659, with a fresh charter from the Protector, the expedition was about to set out to Polu Run, with Captain

John Dutton in command, when the order was cancelled and
the Court of Committees decided to colonize St. Helena
instead, a scheme which had been recommended by Richard
Boothby as far back as 1644, in a pamphlet entitled "A True
Declaration . . ." The Company had taken little or no
notice of this scheme at the time, but since its publication the
island had taken on a new importance quite apart from its
growing use as a place of call for refreshment for East India
ships. The Atlantic from Cape Verde Islands to the Channel
had become dangerous for ships sailing alone, what with the
Civil War, the Dutch War, and the Spanish War, let alone
privateers and pirates, and it had become necessary for the East
Indiamen to complete their voyages in company, if possible,
escorted by one or more men-of-war. In 1649 orders were
first issued that all vessels bound for England from India or
the Far East should wait for one another at St. Helena, and
from 1656 onwards the East India Company annually petitioned
the Protector to send a man-of-war to meet them there and
convoy them home.

A further inducement to the English Company to establish
a permanent colony on the island and to fortify it was the
increasing aggressiveness of the Dutch, who had occupied
the Cape and whose activities in the East were causing considerable alarm in England and who at any moment might
decide to seize themselves this desirable half-way house to
Europe.

An important minute occurs in the Company's records of
15th December, 1658, which runs:

> The Court having several tymes very lately taken into
> their consideration the great conveniencing and concern-
> ment that it might prove, both to the Company and to this
> nation, for to fortify the island of St. Helena, whereon (it
> is believed) many good plantations may in tyme be made,

44

did again this day reassume the serious consideration of that business. And finding so much reason to engage them in this work, as well as encouragement, after a long debate of the whole business, resolved, by a general erection of hands, to send 400 men with all expedition to remayne on the island, with conveniences to fortifie and begin a plantation there.

It is not surprising that the choice of command should have fallen on Captain John Dutton, who had been left unemployed when the expedition to Polu Run was abandoned, and he was ordered to proceed to St. Helena, on the handsome salary of £200 a year, with permission to take Mrs. Dutton, a Dutch lady from Batavia, with him. As his lieutenant the Company appointed Captain Robert Stringer on a more modest remuneration of £40 a year. The fleet set out from the Downs early in February, 1659, accompanied by the *Marmaduke*, a man-of-war of thirty-six guns and one hundred and fifty men, which was ordered to convoy home any returning ships which might be found at St. Helena. To secure the goodwill of the commander of the *Marmaduke*, Captain Peter Butler, the Company gave him a gratuity of £20. The commission given to Dutton, dated 11th January, 1659, declared that having "resolved to settle, fortifie, and plant upon the island of St. Helena" they appointed him to be "Governor in Chief on the said island", and he was required to embark in the *London* and proceed first of all to the island of St. Iago, one of the Cape Verde group, and thence to St. Helena, "where when it shall please the Allmightie to arrive you, we hereby impower, authorize, and require you that, forthwith after your coming to anchor in the roade, you, with the commanders and as many English as convenientlie may be spared from aboard the ships, do repaire on shoare, and in the name of His Highness Richard, Lord Protector of England, Scotland, and Ireland, and the

Dominions thereunto belonging, and for the use of the Honourable English East-India Company, doe take possession of the island, and with drum and trumpett proclaime the same."

All persons then and thereafter appointed to reside on the island were charged to render due obedience to Governor Dutton.

Anyone found guilty of a serious offence, such as felony, murder or treason, was to be confined in chains and sent to England by the next ship for trial, but in the case of minor offences, the governor and his council were authorized to inflict such punishments as were "usually exercised in other English plantations, according to the laws of England". In the event of Dutton's death, Captain Stringer was to succeed him with the same powers. The council was to consist, during the stay of the fleet, of the Governor, the lieutenant governor, and the commanders of the fleet, but after their departure Dutton was to select three of the inhabitants to assist him and Stringer. One member of this council was to write down their proceedings, and these records, signed by those taking part in each consultation, were to be transmitted yearly to the Company in London.

With a view to replenishing the stocks at St. Helena, Captain Bowen of the *London* had been instructed to touch at St. Iago on the outward voyage in order to obtain "all manner of plants, roots, grains, and all other things necessarie for plantation there to be had or procured, but more espetially in those which are to be esteemed your most certaine provisions, as planton rootes, cassandra sticks, large yams, potatoes and bonavist, pease, gravances, and beanes of all sorts, oranges and lemons". Very minute and careful directions were given for the preservation of these roots on the voyage. Also the commander was charged: "In case at St. Iago you can procure five or six blacks or negroes, able men and women, we desire you to buy them, provided they may be had at or under

40 dollers per poll; which service wee hope will not require above three or four daies stay at most."

The Company, then as always, was very solicitous over the spiritual welfare of its servants and for the regular holding of divine service: "to which purpose wee have furnished you with bibles and sundry other good bookes", while Dutton was himself exhorted "by your example and authoritie to suppresse all vitiousnesse in our people, that soe the Lord may prosper you and take delight to dwell in the midest of you".

The members of the Court in London were practical business men, and were concerned with practical matters as well as questions of morals. This is shown by the following order:

> The Allmightie having arrived you at St. Helena, you shall with all speed proceed to fortifie in the most convenient place of Chappell Valley and in such other place or places on the island as you shall judge most necessarie and requisite for the defence of the same and to offend any enemies that shall come into or neare the road or roads of the said island. But while this work is going on, you are espetially to have regard to the first season and opportunitie that God shall graunt unto you to proceede to planting of your provisions, but espetially your plantans and cassada, because they otherwise will be in danger to perish; and this doe in severall places of the island as you shall find convenient. And that you also proceede to set your carpenters and other artificers on worke for the framing and getting up your magazine and storehouse and other houses necessarie for your accommodation within the lynes of your fortifications.

The fleet left England with sufficient provisions to last the colonists for fourteen months, by which time it was estimated that the settlers' crops, together with the foodstuffs they would be able to obtain by hunting and fishing, would be enough for their needs. No detail was overlooked by the businesslike but paternal Court of the Company. A steward was appointed to look after the stores, and all clothing and other goods supplied to the colonists were to be charged to the recipient's account at 20 per cent above the cost of the same goods bought in England. The governor was urged also to take a survey of the entire island and to look for sites for plantations.

> You shall cause an exact draught of the whole island to be platted down in a large scale, after the manner of a land-script, by the most ingenious person that shall be present, by which we may discerne the severall vallies, hills, ridges in the said island; and these to send unto us by the first opportunitie.

The sailors were to be employed on the fortifications and other works, and to encourage them in their labour "a bottle of brandy wine" was to be distributed amongst them and a promise given them that the Company would recompense "any eminent service" they might render.

The *Marmaduke* and the *London* arrived off Chapel Valley on the 5th of May after a voyage which lasted three months. No copy exists of the report which Dutton sent home to the Company on the 23rd of June by the *Marmaduke*.

There are to-day to be seen in the walls of the present castle at Jamestown relics which give us some little information about the first English settlers in the island. These are three stones with the following inscriptions:

CAPT JOHN DUTTON
GOVERNOR OF THIS FORTIFICA-
TION FOR THE ENGLISH EAST
INDIA COMP. JUNE ye 4 ANN DOM. 1658
OPERA TESTANTUR DE M.

THO. COLEMAN WORKMAN IN CHIEF
OF THIS FORTIFICATION FOR THE
USE OF THE ENGLISH EAST
INDIA COMPANY I CAME
IN THE MARMIDUCK
MAN OF WARE
MAY ye 4
1659.

JOHN
JEFREYS THE
MASTURS
MATE OF THE
ADVICE OCTO
BER ye 16. 1659

The Colonists and the sailors appear to have completed the blockhouse or fortification within a month; and the building was called the "Castle of St. John", though whether this was done as a compliment to John Dutton, history does not relate. It did not retain this name for long but was rechristened James Fort, in honour of the Duke of York, who afterwards became King James II. The little town which sprang up in the valley behind the fort was called James Town, and Chapel Valley became James Valley, names which have survived till to-day. Amongst the personal possessions the first Governor took out with him was a portrait of Oliver Cromwell. About this picture and about much else that is interesting we shall learn later on in an account of his visit to St. Helena by the Sieur de Rennefort, in the spring of 1666.

From its start the East India Company took a fatherly interest in the little colony. It soon became obvious that it could not be self-supporting for some years, indeed as it turned out, during the whole colonial history of St. Helena it was, and it still is, unable fully to support itself. By the *Truro*, bound from England to Madras in June, 1659, was sent out a quantity of stores which included flour, peas, beer, brandy, shoes—at twenty-eight shillings per dozen—and fishing tackle. The captain of the *Truro* was instructed to call on his way at the Guinea Coast and there purchase, if he was able, "ten lusty blacks, men and women", as well as grain, coconuts, potatoes, yams, oranges and lemons, for the use of the settlers.

In October of the same year the *Success* man-of-war arrived at Jamestown to convoy home the returning India fleet, and she, too, brought out supplies for the colony as well as more settlers. In the previous January the Company had sent written orders to Surat that every ship coming home should embark a ton of rice for the use of the new colony.

Captain Dutton was not destined to remain Governor of St. Helena for long, for in December, 1660, he received instructions to hand over his charge to Captain Stringer and to proceed to Bantam on his way to Polu Run, though he did not leave the island until the summer of 1661. The restoration of the English monarchy in 1660 placed the East India Company in a somewhat precarious position. Their new charter entitling them to St. Helena "in the name of Richard, Lord Protector" was become of little value with the change of government and the Company had to petition for a fresh royal one, which eventually they were granted. When Captain Dutton left for Polu Run he was instructed to take any of the settlers willing to go with him. The result of this offer was that all of them but two elected to accompany their popular Governor, and this in spite of the Company's offer of grants of land as freemen. In the end twenty-five men left for the East Indies, and as only eleven "servants" came out in the *Africa* from England, the new Governor, Stringer, found himself with a mere thirty able men to look after and to guard the island. When the Company lost their West African possession, Fort Cormantine, in 1662, they sent out word that

any of their servants who wished to return to England were
to be allowed a free passage to St. Helena where it was hoped
some of them might decide to settle and colonize. This
paucity of settlers much hampered Stringer in his work. It is
true that the *Constantinople* brought out twenty-six men in
1663, and the *Charles* another thirty or perhaps more, victims
of the Great Fire of London, four years later, but these and
other reinforcements were largely countered by those others
who returned to England or went on to the East.

The Company caused bills to be set up in London to attract
settlers to St. Helena but with little success, for, as we learn
from Rennefort, there were, in 1666, only fifty white men and
twenty white women in the island, while four years later the
population had fallen to forty-eight whites and eighteen
negroes. Everything was done not only to induce settlers to
go to St. Helena, but to remain there. In Dutton's time there
were no free settlers and therefore no land-holders amongst
the inhabitants, but in 1661 instructions were sent to Governor
Stringer to free all those who were willing to remain in the
island and to give each one a parcel of land as was customary
in new colonies. Acting on these orders Stringer divided up
the island into one hundred and fifty parts, reserving fifteen
for the Company, five for himself and allotting one share to
each planter, his wife and his servant. The arrangement
between the Company and the Colonists was almost a feudal
one, for the land-holder in return for his freedom and land
had to assist in maintaining the fortifications and to take his
turn in the watch and to be ready at the sound of the alarm
guns and the beat of the drum to assemble at the fort whenever a ship appeared, and also to pay a small rent in kind out
of the produce of his ground.[1]

When the *London* brought out provisions to last the new
colony for fourteen months it had been thought that by the

[1] *History of St. Helena and the Route to the Indies, 1659–1702.* W. C. Palmer.

end of that time the planters would have been self-supporting, as far as victuals went. They were not, even in spite of the further supplies brought out by the *Truro* and the *Success*, and a sharp warning came from London that no more supplies need be expected after those brought by the *Constantinople*, and that they would have henceforth to depend on their own exertions. Stringer's position was a difficult one. Towards the close of 1663 he was compelled to write home: "Our stores of provisions are almost spent, our bread ended . . . we have many eaters, and have very little relief from the plantations."

All the comfort the Governor got for this was the reproof: "We cannot but blame you that you should every year take out salt beef out of our returned ships, and in the stead to furnish them with fresh beef at the same price." Three years later the islanders, or at all events the Governor and his household at the castle, seem to have been well provided for in the way of victuals, if we are to believe the writer of the account of Rennefort's visit to the island in the spring of 1666. This record is of peculiar interest and value since it was written by a well-educated observer and is worth while reprinting in full.[1]

We were half a league off shore, when we sighted in a little bay, an important looking English building. We at once gave a salute of three cannons and were answered by one. A long boat having approached within pistol shot, they hailed us in English, asking from whence came the ship. We replied:

"From France."

"From what part of France?"

"From St. Malo."

"Your last port of call?"

---

[1] *Histoire des Indes Orientales.* Rennefort, S. de.   Paris, 1688.

"Madagascar."

"Your captain's name?"

"La Chesnaie."

"Let him come ashore and show his credentials to the Governor."

"Show us a safe anchorage."

We were told that we could safely anchor at this spot and the anchors were cast in twenty-four fathoms. The Lieutenant, whose name was La Poupardrie, made ready to go ashore instead of the Captain, who was at the time far from well, and was recognized by one of the English officers who had just arrived on board and who provided some refreshments. La Poupardrie went with him to the Fort, showed the Captain's credentials and asked permission to draw water, which was granted very civilly.

The next day Rennefort, accompanied by the writer and several of the more important passengers, paid a visit to the Governor, who presented his wife and two of his daughters to them and offered liqueurs while waiting for dinner to be served. He then took them to see a water-fall, which falls between two rocks close to the Fort, and he was kind enough to divert part of the stream, about the thickness of two arms, and to have it run through pipes of a convenient size with which to fill our barrels. The dinner was most cleanly served and consisted of dishes, half of which were French and half English. The ladies sat at table with us and we were free and easy as if we had been in France. The only thing which shocked Rennefort was that when healths were proposed, they were drunk by everyone out of the same glass. La Chesnaie, having had himself carried on to the beach on a bed, was transferred by the Governor's orders to the best room in the fort. The building was on the left hand side, and constructed of wood in the English manner, and roofed with tiles which must have served as ballast to some boat. One gained entrance by a flight of six steps leading to a big armoury. Opening out of each side of this hall, were suites of three rooms, each furnished with Indian materials, Persian carpets, beds and chairs of grey and black ebony, decorated with gold studs. In the most conspicuous position in the Governor's room hung a portrait of Charles II, from which Cromwell's portrait had been removed and hung in the space between bed and wall, with its face to the wall, on seeing which the writer notes that politics still trouble the most distant and solitary places.

On the right hand side, twenty cabins in a line served as barracks for the garrison.

St. Helena is known from many former accounts, but this one seems to be the first to mention that it was regularly inhabited.

To continue the narrative:

The Governor's name was Stringer; a man of about fifty-five. The inhabitants numbered fifty English and twenty women, who were provided with biscuits, oil and salt beef at the expense of the East India Company. Most of the English had houses about the Island and came in turn to the fort to guard and keep watch. There were a few negroes for the heavier labour.

Rennefort admired the quantities of peas, beans, turnips, beetroot, cabbages, bananas, lemons, oranges, grenadines and melons, all most carefully cultivated, even grapes ripen, and there was nothing obnoxious to the amenities of life except vast quantities of rats, on which the Governor wages a sanguinary war. There are great numbers of goats. They did import horses, but these had become so wild that when they were pursued to the ends of the island they threw themselves off the rocks into the sea rather than be caught. Partridges and guinea fowl provided sport for the gun. Mr. Stringer had about twenty-four cows, looked after by his negroes, while four women milked and made the butter.

He showed the Frenchmen the curiosities of his collection, amongst which Rennefort admired the bones of a manatee or sea-cow, the skin of which was made into a corselet supposed to be proof against pistol shots. There was also the biggest example of a flying fish ever caught, though it was no bigger than an ordinary mackerel; ambergris, and all sorts of stuffs and curios brought from India; five lbs. of civet, in a glass bottle, estimated to be worth five or six thousand francs.

The officers of the ship bought during their stay boxes of civet, cornelian rings, agate knife handles, and other Indian merchandise with which the English were well provided. Two musk-cats or two civets cost them sixty piastres. The captain, who had recovered somewhat, had himself transported to the ship to receive the English Governor, his wife, son, two daughters and son-in-law. Once again the healths of the Kings of France and England were drunk.

Eventually, on the 7th of April, after having weighed anchor, and received from the Governor letters for the Eastern Company in Paris, the English were thanked for their kindness by a salute from the guns, to which those of the fort replied shot for shot.

It would be difficult to understand how such friendly gestures were so soon changed into cruel hostilities, if one did not bear in mind that peace was already shattered at that time, between the two countries,[1] and that this disastrous event had already led to much bloodshed in Europe, which news was still not known in far distant places.

[1] France declared war in January, 1666.

In spite of the comforts, and indeed luxuries, at the Castle, the discontent amongst the settlers steadily increased, and not only did the Council in London receive frequent complaints of the shortage of food and other necessities, but also letters from the Governor complaining that in the event of a hostile attack he could not guarantee to defend the island successfully with the handful of men at his disposal. The threat of a general war in 1671 caused the Council considerable anxiety, and they hurriedly despatched eighty men, two hundred and forty round shot and ten barrels of gunpowder.

But these reinforcements, together with fresh stores of beef, wheat, biscuits, arrack, soap, live sheep and deer from England, and rice from Surat, were not enough to stem the rising and dangerous tide of threatened mutiny. In vain did the Governor and his Council meet and debate ways and means of settling what was fast becoming an ugly situation. The government of St. Helena was similar to that at other of the Company's plantations; it consisted of the Governor, who had a casting vote, and three of the islanders chosen by the Governor. Governor Stringer's first Council was somewhat larger than was usual, numbering six members, two of them nominated by the Governor and the rest by the freeholders, but the numbers fluctuated from time to time and from Governor to Governor. It was a Governor's vote which eventually brought matters to a head. Captain Cony, who became Governor in 1672, claimed that his vote over-rode the unanimous vote of the Council, while the Council maintained that his vote, in the case of an equal show of hands, was a casting one, and that a majority ought always to carry the day.

Even in 1664 there had been trouble in the island when Stringer informed the Court of Directors that the last batch of immigrants sent out in the *Constantinople* were full of complaints about the food and clothing, and he forwarded a petition from them. His letter was not received with sympathy, and all he got in answer was a scornful recommendation to keep his people at work and also "to learn how to govern such a handful".

A visitor in 1665, Nicholas Buckeridge,[1] described the island as being in disorder and the time-expired servants clamouring to be sent home to England. In 1670 there was a change of Governors, when Stringer at his own request returned to England and Captain Cony was sent out to succeed him, the gap between the departure of the first and the arrival of the second being filled temporarily by Robert Swallow, a resident in the island since 1669. The arrival of Richard Cony in March 1671, in company with a chaplain Noakes, was at once followed by the first of many unseemly broils. The new Governor was a man of strong will, and for a while his high-handedness curbed the mutinous element. Many charges were brought against him; that he was cruel and arrogant both to the white and black population, and that he defrauded the Company—an old cry often levelled against an unpopular Governor or other servant of the Company. Cony's answer to these charges was that the people drank too much punch made from the arrack which the Company imported so freely and sold so cheaply. He even quarrelled with Chaplain Noakes, accusing him of anti-Royalist opinions in permitting "fanatic" books to the soldiers, which taught that "Kings, princes and Governors may be disempowered by the people". Cony went so far as to name three of his Councillors whom he considered the ringleaders, "two it seemeth old mutineers in former Governors' times"—Henry Gargen and Henry Bennett; and Chaplain Noakes.

With the permanent occupation of the Island, more and more ships called at Jamestown, for water and refreshment, and in time of war, English East Indiamen for convoy home.

[1] I.O., O.C., 3064-1. Vol. 29.

Some of the sailors or passengers aboard these ships wrote down accounts of what they saw at St. Helena, and as almost any first-hand observation by an eye-witness is of interest and value in a history of the island, a few will be included here. Robert Barlow, mariner, kept one of the best sea-journals ever written, and illustrated it with delightful coloured drawings. This diary was recently published under the editorship of Mr. Basil Lubbock.[1] Barlow made two brief visits to St. Helena, the first in April 1671, one month after the arrival of Governor Cony. His ship only stayed for ten or twelve days, and unfortunately Barlow is more concerned in jotting down the news he heard at James Fort of other East Indiamen than in gathering information about the island. He says they watered there and "refreshed themselves with such provisions as the island afforded", that in former times it was inhabited by the "Portangalls" but "their people not liking very well to work, as they must do that intend to live upon it, they left it. Since then our East India Company have taken it in possession and have transported people thither to till it, and keep it for them, sending out of England a stock of cattle with them, which they have increased very much through our people's industry, for the island produceth nothing of itself, only some few oranges and plenty of fresh water, for it is all over very mountainous and rocky; yet there are some valleys which are full of low shrubby wood and very good grass in some places, which keep the cattle very fat and in good case, they multiplying very much on it."

Barlow considered the soil to be very good, and remarked how the inhabitants grew quantities of good potatoes, beans and Indian corn as well as colewort and other herbs such as parsley. "And our English make very good butter of the cattle."

He saw some wild fowl such as guinea-hens and partridges,

[1] *Barlow's Journal.* Edited by Basil Lubbock. Hurst & Blackett, 1934.

and he commented upon the plentiful store of provisions as "excellent good beef" and hogs and goats and hens, "but bread corn they have none, for they cannot sow by reason of the roughness of the ground." A little while before his visit, the English had planted some banana and plantain trees, and he found very good yams, "a thing like a potato but far bigger".

He describes the English fort as being "indifferent well fortified", and the island as being governed by a Governor under the East India Company. He wrote that most of the Company's ships called at the island, and sometimes Portuguese ones bound from Angola to Brazil, and also French ships sailing home from India. Also occasionally English slavers arrived there from Madagascar or the Guinea Coast.

Since the settlers had been made freemen, "you must buy what you have of them, except beef, which the Company hath of their own, which every ship hath some when they touch there, without paying for it."

Except for his description of the fort as being "indifferent well fortified", Barlow gives no hint of the trouble which was brewing. On the 21st of August, 1672, the long smouldering discontent suddenly broke out into open mutiny. On that day the three rebellious Councillors, with the support of the rest of the Council, seized the Governor and kept him a prisoner until October, when they shipped him home in the *Advance*, and in the meanwhile elected Chaplain Noakes to reign in his stead. Luckily for the rebels, though at the time they did not know it, the Company had decided to recall Cony as being unfitted for his post, and had already sent out a new Governor, Anthony Beale, a former ship's carpenter and assistant surveyor of shipping. On his arrival Beale appointed to the Council the turbulent chaplain and Robert Swallow, with two elected planters, but as a reprimand for his late conduct, Noakes was excluded succession in the event of the

Governor's demise. Within one month another and unlooked-for catastrophe occurred. In 1652 the Dutch Company had made a permanent colony at the Cape, largely on the advice of Jan van Riebeck because of his belittling of St. Helena as a suitable place for settlement. But it had not taken long for the Cape-colonists and the Dutch East India Company to see their mistake, for the harbour at Table Bay was not always a safe anchorage for sailing ships, and many homecoming East Indiamen had been blown past the Cape and been compelled to call for water and other refreshment at St. Helena. So the Dutch Company set about searching the South Atlantic for some island which would make a safer and more suitable base than the one at the Cape. Ships were sent out to examine and report on Ascension Island, Trinidad and its neighbouring rocky islets of Martin Vas, Tristan da Cunha and Diego Alvarez, or Gough Island as it is called to-day. None of these was found to be practicable, while the search for New St. Helena, a mythical counterpart to the real island, ended in disappointment, although ship after ship was sent out to look for it. On a map drawn by John Seller and published in 1682,[1] the island of S. Elena Nueva is actually shown, lying midway between St. Helena and the coast of Africa. This mysterious island was believed to belong to Portugal, and several travellers were quite ready to declare they had seen it with their own eyes, while the principal witness in favour of its existence was a carpenter's mate named Lodenwyk Claasz, who turned up one day at Batavia and who swore that in 1652 he had twice been to the island as a prisoner of the Portuguese, who told him its latitude, which was $\frac{1}{2}°$ lower than that of the known St. Helena. He told a convincing story of its flourishing plantations and of its two forts, and how it was so flat as to be invisible but two or three miles away to sea. At last

---

[1] *Atlas Maritimus*: or a Sea-Atlas; describing the sea-coasts in most of the known parts of the World. By John Seller, Hydrographer to the King. 1682.

the Council at Amsterdam came to the reluctant conclusion that no such island as New St. Helena existed, and they began seriously to consider seizing the real St. Helena from the English, or else doing what the Dutch were always partial to, destroying what they could not hold themselves with a view to preventing others—their rivals in trade—from profiting by it. For example, on one occasion the Dutch left on St. Helena twenty dogs and bitches so that they would kill the wild goats, and these dogs, which went wild, increased and became a very serious nuisance.

The English Company who were well posted by their agents in the doings of their Dutch rivals and in their reputed intentions, began to improve the fortifications of the island. Dutton on his first arrival had built sound defensive works at Chapel Valley, or as we must now call it, James Valley, as well as at several other places where an enemy might attempt a landing. The landing at Jamestown was guarded by two small forts, one square, the other triangular, the latter being armed by eleven guns. In February, 1667, a huge tidal wave on the leeward shore carried away the greater part of the fort at Lemon Valley, to the west of James Valley, as well as Stringer's "new sconce". Following King Charles II's declaration of war on Holland in 1672, Cony was ordered at once to repair the fort, and in June, the next Governor, Beale, was urged to fortify and erect guns as quickly as possible wherever required and to prepare the island and the inhabitants for an attack. Alas, the warning came too late, for when in December the enemy arrived, the garrison was undisciplined and dilatory, and the work on the defences incomplete.

The decision to attack St. Helena was arrived at by the Dutch Council at Table Bay on the 30th November, 1672, when they ordered Jacob de Gens to take command of a squadron which included the *Vryheit*, *Cattenburg* and *Vliegende Swaen*, and sail for St. Helena. They left Table Bay on the

13th December, and on the 5th March, 1673, the last-named vessel returned with the joyful news that the English island had been taken after an almost bloodless victory. The Dutch fleet arrived off St. Helena on or about the 20th of December and for two days made unavailing attempts to secure a landing at James Valley and elsewhere. On New Year's Eve a party of soldiers landed at Lemon Valley, but they had been observed by the islanders who met them with such a shower of stones and boulders, which they rolled upon them from the precipices above, that the enemy re-embarked and feigned a retreat. However, returning after dark they observed the light of a fire at another landing place, Bennett's Point, close to Swanley Valley. The light proved to be a signal to the enemy made by a traitor by name W. Coxe, who was waiting there with his slave to guide them. There is a legend that the slave was killed by Coxe after the landing to prevent the possibility of his giving evidence afterwards of his master's treachery.

The party which landed is stated to have numbered five hundred men and was led by Coxe up the steep Swanley Valley, but if this was the case, the valley must have altered considerably during the last two hundred and fifty years, for none but a skilled rock climber could clamber up the valley to-day, even in daylight.

On gaining the pasture at the top they halted to slaughter some cattle, but met no English troops until they reached High Peak, where they came upon a detachment belonging to a small fort there, the ruins of which still stand on one of the most romantic and picturesque spots on the island. A sharp skirmish ensued in which the English were overpowered by numbers and routed. Following up their success, the Dutch marched, without further opposition until they reached the top of Ladder Hill, overlooking Jamestown, where a party was detached to descend and storm the fort. Here they were met by stout resistance and were repulsed each time they attacked. But with possession of the hill above, which completely commanded the fort, Governor Beale saw that his position was a hopeless one, and in order to escape capture he retired with his people and their most valuable belongings on board the *Humphrey and Elizabeth*, a ship then at anchor in the Road, and set sail for Brazil.

The booty falling to the Dutch was meagre, and the only ship they captured was a West Indian slaver from Madagascar, with two hundred and twenty slaves and five hundred and fifty-one pieces of ivory, while the efficient Beale had spiked most of the guns and spoiled the powder before leaving. Commander de Gens immediately took the necessary measures for the defence of the island and put a garrison of one hundred men in the castle. The Dutch had not been long in occupation before three English merchantmen arrived in the Road, and not suspecting what had taken place they dropped anchor, but managed to escape with a shelling and sailed to Barbados. The victors repaired the fort and re-named it "Good Fortune", a name which proved to be a misnomer, for misfortune was soon to follow. First of all both of the officers who had been left in charge of the garrison died, leaving a sergeant in command, whose task was not made easier when he was ordered to return one third of his soldiers to the Cape. "Our watching," he wrote in a letter to the Governor there, Ysbrandt Godtske, "will be in vain, if the Lord Himself, who has granted us this victory, does not watch with us."

The dismal forebodings of the sergeant proved justified. On the 11th of May the Dutch East India fleet left the Cape for St. Helena, the first returning fleet to enjoy the blessings of their new possession, and the *Vliegende Swaen* again sailed with them. On the 23rd of July she was once more back at Table Bay, but not on this occasion the bearer of good news.

Many of her crew were sick after being two months at sea,

and nine of them were dead. She reported that on the 6th of June on a clear moonlight night, she had sighted the towering Barn at the northerly point of the island, and how on approaching the Fort on the following morning she had been met by a heavy cannonade.

Now let us enquire what the English had been doing since the ignominious flight of Governor Beale and the garrison from St. Helena on New Year's Day.

Directly the *Humphrey and Elizabeth* reached Brazil, the Governor hired a sloop for the purpose of cruising to windward of St. Helena and warning all English ships approaching the island of their danger.

Amongst the refugees on board the *Humphrey and Elizabeth* was a planter named Coulson and his family who had with them a negro slave called Black Oliver. This slave was destined to play an important part in the near future. When the ship arrived at Brazil Coulson sold Black Oliver to an English merchant, Mr. Abram, but before the sloop sailed Mr. Abram was prevailed upon to permit Oliver to embark as one of the sloop's crew.

Meanwhile, only fourteen days after the capture of St. Helena, Captain Richard Munden had sailed from England with a squadron, in order to meet the homecoming fleet off James Valley and convoy it home. This precaution of the Company turned out to be a wise one, for the actual news of the fall of the island did not reach England until several weeks after the convoy had sailed. As soon as the sloop was fitted out Beale sailed in her for St. Helena and on the 4th of May had the good fortune, a few leagues from the island, to fall in with Munden's squadron, which now consisted of the men-of-war *Assistance* and *Levant*, the Company's ship *Mary and Martha*, and the fire-ship *Castle*, for the rest had been sent in pursuit of three Dutch men-of-war which they had surprised at St. Iago.

From Beale Munden learned that the Dutch were in possession of St. Helena, and he immediately began making plans
for re-taking it. Hearing that Black Oliver had an intimate
knowledge of the island, he had him removed to his own ship
to act as a guide. On the same night Munden sent his boat to
reconnoitre the Road, which returned with the satisfactory
news that no ships were to be seen. At the same time he
ordered the *Castle*, with four hundred soldiers on board, to
proceed with her consort, under Captain Richard Keigwin, to
Prosperous Bay, on the other side of the island. With this
landing party went Black Oliver. Munden's plan was to
engage the fort at Jamestown from the sea while Keigwin
landed his troops, crossed the island and surprised the fort
from the rear. Although it is possible to land from a boat at
Prosperous Bay on a calm day, the coast there is precipitous,
and seen from the sea appears to be unclimbable, even in daylight. The spot where the Englishmen landed is still called
Keigwin's Point in honour of the gallant and brave captain.
With great difficulty a sailor named Tom succeeded in scrambling up the cliff, an almost perpendicular wall over a thousand
feet in height, and when he reached a secure footing at the
summit let down the end of a ball of twine he carried with
him, to which those waiting below tied a strong rope which
Tom pulled up and made secure to a rock, and then the
soldiers, one by one, climbed up it. This place is known to
this day as Holdfast Tom. Jonathan Higham, a soldier who
took part in the landing and who afterwards settled in the
island, was often heard to say that had twenty men opposed
them, and rolled down stones from above, the English would
never have been able to get up the cliff. As soon as the last
soldier was safely at the top the troops marched in single file
along a perilous goat track until they reached better and safer
going, and then on through Long Wood, until they came to
a farm house called The Hutts, where they arrived at daybreak

and stopped for breakfast. Continuing their march the party eventually arrived at the summit of Rupert's Hill overlooking James Valley and the fort. But they had arrived too late to be of any active assistance, for the fort had already capitulated.

The previous day Munden had bombarded the fort and breastworks, and then withdrawn his squadron, intending to resume the attack the next morning on Keigwin's arrival. While waiting, the commander sent in two of his ships, and on their approach the Dutch—"upon condition they might not be stripped"—surrendered, and thus for the second time within six months St. Helena changed hands, and has remained in English possession ever since. At sunset the English took possession of James Fort, and Beale despatched a trumpeter to inform Keigwin of the Dutch surrender, and so prevent him from damaging property or injuring the inhabitants on his march.

The good fortune which Captain Munden had hitherto enjoyed did not desert him. Within a few days of the fall of James Fort, a ship hove in sight flying the Dutch colours. Munden at once gave chase and at 11 o'clock that night over-hauled and captured her. She proved to be the *Europe*, one of a Dutch East India fleet coming from the Cape, which had outsailed her consorts and expected to find James Fort in Dutch hands. Amongst the passengers was none other than the new Dutch governor who landed at St. Helena, not with honours but as a prisoner of war.

From the *Europe*, the English learned of the approach of the rest of the fleet and prepared a stratagem, so that when in the early morning of the 26th of June, the outlook signalled six sail in sight, a Dutch flag was run up over the fort. The plot would have succeeded better if Munden's order to the gunners to hold their fire had been obeyed. As it was, owing to the impetuosity of some of them, the fleet got wind of the trap and turned about and ran before the gale, with the

English after them. The chase went on into the night, when the *Assistance* drew alongside the Dutch *Vice Admiral* and took her, while the *William and James*, a Company ship, captured their *Admiral*, but the rest escaped. All the same, they turned out to be good prizes, both having large quantities of silver on board. After placing Captain Keigwin in charge of the island with a garrison of two hundred and fifty soldiers to guard the fort, Captain Munden sailed for home in company with five English East India ships and his three prizes, and arrived safely back in England, where King Charles knighted him as a reward for his gallant services.

News travelled slowly in those days. Edward Barlow, who visited St. Helena in 1671, had the misfortune to be captured with his ship a year later off the coast of Java. Not knowing that a state of war existed between the two countries, the English ship had anchored amongst a Dutch fleet, so that escape was out of the question. It was while he was still a prisoner at Batavia that two Dutch ships arrived bringing news of the Dutch capture of St. Helena, and they were followed shortly afterwards by a small English vessel which had been taken when she put in at Jamestown with a cargo of "niggers" from Mozambique. However, more cheerful news reached the prisoner two months later when a Dutch craft arrived from Table Bay with the tidings that the English had re-taken the island.

An interesting visitor to St. Helena in the year 1673 was a Dominican friar, Father Fernandez Navarette, professor of philosophy at the college of Saint Gregory at Valladolid. In 1646 he had been sent by his Order to preach the Gospel to the heathen of the Philippine Islands, though he found China to be a better field for his work. After twenty-seven years of adventure and hardship this remarkable man, who eventually became Archbishop of Hispaniola, returned to Spain, and on his way, on the 20th December, 1673, landed at St. Helena.

He was a man of exceptional breadth of mind and a mighty controversialist. He loved nothing better than a lengthy theological discussion with an antagonist worthy of him, in particular a cultivated and well-educated heretic.[1]

At two in the afternoon we anchor'd at the Isle St. Helena; being so small, it was much we hit it so exactly without missing it. . . . The Portuguese discovered that island; had they kept possession of it and the Cape, they might have easily lorded it in India, for where should ships take in fresh water and provisions? The Dutch took it, but then fixing at the Cape the English made themselves masters of it; the Dutch re-took, and the English again beat them out of it.

The island is small, all encompass'd with rocks rising up to the clouds, it looks like a great fort or castle; it has no harbour, but there is good anchoring and safe from the winds, because at that season they come over the island.

The place where the English were is a small valley, not a musket shot in breadth, without a tree or bush, or a foot of strand; but there is an excellent spring which God has provided for the benefit of sailors; there is no wood, which would have been a great help. . . . In that place there is a little town of the English, who till the ground, sow rice, make butter and cheese; there are some sorts of fruit, swine and goats that were put in by the Dutch and Portuguese, so there is refreshment enough there at present.

There was some dispute about landing, the little Governor was afraid they were going to assault him; he ordered the French should not come within his fort arm'd, and that they should come but two at a time; so that none went ashore but the seamen and two poor fellows.

After Mass I went to get a little biscuit, and saw the

[1] *An Account of the Empire of China. Churchill's Voyages*, Vol. I. 1704.

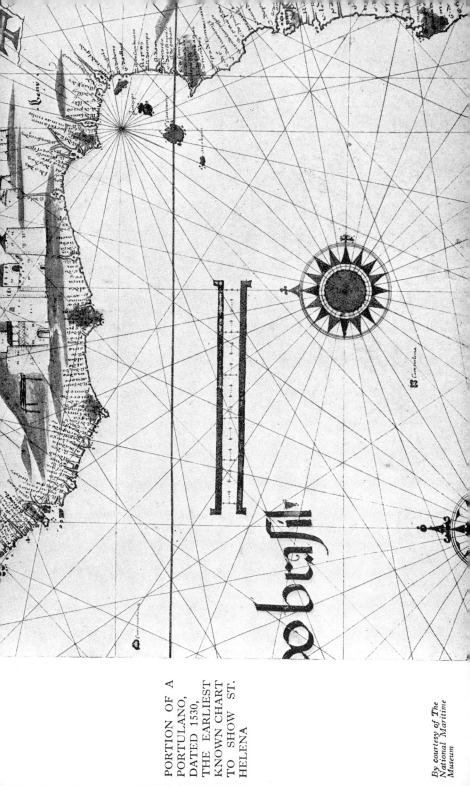

PORTION OF A
PORTULANO,
DATED 1530,
THE EARLIEST
KNOWN CHART
TO SHOW ST.
HELENA

ENTRANCE TO THE CASTLE,
JAMESTOWN

EARLIEST ENGLISH
MEMORIAL ON THE ISLAND

FORMAL CLAIM MADE BY
THE DUTCH TO POSSES-
SION OF ST. HELENA IN
1633

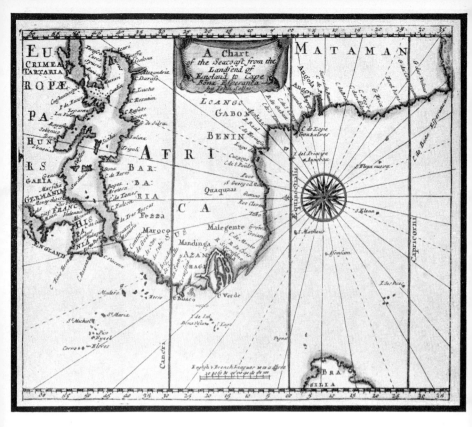

JOHN SELLER'S CHART SHOWING ST. HELENA AND ALSO THE
FABULOUS ISLAND OF NEW ST. HELENA
Atlas Maritimus, 1682

SELLER'S MAP OF ST. HELENA
Atlas Maritimus, 1682

CAPTAIN WILLIAM DAMPIER
from the painting by Thomas Murray
in the National Portrait Gallery

JOHN SKOTTOWE, ESQ.

Governor, 1764-1782
from the Painting by David Martin, 1786

TREE FERNS AMONGST INDIGENOUS FOREST
ON THE RIDGES

Governor who receiv'd me courteously; he had been at Madrid, and valued himself on his *Metaphysicks*: to say the truth, he was an ingenious man, made much of me that day, forced me to stay all night, gave me a good bed.

We discours'd upon several subjects, and he put to me three cases concerning baptism, and [how typical of St. Helena!] was at variance with his parson.

There I found some blacks of Madrastapan, for whom I was concern'd, because they had bin Catholicks at home, and were Hereticks there; there were also two Frenchmen in the same way.

The fort is considerable enough for that place, the garison small, but there is no need of a great one to oppose any enemy. I admire the Dutch should take that island from the English, and much more that they should recover it from them.

After this we had a Treat, and what follows is according to the custom of those nations.

The Governor's name was Richard Cung;[1] he said to the Hugonot (a dear friend and fellow traveller of the friar's), whose name was Foran, "The Father is your great friend." I had, indeed, spoke well of him. Foran answer'd, "There is no trusting of him, for the Fathers don't love Hereticks." I have observed that these men plainly own themselves Hereticks, as I have often heard from their own mouths. Others will not confess it.

After describing the cattle, goats and dogs which earlier travellers had introduced to the island, the Spanish priest remarks on the "abundance of pigeons, and all white; in those parts they call that sort Pigeons of St. Helena, to distinguish

---

[1] This is difficult to understand. Keigwin handed over the Governorship to Field at the end of 1673. Cony—which might be confused with Cung—was governor shortly before the Dutch captured the island and had been sent home in disgrace.

them from those that have been carry'd from several parts of
India". These pigeons of St. Helena were no doubt the White-
birds (*Gygis candida*), one of the most abundant sea-birds in
the island.

The Governor appears to have been as fond of a good
argument as the priest and therefore a man much after his
heart. He was interested also in the supernatural.

> Discoursing concerning transmigration of souls, the
> Governor said, that when he was in Guinea, the interpreter
> told him that in such a house there was a lion, in whom
> was the soul of the first ancestor of that family, as those
> heathens believed. He desir'd to be carry'd to see him,
> they went, and he said he saw a most terrible lion, which
> very tamely pass'd by him into the house, where he took
> two or three turns, and then in his sight went into a room.
> He own'd he quak'd with fear at the sight. Sure some
> Devil was in the body of it, to deceive those people, which
> is the more likely, because they told him it neither eat
> nor drank.

On Christmas morning, after saying three masses at which
"the sailors were very devout, and eight persons communicated" the Father went on board his ship, which set sail towards
Ascension Island.

THE English East India Company had learned its lesson.

After the re-capture of St. Helena, the Committee at London became alive, not only to the importance of their South Atlantic Island, but solicitous for its safety and for the welfare of its colonists. They were anxious to make a new start, and decided on a policy of economy combined with security. The conditions were propitious, for on the 16th December, 1673, the King had granted the Company a fresh charter, which constituted them Lords proprietors of the island with all the rights of sovereignty, and free and common socage "as of the manor of East Greenwich in the County of Kent". In Captain Keigwin, of Munden's ship *Assistance*, they had a reliable and able Governor. Nor did they forget to reward the humble slave Black Oliver, whose services as guide to Keigwin's landing party had been represented to them in so favourable a light that the Company not only refunded the sum spent for his purchase, and sent back his wife and two children to the island, but allowed him the same land and cattle which they granted to European settlers. Those planters who had held land on the island previous to its capture by the Dutch were restored to their estates. In order to ensure sufficient numbers of defenders in the case of another invasion, the Company lost no time in fitting out two ships, the *European* and the *John and Alexander*, and sending

them out with one hundred and ten persons, soldiers and
settlers; provisions, and all sorts of stores as well as a wooden
house in sections, to be used as a storehouse for the Company's goods. To every family which came out in the two
ships, as also to some others who soon followed, were assigned
twenty acres of land and two cows. Those settlers who
preferred to reside on the windward side of the island were
to be granted a double quantity of land. To assist them, the
new planters were to be provided, free of cost, with seeds,
plants, breeding stock, labour and instruction. Provisions were
to be granted gratis to them for a period of twelve months—at
the expiration of that time it was supposed their farms would
afford them a livelihood and they would be expected to pay
for any provisions or other things which they bought at the
Company's stores, at cost price. Yet in spite of all this open-
handedness of the Company, and in spite of the wise governorship of Richard Keigwin, trouble with the garrison and some
of the planters broke out once more. This unruly element
was chiefly due to the policy—or perhaps necessity—of the
Company's recruiting its soldiers (and settlers) from among
the unemployed in England, many of whom were worthless
loafers.

Although Keigwin was a strong Governor he was unable to
keep in order the undisciplined troops and discontented
settlers he had under him.

When Captain William Basse[1] arrived off St. Helena with
a fleet in April, 1674, he did not know whether the island was
in the hands of the English or the Dutch, and in order to
find out, sent ahead his fastest sailing vessel, *The Eastindia
Merchant*, before anchoring in the Road. On going on shore,
he learned that a mutiny had taken place a few days before
and that the Governor, Richard Keigwin, had been seized,
deprived of his rapier and other arms, and carried off up

---

[1] *Journal of Capt. Will Basse, I.O.:* Marine Records. No. LXXI.

into the interior where he was under guard, and "not allowed ink nor paper". The mutineers had invited the Deputy-Governor, Captain Field, to take Keigwin's place, and on his refusal had elected Lieutenant Bird their governor.

The rebels accused Keigwin of the intention to desert the island by the first ship which called, friend or foe, and also of "abusing the soldiers very much without cause".

After much wrangling and argument the mutineers agreed to allow Keigwin to be brought down to the Castle and be examined before Basse and his fellow captains, in the presence of the soldiers.

Sergeant Taylor, a Scotchman and leader of the mutineers, produced a copy of the articles which they had drawn up against the Governor. Captain Basse and his captains then retired to the bastion, where they read the articles, and after a discussion returned to the hall of the Castle which was so crowded by soldiers and settlers that those who could not get in listened to the proceedings from the open windows.

Captain Keigwin was then led in and at once demanded to learn the charges which had been made against him, of which he said he had never been informed.

After reading them through, he was able to clear himself on every one. Then an ugly scene ensued, and Keigwin and the captains had some difficulty in getting out of the hall, for the soldiers hustled and threatened them; one soldier actually thrusting the muzzle of his musket against the breast of one of the captains. There was a good deal of scrimmaging and the situation was fast becoming dangerous, when Captain Basse addressed the mob, and partly by promises of pardon and partly by warning them that they were likely to be hanged for mutiny, brought them to reason.

Lieutenant Bird on being called upon to justify his action in assuming the governorship proved to be "very drunk, and could not say a word for himself but cried like a child".

In the end Captain Basse won the day. The mutineers surrendered, Keigwin was reinstated, and was given back his sword and small arms, while Bird and Taylor were arrested and carried off to the ship.

As for the precious round-robin of the mutineers, Basse ordered it to be publicly burnt by the Marshal at the head of the troops drawn up in the courtyard of the Fort.

Before sailing, the ship's commander offered Captain Keigwin this sound piece of advice, "not to be too harsh in his command, but to moderate his passion and govern with love and meekness, if possible to be done".

The following day the fleet set sail for home, taking with them, besides the two mutineers, two Dutch prisoners from the island, Earick Orea and Henereck Everence.

For the sake of economy, now that the war with the Dutch was ended, and in order to get rid of the more mutinous element amongst the soldiers, the Company devised a system of militia, by granting land to soldiers of good character, and to civilian settlers, on the feudal basis of payment by military service. A code of Lessors was drawn up which compelled every planter to take his turn periodically as a militiaman at the look-outs or in the garrison of the fort, whilst the soldiers maintained the regular watch. By this means, with every ship which brought out new settlers the Company was enabled to dispense with the services of some of their regular soldiers, so that by December, 1674, the purely military forces were reduced to fifty picked men, and yet the total number of defenders in a case of emergency was greatly increased. The population of the island, blacks and whites, had risen by 1675 to three hundred and fifty-seven, and in the following year to three hundred and ninety, while the officers and soldiers under pay numbered only thirty-nine and twenty-seven respectively.

It was often the case that when a really capable Governor was appointed, he soon left again to take up some other post more worth his while than this small island. A letter dated London, 19th December, 1673, from the Court of Directors, reached Governor Keigwin appointing as his successor Captain Richard Field, who was also to be Lieutenant of one of the two companies of foot. As his Deputy-Governor, Captain Anthony Beale was nominated, and he was to command the other company. Amongst other instructions the Governor was told to "take into your possession all the cattle that can possibly be attained, that a distribution may be made to the several inhabitants according to the rules hereafter mentioned. The Three Boats left by Sir Richard Munden to be kept in repair and permit the inhabitants to goe a fishing therein. All fish to be distributed equally amongst the inhabitants."

Besides his duties as Deputy-Governor and Lieutenant of foot, Anthony Beale was to "Husband the Stores", which were to be kept in the wooden frame house which had been sent out, in which Beale and his family were to reside for the first two years "so as he keeps no fire therein". Besides the frame house, there arrived Mr. William Swindle, a Minister of the Gospel, who was reported to be of very good character, and who was to "preach once and caterchize every Lord's Day and to teach or direct the teaching of children as their Schoolmaster and also as many of the Negro children as are capable of learning". He was also to keep a register of all marriages, burials and births. His stipend as minister was £50 a year, with £25 as schoolmaster, and a gratuity of £25, and he was to enjoy the privilege of dining at the Governor's table at the Castle, and to be allotted a plantation. The Company was concerned with the physical as well as the moral health of their subjects, and sent out a surgeon, Mr. Francis Moore, on a more modest salary of £25 a year, but also with the right of dining at the Governor's table. A year later there came a letter of caution on the subject of foreign visitors: "If any European people who are at amity with England arrive at the Island for refreshment use them civilly but do not too far trust them on shore nor to discover the strength of the place."

In place of the higgledy-piggledy collection of shacks which had been erected in Chapel Valley, a regular street of houses was laid out behind the fort, built of stone and brick, to become Jamestown, the capital of the island and still the only town or village on St. Helena: also a church was built and a free market, for the use of the inhabitants and the shipping. More orders came further to defend every possible landing place on the coast, and to see that no houses were on any account erected on the sea side of any fort or fortification.

The Company's lands and plantations were to be looked after by the Governor. From the produce of these lands was maintained the public table, at which the Governor himself presided, and where dined not only the Council and the Company's principal servants and officers, but even the chief blacksmith and other head artificers and the Sergeant of the guard, who all sat in the order of their respective ranks.

This feudal system continued for many years until Captain Poirier, who succeeded to the government in 1697, decided to dine alone with his family. The Records have several minutes concerning this practice.

An extract from the Board Resolution, dated the 8th October reads:

In the Governor's absence, there shall stand a salt upon the table, which shall be placed below the Council and Chaplain. Those who sit above the salt, shall always drink as they think proper, either wine or punch; but those who sit below that salt, shall have, to two persons, one common bowl of punch (which contains three pints); if but three, the same; if four, two; if five, no more; if six persons, three bowls of punch; or in case of wine instead thereof, one bottle for each bowl of punch.

Many of the officers complained to Governor Poirier of having to sit at table with their inferior officers and artisans, and the Governor agreed with them that "nobody ought to sit at table with him that is not cleanly drest, and that has an infectious distemper on him or is drunk." That occasionally one of the guests at the Governor's table became drunk is not altogether surprising when we see the amount of free punch that was allowed to each.

By 1678, Captain Field, worn out with governorship, applied for permission to resign, and returned to England, and Major John Blackmore arrived to take his place on the 19th of July of the same year. Blackmore had been an officer in Cromwell's own regiment, and had gained his confidence, being one of the Council of Officers at St. James's in 1654. It was on account of his military experience that he found favour with the Company, and it was the threat of war with France that led the Court to send out a soldier to govern St. Helena. The new Governor landed with a reinforcement of soldiers to strengthen the defence; and with orders at once to survey all the fortifications and particularly to encourage settlement by the colonists on the windward or south-eastern side of the island. He was to inaugurate a Court of Judicature of which he was to be the sole judge, and which was to be held four times a year. A system of laws, drawn for the most part from those established at Bombay, was at first framed for the island, but it was shortly afterwards changed to a system of trial by jury for cases affecting life, limb and land, leaving matters of less importance to be settled by the Governor and Council who were recommended "not to have their heads troubled with nice poynts of the common law of England; but rather, on considering the reason of things, to adjudge of all cases in a summary way, according to equity and a good conscience, without tedious delays, or countenancing litigious persons in their vexatious prosecutions".

Practising lawyers have always been discouraged from settling at St. Helena from the earliest days.

The semi-feudal atmosphere of the government of the island went a step further with such decisions as that any holder of twenty acres of land had to maintain two English persons over sixteen years of age, one capable of bearing arms to serve in the general defence, and also maintain two cows. On a plantation of ten acres, one man and one cow sufficed. Every inhabitant, whoever he might be, planter, workman or slave, had to work on the public highways for one day in each year, or else pay an equivalent in money.

Two surveyors of highways and two churchwardens, one for each church—for another church had been built in the country near to White Gate—were chosen by the Governor out of persons elected each Easter Monday by a majority of free planters. No lessee, shopkeeper, or artificer had a voice in the election of any island or parish officer. That privilege was confined to the free planters and their heirs, whom the Company, in the following words, declared "they would always esteem and honour as the first occupants, and gentlemen freeholders of the island, for such it was hoped their heirs would prove to be, and to have estates sufficient to maintain the dignity of that title, and defend their country on horseback."

Dr. John Fryer, of Trinity College, Cambridge, who visited St. Helena in May, 1682, mentions meeting Governor Blackmore and bears out his reputation as a military man. When the ship on which he travelled from India arrived in sight of the island, Dr. Fryer wrote in his journal: "By the Grace of God the 19 May, it lay fair before our eyes like a little cloud". He noted the "small white birds floating on the

sea", the lovely little ivory white terns with great black eyes
(*Gygis candida*) which still fly off to meet the monthly Union-
Castle liner, and which are so inquisitive that they come
and flutter within a yard or two of climbers' heads on the
wooded peak of Mount Diana, the highest point of the
island.

As his ship drew near the shore under Munden's Point,
the guns of the fort roared a salute. At the landing place
they were welcomed by the Governor, and the visitors passed
between two ranks of soldiers who stood stiffly at the salute
presenting arms. Dr. Fryer observed that those ships which
were so unfortunate as to miss St. Helena had to sail on to
Barbados, and their crews would be eaten up by scurvy. He
had nothing but praise for the diligence and industry of the
English colonists, but added "here is a mischievous vermin,
sorely vexatious to them, which is Wild Rats." The rats ate
up the potatoes while they were still in the ground, and for
that reason the planters grew yams, which were too bitter for
the liking of the rats, until they had been boiled. The number
of English men, women and children at the time of his visit,
Dr. Fryer gives at four hundred.

After a brief stay at the island, his ship sailed for Ascension
Island—"another meer wart in the sea".

Slavery appears to have been instituted at St. Helena at the
time of, or very soon after the first settlement by the East
India Company. By 1679 there were about eighty slaves on
the island, and apprehension began to be felt of the possibility
of a rising, and restrictions were laid upon further importation, since there were by that time more blacks than whites.
But slaves were still imported from time, to time as in 1684,
when the Company sent Captain Robert Knox—famous for his
twenty years' captivity in Ceylon—to buy slaves at Madagascar
and bring them back to St. Helena, where the Company intended
growing sugar, tobacco and indigo, under the supervision of

a West Indian planter. Knox's account of his adventures at the "Island of St. Lawrence"—as Madagascar was then called—were curious, and curious also were some of the characters he met there; though none more so than King Light-foot, who must have been the most thrifty monarch who ever squatted on a throne. He practised polygamy, and "would with his own hand shoot those of his wives that offended him, and after, bid some cut open her body to take out the bullet". After escaping many dangers at Madagascar, Captain Knox set sail with his cargo of slaves for St. Helena, where he eventually arrived after a terrible voyage, his ship damaged by a "Hurry Cane", and himself so ill with the "sea-scurvie that when I came to land at St. Helena my breath was gone and I was fain to be carried, but this by God's blessing soon wore off". But although "God of his special providence" had preserved the slave-dealer from being murdered at Madagas-car, drowned at sea and dead from scurvy, a new disaster awaited him, one "greater than any of the former, which stript me at once of all my worldly riches and injoyments and exposed me to poverty and contempt that I think I may say never any man saw that Scripture (Proverbs 23, verse 5) plainer fulfilled than myself, vist. 'Wilt thou set thine eyes upon that which is not, for riches certainly make themselves wings and fly away as an eagle towards heaven'."

Knox's ship had reached St. Helena without her main-mast, but after great trouble and at great expense a new one was fitted, and on the evening of the 29th May, 1685, all was ready to leave for India, and Captain Knox was standing on the shore hailing his boat to come and carry him on board his ship, when the crew cut the cables, loosed the sails and, before his very eyes, ran off with the ship.

Poor Captain Knox had to wait on the island a month before a vessel called and took him home to England, and in the meanwhile he had to borrow money to pay for the provisions he had bought for his ship, but the Governor allowed him free diet at the Company's table.

In the year 1676 St. Helena received a distinguished visitor, who was neither concerned with the mercantile activities of the Company nor with its defence. This was the astronomer, Edmund Halley, the first of many scientific men to carry out researches on the island. In the records at the Castle, the astronomer's name is spelled *Hawley*, which makes it probable that his name was not pronounced by his contemporaries to rhyme with sally, as it is to-day. His age was twenty, and he left Cambridge without taking a degree, in order to correct certain defects in the theories of Jupiter and Saturn and to supplement in the southern hemisphere the labours of Flamsteed and Herelius. A recommendation from King Charles to the East India Company obtained for him a free passage out in one of their ships.

Not long after the second settlement of the island, the Company began to be somewhat disturbed by the increasing number of interlopers. These vessels, most of them English, carried on an unauthorised and, in the eyes of the Company, illegal trade with India, in defiance of the Company's exclusive rights. Specially high rates were charged them for water and refreshment, far higher than to Portuguese ships or those of the Dutch East India Company. Every ship which called at Jamestown paid a port duty of two shillings and sixpence for every ton displacement and a sum of five shillings anchorage. An exception, however, was made in the case of Dutch ships so long as a like exception was allowed the English East Indiamen which called at the Cape of Good Hope.

Every English ship trading to Madagascar was obliged to leave on the island one negro, male or female, as the Governor chose.

All ships of the Company were further obliged to deliver, on their arrival, a barrel of gunpowder, a rule which was still in practice in 1824. In 1683 a law was enacted that no interloper should be supplied with water or refreshment until he had paid, in money or goods, the value of twenty shillings per ton, but this was less severe than a regulation passed two years before, that no refreshment of any kind whatsoever was to be allowed to an interloper, unless he agreed to resign his ship and cargo to the Company's disposal. In such a case the commander and officers were to be allowed to retain their private property and to be given the choice either to enter the Company's service with their ship or else to leave their ship and cargo and be sent home to England in a Company's vessel. Until such a surrender had been made, all traffic and communication between the interloper and the inhabitants was prohibited under a penalty of twenty pounds for a Member of the Council, and ten from any other person on the island. Many ships sailing under Ostend colours were refused any kind of refreshment, and allowed barely enough water to preserve the lives of their crews, and were even fired upon to prevent their entry into the Road, or to hasten their departure. But above all things interloping ships were on no account ever to be saluted. This is more than hinted at in an extract from the Company's orders, dated 1st August, 1683, which refers also to one of the many indiscretions of which the early clergymen of St. Helena were so often guilty.

Wee finde, by the list of guns fired, sent us by Capt. Beale, three hundred and odd guns, which is so strange a waste, that we could not think our Governor would have been guilty of; especially considering that island cost us forty thousand pounds, without one penny profit, hithertoo, more than refreshment to ships, which all strangers have had as well as ourselves. But most impudent it was to salute interlopers; as vile of our Minister, Mr. Church (if our information be true), to be first on board an interloper

Pitts, that came in last voyage, and to entertain him at his house.

A tax was levied of six pence on every ox or other beast sold and sent on board any ship, and importation taxes of six pence on every hundredweight of sugar, ten shillings a hogshead of arrack or wine, every piece of calico, six pence, and a similar piece of silk, one shilling. Amongst other taxes was a poll-tax of sixpence a head on all persons above the age of sixteen, which was levied to pay the minister his stipend and to repair the churches.

It was at this early period in its history that the island records began to indicate the anxiety of the proprietors over the wanton and wasteful cutting down of the native forest; a matter which continued to be a cause of anxiety but about which nothing permanent was ever done; nor to this very day has anything been done. Without any thought for the future, trees were felled for firewood, or any other purpose required.

The rainfall of a steep hilly country such as St. Helena is dependent to a large extent on the forest which grows on the highest ridges. If this is destroyed, the rainfall, or in any case the humidity of the atmosphere, is lessened, and also, in a country such as St. Helena, with a light sandy soil, it is the trees and their roots which prevent the erosion of soil which all the world over has turned rich agricultural land into dry desert. When the trees are destroyed on steep hillsides every heavy rain storm will wash tons of good soil into the sea, leaving only a barren, rock-covered surface.

Various regulations began to be framed, all of good intention, but futile, because the planters ignored them.

The worst offenders of all were the distillers of spirits from potatoes, who had their stills working all over the island, producing quantities of spirits which were bought and drunk by the islanders or sold to passing ships. Great quantities of wood were consumed for this purpose. The proper course would appear to have been the withdrawal of all licences for stills, but instead, a tax of twelve pence was levied on every hundredweight of wood used for distillation, as well as one of fourpence for every gallon of liquor produced. Altogether it is not surprising that "secret murmurings" ensued, which soon led to open disturbances. The new taxes, which the inhabitants thought to be excessive, gave offence, the Council was weak and dilatory in insisting that its laws were obeyed, and so raw spirits continued to be cheap and plentiful and became for many years the curse of St. Helena. Seditious meetings began to be held, and as the Government took no decisive or vigorous measures, every unpopular regulation added fuel to the flame.

Thomas Eastings, an orphan of fourteen, one of the noisiest at the meetings of discontents, was proved to have broken into a house for the purpose of procuring arms, and for this and other offences was whipped at the gallows, and was sent away from the island in the *Resolution*, a dangerously leaky vessel which needed extra hands to pump her. The Company blamed the mildness of this sentence in the following words:

Your banishment of Thomas Eastings is likewise such a silly piece of pageantry, instead of a punishment, that we are ashamed our aged Governor should be guilty of so great a folly. We know runagadoes, young fellows, love to be rambling, and believe, if the fellow had committed no fault deserving death or imprisonment, he would have thanked the Governor for giving him such an opportunity to satisfy his humour of changing place. The wise Dutch never banish white men out of India; for, to send home such to any part of Europe, is rather a reward than a punishment. And therefore we forbid you, now and for ever hereafter, to mock the justice of your island with such sham banishments as sending delinquents home to their own country.

Matters became so serious that the Company ordered all the commanders of their returning ships to remain at the island during any period, not exceeding one month, that the Governor should think expedient, so that the ships' companies might assist in maintaining order. One of the most troublesome and turbulent inhabitants was the chaplain, Doctor Sault. The Company seems all too often to have been unfortunate in their choice of clergymen. Over and over again it was the island chaplain or minister who created mischief. It was the chaplain's scurrilous and insulting speeches combined with his "disrespectful and insolent demeanour" to the Council which led to one of the most serious and alarming mutinies that had hitherto disturbed the settlement. It must have been a bitter pill for the committee in London to swallow, when they reflected that although they had spared neither expense, ordinances nor exhortations to promote virtue and religion amongst their colonists in St. Helena, their good intentions were largely frustrated by the unclerical behaviour of a succession of clergymen.

Another of their chaplains was censured in the Company's official correspondence as an "encroaching, avaricious person" and was threatened with dismissal for refusing to marry a couple after the Governor had signed the licence. Yet another clergyman, in a fit of rage against a neighbour, swore to have his blood. A third was fined for performing the marriage ceremony without the Governor's licence and against the consent of the parents. A fourth proved an incendiary and a drunkard, and "persevered in the most aggravating and daring insolence to the Governor, until the reprehension of the Company, and repeated fines, reduced him to better order".

A fifth, a man of very low origin, made the pulpit a channel from which to declaim against the Government, and by his unclerical conduct disturbed the peace of the community and set the whole island in a ferment. A sixth was obliged to relinquish his appointment from habitual drunkenness. A seventh was represented as a sot and a liar. An eighth was notorious for his irregularity of conduct. We cannot do better, in bringing to a close this distressing tale of clerical laxity which extended over a period of sixty years, than to quote the words of the historian T. H. Brooke:

"Without attempting to comment on an extraordinary expression of an elegant author,[1] that 'to a philosophic eye, *the vices of the Clergy are far less dangerous than their virtues*', it may, nevertheless be remarked that even political inconvenience may sometimes result from their vices, however preferable, in the eye of modern philosophy, to their virtues."

The cauldron of discontent amongst the colonists which had begun with the increased taxation, and had been brought to a boiling point by too generous access to fiery arrack, in 1684 overflowed as a result of the heated orations of Doctor Sault the Parson.

The actual trouble seems to have come to a head from an unseemly quarrel between the Deputy-Governor and Storekeeper Holden, and a soldier named Adam Dennison. The latter was what would nowadays be described as "an old soldier", that is to say he had a bad record for boldness of speech to his betters, turbulence and drunkenness.

As in the case of so many great quarrels, this one began over a mere trifle; the cause of it is obscure. Dennison one day demanded of the storekeeper a pound of tobacco, but Captain Holden was too busy at the moment to attend to him as he was stamping some Japan copper bars preparatory for the approaching pay day and told Dennison to come again

[1] Gibbon's *Decline and Fall*, Vol. IX, p. 199.

later on. Apparently the soldier considered, rightly or wrongly, that the Storekeeper had not treated him fairly, and roundly abused him. Such language spoken in anger to his superior officer the Deputy-Governor should have been followed by instant arrest. But instead of taking a strong line, Captain Holden attempted to reason with him, which only resulted in his "reviling the Company in scurrilous terms". Holden pointed out to the angry soldier that he and all the others in the island were amenable to the Company and their laws as well as to the King. For the time being the quarrel appeared to be forgotten, until some five weeks later, when on October 8th at a general muster or parade of the troops Dennison publicly accused Captain Holden of treason by wilfully misconstruing his words, for he declared that he had heard the Storekeeper say: "We are not His Majesty's subjects, but the Company's." Holden had to appear before the Governor and Council to answer the charge, but a very brief investigation was enough to reverse the situation of the accuser and the accused, and Dennison was immediately committed to prison to wait there until the next returning ship should arrive to take him to England. This short shrift on the part of the Council with the ringleader of the malcontents soon brought matters to a stage further. Much of the discontent was fermented by the bad system then in practice of quartering the troops in private houses, instead of in barracks. Many of the soldiers lived in the houses of dissatisfied planters, and this led to the formation of a plot to overthrow the Council and to seize and imprison the Deputy-Governor. After several rowdy meetings some sixty soldiers and planters, most of them unarmed and led by a planter, William Bowyer, who was armed with a musket and sword, and on either side of him Joseph Clarke and Joseph Ousman both with drawn swords, marched to the fort shouting "We are for the King," and to give further appearance of loyalty to the Crown, they carried a King's flag at their head. Hitherto the only flag flown on the island or at the fort was that of the Company.

Although the rioters represented the views of many of the islanders they were in a minority, while amongst their ranks were several well known bad characters. One of these is described in the records as a "fifth monarchy man, engaged in Venner's rebellion", and another as a man who had formerly been accused of felony. Amongst the rebels was also William Coxe, who was said to have betrayed the island to the Dutch in 1672. On reaching the fort the rebels were addressed by Governor Blackmore, who tried to reason with them, and commanded the soldiers to come into the fort and return to their allegiance and obey his orders. But his words had no effect, and one of the soldiers, Robert Moore, shouted out: "If you will not deliver Captain Holden the traitor we will have you too as a traitor, and you are all traitors," whereupon the crowd of excited men began to attempt to force the sally port, but were stopped by two volleys of great and small shot fired by the guard.

Three were killed and fourteen wounded, and sad to relate, one of the slain was Black Oliver, whose services under Munden had been so handsomely rewarded by the Company.

This reception of the rebels seems to have damped their ardour for the time being, and the remainder of the day passed without any further disturbance. In the evening news reached the Governor that a party of the ringleaders had gone up to Bowyer's house at Broad Bottom, so after dark he despatched an armed party under a sergeant to secure them. On knocking at the door of Bowyer's house a voice inside was heard to shout "to your arms, to your arms", upon which the sergeant ordered his squad to fire through the windows, which they did, killing one man, and wounding another. On breaking into the house they seized six others, amongst whom was

Bowyer himself. Thus was brought to an end an attempt to overthrow the Governor and Council and appoint in their place, John Sich as Governor, John Colson as Deputy-Governor, and Thomas Bolton as keeper of the stores. The trial of the prisoners was held on the 23rd December 1684, the day on which the ship *Royal James* arrived. Captain James Marriner, the commander, with six of his officers and six N.C.O.'s from the garrison, were empanelled as an impartial jury.

William Bowyer, Joseph Clarke, jun., Joseph Ousman and Robert Moore were arraigned for sedition and mutiny. The first three refused to plead, objecting to be tried by any other tribunal than the King's Bench in London, while Moore pleaded not guilty and "put himself upon God, his Country and the jury". For two hours the jury deliberated and then brought in a verdict of guilty, and all the prisoners were sentenced to death by hanging. Ousman and Moore threw themselves on the mercy of the Court, and their sentences were reduced to life-long banishment to Barbados, but Bowyer and Clarke, in spite of their continued objection to the legality of the trial, were both hanged. Several more of the insurgents were arrested within the next week or two and likewise brought to trial, when six of them were found guilty and two, Joseph Clarke, sen. and James Johnson were sentenced to death.

Mathew Pouncey, a planter, was imprisoned, fined and given twenty-one lashes for calling one of the Council a "gallows building rogue" and for declaring there was "no justice on the island", while Mrs. Martha Bolton, wife of a planter, received twenty-one lashes, was ducked three times in the sea and then imprisoned for having been heard to say that the rebels were murdered and that Captain Holden was a traitrous knave.

These rigorous punishments appear for the time being to have quelled the spirit of insurrection amongst the soldiers and planters, but as a wise precaution all the troops were hereafter lodged in barracks instead of being quartered on the planters.

By great good fortune, the minister, Dr. Sault, happened to be undergoing a term of imprisonment for debt and was therefore prevented from sowing further sedition and unrest.

As a rap on the knuckles for the Governor, the Court of Directors wrote to him: "Since there hath been four rebellions in the island, His Majesty may justly blame our conduct and we yours, if there should be a fifth, and indeed we must take shame to ourselves that there hath been so many already. All we can say for ourselves, it was too much lenity and compation, but we find too late the verity of the old proverb, 'too much pity spoils a city'."

The Company, not trusting their "weak, good-natured, but honest" Governor, commissioned Sir John Weybourn, newly appointed Deputy-Governor for Bombay, to stop at St. Helena on his way out to try the rebels. With him he took a new proclamation of King James II in case it should be found on his arrival that the mutineers were masters of the island. This proclamation offered a free pardon to all who should return to their allegiance within twenty-four hours. His Majesty likewise directed a commission to the Governor and Council, in conjunction with Sir John Weybourn, Captain Eaton of the *London* and the subaltern officers of Sir John's company of foot, to make war upon the mutineers, if they were in arms, and reduce them by force. They were then to try the aggressors by court-martial and if they were duly convicted (which was extremely probable) to execute twelve of the offenders (whose names had thoughtfully been given beforehand to Judge Weybourn—including that of William Coxe, who "formerly betrayed the island to the Dutch".)

Immediately on the arrival of the *London* at Jamestown, the commission was put into effect and on 20th November, 1685, fourteen of the mutineers were tried and condemned, and five, including Colson and Rutter, were duly executed, the other nine being reprieved until further instructions respecting them should be sent out.

For the next few years the Company pursued a policy of confiscation and repression much on the lines of the "Bloody Assize", and St. Helena was held up to the India councils as a horrid example and a warning of the results of leniency.

If the Court of Directors in London heaved a sigh of relief after this cleaning up of St. Helena, and believed they had heard the last of a worrying and dangerous episode, they were soon to be disillusioned.

Petitions to their Court, and worse still to Parliament, soon began to be made. "The mournful daughters" of John Colson petitioned the Commons to punish all those concerned in their father's "shameful and unnatural death", especially Sir John Child (the virtual ruler of the Company), and Captain Holden —his "instrument". They begged also the return of their father's confiscated property and relief from their financial burdens. This was by no means the only petition for redress from the widows and orphans of the executed rebels. Another was made by Katherine, the widow of William Rutter, on behalf of herself and her four children.

According to Anderson's *History of Commerce*, the House of Commons passed a resolution, declaring the Company to have acted in an arbitrary and illegal manner, which naturally raised a considerable degree of public clamour against them, but nothing further seems to have resulted from the applications, except that the civil code which adjudged the punishment of death was expurgated by the Company in all cases except that of wilful murder.

In the meanwhile a new problem had arisen in the island due to the prolonged imprisonment for debt, of Dr. Sault, the Chaplain. For over a year the inhabitants had been without the benefit of his ministration, and no marriages, baptisms or burials had been solemnized. Therefore it is not surprising that "some persons were glad to take advantage of the services of the Reverend Mr. Buttler", who was on board the ship *London*, to bring up the arrears of marriages. But as ever, the Company appears to have been unfortunate in their clergymen, for no later than 2nd December, Mr. Buttler was in trouble with the government for having married a couple at 9 o'clock at night.

Evidently the Council of St. Helena had by this time learned to deal summarily with delinquent clergymen, for they ordered the minister "to give under his hand a catalogue of all the Christenings, Burialls and Mariages by him officiated on the Island since the coming of the ship *London* by tomorrow morning by nine of the Clock and when so done that the said Mr. Buttler shall be presently (at once) carried on board of the said ship and there remain without coming on shore any more at this place".

One cannot but feel a little sorry for Mr. Buttler because he appears to have acted according to his lights, and also because life for him aboard the *London* must have been anything but congenial. The prospect of being cooped up for several more months in the *London* with Sir John Weybourn must have weighed heavily upon him. As a parting shot he presented to the Governor a petition highly reflecting on Sir John, especially how he had once threatened his life by declaring that as soon as they passed the Cape of Good Hope, when he would become an Admiral, he would try the clergyman before a court-martial and "dead men tell no tales." But all the satisfaction Mr. Buttler got out of his petition was to be ordered to beg Sir John Weybourn's pardon before the Council, and again publicly before the whole ship's company on board the *London*.

The Company's policy of stricter discipline on the island

after the mutiny was felt by all the inhabitants, black as well as white. On 21st June, 1685, a slave called Frank, belonging to Gurling, a planter, was arrested for the murder of another slave. Some discussion ensued whether or not Frank ought to be tried by a jury, but finally it was decided that only whites should be allowed that privilege, so Frank was summarily tried by the Governor and Council. He was duly found guilty and sentenced to have his right hand cut off and nailed to the gibbet near the Sessions House, and then to be hanged and quartered. Two of Captain Johnson's slaves for receiving from Frank some silver buttons were each to have forty lashes under the gibbet and then to carry the quarters of their late friend to the country, and to be branded on their left shoulders with the letter R. That the owner of a slave who was executed might be recompensed for his pecuniary loss, it was ordered that "the masters of Blacks executed or murdered were to have compensation by a Poll tax on other blacks as is the practice at Barbados".

"October 26. Several Blacks punished for plotting to run away with the Company's boat. Ringleader to have 75 lashes and five drops of burning sealing wax on his naked body, the others in proportion."

Several complaints about slaves were made to the Council. Jamey, a slave of the Deputy-Governor, was found guilty of sorcery and burnt to death.

On 24th November, 1687, Peter, a black slave, confessed to having murdered his former master and attempted to poison several slaves by strewing powdered glass in their food. According to the evidence of other slaves, Peter had used powdered glass mixed with earth taken out of dead people's graves. Peter was sentenced to be burnt to death. A proclamation was issued that all the blacks (except young children) were to be present at the execution and that every one of them should bring a piece of wood for the fire.

Two other slaves were shortly afterwards burnt alive for being implicated in the same crime, while Maroa, a black woman, for some crime not stated, was sentenced to be chained to a post near to the bonfire and there to remain until the execution was over, when she was to be given thirty lashes on her naked body, before returning to prison, where she was to be kept in irons until a ship called in which she could be sent away to some other English colony, "but whilst she stays, to receive 30 lashes on her naked body every Saturday afternoon".

After the mutiny had been quelled, further examples appeared of the arbitrary and often dishonest behaviour of Captain Holden, the Deputy-Governor, whose quarrel with the soldier Dennison had started the late rebellion. Mr. Goffe, a member of the Council, reported that Holden had stolen from him a cask of arrack, and as Holden refused to deliver it up, the Governor and the Council, attended by a sergeant and a file of musketeers, marched to the storehouse, which they broke into, and seized and brought away the cask.

In the Council records which follow this incident, occurs this entry: "Capt. Holden had withdrawn himself from our community both in council and in table."

Captain Holden's next move was to refuse any longer to collect the revenues. In the island records from now on until his dismissal in April, 1689, there are continued complaints of the high-handed officiousness of the Deputy-Governor.

A good deal of grumbling went on amongst the colonists over the new currency introduced to the island by the Company. In place of coins, heavy copper bars were issued, stamped with the Company's arms. These were ordered to be the legal currency of the island, but of course were useless elsewhere, nor would the visiting ships accept them in payment. Also the bars were heavy and awkward things to carry about.

On January 6, 1687, in the records is the following minute:

"Some obstruction lately in passing Copper Bars for money. Ordered that in all payments for debts one half may be paid in bars and the other in currant money. Those who refuse such payments to be looked on as turbulent persons and disturbers of the peace."

The same year regulations were issued by the Council for the mixing of punch at the taverns.

"20 drams of strong liquor and 9 drams of sugar with other usual ingredients shall be put into each bowl of punch for which no retayler shall presume to demand any more than five shillings."

These records contain many odds and ends of local happenings, and so do the letters written to the Governor and Council by the Court of Directors in London.

In a letter dated 3rd August, 1687, we read: "Capt. Gregory Field is a mere useless burden to us and therefore we do hereby dismiss him from our service. Give him leave to come home at his own charge and we shall admit him into our almshouse which he petitioned for."

A Mr. Nathaniel Cox was also summarily dismissed—"we are satisfied he has misspent his own time and our money."

One of the liveliest of visitors to St. Helena was the Rev. J. Ovington, whose ship the *Benjamin* called there in January 1690 on her way to Surat. Amongst other blessings brought to the island by the *Benjamin* was the happy news of the coming to the English throne of William of Orange and his consort Queen Mary. Mr. Ovington wrote a book about his travels which was not published until 1698. It is a fund of amusing gossip and matters of minor importance, written in a chatty friendly style which endears the author to his readers, and as his book is a rare one and difficult to come by, no apology is offered for quoting from it at some length.[1]

---

[1] *A Voyage to Surat in the year 1689.* F. Ovington, M.A., Chaplain to His Majesty. 1696.

Amongst the passengers on board the *Benjamin* were several French protestant refugees on their way to St. Helena, and one of them, who had brought his family and several French vine growers with him, was destined to play no small part in the history of the island. This was Captain Poirier who—"stript of all but Freedom of his Thoughts and the Serenity of his Mind"—had been granted permission by the Company to settle, with his three sons and five daughters, in one of the most fertile parts of the island.

The Company's reason for this generous treatment of a foreigner was not altogether disinterested. Before trouble came to him Captain Poirier owned land and vineyards in France where he grew two to three hundred hogshead of wine and brandy every year, and as for some while the Company had in mind the possibility of growing grapes in St. Helena, here was just the man they needed. In their letter to the Governor, the Board of Directors warned him about the way he was to treat the "vineroons" for "we must tell you the French are excellent servants if you keep them under and hold them sharply to their duty, but they are apt to grow insolent and negligent if they be not held to their work as they are in France—and if you give them ear, they will not leave craving and asking. . . ."

M. Poirier was to have a place at the Council and to be given the title of Captain, though he received the pay only of a sergeant. He spoke only a few words of English when he left home, but it was hoped that in the long and tedious voyage out he and his sons would have learned to speak the language well.

But to return to Mr. Ovington, who took an instant liking to St. Helena. He enjoyed its "Air Temperate and serene", he noted how the sky was seldom clouded or overcast, a fact which "produces a General Clearness in the Natives".

The delighted visitor was surprised and gratified to discover that although the island lay well within the tropics, "yet was the heat so temper'd and allay'd by the gentle winds that flew along the land, that the Northernmost parts of the Island made an artificial Warmth very convenient." The climate indeed was so salubrious that the inhabitants were not subject to the most common diseases, "even that of the Small-Pox, but gives them a complexion fresh and beautiful, equal to that of celebrated England". But he was distressed to find how very poor the inhabitants were and how destitute of clothes, except for the few garments which were exported from England, a fact "which makes the Island (to speak the Truth) abate much of the Pleasure of its Habitation".

He rejoiced on landing to find that the island "was well stockt with Inhabitants of both Sexes, whose numerous Progeny shew'd little of Sterility among them; how barren soever the Island was otherwise." This led the inquisitive clergyman to ask some of the women how so many of them came to be there, and Mr. Ovington shall be left to tell the answer in his own words.

The Decoy, they told me, was worth my Attendance to harken to it; and it would not appear strange to see such a number of them there, when they discover'd the Means that brought them thither.

For at their first setting out from England, a Colony for this Island, the current Report that then prevail'd was, that all the single Persons upon the Island were either Commanders, or Lords' Sons, of whom they might have Choice upon their arrival. This made them eager for imbarking for the Voyage, and was Charm enough to make them set forward with full Sail for the remote Island, tho' the distance had been further. No Curse was like a contrary Wind, to check the speedy sight of those gallant Gentlemen that awaited their coming; the ravishing Thoughts of whose

Embraces kept them in Life and Alacrity all the way, and inriched their Fancies with the Hopes of being immediate Mistresses of great Fortunes, and rais'd so far above their Native Birth, that nothing now but Pleasures and Respect should succeed in the room of their former servile state.

The long'd-for Island was at length espied, and now fresh Springs of Love and Delight appear in every Eye and Countenance. The joyful Maids begin to ransack all their Stores for an Ornamental Dress, in which though they cannot much exceed, however they fancied themselves Trim and Gay; and she that could not outvie the other in point of Attire, endeavours to outdo her in Nature's Ornaments, in Chearfulness and Mirth, in a Nuptial Look and taking Air. Thus they stept on Shore, full of Thoughts of a stately Reception, and of the sight of those Gentlemen they had heard so much of.

When, alas! all these Blandishments of Fancy, which were so sweet in the Voyage, carried a Sting in the end of them, which imbitter's all their Joys.

For instead of that Heroick Address which they expected from Men of Wealth and Honour, they were saluted only in the plain courtship of Men employ'd in Agriculture, and ordinary Mechanick Arts.

However the pleasing Expectation they had, gave them this Advantage over the tedious Passage, that whereas the boisterous Waves and impetuous Winds, the Fury of the Sea, and the Dangers of Rocks and Sands, are apt to render so long a Voyage very dreadful, their aiery Hopes made them take Courage, and defie the Power of Storms, and gladly encounter all the Perils that attend such a forlorn Passage.

Mr. Ovington was also surprised and gratified to observe other examples of prolific fertility in the island, as how the fruitful soil was capable of producing many hundreds for every grain of Indian corn "injected into the ground". But unfortunately rats and other vermin too were prolific, and bred in such numbers that they devoured almost every growing thing before it could arrive at maturity, which drove the inhabitants to subsist principally upon yams.

During his walks about the island Mr. Ovington took notice of many things and jotted them down. He noted how the English apple trees bore ripe fruit, green fruit and blossoms all at the same time; as they still do at St. Helena. This phenomenon he accounted for by "the genial heat of the Sun-Beams, to which the Island is happily expos'd, by a constant quick attraction of the seminal juices from the Root to the upper Branches continually".

He spoke well of the public table at the Castle, spread with plenty of provisions, to which all the commanders and mates of calling ships, and passengers of note were made welcome. Mr. Ovington had but a poor opinion of the mentality and manners of the inhabitants of St. Helena, other than the Governor and officers. "The minds of the inhabitants", he remarks, "are generally as Uncultivated as the neglected Soil, their Intellects as ordinary as their Qualities, but what was infinitely worse, the pravity of their Manners compares them with the rankest soil, productive of nothing but noxious Herbs, untractable to all the Arts of Husbandry and Improvement." This deplorable state of affairs the visiting clergyman attributed to the shortcomings of the resident clergyman, who although in receipt of a handsome stipend of £100 per annum, with permission to accept fees and gratuities from his parishioners and the use of a plantation, lived in idleness and neglected his sacred office, so no wonder Mr. Ovington found "the Sacred Administrations but ineffectually used toward the reclaiming of their Enormities and the reducing the lives of the Inhabitants to Sobriety and a Religious Behaviour".

The outbreak of war with France in this year, 1689, was followed by a great diminution in the number of ships calling at the island. Precautions were taken. New fortifications were built at Matt's Mount—or Flagstaff—and at Prosperous Bay, where the English had landed, and wherever else it was thought that the French might attempt to land. By means of small squadrons of fast-sailing ships, the French scoured the home as well as Indian waters so thoroughly that English merchants scarcely dared to send a ship on the long voyage to the East. In addition were the activities of the press gang, which made it next to impossible for a merchant vessel to be manned by a full crew of able-bodied seamen. After the war had been waged for three years and still no supply ship was sent to St. Helena, the shortage of necessities became acute. Cloth, for example, had become so scarce that most of the soldiers of the garrison had nothing to cover their backs but the old red coats they had worn when they came out in the *Benjamin*. The Dutch alliance in 1695 enabled the Company to order their vessels to meet those of their old rivals at the Cape for better security on the homeward voyage. It was not until then, in the sixth year of the war with France, that the Company dared to allow their Captains to touch at St. Helena. It was earlier in this period, on the 1st December, 1690, at six o'clock in the evening, that old Governor Blackmore, while descending the steep path down Putty Hill on his way to Jamestown, fell over the precipice and was killed. He was a big, heavy man, and it was conjectured at the inquest that the bamboo stick which he always used when walking had given way and so he had fallen. On the following day the popular Governor was interred "in as solemn and reputable a manner as possible". Escutcheons were hung on the Castle walls, and the coffin was borne to the grave by six pall-bearers, who were draped with black scarves and hat-bands. The drums and colours were also draped, and four volleys of small arms

were fired at the graveside and afterwards twenty of the great
guns at the fort. All the principal inhabitants were invited to
the funeral feast, at which were consumed one hundred and
seventy pounds of bread and cakes, eleven pounds of tobacco,
two hogsheads of punch, containing twenty-eight gallons of
arrack and forty pounds of sugar, a feast worthy of a good
man who had governed the island honestly and well for twelve
years. The late Governor was succeeded by the Deputy-
Governor, Captain Joshua Johnson, who was not destined to
rule for long.

Soon after this tragic occurrence St. Helena received a visit
from one of the most interesting travellers who ever landed
there. This was William Dampier, the famous explorer,
naturalist, buccaneer and navigator, and as he was a trained
and close observer, and meticulous in his accuracy in describing
all he saw, extracts from his *Voyages*[1] will be taken at some
length, since accounts of the island during this period are few
and far between.

Dampier arrived at St. Helena from Bencoolen, in Sumatra,
where he had escaped from a Dutch prison, leaving behind
him all his worldly possessions but his precious journals and
Joely—"the Painted Prince". This second possession was a
tattooed native of Mindanao, of whose person Dampier had
been given one half-share and of whom he was very fond and
very proud. Being penniless he hoped to get Joely safely
back to England, and exhibit him in public, as a means of
improving his fortunes. When eventually the two travellers
reached England, Dampier was so destitute that he was compelled to sell his share of the Painted Prince, who promptly
died at Oxford of the smallpox.

It was on the 20th June, 1691, that the *Defence* dropped
anchor in the Road off James Valley and Dampier and Joely
were able to go ashore to stretch their legs and see the sights

[1] *Dampier's Voyages.* Edited by John Masefield. 1906.

Unfortunately it rained so heavily during his visit that he was not able to explore the island extensively, otherwise no doubt he would have had many more interesting things to report.

The common landing-place is a small bay, like a Half-Moon, scarce 500 paces wide. Close by the sea-side are good guns planted at equal distances, lying along from one end of the bay to the other; besides a small fort, a little further in from the sea, near the midst of the bay. All which makes the bay so strong, that it is impossible to force it. . . . There is a small English town within the great bay, standing in a little valley, between two high steep mountains. There may be 20 or 30 small houses whose walls are built with rough stones; the inside furniture very mean. The Governor hath a pretty tolerable handsome low house, by the Fort; where he commonly lives, having a few soldiers to attend him, and to guard the fort. But the houses in the town, before mentioned, stand empty, save only when ships arrive here; for the owners have all plantations farther in the island, where they constantly employ themselves. But when the ships arrive, they all flock to the town, where they live all the time that the ships lie here; for then is their fair or market, to buy such necessaries as they want, and to sell off the product of their plantations.

Their plantations afford potatoes, yams, and some plantains and bonanoes. Their stock consists chiefly of Hogs, Bullocks, cocks and hens, ducks, geese and Turkeys, of which they have a great plenty, and sell them at a low rate to the sailors, taking in exchange, shirts, drawers, or any light cloths; pieces of calico, silks or muzlins: arrack, sugar, and lime-juice is also much esteemed and coveted by them. But now they are in hopes to produce wine and brandy, in a short time: for they do already begin to plant vines for that end, there being a few Frenchmen there to manage that affair. This I was told, but I saw nothing of it, for it rained so hard when I was ashore, that I had not the opportunity of seeing their plantations. I was also informed, that they get manatee or sea cows here, which seemed very strange to me. Therefore enquiring more strictly into the matter, I found the Santa Hellena manatee to be, by their shapes, and manner of lying ashore on the rocks, those creatures called sea-lyons; for the manatee never come ashore, neither are they found near any rocky shores, as this island is, there being no feeding for them in such places. Besides in this island there is no brook for them to drink at, tho' there is a small brook runs into the sea, out of the valley, by the Fort.

To continue Dampier's narrative:

We stayed here 5 or 6 days; all which time the islanders lived at the town, to entertain the seamen; who constantly flock ashore, to enjoy themselves among their country people. Our touching at the Cape had greatly drained the seamen of their loose coins, at which these islanders as greatly repined; and some of the poorer sort openly complained against such doings, saying, it was fit that the East-India Company should be acquainted with it, that they might hinder their ships from touching at the Cape. Yet they were extreamely kind, in hopes to get what was remaining. They are most of them very poor; but such as could get a little liquor to sell to the seamen at this time got what the seamen could spare; for the punch houses were never empty. But had we all come directly hither, and not touched at the Cape, even the poorest people among them would have gotten something by entertaining sick men. For commonly the seamen coming home, are troubled more or less, with scorbutick distempers; and their only hopes are to get refreshment and health at this island, and these hopes seldom fail them, if once they get a footing there. For the island affords abundance of delicate herbs, wherewith the sick are first bathed, to supple their joints, and then the fruits and herbs, and fresh food soon after cures them of their scorbutick humour. So that in a week's time men that have been carried ashore in hammocks, and they who were wholly unable to go, have soon been able to leap and dance. Doubtless the serenity and wholesomeness of the air contributes much to the carrying off of the distempers; for here is constantly a fresh breeze.

While we stay'd here, many of the seamen got sweethearts. One young man belonging to the *James and Mary*, was married, and brought his wife to England with him. Another brought his sweetheart to England, they being engaged by bonds to marry at their arrival in England; and several other of our men, were over head and ears in love with the Santa Hellena maids, who tho' they were born there, yet very earnestly desired to be released from that prison, which they have no other way to compass, but by marrying seamen, or passengers that touch here. The young women born here, are but one remove from English, being the daughters of such. They are well shaped, proper and comely, were they in a dress to set them off.

My stay ashore here was but two days, to get refreshment for my self and Joely, whom I carried ashore with me; and he was very diligent to pick up such things as the islands afforded, carrying ashore with him a bag, which the people of the island filled with roots for him. They flockt about him, and seemed to admire him much. This was the last place where I had him at my own disposal, for the mate of the ship, who had (bought) Mr. Moodie's share in him, left him entirely to my management, I being to bring him to

England. But I was no sooner arrived in the Thames, but
he was sent ashore to be seen by some eminent persons: and
I being in want of money, was prevailed upon to sell first,
part of my share in him, and by degrees all of it.

On the 2nd July, 1691, the *Defence* having taken in fresh
water and provisions sailed, in company with the *Princess Ann*,
the *James and Mary* and the *Josiah*, for England.

The poverty and want caused by the island being so isolated
during the war with France gradually led to grumbling and
discontent amongst the soldiers. Principally they complained
of their want of clothing, of poor and insufficient food and the
overdue payment of their wages. Many of them, who had
served their engagements with the Company, claimed the right
to be sent home to England. In order to prevent the soldiers
from deserting, all ships were ordered to leave in the day time,
since several men had got on board vessels at night and so
escaped.

This growing sense of injury led to a sudden mutinous
outbreak on the 22nd April, 1693. A means of escaping first
occurred to the discontented troops when on the 25th February
they saw a volunteer crew set out from James Bay to assist a
vessel too weakly manned to make the island. Though they
reached her, however, the St. Helena men were not enough to
turn the scale and the vessel disappeared, until the 3rd April,
when she arrived back and proved to be the *Francis and Mary*,
an interloper, whose commander, Captain Thomas Pitts, asked
for reinforcement of his crew. The plan then occurred to
some of the soldiers to seize the ship and make their escape in
her. The ringleader in the plot was a Sergeant Jackson, the
commander of the guard, who had been a member of the jury
at the first trial of the 1684 rebels. He laid his plans cunningly.
Being the sergeant on duty it was easy to introduce to the fort
his thirteen accomplices, before delivering up the keys to the

Governor. This he did, and the Governor, quite unsuspicious nor suspecting any treachery, retired to bed. In the middle of the night, when everybody in the Fort was asleep except the conspirators, the apartments of the surgeon, John Stevens, and other of the Company's servants who resided there, were visited by the mutineers who disclosed to each their intentions and offered to take them into the conspiracy. All but four refused to join them and were immediately thrown into a small and airless dungeon. The four who consented or were intimidated into joining, were before long to regret it.

Eventually only the Governor and his family remained to be dealt with. At reveillé Governor Johnson, in his dressing-gown and slippers, came out to deliver the keys to the sergeant, who instantly laid hands upon him. During the scuffle which ensued three shots were fired at the Governor, one of which passed through Jackson's arm and another struck the Governor in the head and he fell to the ground. Their plans had been carefully laid, for immediately every way of access into the country was guarded, in order to prevent the spread of alarm as well as to arrest any who should approach the town.

At the same time messages were sent, in the name of the Governor, to several persons living in the valley, ordering them to report at the fort. As each one entered he was seized and imprisoned in the dungeon which was soon crowded with about fifty persons, whites and blacks, all in a state bordering on suffocation.

One of the mutineers proposed blowing up the prison with gunpowder, but this design was prevented by Jackson. The unfortunate wife of the Governor they dragged naked from her bed, forcing her to carry her clothes under her arm into her closet to dress herself, while they rifled the house and secured the treasure from the Governor's office. Not until two hours after he was wounded would the ruffians permit Mrs. Johnson to visit her dying husband nor allow the surgeon to attend him until the poor man was on the point of death. Meanwhile all the guns were spiked and the two at Munden's Point, which commanded the shipping in the Road, were tumbled down the precipice. Five of their prisoners: Captain Kelinge, the Deputy-Governor, Captain Pitts, John Lufkin, Thomas Goodwin and Richard Gurling, they took out of the dungeon and compelled these unfortunates to accompany them on board the *Francis and Mary*, where they also conveyed the treasure and all the valuables they could collect.

With these five hostages Jackson considered he was now in a position to bargain with the acting Governor, Captain Poirier, for supplies needed for the voyage. One of them, Goodwin, was sent ashore at eight o'clock that Sunday evening to secure supplies and to inform the people that if a single shot was fired at the ship the hostages would immediately be put to death. Early the following morning the supplies had been collected and taken down to the landing stage where Captain Poirier was already waiting, when a boat rowed by negro slaves came off from the ship. In the boat was one of the mutineers, Stephen Lancaster, who told the Governor he had come for the provisions, but he was informed that they should only be delivered half-way between the ship and the shore, and then only if the hostages were sent in a boat to meet them. This was at first refused, but after much wrangling and argument it was agreed to and the two boats met, one with the supplies, the other with the hostages, as well as three of the men who had been forced to join Jackson's party, and they all returned safely to the island. Captain Pitts the mutineers retained on board to pilot them, but before the ship sailed he contrived to get from Kelinge a paper, signed by him, to certify that the Captain was an innocent party to the "horrid transaction", and the *Francis and Mary* departed with twenty-seven of the Company's soldiers.

The men who had been forced to join the mutineers but

who had been sent back to the island, George Lock, Isaac Slaughter and Joseph Davis, were tried for treason and all three sentenced to death. Lock was proved to be one of the party which went to Munden's Point to dismount the cannon, while Slaughter had been seen to go with Jackson into the Governor's office to take the money. As no one on the island could be found willing to act as executioner, the jury reconsidered their verdict and agreed to spare the least culpable of the three, Joseph Davis, on condition he hanged Lock and Slaughter.

Possibly owing to the success of this event, and the escape by sea of so many soldiers, the blacks thought they might do likewise. The first rumour of such a conspiracy being hatched was communicated one Friday night in November, 1694, to a Mrs. Goodwin by her Indian slave, Annah. According to her some of the slaves intended that very night to murder all the whites in the island. First of all they were to go to Lemon Valley and kill the two soldiers there and seize their arms, then return to a rendezvous in the country and starting from there, parties of slaves were to visit each house in the island killing every white man, woman and child. After doing this, according to Annah, they intended to seize the first ship which called and sail in her back to their own country. The whole story was of course fantastic, but on hearing it the terrified Mrs. Goodwin hurried off to inform her brother-in-law, John Goodwin, "who immediately went and took a great horseman's sword that was at his brother's house and thus armed, tied up all the slaves there. Thence he went to Bevians and took his blacks and so to every home thereabout taking all blacks he met withall, tying their hands behind them, so that he with many other white men drove a great many blacks before them to the Fort where they were all secured."

In spite of the fact that not a single slave made any resistance whatever, panic reigned throughout the island.

The Governor on hearing what had happened sent a man post-haste to fire the alarm guns and ordered the guns to be fired at Fort James, Rupert's Fort and at King William and Mary's Fort at Banks's.

By seven o'clock the next morning every man slave in the island was in custody and the whites began to recover from their panic. No time was wasted. Eleven of the ringleaders were summarily tried before a jury of planters, with Orlando Bagley for foreman. All the prisoners at once confessed to everything; not one made the least attempt to excuse or deny anything. Needless to say, all were found guilty, but not all of the same degree of guilt. Jack, Will, Joane, Firebrass, Poplar and Randall were pronounced the greater offenders— Ruface, Hemp, Roger, Peter and Civil, the lesser, but all were to suffer death, the former the more horrible and lingering death. However, vested interests, as so often is the case, and not humanity, intervened. Slaves cost money and the owners of these slaves would be heavy losers if they were executed, so it was decided to put only three of them to death, the others to "receive great punishment, yea even unto death". Jack was hanged alive in chains on the top of Ladder Hill and left there to starve to death. Will and Randall were hanged and then cut down while still alive and disembowelled, after which their bodies were dismembered and their quarters and heads stuck up at the crossway as a warning to all negroes.

The other condemned were to be flogged on the 19th of December, again on the 21st, the 23rd, on Christmas Day, on the 27th, and then to be branded on the shoulders with the letter R.

As Janisch wisely observes[1]: "These cruel sentences were all inflicted and their severity was probably due to alarm caused by the astonishing success of Jackson's conspiracy. But eleven naked frightened slaves who could be so easily

[1] *Extracts from the St. Helena Records.* H. R. Janisch. St. Helena. 1908.

secured in a few minutes by Goodwin with his *'great horseman's sword'* and who at once confessed everything like terrified children, would have suffered quite enough punishment with a dozen apiece at the Flagstaff for their foolish talking."

Having subdued the slaves to a proper sense of respect for their white masters, Governor Kelinge embarked on a campaign of road and path making. Foot-paths and cattle "driftways" were constructed all over the island, to many outlying farms and houses.

The Council continued to sit and try various cases and listen to all sorts of strange complaints.

At a Consultation held on Monday, the 12th day of August, 1695, at Fort James.

Present.   Richd. Kelinge.   Govr.

Capt. Poirier.   Depty. Govr.

Whereas John Sinsnigg, soldier, has had (for some considerable time past) the Hand of God upon him with most violent pains and aches in every part of his body and limbs and whereas information has by sundry persons been given that when in the height of extremity and pain, he has been so unsensible of God's Correction that then he has been so impatient that instead of calling upon the Most High and Merciful God, has blasphemed and cursed his most Holy Name by taking his Holy Name in vain, and uttering most execrable oathes and curses; yea even to call upon the Devil to fetch both his body and soul and cast it into Hell; the which blasphemous words of the said Sinsnigg the Governor and Council this day considered, and thought somewhat how to suppress the said Sinsnigg or any that should happen to fall in the like wickedness (which God forbid) and so again considering that whereas by Divine Providence we have a Minister among us, viz.: Mr. Bartholomew Harwood, it was—that he might the better acquaint us the most

fit proper way and method to proceed against the said
Sinsnigg; whereupon he was sent for and we acquainted
him with the said Sinsnigg's blasphemy and desired him to
put us in the way and usual method that such a person
should be proceeded against; who gave us his advice, viz:—
that the said Sinsnigg should stand at the church door three
several Sundays and in Divine Service be brought in by the
churchwardens to some convenient place in the body of the
church as a person out of the church and then and there
openly to confess and acknowledge his great and enormous
sins to God and desire the prayers of the congregation for
intercession to the Almighty God for his so great offence.

The said Mr. Harwood's advice being conformable to
ours was well approved, and accordingly it was ordered that
the said Sinsnigg be compelled to perform the aforesaid
pennance accordingly.

The next case heard before the Governor and Captain
Poirier also was one concerning a soldier and Mr. Harwood.

Information having also been given by John Long,
planter, that Benjamin Seale, soldier, yesterday in church at
evening service when Mr. Harwood, minister, was administring the Holy Sacrament of Baptism on an infant,
when the said Minister was giving the Godfathers and Godmothers their charge to what they undertook, and asked
them if they believed in the Christian Faith and would, in
the name of the child, renounce the Devil and his works
and they answered that they believed all that and did renounce the devil and his works,—that the said Seale then
said, being within the church, "by God you lie"—or "by
God its a lie".

John Long sworn, saith that yesterday being the 11th of
this instant, in the evening service, sitting by Benjamin

Seale, soldier, (who was then three parts drunk) heard him say, when the minister was administring the Holy Sacrament of Baptism, when he was giving the Godfathers and Godmothers their charge, they took upon them answer, even then said, "by God you lie", or else "by God it is a lie".

The said Seale (whom the Governor upon knowledge of his blasphemy put in prison) was called and asked what was it that could induce him to speak such blasphemy in the Church; who said, if he had, he was sorry, and penitent, but could not remember that he had spoken any such words as Long had deposed nor anything tending unto.

Yet upon mature deliberation, and the advice of Mr. Harwood being herein taken

It is Ordered,

That the said Benjamin Seale do on Lord's Day the 25th of this instant, come into the church when called by the Minister and then and there openly confess his fault as the said Mr. Harwood shall in form draw it.

Consultation held Monday, 26th August, 1695.

Whereas yesterday being the Lord's Day, Benjamin Seale, soldier, was to make his personal appearance at the church or chapel in Fort James Town, to the order of Council held the 12th instant, but contrary thereunto he the said Seale not making his appearance, was this day sent for to know the reason of his contempt, who when he appeared in a humble manner craved forgiveness and declared that he would not have missed to make his personal appearance at the church as aforesaid, but the hand of God being upon him could not possibly come, being then much troubled with Gripps of the Gutts, but promiced not to miss, if God did bless him with his health, when he should be ordered.

It is Ordered,

that the said Benjamin Seale make his personal appearance
at the Church or chapel aforesaid on Lord's Day the 22nd
day of 7br. next ensuing and there perform what was
ordered in the Consultation held the 12th of this instant.

John Sinsnigg, soldier, having also been ordered in the
Consultation held the 12th of this instant to make penance
for his great Blasphemy, as appears in the said Consultation,
but the said Mr. Harwood, minister, came and entreated
that the said Sinsnigg might be remitted upon his promice
to him of reformation, and becoming a new man, and that
with the help of God he would, being the neighbourhood
should take notice of his reformation and becoming a new
man

It is Ordered

That the said Mr. Harwood's request be granted upon the
said Sinsnigg's promice of becoming a new man, but if it
be known that the said Sinsnigg do fall into a relapse, that
then he do pennance as he is ordered in the Consultation
held the 12th instant if the opportunity of a minister presents.

That what was in those days considered to be legal evidence
in a court of law would not be permissible to-day is well
shown by the following extract from the Records:

"John Lamble being sworn saith; that Black Sam told him
that as he was coming from Tombstones Wood he met with
one of Mr. Nichol's sons, named William, who told him that
Orlando Bagley, the son of Edward Bagley, told him at school,
that his father had killed one of the Company's dogs."

On the 23rd December, 1695, "Corporal Grandy who
married Priscilla, a widow, complains of William Marsh
speaking of her as a Witch. Marsh in defence calls Mrs.
Grandy's grand-daughter Jane, wife of Matthew Isaac, who
says, 'that some considerable time since, she lay with her

grandmother and in the middle of the night she missed her out of bed and then saw come at ye window, the apparition of a Black Dogg—so she called "Grandmother—Grandmother"—until at last the Dogg went away and her Grandmother came to her and said "What is the matter child, be not afraid" '."

What decision the Council arrived at in this case is not recorded, but a child's nightmares were things liable to lead to unpleasant consequences in the seventeenth century.

On 30th November, 1697, Governor Kelinge died of a dropsy and was succeeded by the Deputy-Governor, Captain Poirier.

Some unpleasantness occurred when the late Governor's widow took possession of all the plate in the Castle, so that Governor Poirier had "hardly pewter spoons enough to serve ye Company's table". In the end it was agreed to break open a box belonging to the late Governor Blackmore, "and in the presence of the said lady and Govr. Poirier, they took out one handle cup, one porenger, one large sault and one tumbler, weighing together 37 ounces for the lady, while the said Govr. Poirier as his share had several particulars weighing together ninety ounces, valued at five shillings per ounce, which was thought the utmost of its worth it being ould fashion silver."

The new Governor was a good and worthy man, but not one to maintain authority in a community seething with discontent. The island records bear witness to the repeated insults offered to the French Governor, not only by the planters but by the very officers of the Company to whom he looked for loyalty and support. He was continually issuing proclamations urging the observance of morality, but all to very little purpose as might well be expected when even the Chaplain himself was guilty of "debauchery and churlishness". When not employed issuing proclamations or charging juries "to enquire into cases of profligacy" the excellent man busied himself in making more roads and pathways. Mr. Humphreys, the minister, was continually getting into hot water and was eventually dismissed. Several complaints against him were laid before the Council, how he had threatened to thrash Mathew Bazett for being a "nasty French Fellow", and that he abused Elizabeth Bostock and struck her. When sent to the sessions for the assault on Mrs. Bostock he retorted by publicly accusing her mother of selling him several bowls of punch without a licence. Shortly after this, the minister was again before the Council for having declared, before witnesses, that "he did not care a pish for the Governor." If some of the cases which came before the Council were odd, odd too were some of their findings, as on 13 February, 1699, when some twenty "pyrates", who had accepted the King's pardon, arrived at Jamestown from Madagascar in the ship *Pink*, and gave themselves up.

The Council decided to allow four of the pirates to reside on the island in the pious "hope it will prove some considerable profit to the inhabitants"!

Governor Poirier, anxious to combat the "sottish drunken quarrelsome humour amongst the inhabitants" conceived the happy idea of ordering the distillers to pay heavier taxes, but these taxes appear to have had little effect, for six months later an entry in the records runs: "Great increase of drunkenness", and Governor Poirier issued yet another Proclamation beginning:

Said vices have brought and will bring again to this poor island the judgement of God Almighty. We forbid all assemblies upon what account soever to be held in any house whatsoever past 10 o'clock in the evening, whether it be shipping time or not . . .

By the year 1700 the number of stills on the island had

become such a nuisance that they all were suppressed by orders from England.

From time to time the misdeeds of the Company's Chaplains have had to be recorded, but other clergymen also sometimes caused the Governor annoyance. The Rev. Mr. Jethro Bradock, chaplain to the ship *King William*, was fined eighty shillings for solemnizing a marriage between Gabriel Powell and Sarah Rider, not only without the licence of the Governor, but without the consent of the bride's father. The fine was afterwards remitted on account of the parson's poverty and of his being "almost distracted".

Many of the letters written by the Court of Directors in London to the Governor and Council at St. Helena are interesting as showing the almost paternal solicitude the Company felt for the spiritual welfare of its servants and colonists. Such is the one printed below, dated 16 April, 1701.

Our present Governor's continued care for discountenancing vice and promoting virtue we very well approve and earnestly recommend to all of you to lay your shoulders heartily to so good a work as you expect ye Divine protection and blessing and our Favour. When those in authority sett a good example the reformation of their Inferiors is therefore rendered more facil. Your care for keeping ye Lord's Day we approve but must at the same time remember that works of necessity and mercy are allowed at all times so yt when any ships are in danger of losing their passage or otherwise streightened in want of time, they should not be restrained from fetching water and other refreshments on ye Lord's Day nor on the other hand ought they be allowed to do any servile work on that day which can without prejudice be deffered to the next.

Mr. Humphrey (the turbulent minister who had been dismissed) is come here and would faine extenuate ye crimes

you charged upon him. We are sorry he proved so contrary to ye character wch first recommended him unto us.
If we can hear of another of good report we intend to send
him, otherwise we think it far better to send none at all.

We have complaint made to us that our Governor has
laid out some hundreds of pounds in a Tarras walk against
the consent of his Council—send us by the next to what
end and intent it was done.

Our Governor is also complained of as being too arbitrary. We hope the scence he has of our continued kindness to him and his family will engage his utmost zeal to
our service.

In spite of this kind and tactful letter, the strait-laced
Governor continued to deal severely with all breakers of the
sabbath.

One Sunday while he was on his way to attend Divine
Service at the Country church he was shocked to see one of
Mr. Luffkin's slaves carrying a burden on his back. On
the following day he fined Mr. Luffkin the sum of five
shillings.

Eventually the Directors found what they considered to be
a suitable minister for St. Helena in Dr. John Kerr, and he
was sent out but again proved a sad disappointment,—

a most dangerous man, always getting people by the ears
worse than ever Mr. Humphreys did,

also he boasted that he only came out in order to ruin "the
French rogue and refugee—meaning the Governor".

During his ministry Dr. Kerr was a constant source of
trouble to the Governor and to everybody else.

One day while drinking punch with some soldiers he
roundly abused the Governor, accusing him of behaving in
church "like a French Hogonot, proud fool and a rogue".

On another occasion Dr. Kerr was heard to accuse the

Governor of having said "that the Royal race of Stuarts were an unfortunate family and never did any good to England . . . and that the Parliament of England did very ill in choosing Queen Ann to be Queen of England", and other traitrous statements. A less serious remark which he said he had heard Governor Poirier make, was during a conversation about Oliver Cromwell. Someone had spoken of the Protector as "a usurper and traitor", to which, the Governor retorted, "That these things might be left alone, for when he was alive no man durst say so."

During his short period as minister at St. Helena, Dr. Kerr continued to make an unmitigated nuisance of himself. The records are full of complaints of his unclerical goings-on. "Jan. 19, 1704. Mr. Sodington" (the newly arrived Deputy-Governor) "complains of the Chaplain, Mr. Kerr, that he had not been in the Island ten days, before Mr. Kerr used his endeavours to raise an animosity between him and the Governor." He also stated "That he found Mr. Kerr's talent lay much more to Bacchus than his own profession being never better pleased than when his face is of a scarlet dye by his beloved Punch, which makes him very captious. On the 17th inst. being very flushed as usual, he did tell me his black coat was as good as my red, and called me a little fellow."

A week later Dr. Kerr was again in trouble with the Council for having "set up the bloody hand upon a Proclamation, by rubbing his hand in red paint and pressing it on the Proclamation". For giving information about this, the chaplain barbarously beat his servant.

One last, and it shall be the very last, reference to Dr. Kerr is that of Jan. 31, "Dr. Kerr abuses Governor Poirier saying 'You Hogonist, go, go to your Hogonist country to command your Hogonist Ministers'." Exactly what the clergyman meant by "hogonist" it is difficult to decide. May it have been "Huguenot" he meant, but that punch had rendered his enunciation indistinct, or can he have been using a rare and obscure term of abuse which is referred to in the Shorter Oxford English Dictionary? In any case we, and Governor Poirier, have had quite enough of Dr. Kerr.

On February 22nd, 1703, arrived at St. Helena Francis Rogers,[1] merchant, from Surat after a voyage of three months and fourteen days "with only sky and water to direct us". The town consisted then of about sixty to eighty houses and was defended along the shore by a battery of "40 stout guns, besides a small fort where the Governor lives, with more".

. . . Here is great plenty of green trade, as oranges, lemons (the lemons are very large and fine), grapes etc. and all manner of garden trade common with us, besides plenty of potatoes and yams, a large thick root, boiled and eat instead of bread, tasting between a potato and an artychoke bottom, but ruff on the palatte. Our corn will not grow here. The white bread the better sort eat, they have in store ships from England and the ships that touch here. . . .

The Indiamen have 1 or 2 quarters of beef, more or less, as the ship is, 2 or 3 times a week, and a sack or bag of lemons with it gratis. It is reckoned one of the most healthful places in the world, and our sailors just dead with the scurvy and other diseases, with eating nothing but salt provisions and drinking water in these long passages, when carried ashore here, recover to a miracle, rarely any dying though never so ill when brought ashore.

Only once did Rogers—"notwithstanding a great stomach" venture on a walk to view the famous green hills and valleys of the interior of the island.

[1] *Three Sea Journals.* Edited by Bruce S. Ingram. Constable. 1936.

The Chyrurgeon of our ship and myself once made an attempt to go up into the country by one of their best paths, which is bare rugged rocks, and so steep that we were obliged to climb triangularly up. Before I had reached the top one of our men with the Dr. called to me and told me that the Dr. was very sick, his head being giddy with the height and looking down. Upon which I descended to him and we returned down the valley again; after which I never attempted it. The rocks are of prodigious height, 2 or 3 times as high as the Monument and as near perpendicular as it is possible for man to get up them. Some of our sailors did go up, who were better used to climbing than our doctor or I, and the inhabitants make no very difficult matter of it, no more than the goats, use being second nature. The principal liquor here is Arrack punch, here being but little wine and less mault liquor; the place itself affords nothing but water and milk.

They have a pretty deal of fish among the rocks, as crawfish, crabs, eels of several sorts, snappers, rockfish, etc. and in the road flying fish and plenty of a small sort of mackerell, which we call horse mackerell, and take mostly in the night with a candle and lanthorn in our boat, with hook and line, in great numbers.

After spending a month at St. Helena, fishing and perhaps sampling the island brew of arrack punch in the numerous punch houses of Jamestown, but never again venturing to explore the island, Francis Rogers rejoined his ship, for a convoy of nine Indiamen with the *Kingfisher*, Man of War, was ready to sail for England, "leaving this healthful island with pleasant weather and winds".

On the 1st June, 1706, something occurred which was to cause the French Governor of St. Helena far more worry and vexation than all the bickering and backbiting of his officers and clergymen.

At 7 o'clock that morning a double alarm was heard from Two Gun Ridge and soon afterwards a messenger arrived at James Fort with the news that two large vessels were standing in, under Dutch colours. By ten o'clock they were off Banks's battery at the northerly end of the island which had to be passed close in by every ship approaching James Bay.

The Court of Directors had several times expressly ordered the Governor to insist that all ships should send in a boat to Banks' before entering the Bay. They also had ordered every ship of the Company to anchor close in shore.

As soon as the two strange vessels were opposite Banks's, a gun was fired from the battery, when, in accordance with custom, they lowered their topsails and saluted with five guns.

Anchored off the Battery were two Company's ships, the *Queen* and the *Dover*, but neither nearly as close in as they should have been. Then all of a sudden, to the surprise and consternation of the onlookers at Banks's, one of the Dutch ships stood towards the *Queen* and running alongside, poured into her a volley of small arms from the tops, which the *Queen* returned with a broadside; but she was quickly boarded and taken. Not until then did the enemy haul down their Dutch flags and run up French colours instead. As both the enemy ships were two-deckers, the *Dover* had no choice but to strike. At this gross breach of the law of nations, the battery opened fire, but unfortunately there was neither sufficient powder nor match in the forts, nor did many of the sponges fit the guns. Not unnaturally this caused so much confusion and delay that the French were able to cut the cables of their prizes, and after firing a few broadsides at the batteries, haul out of gunshot, and so escape.

Monsieur Desduguières, the French commander, had some

years before visited St. Helena in time of peace, and had been fêted by Governor Poirier and allowed to take soundings about the coast whenever he pleased, and to send his officers into the country, on the pretence of shooting, though it was now suspected that the real object was to survey the island.

O NE of the principal and growing anxieties both to the Governor and Council of St. Helena and to the Court of Directors in London was the increase in the number of interloping vessels which called at the island for water and refreshment, and if they could, to get permission to trade. At first these interlopers had been few and far between; but as they grew in number, the Company endeavoured to discourage them, either by altogether refusing them refreshment, or else even when water only was asked for, selling it at exorbitant rates. By 1691 the interlopers had formed themselves into a trading company or society and in 1698 an act of Parliament was passed creating them the New East India Company, to which the original company subscribed £315,000, and so became the dominant factor in the new body. Even after this, rivalry continued between the two companies until they were finally amalgamated in 1708 under the title, the "United Company of Merchants of England, trading to the East-Indies". St. Helena was then transferred from the old to the United East-India Company, in whose possession, as Lords Proprietors, the island remained until 1834 when it was taken over by the Crown.

Captain Goodwin became Deputy-Governor of St. Helena on September 8, 1707, when Governor Poirier died, but he held office only for eleven months, until the arrival from England of Captain Roberts, on August 24th the following

year. When the new Governor came he found the island in a
state of disorder and corruption, but being an able and energetic man his wise administration makes a striking contrast to
that of his predecessors. As the security of the island was the
first object of importance, he lost no time in putting it into a
thorough state of defence. The very day he set foot on St.
Helena he ordered the chief engineer to draw up a plan for a
new battery to be erected at Munden's Point. Two days later
he got a resolution passed in Council for the construction of
the present square in Jamestown and also of a new government house. Almost all the buildings on the island were in
a state of ruin, many of the walls of the houses and of the
Castle itself being shored up to prevent them falling down.
This was principally due to the lack of cement, a shortage
which had led to the use of mortar made of mud. Hitherto
chalk had been imported from England to be burnt into lime
on the island, a very expensive method, and now Governor
Roberts began to enquire whether it would not be possible to
obtain lime on the spot. A reward of one hundred dollars
was accordingly offered for the discovery of lime, and a few
weeks later Aaron Johnson, a soldier, reported finding some,
but as the quantity he was able to procure was inconsiderable
he was granted only a smaller reward, and another offer of a
sum in proportion to the capacity of the quarry was proclaimed, to stimulate further exertion. The next excitement
was the reporting by Captain Mashborne, a member of the
Council, of his discovery of gold and silver ore in Breakneck
Valley, while searching for lime. Another soldier, Charles
Rothwell, stumbled upon what was believed to be gold
and copper. The excitement increased and from the next
proclamation we can well believe that little work was done
on the plantations, for every able-bodied man, white or
black, who could wield a pick or handle a shovel, was out
prospecting.

22 Feb. 1709. A Declaration by the Governor and Council . . . For the encouragement of any person that shall be industrious towards finding a mine (of Gold or copper) he shall have as a reward for his trouble, two hundred and fifty pounds for the gold, and one hundred and fifty pounds for the copper mine; and this rainy season being the most proper time for looking into all the water-falls and streams, we desire they may apply themselves diligently thereabouts, being assured there are such mines upon the island.

Alas for false hopes, Captain Mashborne's gold proved on being assayed in England to be nothing but iron pyrites, and no further signs of gold or copper were found.

The offer of such big prizes had another result which in the end was probably of greater value to St. Helena than mines of gold, silver or copper, for in Sandy Bay were discovered "mountains of extraordinary limestone, and, providentially, lying on the hillside, and nearby huge quantities of dead ebony wood for burning the lime". When St. Helena was discovered, ebony trees grew all over the island, but already had become almost extinct from two causes—the herds of goats which roamed at large and nibbled up almost every growing sapling, so that very few grew to maturity; and the stupid lazy practice of the islanders, who when stripping the bark for tanning hides for export to England, stripped only the trunks of the trees and did not take the trouble to remove the bark from the branches, a practice which caused a shameful destruction of three trees where one would have sufficed.

For some time the work on the defences had been held up owing to the dismissal of the engineer, C. F. Vogell. Several references to him occur in the records, and few to his credit. One Newman was fined in March, 1707, for abusing Vogell, by saying "the Engineer knew no more than a cat . . . he was

a fool and would go off the Island in disgrace . . ." a statement of opinion which was shortly after to be proved so true
that one can only hope that Newman had his fine remitted.
On April 1st we read: "The Engineer Vogell tried for profligate
conduct and acquitted. But the Governor (Goodwin) on
hearing from John Alexander, Clerk of the Council, that
Vogell had asked a slave girl at the Castle who were the sweethearts of Mary and Martha Goodwin, was very angry and said
if this declaration had been given in before, he did not think
Vogell would have got off so well."

Under the rule of the capable new Governor Roberts, the
engineer was doomed. On October 12: "The Governor
reports to the Council that he observes the Engineer to be
useless, running headlong into business, rather a Pioneer than
an Engineer and no gentleman—Idle, ignorant and lazy—to
be dismissed the Honourable Company's service from this
day. . . . Mr. Vogell the Engineer prays he might be allowed
time till next ship arrives from England expecting to be
employed in India. That his salary be continued to enable
him to pay his debts and to carry him off like a gentleman.
He is answered—it was the opinion of the Council that if he
carried nothing off with him he would in that point go off as
much like a gentleman as he came on."

Poor Mr. Vogell. He really does not concern the history
of St. Helena any further, but a worse calamity, and his last,
was on its way. He embarked on the *Despatch* for England,
and when off the North of Scotland the ship was sunk by a
French privateer and every soul on board, except the doctor,
perished.

Even if the work on the buildings had to be postponed
until another engineer arrived, the energetic Governor was
not one to sit idle by himself, nor to allow others to do so.
He at once issued orders for improving pasturage, planting
trees for wood and fruit, fencing all the Company's lands and

renovating the Company's farms. The regulation which obliged the land-holders to pay the Company one shilling annually for every beast pastured on the waste lands had become entirely ignored until Governor Roberts put an end to any further violation of this law by confiscating some cattle belonging to Mrs. Elizabeth Johnson, the widow of the late murdered Governor. Groves of gum-wood and lemon trees were planted, as well as castor-oil plants. To do all this extra work the Governor concluded that two hundred more slaves were needed, and to feed them, suitable ground had to be found for the cultivation of yams, a coarse, unappetizing root considered suitable diet for negro slaves and pigs. Many difficulties were raised, but he swept them all aside. By an ingenious method he had water carried by a canal from the spring at Plantation to irrigate some sixty acres of bare waste land lying between Breakneck Valley and Friars Valley, which to this day goes by the name of New Ground. Its main advantage was that the slaves working there could be overlooked from Plantation House, for "one Black under Eye does more work than four out of sight."

Here in a short while were growing in profusion, not only yams, but beans, Indian corn, sugar canes and grape vines, and the Governor had the satisfaction of being able to report his success to the Council and to exhibit samples of sugar, rum, wine and brandy, all the produce of New Ground. He also ascertained the practicability of making bricks and tiles, thus saving the enormous expense the Company incurred by importing these from England. The Council was fully impressed by the Governor's exhibits and particularly by the sugar and passed the following resolution: "That a pound or two be sent to our Honourable Masters, by the next shipping and that they may be acquainted that we have found the following articles since Governor Roberts came here, viz:

Lime,
Tyles,
Brick,
Cut-stones, for building,
Sugar,
Rum,
Minerals of severall sorts.

Upon which we are now resolved to fire nine guns; to drink our Honourable Masters' good health, and success to the island."

One of the Governor's chief ambitions was to persuade or compel the land-holders to fence their properties. Crops were ruined and trees were being exterminated by the wandering herds of goats, sheep and cattle, and unless the cultivated land was quickly protected, there would soon be scarcely a tree left growing on the island.

Many of the inhabitants derived a considerable income by hiring out their slaves to the Company at one shilling and sixpence a day, but the Council now resolved that no black should be hired until his owner could satisfy them that his land was properly fenced and planted with the required proportion of wood. The result of this wise edict was that soon decayed fences and ruined plantations began to give place to well-managed farms, while "sloth and intemperance were succeeded by sober habits; and the face of the country soon wore a new appearance."

Another serious problem which Roberts took in hand was the almost entirely neglected laws and orders which had been from time to time transmitted by former governments. It was questionable whether many of them had not become obsolete, nor was it certain which were still in force. Many of the land-holders were quite ignorant even of the terms by which they held their lands. Two members of Council were,

therefore, instructed to examine the various orders sent out
and to write them down in a book to be entitled "Laws and
Ordinances". At the end of three months the work was
finished and a meeting of thirty-six principal inhabitants was
convened at the Country Church, that the code might be read
to them and copies delivered to the churchwardens for general
distribution.

The list of names of the principal inhabitants in 1709 is
interesting because there is only one name, Orlando Bagley,
which still exists on St. Helena, for Mr. Orlando Bagley, a
direct descendant, is to-day a landowner on the island. All the
other families named appear to have died out or left the island,
though some have left their names behind to places on the
map such as Cason, Powell, Lufkin, Seale, Francis and
Wrangham.

At the same meeting notice was given, with the sanction of
the Company, that any observation, suggestion or proposal
offered by the inhabitants might be delivered in writing and
the Government would take them into consideration.

This unheard-of indulgence resulted in a list being presented
of nineteen proposals for alteration or modification of certain
ordinances the inhabitants considered oppressive, and most of
these were either struck out or modified.[1]

Under the vigilant eye of the Governor, rapid progress was
made on the work at Munden's Point, and the Company's
orders for erecting barracks, which had been very incom-
pletely effected under Governor Blackmore, were completed.

Only a part of the improvements carried out by Roberts
have been stated here, and it was an unfortunate day when
one of the best Governors St. Helena ever had resigned
his office in August, 1711, and Captain Boucher was sent out
to reign in his stead.

Captain Roberts's government may well be said to have

---

[1] See Appendix II.

begun a new era in the history of St. Helena. Out of disorder
and chaos he evolved a law-abiding, temperate and flourishing
little colony.

At a meeting of the inhabitants held shortly after he assumed
governorship he made the following declaration, which gives
a vivid picture of the kind of man he was, and largely explains
the secret of his success.

Gentlemen, I am very jealous of my Masters' honour, and
it is not in my power to receive any affront if I would; for,
as I and these gentlemen of the Council represent them, so
no affront can be put upon me, but must immediately fall
upon the Lords Proprietors. No man shall come to me
with a civil question but shall receive a civil answer; and I
would have you assure yourselves that sudden affronts
shall receive sudden punishment.

After all the hard things which have had to be recorded of
many of the clergymen at St. Helena, it is pleasant, and only
just, to quote the words in which Brooke the historian concluded his chapter on Governor Roberts: "His labours probably derived some aid from the chaplain, Mr. Tomlinson, who
is mentioned as a worthy character, and is the first instance
of such a clergyman that appears on record for thirty years
back."

When the new Governor, Captain Benjamin Boucher,
arrived at St. Helena on 7th August, 1711, he brought with
him as Deputy-Governor a sinister character, Mr. George
Hoskinson. The latter, who was a wealthy planter and one
of the biggest landowners on the island, had incurred for-
feiture of his lands owing to a statute which laid down that
any person holding lands from the Company who went away
for more than six months should be deprived of such lands,

houses, etc. In a minute dated 7th January, 1710, Hoskinson
had been described as a person who, with the exception of
murder, "it would be no hard matter to prove had broke
through all the laws both of God and man." In the July
following Hoskinson had clandestinely left the island, without
the knowledge or permission of the Governor, and his
property was therefore forfeited. At the same time the
Council, out of pity for his wife, granted her permission to
live on a good property, with a farm, called Bowmans, for
which she was to pay the Company a nominal rent. Hoskinson had powerful friends in England, and by means of a
plausible tale they persuaded the Directors to allow him to
return to the island and to re-possess his lands, and even to
appoint him Deputy-Governor.

Governor Boucher was soon at loggerheads with his deputy
as we learn from the following entry in the records, dated
5th February, 1712:

> The Governor, having ordered the colours to be half-
> masted on 30th January, being King Charles Martyrdom,
> Capt. Hoskinson further caused eight guns to be fired,
> for doing which the Govr. requires an explanation in
> writing.

But a month afterwards, fortunately for the island, Hoskinson died.

Captain Boucher on assuming the government pursued a
line of conduct in exact opposition to that of his predecessor,
and no more is heard of sugar-works, the manufacture of
wine, brandy, bricks or tiles, nor of endeavours to promote
improvements of any kind. For some unexplained reason he
began buying up for the Company every plantation which
came into the market, until the decreased number of land-
holders became a subject of extreme anxiety and alarm to the

Court of Directors at home. By extravagance he wasted the produce of the Company's farms and allowed to be exterminated a fine herd of deer. The gardens at Plantation House, the principal estate of the Company, and the apple of his eye to Governor Roberts, were allowed to run to waste and were thrown into pasture for Governor Boucher's donkeys, of which he kept a large stud. His favourite exercise was riding donkeys, though he insisted they should be always referred to as his horses; and in order that he might indulge in this pastime in all weathers he had erected, at the Company's expense, a covered shed four hundred feet in length. In addition he made a riding-field four hundred feet long in the garden of the Fort, and turned the remainder of it into grazing land for his "horses". Governor Boucher believed himself to be in a delicate state of health and that the exercise of riding was the only means of preserving his constitution. He spent six hours a day in the saddle, three before and another three after he dined at noon.

The misconduct and bad management of this man were all the more pernicious in their effects as the island was at that period suffering from an unusually dry season. Two thousand five hundred head of black cattle perished for want of water and food, and meat became so scarce that the inhabitants were allowed the use of the Company's yawl to go fishing. To such extremities was the island reduced that a conspiracy was planned among the garrison to seize the Governor and Council and then to plunder the stores of food. This plot was happily discovered in time for steps to be taken to frustrate it. A pretext was found for extracting the flints from the firelocks of the suspected soldiers, and on the following morning secret orders were given to fire an alarm at Prosperous Bay. When the armed militia assembled at the rendezvous they far outnumbered the garrison of only one hundred and twenty soldiers, so that the ringleaders were easily secured and

shortly afterwards sent away to the Company's factory at
Bencoolen in Sumatra.

After a government of three years, the Company gladly
accepted Captain Boucher's resignation, but ordered him to
refund the money spent on building his riding-house. On
29th June, 1714, Governor Boucher embarked for England
on board the *Recovery*, and was succeeded nine days afterwards
on the arrival of Governor Isaac Pyke and a new Council, to
which Captain Bazett, in addition to the office of store-keeper,
was appointed to take his seat as fourth member.

Matthew Bazett, a Huguenot refugee, arrived at St. Helena
on 8th January, 1684, in the ship *Charles II*, as a cadet in the
H.E.I.C. service. Many references to him and his family occur
in the Records. His great-grandson, Bazett Knipe, was
Assistant Colonial Secretary and Treasurer Officer in 1882.
Four generations of Bazetts played an important part in the
history of the island.

Governor Boucher's parting act was to strip Government
House of everything portable, even to the locks on the doors.

It was the practice of the Company, whenever a weak
Governor had allowed the island to deteriorate or the inhabitants to become unruly, to send out a strong man in his place.
Such a man was Isaac Pyke. He arrived at St. Helena during
a difficult period. The island was seething with discontent,
bordering on rebellion, and he found many obstacles to contend with.

The long, unprecedented drought continued. There were
tremendous gales which caused great havoc.

Then appeared a mysterious epidemic which none could
understand, which spread death amongst both whites and
blacks. When at last the drought ended in 1718, a water-
spout broke over Sandy Bay Ridge occasioning serious and
extensive damage. It must have terrified those planters and
their families who lived in that lovely Bay, for the water is

described as having "descended with mighty floods and torrents, carrying away the soil in an incredible manner, with
both grass, trees, yams and stone walls before it. It brought
down rocks of a mighty bulk, and covered abundance of
fruitful land with stones."

The sea for many miles around was discoloured by mud,
many families were almost ruined, and it called for all their
industry to repair the mischief.

Governor Pyke, who was particularly interested in agriculture, was anxious to encourage the cultivation of yams on a
far larger scale than hitherto. The ambition of Governor
Roberts had been to grow enough of these useful, if unpalatable, roots to supply the Company's slaves and cattle
without having to purchase any from the planters, but the
prolonged drought had sadly depleted the stock. With this
object in view Pyke imported a considerable number of slaves
during his governorship. To the planters this scarcity of
yams was little regretted for it was a popular belief amongst
them that during the rainy season the yam was a very unwhole-
some food, and in any case the cultivation of potatoes had
lately become general and to some extent superseded the
other.

The planters employed an almost infallible antidote to the
evil effects of eating yams, and this was the free use of strong,
distilled spirits. The Governor refers to this in a letter to
the Court of Directors, dated March, 1717:

As an alteration of weather often happens here in less
than an hour's space, from sultry heat to very cold, and the
mountainy part of the country is not only windy, but
always exposed to great damps and fogs, we are apt to
think it easier to drink water for a constancy in England
than in this place. The physical people we sometimes
converse with [that is, the ship surgeons] tell us, that

strong liquor is necessary to all people who have no other bread but these watery roots (for a yam is called the water-parsnip); and we also find it so; wherefore, tho' we shall encourage temperance and sobriety, as well by our example as our precept, yet it is in vain to dissuade the use of arrack among these people, who prefer it before the choicest wines.

Not without cause did the Directors write on one occasion, when remonstrating with the Council, "People will be apt to say that at this island the old proverb is true about settlements, that where the English settle they first build a Punch House, the Dutch a fort, and the Portuguese a Church."

Owing to the indolence of the late Governor Boucher, combined with the long drought which was followed by an epidemic amongst the cattle, the live-stock had decreased to an alarming degree. Shortly after Pyke's arrival a census shewed that there were only sixty head of cattle, twenty-four swine, three sheep and twenty-six fowls on the island, and he ordered that until the stock had increased, the white inhabitants were to eat salt meat on two days in the week and fish on two others. As to the blacks, they were to sub-sist as best they could on a diet of yams. Any ship calling at the island might be supplied with anything except fresh beef. Eggs of seabirds were also much eaten, and the inhabitants were permitted to collect them on certain days in the week, but they began taking them on the prohibited days, and some men who landed on Egg Island, a rock still a favourite nesting site of Noddy terns, lighted fires which drove away the birds to nest on the steep cliffs on the mainland where it was ex-tremely difficult and dangerous to reach their nests.

It did not take the islanders long to discover that although their new Governor could be a hard and strict man when the occasion required, he had his softer moments, as when Mr. Tovey, the clerk to the Council, on being reprimanded for his arrears of work, excused himself by pleading the want of ink, to which the Governor answered, "This is only his pretence—and friendly advises him to be more careful." Others may have considered him a harsh man, though the Governor seems to have considered himself a tolerant one, for when Thomas Bevian was tried before him for stealing a silver-headed cane, the Governor directed the jury to arrive at a lenient verdict, the accused being a *white* man. Their verdict was: "found guilty to the value of tenpence" and the judge thereupon sentenced the culprit to receive thirty-nine lashes!

Many accusations were made against Governor Pyke of arbitrary conduct, one of which brought him a sharp reproof from the Court of Directors. Whenever a soldier had served his time at St. Helena, he had the right to claim to be sent back to England. Four time-expired men, Bates, Flurcus, Shoales and Poulter applied to the Governor to be given their discharge, but were refused it. They then stole an open boat one night, and with enough food and water to last them about one month set sail out into the Atlantic, and by the greatest good fortune eventually reached the island of St. Nevis in the West Indies, after a voyage of some four thousand five hundred miles.

The Court of Directors, in a letter dated 22nd May, 1717, referring to this event, wrote:

At first sight it would appear you were too arbitrary in the case of Flurcus and the other three men who ran away with the Long Boat because nothing but death was likely to be the reward of that attempt. Flurcus and Shoales came to England and were here last July to justify themselves and to complain of the severities which forced them upon that desperate adventure. By the journal they gave in, which contained a voyage of 1,428 leagues run, it appears Flurcus who kept it is an able mariner.

Flurcus, the hero of this remarkable voyage, must have been a man of unusual ability. He came out to the island as a tailor, but making friends with some stone-cutters who could not write, and being himself "expert with his pen and Ingenious, drew out and marked their work and learned their trade". After a while he made friends with "one Welch, who had made some proficiency in numbers and practised some parts of the mathematics and so to navigation which when he had gained some knowledge in, he put into practice", and no mean practice either, to sail an open boat with a crew of three soldiers from St. Helena to the West Indies.

For all his ruthlessness, Pyke restored the island from a ruinous to as flourishing a state as could be expected under the circumstances. He made the first safe roadway up the steep side of Ladder Hill, which leads from Jamestown to High Knoll and Plantation House. He introduced fir and pine trees to the island and brought it many other benefits. That he was a man of intelligence and wide outlook is shewn by the following letter written to the Court of Directors on 19th February, 1715:

We hear that the fruitful island called Mauritius, that was lately left by the Dutch is yet uninhabited and has not had any dearth upon it but abounds plentifully. There is deer and other cattle with fruit of every sort and plenty of many sorts of timber, with commodious harbours for ships and a fine temperate air which usually preserved the former inhabitants to a very great age. But now 'tis wild, the land unoccupied and almost overgrown with wood as well as overstocked with cattle—be pleased to pardon us for this freedom who had not troubled your Honours with such accounts as this, but Capt. Litten making this report and our Governor having formerly been in several parts of this island . . . and being able of his own knowledge to confirm all that Capt. Litten has said about Mauritos was desirous of writing to your Honours concerning this place for the following reasons.

First that we have several young people here more than we can supply with plantations, that would be very proper inhabitants to settle in that place, and because that place is naturally so well supplied that it would maintain a very great colony without any charge to their Patrons more than sending them out, and the place lies in the root or tract of all the homeward bound shipping.

But our great and principal reason is the Government and people of Don Mascarenas[1] say they have been sent to France for liberty to transplant themselves to this neighbouring island, which is not only more commodious than Mascarenas in regard to shipping but it exceeds it so much in fertility that it is a paradise to the other. The consideration of keeping out the French or the Indian pirates from an island of much consequence as the Isle Mauritos may be to us, will, we hope, excuse us to your Honours for making this digression, because we believe ourselves bound by the ties of gratitude and duty to acquaint your Honours with whatsoever has an apperance of yours and our country's interest.

Had the Company taken the advice of their Governor at St. Helena they would have saved themselves and the country a vast amount of future trouble and expense. The Dutch abandoned the island in 1710, but it was not colonized by the French East India Company until 1721, so that Pyke's suggestion was not only a good but a timely one.

The subsequent history of Mauritius proved how advantageous would have been its occupation by the English, and how many disasters might have been avoided. During

[1] Réunion Island.

subsequent wars it became so increasingly a source of mischief to English merchant vessels and East Indiamen from the sorties made by French men-of-war and privateers, that its capture became essential, and was effected in 1810 by an expedition specially sent out by the British Government. Had Pyke's hint been taken at the time, instead of being pigeon-holed and forgotten, this expedition would have been unnecessary.

Governor Pyke was in many ways a remarkable man. When he first arrived at St. Helena, the soldiers were dying in considerable numbers from some disease, possibly dysentery, believed to be due to their drinking impure water, which had become contaminated during the rainy season. Pyke gave orders that in future tea should be the soldiers' ordinary drink, in place of water, "in the same manner as the Dutch soldiers at Batavia", who had, he learned, been in much better health after they took to drinking tea instead of water. In the official report which he wrote on the epidemic, he suggested that perhaps the beneficial effects of tea-drinking might not be due to any virtue of the tea but to the boiling of the water, and so anticipated by many years the discoveries of Pasteur and other nineteenth-century scientists.

An appreciative and observant visitor to the island was Captain Daniel Beeckman who landed there on a voyage from the East, on the 9th June, 1715.

In a book he wrote,[1] he tells us that all the white inhabitants were English, who owned a large number of slaves. "They all have a great desire to see England, which they call home, though many of them never saw it, nor can have any true idea thereof."

Beeckman was impressed by the fortifications which he described as "in a manner impregnable".

He met Governor Pyke "whose study is employed to the advantage of the island, and the Company's interest", and

---

[1] *A Voyage to and from the Island of Borneo.* D. Beeckman. 1718.

mentioned the path which that energetic man had just made up Ladder Hill, so that no longer had the inhabitants to use the rope ladder which gave the hill its name.

Like every visitor to St. Helena, excepting the French exiles at Longwood a century later, Beeckman held the climate in high esteem. He gave a list of the birds he saw, or thought he saw, which included larks and moorhens, birds which certainly do not exist to-day. He also described "a sort of long-legged bird like our wheat-ears which eat very sweet, but not so fat as ours"—which evidently were the native wire birds.

Concerning the multitudes of sea-birds that nest on the rocky coast he wrote: "At certain seasons you may fill your boats with eggs of sea-fowl, so tame, they suffer you, when they lie on their eggs, to take them up with your hands."

The gardens abounded with fruit trees, but unfortunately the island abounded with rats, so that the farmers found it to be useless to grow corn, because the rats ate up all the grain as soon as it was sown, and this in spite of "vast numbers of cats, that went away from the houses, and became wild, living among the rocks, where they find good prog, feeding on young partridges, so that they became as great a plague as the rats".

Jamestown contained some seventy to eighty houses, most of which were owned by planters, who only occupied them when a ship called.

He gives a minute description of the elaborate procedure which took place on Sundays when Governor Pyke and his lady attended divine service.

They use great formality in going to church; for about nine o'clock in the morning, the council, the minister, and their wives, together with such commanders of ships as have a mind to it, do wait on the governor in the castle. After which a bell being ordered to ring, a company of soldiers, with a serjeant, in good liveries, are drawn up in the castle, where they make a lane (resting their arms) as a passage to the gate, where there is another serjeant and a company, which march with beat of drum before the Governor into church. After follow the gentlemen and their ladies in their respective order. As soon as the soldiers get into the church-yard, they fall off to the right and left, making a lane to the church-door. The Governor has a handsome large seat, with books, where he generally desires the commanders of ships to sit, the ladies being seated by themselves.

While Captain Beeckman was on shore, attending church parades, and admiring the country, some of the crew of his ship, "restless villains" from Batavia, "with wicked designs" plotted a mutiny. But some of them got drunk in the taverns and were overheard "cursing and damning the ship and the voyage" and "laying their heads together" to carry off the ship. Governor Pyke, being informed of this arrested "a Knot of 22" of the conspirators, had them tried before the Council and whipped at the flag-staff and then put in irons on board another ship which took them to England.

The Company appears to have employed some queer doctors as well as queer clergymen. One of these, Dr. Du Nay, is interesting principally from a medical point of view, as a sufferer from a chronic indisposition. He was credited with being a "well qualified, sober man, with a good judgment in his business", though it was not thought he would long survive on account of his delicate health. His own treatment for his malady was drastic, for we are told "he takes at least a gallon of blood a week from himself, so that he is brought so low as we can't expect he can continue long in this world."

It may well have been this generous auto-phlebotomy which was the cause of his very curious and unusual train of symptoms.

Evidently the members of the Council were much interested in the health of their medical officer, for all kinds of medical details about him occur in the records.

> August 12, 1716. Dr. Du Nay has been a long time sick. We allow him diet money because he can't eat at the Fort because the half part of the provisions is usually Pork, *and if he sees any pork he faints away*, let it be where it will, and is very ill, so that we are forced when he comes down to the Fort to have everything of that nature taken out of sight. He is in other respects an honest and, we think, skilful man.

There had been some trouble with mutinous sailors on the *Eagle* galley, a ship which called in on her way home from Madras. A conspiracy was discovered just in time to arrest the ringleaders and imprison them. When the *Eagle* arrived in England all sorts of untrue stories and complaints to the detriment of Governor Pyke were taken to the Court of Directors, the principal informer being one Swartz, a German, but any credence the Court may have given to his story was entirely wiped out when they received from St. Helena the following report by the Council.

> We think we know the fomenting of this complaint comes from Bartholomew Swartz, a German, who is none of the best nor wisest of men, tho he had once the honor to be appointed your Supra Cargoe on board the *Borneo*. He is a vain man who pretends to be intimately acquainted with King George, and was used when here to carry a bundle of papers in his pocket wherein he told were 20 letters from the Princess Sophia and some from her son (our present King whom God preserve) that they had sent to the Cape and left some of these letters for him there.

But the misfortune was that the Princess Sophia dyed about six months before she sent him the last letters. A man who would tell us such gross absurdities without any colour, ground or reason will never stick to frame a story for your Honours.

Some of the strangest reading in the Council's record books is about the trials held for various misdemeanours, and the incongruous and generally brutal punishments inflicted for quite trivial offences. Thus, in November, 1716, we read:

Sentence against Huff, a soldier, for having a child by one of the Company's slave women, that he be set this evening as soon as the heat of the day is over, publicly on the Wooden horse, *with his face blackened*, and that henceforth he be looked upon as no other than a Black.

Another later:

Peter and Moll, two runaway slaves belonging to Sergt. Slaughter, accused by Capt. Haswell of robbing him, sentenced—that they have forty lashes a piece, which is less by seventeen than the law prescribes—and the reason for that is because *no witness appeared against* them.

From a letter to the Directors, 12th January, 1717:

The people here are peevish and vexatious and some of them turbulent. . . . They are all Lawyers here, Mr. Powell and Parson Tomlinson and Richard Swallow, sen., are usually the Directors of the Public on one side or other of every contention.

The inevitable trouble with the Company's Chaplain is referred to in a minute dated October 8:

Of late our parson has been more troublesome than usual and has several new notions. Last Sunday there was a great omission of several parts of the Liturgy, the Nicene Creed, the prayer for the Company and Shipping, and there was only a Collect and the Lord's prayer before sermon.

Mr. Tomlinson, sent for and questioned, is informed:

The Governor and Council are resolved to have no more of these Fopperies nor alterations in the established forms of the Church prayers, and if you go on in these whimsical methods of altering the established prayers by halving them, you will render yourself incapable of acting as a Minister of the Church of England here and must expect to be sent home.

For the first time in the history of the island notes or bills were now issued by the Company to overcome the shortage of metal currency. "The people begin to like them, though we have some difficulty to establish them in their good opinion." With the bills, which amounted only in value to £400, the Company sent out £100 in "bits", £100 in fanams, and £100 in copper pice. The question of currency in the island had always been a troublesome one. Later on the Company issued its own copper coins, but until then all kinds of small Indian coins were in circulation, and the only currency actually issued by the Company were large and heavy copper bars, to which the inhabitants strongly objected, for, apart from their cumbersomeness, no customer on a passing ship would accept them.

It goes without saying that a strong Governor of the type of Isaac Pyke made enemies in the island. Some of these wrote letters of complaint about him to the Directors, in which they did not mince their words, calling him "Rogue" or Villain", or accusing him of driving a great trade with visiting ships, or of wasting the Company's money on useless extravagances such as the new banqueting house or a ground for the game of nine-pins. He was accused of taking away the Company's slaves from doing useful work on the plantations in order to make paths "the better to carry the Ladies in their Sedans up and down hills for visits and diversions".

Pyke was ready with his answer to this last complaint. "Sometimes (about once a week) the blacks carry a chair and sometimes in shipping two or three chairs into the country, and can be no great loss of time. The chairs were never carried here till Governor Roberts' time, yet before then there were on such occasions as many blacks employed to carry hammocks as now to carry a chair."

A more justifiable complaint against the Governor was that he had employed the Company's stone-cutters and work-men for eight months building a tomb ten feet in height by seven broad, for his wife, Mistress Ann Pyke, and that he had charged this as spent on the fortifications. The Directors took a serious view of this and ordered him to refund the cost of building the tomb. To these accusations the Governor, never at a loss for an answer, replied, though he had to admit to the truth of the one about the family grave:

As to the Governor driving a great private trade we assure your Honours we know of none, and the Governor says he never sold anything to the garrison at all unless when three of his servants died, their goods and cloaths were put up and sold by public outcry. As to the path, the ban-queting house and the nine-pin place there is no such thing. Nine-pins is what the Governor never plays at, so its not so likely he should bestow charge on that. The value of the tomb has been referred to Capt. Haswell and Bazett who have not yet brought in their report, but as soon as it is done the Governor shall be made debtor for it.

This tomb still stands at Jamestown; neglected, sad, unnoticed, in a desolate and dirty place, the lower graveyard: a playground for ragged children and the resort of goats.

Built into the side of the tomb, one of the most treasured possessions of the island was recently discovered by Mr. G. C. Kitching, the Government Secretary, and Dr. Paul Wilkinson, the Medical Officer. St. Helena is, or should be, ever grateful to these two enthusiasts for rescuing it and placing it where it now stands, at one side of the entrance to the Castle. It is the stone commemorating the visit of Commander Fremlin in the *Dolphin* in 1645, and is illustrated in this book.

So much has been recorded to the disparagement of the clergy of St. Helena that it is a pleasure to find the Rev. Mr. Tomlinson well spoken of, in the recorded minute concerning the ruinous state of the church at Jamestown, "a very scandalous place to look upon, being worse in appearance than a poor mans barn". It then goes on to state: "The Minister who is a very honest good man has been industrious in getting subscriptions. He is a useful man, and since our best doctor died he has offered to prescribe in physic for any of the garrison gratis, being always ready to do any good if he can."

There seems to have been something about St. Helena, some sort of spell, which had a disastrous effect upon clergymen. Only a few months later we find the following entry: "Parson Tomlinson having sold arrack to a soldier, the Governor says the Parson has engaged himself to him never to sell any more arrack, and the Governor is resolved he never will look upon him nor his wife neither, if ever he does."

A fortnight later, September 17, 1716, there is more trouble between the Governor and the parson.

Parson Tomlinson demands that a petition sent in against him should be torn. The Governor answers that his own petition ought rather to be torn because he hauls in all his sacred Function to the scrape, and to help out with his clamour; but so it has been too much of late, when a churchman can't justify his actions then he cries out and makes his church in danger, and for lugging in his church into the brawl or contest, it ought to be disregarded.

For more than two years Mr. Tomlinson's name is not mentioned in the records either in praise or censure, until May 26, 1719, when "The Governor orders that no gratuity be paid without his particular order because he thinks where persons have done less than their duty instead of more, the salary itself is scarce due. For instance the parson who never of late goes up to bury any of the garrison but leaves the Dead to bury the Dead. And whereas before it used by all chaplains that has been here to insert immediately after the petition for those in the Company's service abroad these words, 'more especially the Governor and Council of this place', and since he constantly omits that sentence and has given out by his brother that he don't think them worth praying for, the Governor says there is an old proverb, 'No Penny, no Pater Noster', so we say, 'No Pater Noster, no Penny', and are very well contented because as we think the prayers of such a fellow can do us but little good."

One more mention of the quarrelsome Mr. Tomlinson, and only one, shall be made before he disappears forever from the pages of the books of records and the shores of St. Helena. It occurs in a copy of a letter addressed by the Council to the Board of Directors, dated May 5, 1719.

As to Dr. Tomlinson, the Governor knows too well the trouble that attends disputing with any that have the privilege of wearing a parson's gown, and therefore he always endeavours to avoid it, for if any of them think they

meet with the least slight or disappointment, they cry out
at once for the help of their tribe, and their Church must be
in danger of everything which crosses their covetous or
ambitious humours, and for that reason the Governor says
he never cares to have too much to do with the parsons.
Some of them are good men while in a pulpit who are
indifferent out of it.

In this same letter we get a curious sidelight on the lives at
St. Helena of members of the learned professions of medicine
and the Church. Members of the other learned profession,
the law, were always rigidly excluded from the island. The
passage is about a man called Beale, a well-known island
name, who

arrogantly assumed or pretended to great skill in physick,
but is indeed very ignorant. He was a taylor but when he
could not live on that trade, he had licence to keep a punch-
house. One, Dr. Porteous, who was surgeon here, among
other medicines gave one particular pill with good success.
Beale learnt the method of making that pill. About a year
ago his success obtained him a great deal of credit here, but
his vanity lost it again, for he bought three sick blacks for
£27—which he vaunted he could cure, but they all three
died and he lost his fame and his money together.

When Governor Pyke made a law he saw that it was enforced, but although laws were passed to reduce the enormous
number of stills in the island and a tax of one shilling was
levied on every gallon of arrack imported, yet drunkenness
amongst the inhabitants continued. The annual death-rate
hitherto had been about five per cent amongst the population
—to-day it is 1.5 per cent for the whole population, white and
coloured—but in 1719 it rose to ten per cent, which was

accounted for by the enormous quantity of rum punch consumed. It might be expected that a good example of moderation in drinking would be set by the medical practitioners, but on the 3rd June of that year we read: "Doctor Hicks for being drunk and breaking the peace in the street, with his sword drawn; fined and his sword ordered to be sold for the use of the guard"—which windfall the guard no doubt spent on rum punch.

From the very beginning St. Helena had been a favourite place of exile for political and other prisoners, keeping them out of the way of doing further mischief. As will be remembered, the first resident on the island was a Portuguese renegade officer, and on May 24, 1719, another prisoner of the same race arrived in the ship *Morrice*. This man is described as a Portuguese Admiral, and with him were three other Portuguese prisoners from Bombay, who had been found guilty of treason, in the Company's war against the pirate Angria. He landed at Jamestown in handcuffs, and in contemporary records is described as "the one-legged Portuguese villain".

According to Clement Downing,[1] he came with orders from the Company that he was to work as a slave for the remainder of his life. There is no mention made of this picturesque prisoner in the island records, but Downing, our only authority, states that "by his fair speeches and behaviours" he so far succeeded in gaining the good opinion of Governor Pyke that he appointed him overseer of the Company's slaves. He abused this good opinion, and "infus'd such notions into the heads of these slaves, that they were near upon rising and cutting off all the inhabitants in the night; but by the providence of God, Captain Sclater[2] was informed of this plot by one of his own servants, and prevented the intended mischief."

[1] *A History of the Indian Wars.* London. 1735.
[2] Ensign William Slaughter—the Town Marshal.

The Governor at once had the villain arrested and confined in the Castle dungeon until the arrival of the next Company ship which took him to Bencoolen "where the rogue had like to have raised all the Malays and to have been the cause of having the whole settlement cut off". As this is a history of St. Helena we must not follow any farther the exciting life story of this one-legged Portuguese Admiral, except to add that from Sumatra he was transferred to Madras and eventually escaped from there to join the pirate Angria, and become one of his "Head Gunners".

In the summer of 1719, Pyke was transferred to the Company's settlement at Bencoolen in Sumatra, and he left St. Helena much improved in every way to the state in which he had found it five years before.

In that year, the population of the island, exclusive of the garrison, was three hundred and twenty whites and four hundred and eleven blacks, while the number of cattle, other than those owned by the Company, was one thousand, seven hundred and sixty-five.

Isaac Pyke was succeeded by Mr. Edward Johnson, who arrived at Jamestown in the "good ship *Craggs* frigot" on 13th June, 1719. Also on board was the Reverend Mr. Jones, the new chaplain.

Hitherto every Governor had been a military man or at all events had assumed military rank on taking office, but Mr. Johnson was a civilian. In England he had acted for many years as a Justice of the Peace and for this reason was considered by the Court of Directors to "well understand what is proper to be done" in the administration of law and justice.

Another innovation was the annulment of the office of Deputy-Governor. The emoluments of the Company's servants were increased and a re-arrangement made of the various duties allotted to the members of the Council, as follows:

Governor Johnson, one hundred pounds salary and one hundred pounds gratuity.

Captain Bazett, second in Council and Store-keeper, seventy pounds and thirty pounds gratuity.

Mr. Byfield, third in Council and Superintendent of the Company's plantations, sixty-five pounds salary, thirty pounds gratuity.

Mr. Antipas Tovey, fourth in Council and Accountant, fifty pounds salary and thirty pounds gratuity.

Captain Alexander, fifth in Council and Secretary, forty pounds salary and a gratuity of ten pounds.

It is only with genuine regret that the chronicler of this history is compelled, once again, to refer to the misdeeds of the clergy of the island. He would have preferred to pass over in silence the activities and even the very existence of the new chaplain, Mr. Jones, but in a work such as this, of fact, not fiction, veracity must have preference over the personal wishes of the author.

Within one month of his landing at St. Helena the new chaplain was up before the Council charged with having torn the gown off Mr. Tovey and with having struck him with his fist in the eye, causing it to become black and swollen. In his defence Mr. Jones replied that Mr. Tovey had called him "a scoundrel with other abusive words"—and pleaded that "flesh and blood was not able to bear" such insults, though he owned up to the blow and made a handsome apology "upon which they shook hands".

On November 24th following, we read:

Parson Jones refuses to attend Council when summoned and is brought up by a warrant for neglecting to use the prayer for the Company on 22nd November. He behaved very insolently and his gratuity was ordered to be stopped.

The next entry in the book of records is a copy of a long letter addressed by the Council to the Board of Directors, on 21st December, 1719. It is headed:

A true state of the case of Mr. John Jones, Chaplain.

To draw him off from associating himself with those of too mean a rank for him now as a clergyman, though his equals when he was in the island before a private soldier, the Governor attributed his too familiar phrases and expressions he used to let fall at the table before him in some measure from his not conversing with a better sort, therefore invited him to be his companion and allotted him an apartment at the Plantation House (the Governor's country residence) to be there when the Governor was there.

On the 22nd September at the Plantation House a wedding took place, one of the gentlemen of the Council to a young gentlewoman. The account of what fish the fishing boat had taken was brought to the Governor as usual. The account was, twelve fishes called Jacks, and twelve fishes called Old Wives, which occasioned the Governor to joke with Mr. Jones by saying, "Parson, you and I need not despair, for the old English proverbe, a Jack for every Gill, is verified, even by the fish you see here—twelve Jacks to twelve Old Wives"—which expression put Mr. Jones in mind of the old woman he married when he went off from hence to England before, and raised his passion, which the Governor took no notice of at first but endeavoured to overlook it.

But when he grew noisy, the Governor asked him what was the matter; who had angered him?

He in a surly loud way, replied, "Why you have. If I had the misfortune to marry an old woman must I always be twitted in the teeth for it?" When the Governor told him he did not design any reflection on him, it was a proverb agreeing with the fish was the occasion, but that answer not assuaging his fury, the Governor told him, since he could not be easy he should quit the house to-morrow, to which he replied, "Aye, that I'll do now, I won't be beholden to you", and so went his way.

The pulpit he hath several times made the stage to reflect on the Governor's administration, and harangue the people, which might have proved of ill-consequence had not the whole island been better satisfied.

On the 27th the Governor sent Ensign Slaughter to Mr. Jones to let him know, and not be surprised if his neglect of attending on the curtain[1] as belonging to the garrison, should be punished when the Governor from the country entered the garrison as the rest of the gentlemen of the garrison did. Mr. Jones sent back word "he knew no obligation, neither would he".

On the 28th, an alarm being made, he took his post on the mount, when the Governor told him that by his answer to Mr. Slaughter he refused to do the duty belonging to the garrison in paying the respect to the Governor thereof and therefore he ordered him out of the garrison.

On the Sunday following, in his reading Divine Service, he mistook the Collect for the day, when the Governor said to Mr. Jones "you are wrong, this is the second Sunday in Advent", which he soon recollected.

Before the Litany he read the form appointed for the Hon. Company and then the Collect for the first Sunday which never was done in that place before, nor enjoined by our Church.

When he came to the Communion service he began to read the wrong Collect, notwithstanding the Governor again reminded him, and persisted and read the Epistle and Gospel in open defiance of the Governor. Whereupon

---

[1] The wall connecting the two bastions at the Castle.

for his insolent behaviour as well, before the Governor and Council as before, he was confined in his chamber until the departure of the *King George* or the *Addison*, then in the Road, and then to be put on board for England.

The scandalous libel fixed up in the valley reflecting on the Governor the same night, the concource of the people to visit the parson, the false reports of what the Governor should say.

Another libel two nights after, mentioning the Governor's name, both writ in a hand unknown, began to make some people so uneasy that the Governor was forced to send for several people to trace the author and which was found to be the Sachevaralties of this island.

The thoughts of the unhappy state of this island may be reduced to, by this unstable, ill-designing, ignorant but haughty priest, by his insinuating himself into the tender minds of a weak and undiscerning people by that fallacious mistaken pretence of the Church being in danger.

His Holy order is affronted, when indeed the vile practices of the man is punished, will justify our proceeding herein to your Honours.

Even when punctuations have been inserted, the meaning of the above letter is not always clear, and the Council evidently were aware that their literary style was at fault, for at the end of it they added the following apology, which has been transcribed without any added punctuation:

We believed your Honours sometimes have been tired with the too great length of our letters which we would remedy if we knew how, but find it requires more ingenuity than we are master of. Your Honrs. are at London where all your directions are penned by men of the brightest parts. We have nobody but ourselves and though we take your

Honrs. letters to us for Copys to write ours by yet when we have answered them the best we can we have judgment eno to find we are vastly short.

The whole island was soon in an uproar over the quarrel between the Governor and the parson. The parties in favour of the parson held public meetings and wrote letters to the Court of Directors giving their version of what took place in the church.

Six leading inhabitants, including Mrs. Southern and Doctors Leigh and Civil, were taken into custody for writing and sending home the following document:

Whereas on the 29th Nov. 1719, the Rev. Mr. Jones, the Right Hon. Company's Chaplain on the said island was celebrating of Divine Service according to his office, the Collect of the day was interrupted by Governor Johnson saying very outrageously: "You are out to-day as you were last Sunday, for this is the 2nd Sunday in Advent"; the which the Rev. Mr. Jones read to prevent any further indecency, but informing himself while a psalm was sung, and finding he had committed no error, proceeded on his duty till he came to a second time to read the Collect for the first Sunday in Advent, was instantly interrupted by Governor Johnson saying: "Why do you make these mistakes?" To which the Rev. Mr. Jones made no reply but went on to the end of the Communion Service and published the holy day, viz: St. Andrew's, being the next day, adding that prayers will be at Church—then the Rev. Mr. Jones had no sooner exprest himself thus, but Governor Johnson said "Not by you, Sir"—calling out very furiously "Officer, take him prisoner, bring him before me. I'll see who is Governor, Mr. Jones or I." The order was immediately executed.

Six other principal inhabitants, Messrs. Gurling, Johnson, Rider, Powell, Greentree and Long were summoned for criticizing the administration of the Government relating to Mr. Jones and for signing the following paper:

These are to certify whom it may concern that the Rev. Jones did formerly reside here for some years and behaved himself soberly and civilly and did much good in his station as schoolmaster and being since sent as the Hon. Company's Chaplain has in that function carried himself to the satisfaction of us the inhabitants.

For this public expression of opinion the signatories were bound to appear at the Sessions under a bond of £100 each. At the trial of Mrs. Southern and her fellow conspirators, she and Doctor Civil were found guilty, and both sentenced to be set in the pillory for one hour. The pillory was erected for the occasion in the middle of James Valley opposite the Store House.

The last echo of what had come to be known as "the affair of Mr. Jones the Chaplain" occurs in a letter from the Court of Directors in England, dated 31st May, 1721. It is a long letter, and is full of references to "the affair", but only one paragraph shall be quoted, in which the Court expresses its mind quite freely on the Governor's conduct in church on that memorable St. Andrew's Day:

The affair of Mr. Jones the Chaplain, taking him out of the desk in the time of Divine Service in that outrageous and unprecedented manner shockt us at the first hearing of it, and more so when it was further explained, and the causes of it particularised.

We are surprised that Mr. Johnson who knows so much better, could be capable of doing it. We tell you we will never endure it. It seems he did while officiating in his office act unbecomingly and the language thereof might be interpreted "Thou art the Man".

Another tiresome case to come before the Governor and Council occurred when a marriage was performed without the Governor's permission:

August 8, 1721.

Joseph Bedloe a soldier and Widow Mary Swallow were married by Dr. Middleton of the ship *Hartford Francis*. Bedloe and Widow Swallow being sent for by the Marshal, Bedloe led her down the valley and introduced her into the Hall of the Castle by the hand as his wife. They both owned the fact before the Governor and Bedloe offered to shew his certificate. The Governor ordered Bedloe to be whipt and to receive fifty lashes on his bare back at the flagstaff and to be confined in prison till the departure of the next storeship, and the said Widow Swallow was ordered to receive twenty lashes on her naked back, but when she was affixed to the flagstaff the Governor ordered the whipping to be remitted, hoping the shame of being so publicly exposed would have the same effect on her as the smart had on some.

Doctor Middleton having returned on board the ship *Hartford Francis* was again brought on shore by order of the Governor and whipt at the flagstaff with twenty lashes for disorderly behaviour.

Governor Johnson's tenure of office was not a long one, nor is very much known about his administration. Certainly he completed the barracks which Governor Roberts began, and built a wall which ran from the landing-place to the draw-bridge of the Castle, as a safeguard against the surf. He also completed the warehouses in Jamestown and made further additions to the defences of James Valley.

One of the principal reasons for his appointment by the Company being the fact that he was a magistrate and had some knowledge of the law, makes some of his judicial findings all the more surprising. On one occasion the inhabitants had represented to the Council the injury the public sustained by the depredations committed by runaway slaves, and petitioned for a law to permit the offenders when caught, being punished at the discretion of their owners. To this extraordinary proposal the Governor gave his assent, and so combined in the slave-owner the offices of judge, accuser, and executioner, and did so in spite of the Company's strict injunctions to adhere as closely as possible to the spirit of the laws of England. The Governor's assent in granting this privilege to the planters is all the more odd since he had the reputation of being humanely disposed towards the blacks, as is borne out by a complaint sent home against him that his leniency towards the slaves would be likely to lead to an insurrection, though the principal complaint of all was his having referred to the blacks as "his children".

On 16th February, 1723, Johnson died of a "Bloody Flux", and the then senior member of the Council, Edward Byfield, acted as Governor until the arrival three months later of Captain John Smith.

There is little of interest or importance to record during the short period of Edward Byfield's acting Governorship, except that on the 17th April the Council indented for two hundred pounds of hair powder and that the census returns shew the population of the island to have been 1,128, consisting of: Whites, fifty men, seventy-nine women, and the surprisingly large total of two hundred and fifty-one children. Officers and soldiers, one hundred and twenty. Free blacks, eighteen men. Slaves, six hundred and ten.

The "Worshipful John Smith, Esq.", the new Governor, arrived from England in the *Essex* on the 28th May, 1723, and on landing his commission was published, as was the custom, by beat of drum. He was an Elder Brother of Trinity House and resigned in order to take up his new appointment. After his recall to London from St. Helena he was re-elected.

According to Brooke, "The new Governor was desirous of recommending himself as a moralist, and a reformer of manners, and was loud in his public declarations against vice and debauchery." "This endeavour," continues the historian, "might probably have been followed with success, had moderation, justice and a little Christian charity constituted any part of his character. It would have been well, also, if he could have excluded all appearances of private pique or resentment from his zeal for the suppression of immorality. But unfortunately while insensible of the beam in his own eye, he very clearly discovered the mote in his brother's."

The very first person to catch the attention of the godly Governor was Parson Giles, who was summoned before the Council for being drunk and disorderly on many occasions through daily drinking two to three quarts of rum punch. The Council "willing to shew our leniency towards him and the cloth he wears, will try him one month longer".

On August 31st, 1724, Totty, a slave, was tried for repeatedy running away and leading a "free-booter's" life. "The Gentlemen of the jury, *several of whom have already been great sufferers by the said Totty*, petitioned to have him executed", thus constituting themselves plaintiff, jury and judge. The wretched Totty, who hated working as a slave and preferred to live quietly in the woods, was sentenced to be drawn in a cart to the gibbet by other runaway slaves and there hanged.

Shortly after this occurrence, Governor Smith got wind of a very unsavoury scandal and took immediate steps to nip it in the bud.   Mr. Benjamin Hawkes, a respected officer of the Company, had an intrigue with a widow, Mrs. Tovey. News of this coming to the ears of the Governor, he at once ordered Mr. Hawkes to be brought before the Court of Jurisdiction.

At the Sessions, Mr. Hawkes took offence at certain reflections on his conduct and character made by the Governor, and replied in language which the latter considered to be threatening and impertinent, and so condemned the gallant Hawkes to a term of imprisonment.

The sentence, to modern ideas, seems excessive and out of all proportion to the crime.

> That he be degraded, and rendered infamous, and incapable ever to serve the Honourable Company; that his sword be broke over his head at the front of the garrison, as unworthy to wear a sword or bear a commission, that he afterwards stand in the pillory from the hour of eleven till twelve at noon; and that Margaret Tovey be placed in the pillory with him, there to continue during the time aforesaid.

Very unfortunately for Mrs. Tovey, some of her love letters had been found amongst Hawkes' papers in which the Governor was described in such terms of abuse as—"old rogue"—"partial doting old fool"—"monster"—"brute"—"beast and serpent". For this she, too, was committed to prison.

In order that the aiders and abettors of such lewdness should also be punished, Smith ordered that Mr. Free, the proprietor of the house at which the lovers used to meet, should be placed in the stocks.

In all fairness to Governor Smith it ought to be admitted that on some occasions his punishments were less severe; only in cases of personal immorality he could not relent.

There was the case of Martin Van Oesten, the Company's

accountant, found guilty, at a coroner's inquest, of the murder of his black boy. To the amazement of the whole settlement the affair was hushed up by their conscientious Governor, who punished offences which, comparatively speaking, could hardly be classed as crimes.

Van Oesten was a native of Holland, where he was supposed to have committed several murders, which included drowning his infant sister in order to acquire her property, and poisoning his first wife. After robbing his father he fled on board a Dutch East-Indiaman to the East. When on his return he arrived at the Cape, he decided it would be rash to re-visit his native land, so he endeavoured to pass himself off for an Englishman, and to enter a Company's ship there. His broken English, however, led the captain to suspect an imposture, but Van Oesten explained that he had lived so long amongst the Hottentots he had almost forgotten the use of his native tongue. So the captain agreed to take him to St. Helena where he landed under the name of Breasy and enlisted as a soldier. Possessing some talents and being tolerably well versed in business he soon made himself so useful as to be employed in a civil capacity and rose to become accountant, an office of trust which enabled him to carry out several frauds. Such was the villain to whom the favour and protection of the Governor was extended.

February 27, 1727, was a day of rejoicing at St. Helena, when the *Princess Anne* arrived with a commission appointing Mr. Byfield Governor in place of the unpopular and tyrannical Smith.

Now commenced a new era of peace and justice. For once the inhabitants were united, and in July presented the new Governor with an address, in which they declared: "'Tis to this happy and agreeable change that we owe the preservation of the small remains of our Liberty and Property, which in many instances, by the late violent and arbitrary proceedings was destroyed by Force, and in others rendered uncertain and precarious."

Two months later a minute appears in the St. Helena records, which is unique:

> Sessions. There being a very good harmony and agree-
> ment among the inhabitants and no person having entered
> any action against his neighbour, Sessions adjourned.

As some doubt existed as to the number and position of the guns defending the island, Governor Byfield had a list made of them, as follows:

The Castle	79
Munden's	14
Banks's	7
Rupert's	9
Lemon Valley	4
The Crane	2
Prosperous Bay	4
Two Gun Hill	5

making a total of one hundred and twenty-four.

In October the island was visited by several strange birds which it is impossible to identify from the description in the records; they were "birds of a different species from those that frequent the island, lately come hither, the bodies of which are as large as a pheasant, their legs long and black but their claws open and not webbed like sea-fowl, with long bills resembling those of a snipe but thicker and longer in propor-tion to the bulk of their bodies."

In spite of an order of the Council "that all persons be publickly forbid by advertisement either to kill or disturb any of the said birds or destroy any of their eggs", the birds do not appear to have remained on the island.

One of the first things which Byfield undertook was to make a thorough survey of the plantations of trees which Roberts had been so instrumental in getting planted. The regulations which had been made had not been strictly enforced by the Governors who followed Roberts, particularly that one which bound the land-holders to rail off one tenth part of their land for growing trees. The planters complained that if they did this, it would be quite impossible to pay their rents. The farmers allowed their cattle and other stock to graze where they would on the Company's lands and woods, barking trees and nibbling seedlings, while they themselves continued to cut down the mature wood for building and fuel. Within the memory of several persons living in 1718 the whole district between Long Wood, Flagstaff and Halley's Mount as far as Alarm House, had been one vast forest, and now it was become almost bare of trees. James Valley, too, once so thickly wooded, was become almost denuded of trees and bushes. One result of all this wanton denudation was the erosion of soil which followed every heavy fall of rain.

When the survey was completed twenty-three persons were summoned for neglect and several fined and the rest excused upon promising to plant trees on enclosed portions of their lands. To show to what lengths this neglect and destruction had gone, about five years previously the Governor procured, after great trouble, two young plants of the red-wood tree, neither of them above an inch high, which he planted in his own garden, and after tending them carefully they grew and flourished, so that by 1727 they were producing seed in great abundance.[1] The idea of fencing in Long Wood had been revived during the governorship of Isaac Pyke, and the work was commenced by Governor Smith. Actually this was an infringement of the conditions on which the law had been

[1] To-day there are exactly six examples growing in the Island, yet with a little trouble and forethought there might be hundreds of this beautiful and almost extinct native tree.

passed for planting one acre in ten, and consequently the land-holders were released from that obligation so far as the *free* lands were concerned.

In the year 1728, about one hundred and fifty acres of Long Wood were completely enclosed, sixty-four of which, on the part called Horse-Point, were appropriated to forest. The remainder were divided into three portions, and were found, for nine months in the year, to be capable of maintaining the Company's whole stock of black cattle.

Much attention was also bestowed on the Company's other lands. Hitherto the potatoes cultivated on the island were of the red kind, but since the prohibition of the distilleries they had been neglected. A new sort of Irish potato was planted in Long Gut, now called Mulberry Gut, a valley which runs between Long Wood and Dead Wood. Five acres of the Plantation House grounds were enclosed within a wall and used as a nursery, and here the red-wood, which had become so nearly exterminated, was preserved and protected. One of Pyke's innovations had been the planting of hedges of gorse, which not only acted as a fence to restrain straying cattle, but made most valuable wind-breaks in a high hilly country where a gale blows on most days throughout the year. From this gorse a considerable quantity of fuel could be collected, which probably prevented the total extermination of the few remaining trees. Governor Byfield ordered annual surveys to be made to ascertain whether the tenants were planting furze and keeping up their fences and planting the proportion of wood as stipulated in their leases. No defaulter escaped, and it was not long before the tenants perceived that until the depredations committed by goats and sheep on the plantations were prevented, they must be perpetually liable to be fined. At length a general meeting of the inhabitants was held, and after some deliberation, it was agreed by a majority of fifty-one to eleven to beg the Governor and Council to pass a law for the destruction of all the goats and sheep over the period of ten years, to commence from the 1st of February, 1731, so allowing the owners time in which to reduce their flocks. This was the very idea which had been suggested by Roberts, but he had been afraid to enforce it in opposition to the inclination of the planters. But the wise Byfield saw to it that the proposal should originate in the inhabitants themselves, rather than from the Government. When the proposal was forwarded to London the Court of Directors expressed much satisfaction, and the law was duly confirmed and was followed by the greatest success, for the indigenous trees shot up spontaneously in great number. An inhabitant who died in the year 1805, at the age of eighty-three, informed Brooke that many parts of the island where no trees had grown for many years before became covered with wood after the enforcing of the act.

During the four years that Edward Byfield was Governor, he saved the Company twenty-five thousand pounds, and the Company, ever generous to those of their servants who served them well, raised his salary by one hundred pounds, gave him a gift of plate valued at a hundred pounds, as well as four hundred pounds in cash. The inhabitants at the same time again expressed their high sense of the Governor's just and lenient disposition.

The news of the death of King George I did not reach St. Helena until many months after the event, but when it did the new King's accession was announced at the Castle by the Governor and all was merriment, which was not marred by the fact that a few days earlier seven slaves in a fit of despair had seized a boat belonging to Captain Goodwin, put off to sea, and to inevitable death. Another loss was sustained at seven o'clock on the evening of the Proclamation, when a long-boat with a crew of seven blacks was overturned in a sudden gust of wind on its way to Sandy Bay for cement and five of the crew drowned.

Although Governor Byfield had been so respected and held in such high esteem by the inhabitants while they still had in memory the galling yoke of Governor Smith, as time wore on they forgot this and began to abuse him. Their animosity appears to have originated from his attempting to support the cause of the poorer class of planters against the few opulent land-holders, who wanted to be allowed to sell their beef to the ships at a rate below the established price. Nor would the Governor ever agree to sacrifice the Company's interest to obtain popularity.

At all events his enemies were determined, if possible, to procure his dismissal. A powerful party was formed against him, and a deputation of two of its members was sent home to lay their pretended grievances before the Court of Directors. Among a variety of complaints brought forward, it was alleged that the farmers were debarred the privilege of selling beef to the ships, that they were prevented from going on board to dispose of and barter their commodities, although this was a right granted to them by the Company. It was also affirmed that they could not procure necessaries from the stores except on condition that they purchased articles belonging to some of the Council, and that the Governor sanctioned the Surgeon to charge his patients exorbitant fees.

The Directors made a careful investigation of the charges and very quickly came to the conclusion that they were totally unfounded. For example, the only sum that the surgeon had ever received from the inhabitants during his whole residence on the island was exactly one half-crown. Brooke accounted for this extraordinary state of things in that "most of the original settlers were of inferior rank, that their offspring had no other religion or moral instruction than that which could be obtained within the circumscribed society of the island. "Their spiritual teachers," he pointed out, "far from inculcating sobriety, submission to the laws, mercy, charity, and other

Christian virtues, were foremost in scenes of debauchery and infamy; and when it was considered that rebellious revenge, hatred and duplicity, blackened the character of the St.Helenian chaplains for more than sixty years, might it not have been expected that both religion should be put out of countenance, and morality out of practice?"

That Governor Byfield was indignant at this change from gratitude to abuse and thanklessness can well be understood, and it is not surprising that he immediately handed in his resignation in disgust. No doubt the intriguants who had brought this about were elated at their success, but their exultation was to be short-lived, for on March 15th, 1731, arrived back their old and ruthless enemy, Isaac Pyke, sent to resume the Governorship, though the Directors gave orders that Byfield was to hold his position up to the time of his departure.

If Pyke had been a harsh dictator during his previous administration the people of St. Helena were soon to learn that those were days of mildness in comparison to what was to come. The white inhabitants were ignominiously whipped and imprisoned for the most trivial offences. The military officers were fined and suspended by the Governor without courts-martial. The tyrant ruled with a rod of iron, and ruthlessly crushed at its birth any hint of disturbance or opposition.

One thing even Governor Pyke was not able to quell—the rats. These vermin had of late increased to vast numbers and did great damage to stores, crops and trees. Mr. Goodwin reported to the Council that he had observed several of the top branches of the gum-wood trees behind Plantation House to have been barked and killed by rats, and Mr. Crispe that in Great Wood he had frequently seen nests, like birds' nests, built by the rats at the tops of the trees, each nest two feet across and containing six or seven young ones, and that the whole country thereabouts was overrun with rats: evidently the old English or black rat, which is an agile climber.

Although Pyke was ruthless in his punishment of the whites, he now and again showed surprising leniency towards the blacks, to whom hitherto no mercy had ever been shown. When one of the Company's slaves was brought before him for breaking into the Storehouse, instead of ordering him to be flogged almost to death, as had always been the rule, Pyke ordered the man to be fitted with irons and set to work and to be exchanged for another slave when the next slave-ship called at the island, for he considered such treatment very much better than severe corporal punishment, "as we find by experience among the planters who are most of them very severe to their slaves, but we can't perceive that it does them any good, but rather makes them worse, always solemn, often desperate, and in their despair they sometimes hang or drown themselves, or run away". Whether the punishment imposed upon the slave Caesar for stealing a surplice from the Church was considered harsh or lenient it is difficult for us to judge, for the standard of values in such matters has changed.

Caesar was sentenced to be led with a halter round his neck from the Church Gate to White Stone and back, while he pushed a wheelbarrow containing the stolen surplice, and to be flogged on his bare back, all the way, by the Marshal.

In January, 1733, the Governor ordered a survey of the various plantations of trees to be made, and it was reported that many of them had been wantonly destroyed. He found that over one thousand young trees which had been planted in one of the Company's plantations had been cut down and carried off, and that all over the island the same destruction was going on.

During his previous term of office Governor Pyke had made the interesting and important discovery that if the soldiers drank only boiled water they no longer suffered from dysentery. He now observed and made a minute of it in the Records, that "water in tubs breeds such swarms of Muskittoes that the Castle and every house in the valley are filled with them"; but he did not say if he ordered any steps to be taken to rid the town of these dangerous and annoying insects.

He started planting coconuts which were sent from Bombay and reported that they were thriving, and coffee plants as well.

In the summer of 1734 he made a thorough inspection of the various defences of the island. At Sandy Bay, on the windward coast, the old battery had been built too low down, so that in rough weather parts of it were washed away, and four guns with their carriages fell into the sea, where on calm days they might be seen lying on the bottom.

Prosperous Bay had no guns, for in spite of it being the place where the English landed in 1673, it was considered unnecessary to fortify it. Banks's, which is said to have got its name from the man who built the battery there, was well armed.

Officially it was called King William Fort, but to-day both on the maps and by the inhabitants it is known as Banks's. The name of Rupert's Bay, which lies immediately to the north of James Valley, is thus accounted for in the Records:

Here Prince Rupert, son of the King of Bohemia and nephew of King Charles the First, on his return from India came to anchor and stayed here to refresh his ships company which gave to this place the name of Rupert's Valley.

Although it is quite possible that during his piratical cruise off the West Coast of Africa and to the West Indies, Prince Rupert may have put in at St. Helena, there appears to be no historical evidence of his having done so.

The Main Fort by the Castle which overlooked the principal

landing place on the island at James Valley was defended by two large curtains and two half-bastions. On the east half-bastion were twenty-three small guns, called falcons, falconets and rabinets, but they were too small for anything but to fire salutes.

On the Mount, in front of the Main Fort, were six "very good" demi-culverins.

The next spot mentioned in the report is Breakneck Valley, which lies immediately south of James Valley, between Ladder Hill and Donkey Plain. An account is given of an adventure which happened to a sailor off a ship, the *Wyndham*, who had been up in the country with his shipmates but got lost and rashly attempted to reach the shore by climbing down the cliff in the dark. He got a good way down when he found he could get no lower nor yet retrace his steps. There he had to stay all night, but when it became light and he could see the precipice above him down which he had climbed in the dark, he dared not attempt to scale it. At last he saw a boat down below and shouted to the men to shew him a way down. In the end a rope had to be lowered to which the sailor made himself fast and was hauled up to safety. The account ends: "He lost a china bowl and a catty of tea which none of our people, not even the blacks, have ventured to go there and fetch it."

The drilling of the garrison and militia was under the charge of Captain Cason—there is still a place named Cason's Gate—who drilled his troop "according to Colonel Blunt's method, who is Colonel of the King's Guards", with such evident success that visitors calling on their way home from India used to say "that no soldiers in India exercise so well as our men." This Captain Cason had served in the army under King William and Queen Anne, and had been chief military officer on the island with the last seven Governors, and "was esteemed by all the Governors and is beloved by the people".

The strength of the garrison on the 31st January, 1734, was as follows:

Whites:	Officers and men	134
	Planters—militia	31
Blacks:	Belonging to the Garrison .	75
	Belonging to the Planters .	102

making a total of 342 armed and trained soldiers.

Governor Pyke tended to unorthodox decisions when he tried cases in the Court. When Eleanor Isaac was sentenced to be whipped—her misdemeanour is not stated—one Nathaniel Cressener expressed his sympathy for Eleanor by offering "to save her being whipt he would be willing to lye two hours neck and heels to save her each lash". Governor Pyke, quite ready to oblige, said that "since he is so desirous to bear some punishment of his wench he would order him to be tied neck and heels in the usual manner an hour, and if he liked it and continues in the same mind he, (the Governor), would make a bargain with him and excuse the wench one lash for every two he was tied neck and heels".

Nothing was too trivial to excite the curiosity of Governor Pyke, and even an epidemic amongst the poultry he considered important and interesting enough to enter in the record of Consultations.

April 8, 1735. Governor reports that the Poultry in all parts of the island has been lately seized with a strange distemper that kills multitudes—their head first begins to swell, soon after they become blind, and they are presently taken with a giddiness of which they die.

A happy event is recorded in the minute which follows. It was the celebration of the one hundredth birthday of "Old

Will", who had faithfully served the Company during the administration of twenty-one Governors. When he came to the island from Madagascar he brought with him three yams, nine head of cattle and two turtle doves. Brooke in his history supposes from this that Old Will came to the island a free man, but Janisch points out that if he did so, he must have fallen among thieves, who not only robbed him of his yams, cattle and doves, but of his freedom as well, for in all the Old Returns he is numbered among the Company's slaves. Old Will lived on for another two years, and such was the love his fellow slaves had for him, that at his funeral his coffin was followed to the grave by a procession of more than two hundred blacks.

One day the *Drake*, Captain Pelly, arrived and reported that when a distance of 450 miles from land, she had picked up a boat containing ten natives of the Maldive islands, who had been driven out to sea and were in the last stage of exhaustion. Three of them died on board the *Drake*; and the survivors, five men, one woman and a boy, were landed at St. Helena. The price the castaways paid for the saving of their lives was their freedom, and the men were put to work making a new plantation garden at the upper end of Jamestown, which still goes by the name of Maldivia.

When studying the early records of the Company at St. Helena one cannot but be struck by the frequency with which incompetent or unqualified persons were sent out from England to occupy posts for which they proved quite unfitted: round pegs, in fact, to fit square holes. But of them all not one was ever more aptly named than the French Engineer, who was handicapped through life by bearing the most unfortunate but very suitable name of Monsieur Gausherie. "We look upon him as a useless person," the Council reported on July 24, 1735, and continued: "Even tho' he had as much skill as he pretends to in Fortifications, his way of designing them will do the place no good, for he does not care to go by land, and when we supplied him with a good boat, he did not venture to go nearer than within half a mile of the place, as he did at Turk's Cap Valley and Prosperous Bay, which will not do here."

All sorts of odd cases were tried before the Governor, who had a rough and ready way of dealing with them. Such was the case when Mr. Bates appeared before His Excellency, to complain that his black slave was trying to poison him by witchcraft, by burying a phial under his chair. To strengthen his case Bates produced for the Governor's inspection a copy of Captain Hamilton's book of Voyages in which he turned to several fabulous stories of charms, spells and talismans, which had frightened Bates almost out of his wits. But Governor Pyke was not at all impressed and told the court "if he troubles us or his neighbours with any more of these idle fancies we will dose him with hellebore and furnish him with a dark room and some clean straw"—another instance of the Governor's knowledge of contemporary medicine, for his threatened treatment of Bates was the approved method of dealing with the insane. All the same poor Bates was fortunate to escape a sound whipping.

Many of Pyke's decisions on the bench were not so wise nor successful as this last one. A free black woman had a child by a soldier. For this offence, if offence it can be called, the wretched woman and her child were both made slaves on the pretence that such was the law in some of His Majesty's plantations.

John Long, a prisoner, begged the Council that owing to his suffering from the flux he might be excused working on the fortifications until he was better. Two of the councillors, Alexander and Goodwin, thought he should be allowed time to recover, but not so the other councillor, Mr. Crispe, who was of the opinion that the most effectual way to cure him would be to hang him.

Poor crazy Mr. Bates, who thought he was being bewitched by his slave, was soon in trouble again, for in August, 1736, he was before the court charged with coining counterfeit pagodas, a small gold coin current in Southern India. The prisoner informed the Court he had found a gold mine, but the well-informed Pyke satisfied himself that the gold which Bates had found was only "marchasites". Shortly afterwards Mr. Bates was once more in trouble on a much more serious charge, that of saying he believed it was no sin to shoot the Governor. "Ordered to be whipped with thirty stripes at the common whipping post"—no nonsense now about hellebore and a darkened room.

Another delinquent before the court was Elizabeth Edwards, mother of a child of eight months. On being cross-examined she stated that the father of her child was one Beale, the husband of her deceased sister, who had promised to marry her. The learned Judge, Governor Pyke, informed her that such a marriage would be illegal, but in answer she referred him to Deuteronomy XXV: 5. After studying the passage in the Bible, Pyke declared himself as follows: "This fault seeming to us to be in some sort the effect of ignorance, we are willing to be as favourable as we can—ordered ten lashes at the Common Whipping Post."

Having delivered himself of his sentence, the Governor, after observing that the young woman appeared to be "very ignorant and to have grossly mis-applied the 5th verse of 25 Deut." sent for Mr. Fordyce the Chaplain, to explain the matter to her. But the Chaplain "after he had heard the examination and the 5th verse aforesaid read, he said there were some places of Scripture that seem to favour that opinion, though as to the crime of it he could say nothing." This answer was not at all what the Governor had expected, indeed it "surprised us, expecting to hear something more decent of him, but indeed he himself seems as ignorant of these matters as anybody who is permitted to wear a gown". But the Governor was not one to be out-argued by the logic of a parson, for he "cleared up the matter and told them that this was an extraordinary case, and in King Henry the 8th time the Reformation of Religion from Popery depended on it, and our laws made this offence Incest." And so in order to make his meaning quite clear, he ordered Beale to be whipt as well as Mistress Edwards.

It was unfortunate for the persons concerned in the case which followed that the Governor had been put into a bad temper. The accused was a soldier, Thomas Swindle, who was up before the court for having a child by a free black woman. He was quickly found guilty and sentenced to ride the wooden horse for two hours, with his face blackened all over. The wench "as soon as she was out of the straw"—all blacks, free or slaves, and cattle were much the same to the whites—was to be publicly whipped and *herself and child* made slaves *to the Company*.

In fairness to the Governor it should be explained that his health was rapidly failing. In March, 1737, owing to a severe attack of gout in his right hand, he was unable to sign his name, and on 28th July he died "in violent convulsions which we imagine was occasioned by the morbid matter of the Gout lodging upon his Brain. Nature being much worn and decayed and not strong enough to throw it off."

So departed this life one of the most capable Governors St. Helena ever had. He was ruthless, arrogant and despotic, but he probably appreciated that by no other methods would it be possible to rule the turbulent subjects of his little island. He was energetic and always insisted that the law should be carried out to the letter.

The next Governor was Mr. Goodwin, the senior member of the Council and a native of St. Helena. Shortly after being proclaimed, the island met with another misfortune, by the untimely death of the Chaplain, Mr. Barlow. In those days good chaplains were few and very far between at St. Helena; and the Council marked their appreciation of him by the following entry in the Consultations: "The most acceptable of his profession of any we have had among us for a great number of years past."

To make up for the loss of the services of Mr. Barlow the Council in its wisdom decided to supply his place with public readings from Archbishop Tillotson, Dr. Smith, Bishop Fleetwood, Dr. Calamy and "other eminent English Divines from whose discourses wee are sure we shall be much more improved than by the crude, uncouth compositions we have commonly met with for several years past, and such as were so far from edifying that often times they were not intelligible".

A good idea, no doubt, but scarcely kind or tactful to the memory of the lately departed and "acceptable" Mr. Barlow.

The new Governor was Governor only in name, for the real power on the Council was the second member, Mr. Duke Crispe, described by Brooke as "a man not deficient in talents, but possessed of no common share of knavery and cunning". He had formerly held the situation of Governor's steward, from which he had risen to a civil appointment in the year 1726 and afterwards was promoted to a seat in Council. For a long while he had been concerned with Goodwin in shady and dishonest transactions and had a strong hold over him. Together they disposed of the Company's lands for a tenth part of their value, embezzled the stores, and carried out frauds by erasure and false entries and managed to rob the treasury of nearly four thousand pounds. Goodwin died in August, 1739, two years after becoming Governor, and was succeeded provisionally by Crispe. All might have gone well if Crispe had not incautiously omitted to allow a due share of the plunder to George Gabriel Powel, one of his colleagues on the Council; a man "still more artful than himself and equally devoid of principle". Powel turned informer, but without revealing to his employers his real character. As a result of his secret letter to the Court of Directors, a man of unassailable character and honesty was sent out, with extraordinary powers, to investigate the charges, and even, if he should so decide, to supersede the acting Governor and Council.

The man of integrity chosen by the Board of Directors for this delicate and important task was none other than Mr. Robert Jenkins, master-mariner—of "Jenkins' Ear" fame.

It was when off Havana in 1711, that his ship, the *Rebecca*, was boarded by a Spanish guarda-costa and plundered, and one of Captain Jenkins' ears cut off, and the vessel left "with the intent", it was alleged, "that she should perish on her passage". The *Rebecca*, however, did not perish, but reached England, and later on Jenkins was examined before a committee of the House of Commons. His story lost nothing in the telling, and when he produced something from his pocket, wrapped up in a piece of paper, which he asserted was the very ear which had been cut off, and was asked "What were your feelings when you found yourself in the hands of such barbarians?", he made his famous reply, "I committed my soul to God and my cause to my country." Instantly the whole country was raised to the utmost indignation, which led to the war with Spain the following year.

When on the 9th May, 1740, Captain Jenkins arrived at St. Helena he went ashore in the first boat and immediately proceeded to the Castle, accompanied by Mr. John Godfrey, his assistant. Upon his announcing that he carried despatches, a Council was instantly assembled. Jenkins then opened his commission, summoned the chief supercargoes and captains of the Company's ships then at the island, and in their presence demanded of Messrs. Duke Crispe and Bazett the keys of the treasury. The cash, counted on the spot, amounted only to six pounds and nineteen shillings!

Duke Crispe and the rest of the Council, with the exception of Powel, were declared no longer in the Company's service, and Jenkins assumed the government and formed a Council consisting of two supercargoes, with Godfrey and Powel. A thorough investigation of the Company's finances gave ample proof in support of the accusations made by Powel, who was in consequence promoted to second in Council, while the estates of the guilty parties, to the extent of £6,284, were seized to refund the Company the money stolen from them.

When Jenkins perceived that his investigations were likely to be unduly protracted—since most of the papers had been burnt, he "shut up Crispe for a few days, and gave him a book of divinity to assist him in his meditations".

His next task was to muster the garrison, and it was found to be short of one corporal, three "matrosses"—i.e. gunners' mates, one drummer and twenty-one sentinels.

But the twenty-six soldiers had all drawn pay; and all Mr. Crispe could say was that it had long been the perquisite of the Governor to draw four men's pay, in addition to his emoluments, and the Members of Council pro rata.

No department of the Government escaped Jenkins' energetic investigations. On the 19th June, Crispe was brought before a special Council, reinforced by two "supra cargoes" and three ships' captains, when he was adjudged to have "appeared in such colours as is not possible for us to paint", but being unwilling to proceed against him with the rigour he richly deserved, the Council decided that he was to be left alone until receipt of the Company's orders.

For the rest of his time in the island, Jenkins devoted himself to the repair of the fortifications—they were so dilapidated that when the guns were fired from the Castle, part of the walls fell down—and the development of the Company's lands in Sandy Bay.

He was, beyond question, a most able man, and all his

minutes and correspondence provide abundant evidence of his clear and business-like disposal of public affairs.

Before his departure he was to have one more encounter with Duke Crispe. They both attended the wedding of Ensign Scott to Miss Martha Doveton, to which had been also invited the two daughters of a Mr. Johnson.

"Everybody was very cheerful all the morning, but after dinner somebody took it into their heads to arrange a kissing dance", in which Mr. Crispe took a leading part. The movements and nature of this interesting dance have not been handed down to us, but Jenkins was incensed and deeply shocked so that he called for his horse and carried away the two young ladies with him, with a parting shot that certain of the male guests were "likely to pay dear for their share of the kisses for he was very near putting them under arrest".

As Mr. Kitching has justly observed:[1] "As might have been expected from one who when confronted by the horrors of torture commended his soul to God and his cause to his country, Jenkins was an austere and upright man."

His memory is perpetuated in St. Helena by a stone built into the side of a house in Sandy Bay called "Lemon Grove" that bears the following inscription:

Robert Jenkins Esq.

Dec. 16

A.D. 1741.

Having made a thorough clean-up of the island's affairs, Governor Jenkins handed over the government to Major Thomas Lambert who had arrived as his successor on the 22nd of March, 1741, in the ship *Harrington*, of which Captain Jenkins was directed to assume the command for the remainder of her voyage.

[1] G. C. Kitching, *Papers relating to the History of St. Helena*, 1937

The new Governor lived only four months, but in that brief period he established the first hospital on the island, at Maldivia, on the site of the present one. Mr. Duke Crispe, unabashed by his exposure by Governor Jenkins, on the 1st June wrote a letter to Governor Lambert in which he referred to the friendly feelings the late Governor had for him, up to the day of the wedding, and gave his own account of what happened on that occasion.

However, the Council thought little of the letter, which they entered in full in the records, for all the comment they made on it was: "We think Mr. Crispe's long letter seems calculated rather to fling dirt at Mr. Jenkins than to clear himself."

Three days later we read that Mr. Crispe found bonds for £1,145 and was granted permission to leave the island in the next ship which should call. In the same month Governor Lambert died and George Gabriel Powel was proclaimed Governor in his stead, with John Godfrey second and Christopher Dixon third in Council.

In the early part of the year 1742 the island was visited by an epidemic.

> We have had abundance of mortality in this island. The inhabitants have been seized with a violent distemper very little inferior to the plague that hath carried off abundance of them. . . . They are seized with violent oppression at their stomach and pain in the small of the back, and bowels attended with a strong fever and generally die in four or five days.

Post mortem examinations were made on two slaves, Harry and Dick, to discover if possible the cause of this alarming visitation. The one on Harry was reported as follows:

> Pericardium much extended with a greater quantity of water in it than usual. The right ventricle very large. On

opening it, extracted three distinct pieces of flesh about an inch and a quarter in length, not adhering to any part of the ventricle, with a large quantity of coagulated blood. Right lobe of lungs adhering closely to pleura, a little imposthumated.

Whether or not this disease was plague is for experts to decide, but it is significant that at this time the island was over-run with black rats, by which the plague flea is carried, and that constantly ships were arriving at St. Helena from plague-infected ports in India.

Governor Powel ruled St. Helena for two years when he was dismissed the Company's service. During this brief period he embezzled the Company's money, stole their brandy, wine, beef, pork and other property from the store, which he sold privately, and he leased their lands for his own gain. The Company's farms he appropriated to his own use, and their timber, lime, purbeck-stone and other building materials to construct a commodious dwelling-house on his estate in the country. The wages of the builders, carpenters and labourers employed on this work he charged to the account of fortifications and other public works. When the Company's slaves had finished their day's work, instead of returning to their homes, they were compelled to carry heavy loads from Sandy Bay and James Valley to his new house.

If they did not return to their work before daylight the following morning, he had them severely flogged. As a result of this brutal treatment they seldom slept in a house but usually lay all night by the roadsides. Like so many rogues, Governor Powel was no fool, and not without a measure of cunning. This latter quality was well brought out one day when two slaves (brothers) were brought before him, one for having run away and hidden in the woods, the other for having supplied him with food while he was in hiding. Against the first brother there was clear proof, but against the second none whatever. As the first refused, even under the lash, to implicate the other, the latter naturally refused to confess the fact. The Governor on this occasion said to the Council, "Gentlemen, this villain should be flogged severely. A wretch who would not give his poor brother a morsel when starving, deserves to be hanged." This declaration induced the intimidated creature to confess, and he was immediately and unmercifully flogged. Powel was a bully. Once he employed a man to make him a new wig, and when it was finished he did not like the material used, so flew into a passion and ordered the unfortunate wig-maker into his own room, where he was placed on the back of a soldier and whipped by a slave with fifty lashes. He must have been an exceedingly ill-tempered man, for constant quarrels are reported in the records between the Governor and Mr. Dixon, the third in Council. On June 27th, 1743:

Governor Powel complains that Mr. Dixon insults him whenever he happens to meet him. That last Sunday in the Church, Mr. Dixon, who sat in the pew, took the liberty when the Governor's eyes and attention were otherwise employed, to point at him at sundry times, to sneer at him and then wink and smile to one of his acquaintances who sat at another part of the Church. That whenever he has passed Mr. Dixon in the street, instead of paying the compliment of the hat, Mr. Dixon cocks his hat upon his head staring him in the face, strutting by in a more bullying, insulting and rude manner than can possibly be expressed.

In the records of this period there occur over and over again accounts of slaves stealing boats and escaping to sea. Nothing exemplifies more their miserable and hopeless lives than these desperate attempts to escape. Not one boat ever reached another land, nor could it when the nearest point of Africa was twelve hundred miles away. Every slave who left St. Helena in an open boat died either of thirst or by drowning.

March 16, 1744. Ten men slaves run away with the Long Boat.

Feb. 19, 1745. On Sunday night last nine of the Planters slaves run away with the Company's boat though the Rudder, Sails and Oars were on shore.

Feb. 22, 1747. Four Blacks of the Company, one of Powel's, went off from Sandy Bay in the night in a small fishing yawl with a very small quantity of provisions so that in all probability they are perished.

June 16, 1747. Two of the Bencoolen slaves enticed several others and went away with a boat from Sandy Bay.

Dec. 4, 1747. Fifteen slaves of the Company run away with the Long Boat.

On 11th March, 1743, Colonel David Dunbar arrived as Governor, with orders to enquire into certain private allegations which had been made to the Court of Directors concerning Governor Powel. When charged with his crimes, Powel refused to make any statement or to defend himself. In the end he gave full security to meet the Company's claims, and was allowed to go to England. Needless to say the Company employed him nò more, and he went to America where he became conspicuous as a patriot in Carolina, and, it was said, even became a member of Congress.

Colonel Dunbar proved an honest and hardworking Governor, but owing to his violent temper and high-handedness was continually quarrelling with the Council. There must have been something in the atmosphere of St. Helena which tore tempers to rags.

He did much to improve the fertility of the island and carried out experiments at Longwood in the cultivation of oats, barley and wheat. At first the results were so promising that a barn was built there, which was later converted into a house for Mr. Hutchinson, the Lieutenant-Governor, and was destined some sixty years later to become the residence of St. Helena's most famous inhabitant. It was Governor Dunbar who planted the avenue of peepul trees which ran along the middle of James Valley up to the hospital, which in Brooke's day was so much admired for its appearance and the shade it gave.

Perhaps St. Helena may yet be blessed with another Governor who will plant avenues of trees in Jamestown, for trees are badly needed in that sweltering, shadeless valley.

Unfortunately Dunbar resented the least hint of opposition from the members of his Council or from the army officers, and would on the slightest pretext and entirely unlawfully, fine them, sometimes a month's or sometimes even a whole quarter's salary, or he would suspend them at pleasure. Needless to say he almost immediately quarrelled with Mr. Dixon, whom he imprisoned, and did so in spite of the fact the Council denied he had authority to confine any member of their body. When Mr. Hutchinson begged that his parlour might be ceiled, the Governor refused on the ground of it being unreasonable. Put to the vote, the Council—with the Governor dissenting—thought the request reasonable and granted it. But the Governor would not give way. His reason for objecting was that lime could not be made fast enough for the fortifications and "if the gentlemen who so readily voted to make a ceiling for the Lieutenant-Governor meant that vote to be respected as an order, I do tell them I shall show no regard to it, and that no ceiling shall be made:

even in the Castle hall and our common eating room having never been ceiled to this day."

By way of bringing the matter of the ceiling for the Lieutenant-Governor's new house at Longwood to a satisfactory and final end, the Governor fined him, Goodwin and Purling each a quarter's salary.

Shortly afterwards the long-suffering Mr. Hutchinson was once again fined, for no better reason than that he had dared once more to vote against the Governor at a Council meeting, which was brought to a close by His Excellency shouting ". . . and I now caution the Lt. Governor to be on his guard that he forebears his illtreatment of me, and he may be assured that if he perseveres I will make myself easy by suspending him and perhaps sending him home."

However, the wise Directors who by some means or another always seem to have had a shrewd idea of how matters went at St. Helena, solved all the difficulties of the Council, by sending out the following brief and concise letter, dated December 23, 1746.

We direct that immediately on receipt hereof, David Dunbar, Esq., do resign our service, and deliver over the Government to Charles Hutchinson, Esq.

CHAPTER V

1746–1787

O N the 13th March, 1746, the *Swift* arrived bringing a
formal commission appointing Mr. Charles Hutchinson Governor of St. Helena. She also brought an
order from the Court of Directors that the various fines
illegally levied by Governor Dunbar on the members of the
Council were to be refunded.

Little of particular interest or importance appears to have
occurred during the next few years. True, a woman slave
was beaten to death by three white men, egged on by her
owner, Mr. Meacocks; but as the four murderers were fined
only £6.10*s* between them, it cannot have been looked upon
as an event much out of the ordinary.

The close season for shooting partridges was extended from
January 1st to February 1st, and a new burial ground, for
whites, was made at the Country Church.

The principal subjects with which the records are concerned
during the first years of the Governorship of Charles Hutchinson are the climatic conditions and the deterioration of the
crops and live-stock. Such had been the neglect for some
time past of the fruit trees of the island that by now most of
the lemon trees were dead, even those in the lower part of
James Valley, where formerly they throve best—"There hath
not been for some time a lemon fit for use in the island." St.
Helena was passing through one of those periods of drought
to which the island has always been subject. Everywhere the
pastures were burnt brown, while several springs had dried

up, though never before within the memory of the oldest
inhabitant had they been known to fail. The cattle were
dying of starvation, a distemper had played havoc amongst
the poultry, killing a thousand turkeys and most of the fowls.
Even the yams failed, that unpalatable tuber, which formed the
staple diet of the cattle and slaves, from which the St. Helenian
gets the nickname of Yamstock. The Company had to put
the white population on a ration of three pounds of bread a
week a head, and even then it was calculated there was not
enough flour and biscuit in the Company's store to last longer
than one month. When at last the drought broke, the island
was deluged by heavy rain storms which caused great damage.
The military stores were washed away at Sandy Bay and so
was the guard house at Lemon Valley, and also the breastwork at Breakneck Valley. Such torrents of water rushed
down Banks' Valley as to cause great damage to the lower
platform there. At the same time, heavy seas with huge
breakers, such as had never been experienced before, smashed
the old battery at Sandy Bay and washed away the crane on
the landing-place at Jamestown, and water even penetrated
into the Castle powder magazine. The high surf washed away
the earth and undermined part of the works at Rupert's Bay,
and did considerable damage to the main fort. On June 29th,
1756, the Council was unable to hold a meeting, being cut off
from the Castle by a great torrent of water which rushed down
James Valley and through the town.

It ran with such rapidity out of its common course that
it was not possible to turn it until the rains abated and
therefore it had done great damage to the fortifications and
plantations, as well as to many of the possessions of the
inhabitants. It made two breaches in the wall of the
Maldivia Gardens, covered up several thousands of yams
with large stones and rubbish—broke down part of the

fence of the new burial ground, overflowing that which was prepared for erecting barracks upon, making its way towards the bridge with several large rocks, which not having width to vent them fast enough, part of the torrent run over one side of it which came down the public street which nearly destroyed several people, carrying with it everything that was in its way, gullying the street, rushing into houses, tearing one of the gates that leads to the line off the hinges, and damaged the other very much, forcing a vast deal of mud and rubbish along with it filled the work up to the ambrasures and run over into the ditch which was almost two-thirds full.

That part of the torrent that went behind the houses next to Ladder Hill has almost destroyed every person's yard walls on that side and has thrown down some buildings and carried many things out of the people's houses, greatly hurting one and destroying another of the portcullis through which it was to pass.[1]

Each year more and more ships called at Jamestown, and the Company's South Atlantic island gained steadily in importance as a place for rendezvous and refreshment.

Much excitement was caused amongst the inhabitants when on 5th March, 1758, a "double-alarm" was fired to report three big vessels in view, to the windward of the island. At noon they were lost sight of, and did not reappear until the following day, when again they stood away to windward. Eight days afterwards the ships could be made out cruising in the same locality, and as it was suspected that these mysterious ships were Frenchmen and were lying in wait for East Indiamen bound for St. Helena, Mr. Richard Bendy, a midshipman of one of the Company's ships was ordered to take the long boat and cruise to the windward of

[1] *St. Helena Records.*

the squadron, in order to warn the expected Indiamen of their danger.

He succeeded in gaining his station unperceived by the enemy, but unfortunately a few days afterwards seeing some ships to leeward, and taking them to be English, he bore down and did not discover until too late that they were the French men-of-war, *L'Achille*, *La Syrenne* and *La Zephyre*, and was taken prisoner. Early in May, four of the Company's China ships, *Prince Henry*, *Hawke*, *Osterly* and *Tavistock*, were chased by them, but after an obstinate running fight, escaped under cover of darkness. On the 15th of the same month, the *Boscawen* and *Fox* also fell in with the enemy but got clear of them and made for the Bay of All Saints in Brazil, where they found the four China ships. For a while they were blockaded by the French who had followed them, but the enemy soon quitted their station for want of water, and afterwards St. Helena was no longer molested. The failure of this enterprise seems to have discouraged the French from any further efforts of the same kind.

Some little while after these exciting events a visitor, unknown and anonymous, "passed three most agreeable weeks" on the island and wrote an account of them for the *Gentleman's Magazine*, in November, 1759. The writer, who hides his identity under the pen-name of *Susannicus*, was on his way from India to England, and like every other visitor to the island, left it with pleasant memories.

He was particularly impressed by the appearance of the main and only street of little Jamestown, with its two rows of handsome sashed houses which formed a neat and pretty street, and the pleasant walk of nearly a quarter of a mile at the end of the street, between an avenue of trees, always green and blooming, leading up to the Maldivia Gardens. He admired the ingenuity which had been shown in making the new winding road up the steep side of Ladder Hill, "to ascend which—though not without difficulty, is yet safe, having a wall on the side next the precipice, and the inhabitants of both sexes commonly ride up it on horseback".

He found the prospect "infinitely grand and agreeable: as, from a sterile, brown, barren rock you view the most lovely verdure in nature; beautiful lawns, with sheep and cattle feeding in different places, intersperced here and there with cottages and little agreeable retreats".

He tells the reader how "the present worthy Governor, Mr. Hutchinson", had about five years previously begun to build himself a small villa by a "delight natural cascade, far excelling the celebrated valley called Arno's Vale, in Italy", but how his attention to the far more important matter of the fortifications had led him to postpone the work.

He then draws attention to another building, "a large and most expensive pile", which had been erected by a previous Governor, [Powel], "while he suffered the fortifications and dock to go to ruin".

Susannicus went into ecstasies over almost everything to do with St. Helena; its appearance, climate, buildings; but most of all the roses "which grow here in surprising abundance, and form in many places the most fragrant and beautiful hedges in nature".

This indefatigable tourist did not miss one of the principal natural curiosities of the island, the Bell Stone which "when struck with a stone, produces so sonorous a noise, as to be heard near 3 miles away". If *Susannicus* is generous in his praise of the natural beauties of the island, he is lavish in his admiration of its inhabitants. "The manners of the inhabitants are such as poets have fabled of the golden age; they are to the last degree kind and affectionate to one another, and extremely hospitable to strangers; detraction and every other vices they have no idea of, and so little do they know of the litigious disputes and chicanery of the law, that there is not a single person of that profession upon the island."

All of which leads one to suppose that Governor Hutchinson had brought about a striking change in the character of the St. Helenians since his arrival sixteen years before.

"They are in general polite, honest without the effection of it, and sincere in their protestations of friendship"—sentiments which, if *Susannicus* to-day revisited St. Helena, he would have no reason to alter.

Under the governorship of Charles Hutchinson, St. Helena for the first time in her history since the English occupation in 1673 began to enjoy a prolonged period of peaceful tranquillity combined with prosperity. No longer do the records of the Council abound with accounts of personal quarrels, bickering and strife.

In 1760 His Majesty King George III came to the throne and "was graciously pleased to encourage the making observations on the transit of the planet Venus over the Sun's disk", which was calculated to take place on 6 June the following year. To make such observations, the Royal Society sent out Dr. Nevil Maskelyne, the future Astronomer Royal, and Mr. Robert Waddington. An observatory was constituted for their use on the top of the high ridge behind Alarm House. Unfortunately when the long-expected hour arrived a passing cloud obscured the phenomenon from the astronomers' sight, although it was distinctly seen by several persons down below in James Valley.

The continual desertion of slaves, added to suicides and occasional murders, had so reduced the number on the island that it became necessary, if the supply of coloured labour was to be maintained, to import more blacks. With this end in view ten men from Malabar were brought over in 1757, who were reported to be officers of the army of the King of Travancore. One of these prisoners of war died on the voyage, but the other nine were landed, and after being dressed in slaves' clothes, were sent up into the country to work on the plantations with the other slaves. A few days afterwards five hanged themselves and the remaining four threatened to commit suicide if they were put to any kind of work. It was then decided to procure blacks from Madagascar, which had been the favourite depôt for slaves, for of all blacks, those of Madagascar had always proved the best and most docile. So the *Mercury*, a snow[1] of 140 tons and eight guns, and the cutter *Fly*, were despatched to Madagascar to obtain slaves, rice and paddy and live canaries. The slaves were all to be able-bodied men under twenty-five or well-grown boys. To act as interpreter between the slaves and the English, they took with them a St. Helena slave, Cupidore.

In the following January the two ships returned with sixteen men slaves and ten boys, 107 cwt. of rice and a flock of canaries. When eight days out from Madagascar, at two o'clock in the morning, the slaves in the *Mercury* mutinied, killed the captain and seriously wounded the mate. The riot was eventually quelled by musket fire, but not before two slaves had been killed and three wounded. The cause of the uprising was attributed to Cupidore, the interpreter, who "by filling their heads with shocking notions of their wretched fate as slaves" excited the blacks to revolt. For this Cupidore and another slave called Winchester were "tried" for murder on their arrival at St. Helena and executed.

With the more settled condition and increasing importance of St. Helena, certain changes were evolved in the administration of the island, both civil and military, and many of the old laws were annulled or else modified to be more in harmony with the laws of England. The two services, civil and military, were made more distinct, and no longer did officers of the Company hold at the same time posts in each. In the

---

[1] A small sailing-vessel resembling a brig, often employed as a warship.

civil department a regular rule for promotion and graduations of rank was fixed, and from the year 1759 one or more seats on the Council were invariably filled by senior civil servants. In fact, all members of Council, as such, were upon the civil and not the military establishment; even if they were army officers holding a military commission of the Company they sat as civilians.

In future the Governor and Council were not to have the power of dismissing any servant of the Company, civil or military, but could only suspend him from the service, until the Court of Directors' pleasure was known. The early laws of St. Helena had been so grossly unfair to the blacks and so very partial to the whites, that a black would be condemned to death for the same crime for which a white would only be lightly punished. The power vested in the Governor of trying cases, either by jury or before Council, according to his discretion, was often abused. Also, in violation of the Company's orders, persons were deprived of their lands without the verdict of a jury, and frequently unwarrantable fines were imposed. Many daring felonies, burglaries and other serious crimes were committed by both whites and blacks. After repeated representations on this subject by Governor Hutchinson the Court of Directors took the matter up and consulted the most eminent egal authorities in England, who gave as their weighed opinion that the East-India Company "had a right by themselves, their ministers and officers, to govern the island of St. Helena, and to hold courts of justice therein for trying all kinds of crimes, offences and misdemeanours, and also for determining all civil actions". The Governor and Council were to continue to act as judges and magistrates, and they were in consequence declared Judges of the Courts of Oyer and Terminer and Gaol Delivery; which courts were established in the year 1762. The offices of Sheriff and Constable were at the same time instituted, but the Court of

Directors in their wisdom disapproved of the proposal to send out a professional lawyer to be Clerk of the Peace, and enjoined the Governor and Council to discourage litigation as much as possible. "This wise admonition," remarked Brooke in 1808, "has been attended with the happiest effects, for in general, no people are more averse to law-suits than the natives of St. Helena." The grand juries were usually composed of civil servants, military officers and principal land freeholders, while the petit juries were drawn from the smaller free and lease-holders, but any Englishman at the island was liable to be empaneled as a juror. All convictions and punishments were now required to conform with the laws and statutes of the British realm, or as nearly so as the nature and circumstance of the cases admitted.

There were a few exceptions, such as in the case of those crimes which in England would condemn the offender to transportation, but which at St. Helena were punished either by burning in the hand or by whipping. Until 1787 the evidence of a black, although deemed competent against other blacks, was not admissible against whites. This differentiation often led to the most gross miscarriage of justice, as in the year 1785 when Elizabeth Renton, a white woman, in a fit of passion stabbed one of her female slaves with a carving knife. The slave died in a few moments. The verdict of the coroner's inquest was wilful murder against Elizabeth Renton. The grand jury at the following quarter sessions presented a bill of indictment to the same effect.

When the case came to be tried, the only witness who could have sworn to the fact was a person of colour who was not examined at the trial because the evidence of blacks against whites was inadmissible. Thus, because of the colour of her skin, the murderess escaped scot-free.

The following is a similar case. A planter named Worrall and his slave, Yon, were detected in the act of sheep-stealing.

As all the witnesses in this case were blacks, Worrall could not be brought to trial, but his slave was tried, convicted and sentenced to death, notwithstanding that he had acted under the coercion of his master. Such a flagrant outrage of justice was too great, even for St. Helena, but as there was no authority for pardoning criminals in the Company's charter, Yon was reprieved and recommended to his Majesty's royal mercy, and in the end received from England a free pardon.

An interesting legal quibble arose over this case. It was the rule, when a slave was executed, for the Company to pay fifteen pounds compensation to his owner. When Yon was reprieved and later pardoned, Worrall claimed the return of his slave, but the Council decided to keep him for the Company, and to pay Worrall the fifteen pounds as if he had been executed. It was this case which eventually induced the Company to alter the law so as to allow blacks to give evidence against whites, as well as against those of their own colour.

Amongst other reforms and improvements was the increase of salaries paid to the Company's servants.

Ever since Governor Poirier's appointment, persons below the rank of gentleman had been excluded from the general table, but it was found that the right enjoyed by civil and military officers of constantly dining at the same table as the Governor did not always tend to establish a proper sense of respect for that supreme official, and at the end of 1743 the general table was abolished, and in its stead an allowance, under the title of diet-money, was granted to those entitled to it. New regulations were adopted in the store department, by which bread and flour were sold to the military at cost price; clothing and all other stores at 10 per cent; and to the inhabitants at 40 per cent above it. In 1772 the privilege of purchasing articles in the stores at no more than 10 per cent was extended to the planters and other inhabitants not in the Company's service.

During the government of Mr. Hutchinson many new trees were introduced to the island, both useful and ornamental. Thus, in 1749, the Scotch and the spruce fir were first planted and did well, and some acorns which were sent out from England produced fine oak trees, but in all these cases trees only grew into good specimens if planted in situations sheltered from the prevailing winds. The numerous attempts to establish the coffee plant failed.

So pleased was the Court of Directors with the ability with which Governor Hutchinson had governed the island for eighteen years that they notified him of their intention to settle upon him an annuity of £300 whenever he decided to retire, though they were careful to explain that this offer was in no way to lead him to suppose they wished him to resign. However, the Governor was becoming old and infirm, and was anxious to re-visit his native country, so on the 10th March, 1764, he delivered over his charge to the Lieutenant-Governor, Mr. John Skottowe.

One of the new Governor's first transactions was an attempt to regulate the sale of arrack and punch, a matter which for many years had caused the government considerable trouble. A "Society for vending Arrack and other Spiritous Liquors" was inaugurated and made the monopoly of the four Senior Civil servants and the senior military captain.

Another very useful undertaking which Skottowe carried out was the laying down of leaden pipes to carry water from Chubbs Spring, opposite the Briars in James Valley, down to the Wharf, a distance of a mile and a half.

It was during the same governorship that the island received a visit from the great circumnavigator, Captain James Cook. He sighted St. Helena in the morning of the 15th May, 1775, at a great distance, and at midnight his ship anchored in the Road in front of the town. At sunrise the following morning the Castle and the *Dutton* fired salutes of thirteen guns each,

HON. EAST INDIA COMPANY'S SHIP, *GENERAL GODDARD*, ATTACKING DUTCH FLEET,
JUNE 14, 1795

from the painting by Thomas Luny

COLONEL ROBERT PATTON
Governor, 1802-1807

Top: St. Helena Halfpenny.

Centre: Token issued by Messrs. Solomon, Dickson & Taylor.

Bottom: Silver Medal, awarded to diligent slaves by Governor Patton (by courtesy of G. C. Kitching, Esq., and *Notes and Queries*).

ROBERT BROOKE
Governor

THE *NORTHUMBERLAND* OFF JAMES VALLEY

from the painting by Thomas Luny

MAJOR-GENERAL ALEXANDER BEATSON
GOVERNOR OF ST. HELENA, 1808-1813

MR. PORTEOUS'S HOUSE AT JAMESTOWN, WHERE
NAPOLEON SPENT HIS FIRST NIGHT ON THE ISLAND
Photograph taken before 1865

MOUNT
PLEASANT,
SANDY BAY,
SHOWING LOT
AND LOT'S
WIFE IN
DISTANCE

TURK'S CAP
AND THE BAF

and on landing, Cook was saluted by the Castle with the same number, each salute being answered by the ship, gun for gun. The Governor with the principal gentlemen of the island was on the landing-step to receive the distinguished visitor, and during his stay he was treated with the greatest politeness, "shewing me every kind of civility in their power". Captain Cook, like all visitors to the island, was attracted by it. "Whoever views St. Helena," he wrote in his journal, "in its present state and can but conceive what it must have been originally, will not hastily charge the inhabitants with want of industry. Though, perhaps, they might apply it to more advantage, were more land appropriated to planting corn, vegetables, roots, etc., instead of being laid out in pasture, which is the present mode." This might well be said of the island to-day, and if in the place of the "Company" we say "a few landowners" the sentence which follows would equally apply to modern conditions. "But this is not likely to happen so long as the greatest part of it remains in the hands of the Company and its servants." Cook admired the new church, and several buildings which were then under construction, the commodious landing-place for boats, and several other recent improvements. During their visit some necessary repairs were done to the ship, they filled their water-tanks and the crew were served with fresh beef, for which they paid five pence a pound. "Their beef is exceedingly good, and is the only refreshment to be had worth mentioning."

In the evening of 21st May, after a stay of six days, Captain Cook took leave of the Governor, repaired on board, and with mutual salutes between his ship and the Castle set sail for Ascension Island, on his way home to England.

A far different visitor to the island from the famous Captain Cook was John Macdonald, a footman, who spent a few days there in the year 1773. He wrote a most entertaining book[1]

---

[1] *Memoirs of an eighteenth-century footman, John Macdonald.* G. Routledge. 1927.

about his travels with his various masters, and one wishes he had been more discursive on his impression of St. Helena, as his viewpoint as a footman was quite different from that of most travellers.

He arrived in the East-Indiaman, the *Hampshire*, bound for England from Anjengoe, to whose commander, Captain Taylor, Macdonald was acting as footman.

Here is what little he has to say about St. Helena:

> We came down with pleasure to St. Helena, and stopped 10 days. On shore I was Acting Steward, and Captain Taylor's servant. As they dine early at St. Helena we walked every day after dinner up the country amongst the white farmers. As the country is very high, we could see a great way at sea; and up the country we saw a great many white girls, farmers' daughters.
>
> St. Helena is a wholesome, pleasant place, and a fine, keen searching air. If noblemen and gentlemen of Great Britain and Ireland would go to Madeira and St. Helena for their health, instead of going to France and Portugal, they would be sure to re-establish their health.

One interesting character who visited St. Helena was Philip Francis, the reputed author of *Letters of Junius*, and one of the four councillors of the Major General of India. He arrived there in 1781, and had to kick his heels for five months waiting for a convoy to England, owing to the war between England and France, Spain and Holland. The little island was no place for an energetic man like Francis, with nothing whatever to do. Ever after his sojourn there he used to say that the patron saint of St. Helena was *Ennui*. During his stay he was the guest of Mr. and Mrs. Wrangham, whose daughter Emma was well-known to Francis as the reigning belle of Calcutta, her hand being sought in marriage by all the rich bachelors of that town.

Wrangham's, as their house is still called, stood embowered in roses and flowering trees and shrubs on a little eminence in the lovely Sandy Bay. When at last Francis reached home he wrote the following letter to his friend Mr. Livius of Calcutta, in which his usual cynical acidity discloses itself:

If you literally married the Wrangham (Emma) or if Mackenzie should have married her or Collins or Archdekin, I must beg leave to decline your society in future, at least until the death of her father and mother, whom Heaven confound. I spent five months with them very agreeably in the middle of the Atlantic and most devoutly pray that I may never see the face of either of them again. You need not mention this affair to the daughter or to Mrs. Stevenson. I should be sorry to wound their delicate sensations or any of the refined sentiments they derive from St. Helena. If ever you visit that Island keep your hands on your pocket.

As he drew a salary in India of £10,000 a year and made much more besides by gambling and other distinctly shady methods, this warning about the rapacity of the St. Helenians bears out the reputation which Philip Francis had for parsimony.

Another but a very obscure visitor to St. Helena at this period was John Nicol, Mariner, who during a long life at sea as an ordinary sailor kept a journal.[1] His ship, the *King George*, was on her way to England with a cargo of tea from China and called in at St. Helena in 1788. He has little to record beyond the interesting fact that the Captain of the ship presented the Governor, Skottowe, with a number of empty bottles in return for which he was given a present of potatoes —"a valuable gift to us".

[1] *Life and Adventures of John Nicol—Mariner.* Cassell. 1937.

While here (he writes) I and a number of the crew were nearly poisoned by eating albicores and bonettos. We split them and hung them in the rigging to dry; the moon's rays have the effect of making them poisonous. My face turned red and swelled; but the others were far worse; their heads were swelled twice their ordinary size; but we all recovered.

At this period great numbers of vessels called annually at St. Helena, and so we get more and more documented evidence about the island from various sources.

One of these is the sprightly and charming Mrs. Eliza Fay, whose *Original Letters from India*[1] is one of the gems of obscure autobiography. She landed there on her way to England from Calcutta in September 1782. Her letter from St. Helena, addressed to her sister, is a long one and mostly concerns the hardship encountered by the passengers on board the ship *Valentine*:

A more uncomfortable passage than I have made to this place can hardly be imagined. The port of my cabin being kept almost constantly shut and the door opening into the steerage: I had neither light nor air but from a scuttle: thereby half the space was occupied by a great gun, which prevented me from going near the port when it *was* open . . . Judge if I did not rejoice at the sight of this romantic Island; though its appearance from the sea is very unpromising— inaccessible rocks, and stupendous crags frowning every side but one. The town is literally an ascending valley between two hills, just wide enough to admit of one street. The houses are in the English style, with sashed windows, and small doors. Here are back gardens, but no gardens:

[1] *Original Letters from India* 1779–1815. By Mrs. Eliza Fay. Edited by E. M. Forster, 1925.

which makes the place intensely hot for want of a free circulation of air; but when once you ascend Ladder Hill the scene changes, and all seems enchantment. The most exquisite prospects you can conceive burst suddenly on the eye—fruitful vallies—cultivated hills and diversified scenery of every description. The inhabitants are obliging and attentive, indeed, remarkably; so altogether I find it a most welcome resting place. After being kept on salt provisions for a month, one is not likely to be very fastidious; former abstinence giving more poignant relish to the excellent food, which is set before us.

One thing Mrs. Eliza Fay quite forgot to tell her sister in this letter was the method by which she paid Mrs. Mason her bill for board and lodging during her two months' residence at Jamestown.

That all came out when next she called at the island nine years later. She was then a passenger in an American ship, the *Henry*, belonging to the famous Salem family of Crowninshield—pronounced Grounsell—and commanded by the twenty-one year old Jacob Crowninshield. The *Henry* was on a voyage from Calcutta to Ostend and put in to St. Helena for refreshment on 2nd July, 1791.

In this letter which is addressed to a Mrs. L——, Mrs. Fay writes:

I went on shore in the afternoon and learnt with some vexation that a large fleet had sailed only the day before. I wished to have written, especially as we are not bound direct to England. Many changes had happened in this curious little island, during my twelve (sic) year absence. Few recollected me; but Captain Wall of the *Buccleugh* formerly chief officer of the *Valentine* behaved with the greatest attention—I shall ever acknowledge his kindness.

Fresh provisions were very scarce, a drought had prevailed until this season for four years, and it would require three good seasons to repair the damage sustained, by their stock perishing for water. A circumstance happened during our stay, the like of which was not remembered by the oldest inhabitant, though from the appearance of the place, one would conclude such events were common: a large fragment of rock, detached by the moisture, fell from the side of Ladder Hill, on a small out-house at the upper end of the valley; in which two men were sleeping in separate beds. The stone broke thro' the top and lodged between them, the master of the house[1] was suffocated, it is supposed, by the rubbish, as no bruises were found on his body; the other man forced his way through, and gave the alarm, but not in time to save his companion. This accident caused many to tremble for their safety, since all the way up the valley, houses are built under similar projections, and will some time or other probably experience the same fate. Amongst the Alps such things are common.

Early in her letter Mrs. Fay had remarked how few of the inhabitants recollected her. What a happier woman she would have been if only Captain Wall and no others had remembered her. After recounting the calamity of the falling rock she continues:

An unpleasant affair also occurred to me. I had, when last here, given a girl who had attended me from Calcutta and behaved very ill, to Mrs. Mason, with whom I boarded, under a promise she should not be sold, consequently no slave paper passed. Mr. Mason, however, in defiance of this prohibition, disposed of her for £10. This act mitigating against the established regulations, advantage was

[1] Henry Powell, a publican.

taken of my return to the Island, to call upon me as the original offender, not only for that sum, but a demand was made of £60 more, to pay for the woman's passage back to Bengal with her two children!!! After every effort I could only get a mitigation of £10, being forced to draw on my brother Preston, for £60, a sum that I could ill afford to lose, but the strong hand of power left me no alternative.

This account of the episode was not entirely accurate, for in the India Office Records is to be found the other side of the story.

In 1782, Mrs. Fay stranded the girl on the island probably in payment of a bill to Mrs. Mason. The case roused great indignation in St. Helena. The girl was no fool and, on discovering that her late mistress was passing by on the *Henry*, she at once went to the Governor, Robert Brooke, and denounced her. In her deposition she "made oath on the Holy Evangelists that she was called Kitty Johnson as her supposed Father was Johnson the Governor's Groom at Calcutta, that her Mother's name was Silvia, a Free Woman, half cast, and she believes that a woman, called Peg Chapman, her supposed godmother, sent her to service to Mrs. Fay, then Mantua Maker at Calcutta". Kitty goes on to say that Mrs. Fay was following her husband to England and "was intimate with the Doctor of the Ship going home, and as the Deponent knew of it, Mrs. Fay did not like to keep her. She further complains that she has been left without her consent, sold into slavery, and ill-treated: and now has two children and wishes to return to her mother who is said to be alive". The Governor then summoned Mrs. Fay. In her statement she keeps a dignified silence about the doctor, merely remarking she left Kitty on the island "on account of her bad behaviour as a present to Miss Betty Mason, but did not suppose she would have been sold". The Governor took a serious view, and told Mrs. Fay she must either settle the matter or remain at St. Helena to stand her trial.

Accordingly she drew a Bill for £60 on "my brother Thomas W. Preston" (presumably her brother-in-law): £10 were to purchase Kitty's freedom, £40 for her passage with her babies to Bengal, and £10 for maintenance on arrival.

Largely as a result of this scandal, regulations were passed which compelled the owners of slaves to teach them some useful profession and produce them at Divine Service at least once a fortnight.

Governor Skottowe, like his predecessor, held the reins of government successfully for eighteen years and retired in 1782, to be succeeded by Daniel Corneille, the Lieutenant-Governor.

Skottowe's time had on the whole been undisturbed by irregularities or trouble, his principal anxiety being the frequent desertion of the soldiers of the garrison. That the soldiers had, or considered they had, some genuine grievance there can be no doubt, and as this spirit of unrest and discontent was shortly after to break out into open and dangerous mutiny, particulars of some of these desertions will not be out of place.

On the 28th July, 1770, a sergeant of artillery and six soldiers and a slave stole the Company's long boat and seven muskets and provisions and slipped away during the night.

The following year Sergeant Moon and four soldiers at Lemon Valley plotted to seize the long boat and desert. This came to the Governor's knowledge and the long boat was secured, but the deserters nevertheless escaped in a small jolly-boat, and were never heard of again.

Then an exciting piece of news was brought to St. Helena by a black woman who had returned from England. She declared that she had actually seen and spoken in London to some of the men who deserted in the long boat on the 28th July, 1770. They told her they had sailed to Brazil and from there eventually returned to England. This so excited other malcontents that on the 30th September, 1771, on a dark windy night with a very high sea running, six men of the garrison embarked in a small boat. They were never seen again and it was presumed that they perished. It was this series of desertions which caused the Court of Directors to write a letter of sharp reproof to the Council at St. Helena ending: "until we shall be fully satisfied that there has been no neglect in garrison duty we shall impute the blame to our Governor and Lt. Gov., as they are more immediately entrusted with the Military affairs of our settlement."

In 1772, John Fortune arrived back at the island. He was the slave who had deserted with the soldiers who escaped to Brazil in 1770. He had surrendered himself voluntarily to the Company at London, and said he had been fishing in a boat when the runaways forcibly seized him and carried him off in the long boat.

The next deserters were six soldiers who one night went off in a yawl and a jolly-boat. They were still in view of the island at daybreak the following morning, but too far off to pursue and soon were out of sight. They were described as being "illiterate men of bad character, and having only a few days' provisions must inevitably perish".

The Council made searching enquiries to discover the cause of the discontent amongst the soldiers which induced them to desert in open boats, with but the barest possible chance of ever reaching land alive. The Lieutenant-Governor, Daniel Corneille, attributed the trouble to the slackness of Lieutenant Leech, the officer in charge of the garrison, "that for the nine years he has been here the Garrison were never under arms for a field day or exercised together". The Governor, on the contrary, did not take this view, but attributed the whole trouble to drink. But now the troops were at once put through a course of the "new Prussian exercise and better disciplined than ever". This satisfactory improvement lasted for a while, until in 1778 a corporal and three privates ran away with a cutter, the property of Captain Harper, and escaped, though "we judge they must have perished," and a little while after, another corporal and a soldier deserted from Lemon Valley in a fishing boat. The *Glattor* sent in pursuit did not succeed in finding them, but instead captured two slaves who also were attempting to escape in an open boat.

On the same day, October 25th, 1779, one Winter Benis was tried by a court martial for writing a letter to the Court of Directors "tending to promote mutiny and for accusing the Garrison of mutinous intentions". For this he was ordered to be flogged and drummed out of the garrison with a halter round his neck. As it afterwards turned out, Benis's warning of impending trouble was not without foundation.

Again six soldiers stole the cutter and deserted in her, one of them being the sentry on duty. When Skottowe retired and Corneille took over the administration of the island, in 1782, although there were still a few desertions and a few cases of insubordination amongst the soldiers, nobody suspected the sudden trouble which was impending.

As in so many mutinies amongst disgruntled sailors and soldiers, the actual incentive was interference with the men's liquor. Hitherto the soldiers of the garrison were free to go and drink at any of the numerous punch-houses and taverns they chose. Then the Company put the punch-houses out of bounds, which had also been done at Gibraltar, and allowed them to drink only at the military canteens. This was much resented by the troops who preferred the punch-houses which reserved special rooms for soldiers to drink, sing their songs and enjoy themselves in any way they liked. The punch-houses being put out of bounds, the only alternative was the

canteen, where there was no place to sit down, and where each
man was allowed only to drink an allotted quantity of liquor
at certain hours, and had to leave directly he had finished his
drink. To add to the humiliation, the blacks were allowed to
regale themselves in the punch-houses without restriction.
The ugly temper of the soldiers first showed itself on the day
before Christmas, when they refused the usual extra allowance
of flour and other articles which were always issued at this
season. This being reported to the Governor, he agreed to
increase each man's allowance, and Christmas Day passed off
quietly. But on the 26th a disorderly body of them assembled
and loudly complained of their grievances. The disturbance
was for the time being quelled when the Governor promised
to take their complaints into consideration and to redress any
which seemed to be justified. But on the 27th, after they had
consumed their issue of spirits, trouble again broke out and
they demanded more from the officer of the week. They were
quieted temporarily by this officer's promise to go personally
and put their case before the Governor. On learning that the
Governor would not agree to their demands, two hundred
soldiers armed themselves and marched out of barracks with
drums beating and fixed bayonets, with Sergeant Tooley at
their head. Their object was to gain possession of the post
on Ladder Hill, where field pieces, mortars, and ammunition
were kept, and from where they would have complete command of the town below. The Governor and the Lieutenant-
Governor, Major Grame, were coming down Ladder Hill from
the country when they saw the rioters, and by hurrying were
just in time to reach the terrace overlooking the town before
the soldiers arrived at the foot of the hill.

The Governor, who saw how desperate the situation was,
at once threw himself (alone except for his groom) amongst
the rabble and tried to persuade them, by promises of forgiveness, to remove their grievances if they laid down their arms

and returned to quarters. This had the desired result, and they returned the field pieces which they had drawn out and loaded, and with the Governor at their head, marched down the hill again. But on the way they noticed Major Grame was bringing cannon up the parade, and at once halted and refused to resume their march until the Governor sent instructions to remove the cannon. When this had been done, Sergeant Tooley gave the word of command to march. The Governor flattered himself that he had got the men under control and that their confidence in him would be a safeguard against any further trouble, and he very imprudently returned to his country house. But the inhabitants were far from being satisfied, for although most of the soldiers were sober, there was a dangerous and sullen spirit amongst them. Major Grame, too, was alarmed not only at the mutiny but by the insolent messages sent him by the garrison that night and the following morning, and strongly advised the Governor to take military measures to prevent a possible recurrence of the riot. The Governor, however, declined to take this excellent advice on the ground it might lead the men to suspect he did not mean to keep terms with them.

On the 29th the Council removed the principal grievance about the canteen and directed that the punch-houses should be opened on their former footing, though limiting the soldiers to what they considered a sufficient quantity of spirits for their daily consumption.

By five o'clock in the afternoon the soldiers, having finished this allowance, became riotous and demanded more liquor. Several of the officers went amongst them endeavouring to bring them to reason, but with no success. The Governor, at last recognizing that sterner measures must be employed at once if serious trouble was to be averted, arrested Sergeant Tooley, called out the main guard who had not gone over to the mutineers, and marched up the street at their head. On seeing what was happening the rioters rushed into the barracks, seized their arms and marched off in the direction of the Alarm House.

A race then took place up the almost perpendicular side of Ladder Hill between the small party of the loyal troops, headed by Major Grame, and the mutineers to reach Alarm House. The small party scrambled up a steep side path in order to get there first, but Major Grame "with that ardour and alacrity for which he was remarkable" spurring on his horse, forged ahead of them, riding along a narrow, steep, but shorter path, called the Saddle, doing so at immense peril, for apart from the danger of falling over the precipice he was in full view of the mutineers, who kept up a running fire at him with their muskets. It was dark by the time Major Grame reached the Alarm House, but he got there just in time to order the six men of the guard to load and fire five rounds at the advancing mutineers who were now close up to the house. By keeping up a rapid musket fire the seven soldiers held up the enemy for a while, but at last when the block house was almost surrounded, Grame made his escape. A party of the mutineers pursued him for some distance, firing at him several times. At ten at night, after making a long circuit, he got back safely to James Valley. In the meantime the Governor had sent Major Bazett with three officers and about seventy men in pursuit of the mutineers. On finding that Alarm House was in the hands of the insurgents, Major Bazett decided to attack it from the ridge at the rear, so as not to expose his men advancing up the open hill-side.

The mutineers who were now under the command of a Sergeant Burnet, had drawn up the field pieces in different directions, and placed one to sweep the ridge, rightly suspecting that Major Bazett would attack from that quarter. Owing to the darkness the mutineers in the Alarm House did not see the loyal troops until they were quite close up, so that when they discharged their piece it had no effect, owing to its too great elevation. Major Bazett's men immediately rushed forward, seized the field-gun and drove off the men in charge of it. Irregular firing on both sides took place for ten minutes or more, when the mutineers broke and ran for refuge into the house. The casualties in this action were two killed of Major Bazett's party and three wounded among the mutineers, with one hundred and three prisoners. This number by no means represented the total number that took up arms, for many of them had slipped away in the darkness and mixed unobserved with the Governor's loyal troops.

At the court martial which followed, ninety-nine of the prisoners were condemned to death, but as such a wholesale slaughter was deemed too sanguinary a proceeding, the condemned were "decimated", that is, lots were drawn and one in every ten prisoners was shot, amongst the victims being Sergeant Burnet. Sergeant Tooley was shortly afterwards sent off the island in a packet bound for England, which on her passage was wrecked off the Scilly Islands and every soul on board drowned.

One good thing resulted from this rebellion, for now it was known who were the ringleaders amongst the soldiers, and as those of them who were not shot were sent away, the garrison was thoroughly purged of all its seditious characters.

Governor Corneille resigned in June, 1787, and returned to England, and Mr. Robert Brooke was appointed in his place, with Major Francis Robson Lieutenant-Governor, Major Bazett, William Wrangham and Henry Bazett to the Council.

T HE new Governor came from Bengal, where he had distinguished himself in the Company's service, both in a military and a civil capacity.

To whatever causes the late mutiny in the garrison might be traced, it certainly did not arise from any want of frequent and severe corporal punishment. Governor Brooke considered that the repeated application of the lash, often for the most trifling offence, had the effect of brutalizing the soldiers, and with the object of rousing in them a sense of shame and self-esteem he ordered that in the future lesser offences should be punished not by stripes but by labour. Instead of appreciating this humanity and leniency, the rougher element refused the labour and demanded to be flogged. The Governor, who was not to be baulked, took a new line for dealing with this difficult problem. All the bad characters he separated from their comrades, under the designation of the *miscreants' mess*. The worst provisions were allotted to them and they were deprived of many of the privileges the soldiers valued most. This ostracization, and the sense of contempt it brought upon them from their comrades, proved to have a far greater effect than lashes, and very soon the members of the "miscreants' mess" were imploring to be allowed to rejoin their companions and to undergo labour, however hard, for their misdemeanours rather than continue to be a by-word and a mockery.

The wily Governor took time to consider his decision, pretending the situation was a difficult one to alter, but eventually he agreed, and from that period there never was any occasion to renew the "miscreants' mess". With the extra labour obtained by this means, whole tracts of waste land in the town which hitherto had been an offence to the eye and the dumping ground for filth, were converted into a handsome parade ground for the soldiers, and into gardens which did credit to the town and were a benefit to the hospital. But of even greater advantage than gardens and parade ground was the improved appearance in the personnel of the garrison, a change which was noticed and commented on by every passing traveller who revisited the island. Infantry manœuvres and sham fights were started, greatly to the benefit of both officers and men. Such was the improvement in the moral and general well-being of the garrison that recruits were no longer difficult to get. Numbers of discharged soldiers returning from India, perfectly restored to health on the passage to St. Helena, now offered with eagerness to renew their term of service. By this means about nine hundred men were obtained during Brooke's term of office. These, with the recruits received from England, made it possible for the Governor to send drafts to India, amounting, at different periods, to the number of one thousand and two hundred men, all of them disciplined and trained soldiers, prepared for a hot country by a seasoning in the moderately tropical climate of St. Helena. These detachments sent from St. Helena were much appreciated in India at that time when good soldiers were in great demand.

In a letter from Madras, written in 1791, Lord Cornwallis wrote to Governor Brooke:

I have been favoured by your letter and am truly sensible of the earnest and meritorious zeal with which you have been actuated in preparing and embarking for the service of this country so considerable a part of the force of your island.

From the very first settlement in St. Helena the military establishment had been a restricted one. At the commencement of Robert Brooke's government it consisted of four companies of infantry and one of artillery, and as the transfer of officers from one Company's settlement to another was not allowed, promotion of those on the island was of course very slow. At the urgent desire of the Governor, the Court of Directors increased the garrison in 1796 by a battalion of infantry and a corps of artillery. This had the effect of making promotion much more rapid, so that junior officers who had up till then no higher expectations than of one day becoming captains now looked forward to reaching the rank of field-officer.

The security of the island was further increased by the organization of the whole of the male population into disciplined militia. The force under that name had previously consisted of thirty or forty white men. The encouragement given by Brooke to discharged soldiers of good character to settle in the island, combined with the increasing population, made it possible in time to form two companies of white militia, and afterwards two companies of blacks were embodied, and the whole organized into a corps, officered by the Company's civil servants, and commanded by a member of the Council.

Until they became sufficiently trained, the corps was drilled twice a week. The importance of this measure was later to be appreciated when a fresh mutiny amongst a part of the garrison broke out in 1811.

When, in 1673, the Dutch seized the island and drove out the English, the ultimate reason of their success had been their possession of the higher ground and ability to fire on to the fort below, where the English were helpless to retaliate or defend themselves.

It might be thought that during the one hundred and more

years which had passed since the English regained St. Helena, the lesson would have been learned, that however well a place was fortified, and however many of these forts there might be down in the valleys or by the sea coast, they would be helpless if an enemy managed to win his way to any of the numerous high hills or ridges which overlooked every one of the forts. It was not until Governor Brooke arrived, with his expert military knowledge gained on active service in Southern India, a country in some ways not unsimilar to St. Helena, that the defences of the island were thoroughly reorganized on up-to-date lines.

New forts and defences were built on high positions and at different passes and defiles from which they could command the valleys lower down if an enemy should land. Many of the field guns and mortars were removed from their old positions where they would be of little use and placed in more suitable localities.

To the islanders, any innovation or any change from the routine they were accustomed to, was always likely to start a lot of tongues wagging. Over the new fortifications they wagged so loudly and so persistently as to reach the ears of the Court of Directors in London, who suspended all work on them until General Sir Archibald Campbell, who was expected to call on his return from India, should inspect and report on both the works which had already been constructed and on those in contemplation. On his arrival the General made a careful inspection of what had been done, and as good luck would have it there was a general alarm during his stay, so that he had an opportunity of observing the disposition of the island troops in the event of an expected attack. In his subsequent report, General Campbell was all in favour of the new system of fortifications but lamented the parsimoniousness of the Company which had considerably cramped the Governor's schemes. Shortly after this, Lord Cornwallis arrived at St.

Helena and he also made a tour of inspection, and his report was strongly in praise of the work the Governor was carrying out.

The only method used hitherto in announcing the approach of ships to the island was by firing guns, after which the commander-in-chief at the fort at Jamestown had to wait until further particulars were brought by runners a distance of seven or eight miles. Now a code of signals was substituted, which though far from perfect, was a great improvement on the old system and one of the utmost importance.

In spite of the murmurings of a handful of die-hards amongst the inhabitants Governor Brooke continued to bring about improvements in the island. Owing to the tremendous surfs which break against the shores of St. Helena, landing was often a dangerous adventure and many fatal accidents occurred in rough weather, and as there was only one crane on the jetty much delay and inconvenience was caused when landing passengers or goods from ships. Governor Brooke had noticed that the fishermen could often land on a rock which jutted out beyond the end of the jetty when the common landing place at the stairs was impracticable. With great ingenuity and some difficulty he prolonged the wharf to this rock, and thus was able to erect an additional crane, and at the same time provide a landing place which was safe: so safe indeed that when the Governor's nephew wrote his history of the island in 1823 only one life had been lost in landing, although previously serious accidents were frequent.

From time to time mention has been made in these pages of visits to the island by distinguished travellers or others. One of the former who arrived on 17th December, 1792, was Captain Bligh, the hero of the *Bounty*, returning from his second voyage to the South Seas with his ships, *Providence* and *Assistant*, laden with breadfruit trees for Jamaica.

Bligh tells of his coming to St. Helena:[1]

[1] *Captain Bligh's Second Voyage to the South Sea.* Ida Lee. Longman, 1920.

At noon after I anchored, an officer was sent from the Governor, Lt.-Colonel Brooke, to welcome us. I landed at 1 o'clock when I was saluted with 13 guns, and the Governor received me. In my interview with him I informed him of my orders to give into his care 10 breadfruit plants, and one of every kind (of which I had five), as would secure to the island a lasting supply of this valuable fruit which our most gracious King had ordered to be planted there. Colonel Brooke expressed great gratitude and the principal plants were taken to a valley near his residence called Plantation House, and the rest to James Valley.

On the 23rd, I saw the whole landed and planted; one plant was given to Major Robson, Lt.-Governor, and one to Mr. Wrangham, the first in Council. I also left a quantity of mountain rice seed here. The sago was the only plant that required a particular description. I therefore took our Otaheitan friends to the Governor's House where they made a pudding of the prepared part of its root, some of which I had brought from Otaheite.

Writing of St. Helena further, he says:

Few places look more unhealthy when sailing along its burnt-up cliffs—huge masses of rock fit only to resist the sea, yet few places are more healthy. The inhabitants are not like other Europeans who live in the Torrid Zone, but have good constitutions—the women being fair and pretty. James Town, the capital, lies in a deep and narrow valley, and it is little more than one long street of houses; these are built after our English fashion, most of them having thatched roofs. Lodgings are scarce, so I was fortunate in finding rooms with Captain Statham in a well-regulated house at the common rate of twelve shillings a day. The Otaheitans were delighted with what they saw here, as

Colonel Brooke showed them kind attention, had them to stay at his house, and gave them each a suit of red clothes.

A letter from the Governor and Council was despatched to Captain Bligh before he left, conveying thanks for the gifts which they declared

> had impressed their minds with the warmest gratitude towards His Majesty for his goodness and attention for the welfare of his subjects; while the sight of his ships had raised in them an inexpressible degree of wonder and delight to contemplate a floating garden transported in luxuriance from one extremity of the world to the other.

On December 27th, after taking on board "all needful refreshment" the ships left St. Helena, receiving a salute of thirteen guns from the battery on Ladder Hill.

It was a little while after Bligh's visit that a ship arrived from India carrying French prisoners of war to England. They were permitted to land, but the action of a French officer in swaggering about the street of Jamestown wearing in his hat a cockade, "the present insignia of Rebellion", caused no more French prisoners to be allowed to leave the ship.

A month after this incident another vessel arrived bringing an Arab thoroughbred for the Governor, which he had bought for the exorbitant price of £400, in order to improve the breed of horses in the island.

Another visitor to St. Helena must not be passed over without mention. This was the famous, or infamous, William Hickey, who made up for an ill-spent life by leaving behind him one of the most entertaining books of memoirs in the English language.[1] In 1793 he was returning from Calcutta in the *Eden Castle*, one of a fleet of the East India Company's

---

[1] *Memoirs of William Hickey* (1749–1809), 4 vols. Hurst & Blackett, 1919.

ships. The voyage had been a very stormy one and Hickey and his fellow travellers were delighted when

At noon we had the gratification of seeing the land from the deck, and never did I feel more pleasure than in beholding that little speck in the midst of an immense ocean. . . . By the time we had got close under the land it was so dark we could not see a ship's length in any direction, nevertheless we stood on. Before rounding a point which opened the valley in which the town stands, we steered by the lights of the houses.

At eight o'clock we let go our best bower anchor and Captain Colnett immediately sent his purser on shore to secure lodgings for himself and me. These he secured at Mr. Dunn's, the principal Surgeon of the Settlement, where we were also to mess.

On Sunday morning I accompanied Captain Colnett on shore, taking with me my faithful servant Munnoo, and we took up our abode at the very comfortable apartments of Mr. Dunn's. After an excellent dinner, at which we had abundance of fine fish of different sorts, and spending a cheerful evening we retired to our respective bed-chambers and I enjoyed a better night's rest than I had done for several weeks. . . . At dinner we had sitting down, I think, twenty-eight in number, Mrs. Dunn presiding at the head of the table, the honours of which she performed with much credit to herself.

At four o'clock on the 19th, the fleet left the island with a fine, fresh breeze, and Hickey continued his journal:

St. Helena is much more beautiful and picturesque in sailing from it than in approaching towards it, as in departing you have in view the rich and fertile valley with a remarkably neat and handsome town as well as a variety of country houses and gardens in different directions, forming an interesting and agreeable appearance of verdure or capacity of cultivation.

One wishes that William Hickey had been more informative about what he did during his eight days on land, for he managed in that short space of time to spend the large sum of two thousand rupees.

When the British code of laws was introduced to supersede the unsatisfactory island one, the legal status of master to slave was overlooked. As no special laws had been framed for the protection of slaves, too much power remained in the hands of the proprietors. Although the large majority of slave owners treated their blacks with humanity, yet the records shew sufficient evidence that all did not do so. Under Governor Brooke cases of unwarrantable severity to or unjust treatment of a slave met with immediate redress, and the offender was heavily fined.

In 1792 the Governor drew up a code of laws for the control and protection of slaves, which limited the authority of the master, and extended that of the magistrate. This code was submitted to the Court of Directors for their consideration. Though the Court did not approve of Brooke's system in all its parts yet they passed a set of laws nearly similar. By the new code a master was allowed to punish his slave with twelve lashes of the cat-o'-nine-tails, but if he considered the fault to call for more severe punishment a magistrate was to be appealed to, who, with the Governor's concurrence, could award such chastisement as appeared expedient. If a master exceeded his powers, he was liable to be prosecuted by his slave before the justices, and on the other hand, a frivolous or unfounded complaint by a slave incurred punishment at the discretion of the magistrates.

When Dunbar was Governor, the use of the plough which had been introduced to the island some years before was given up. Governor Brooke re-introduced it upon some of the Company's lands, but not at Longwood, as the good farming land there had been given over to the raising of trees.

Amongst other improvements to the credit of this energetic and longsighted Governor was the conducting of water from some springs below Diana's Peak to Deadwood, which proved invaluable during a long drought and saved a large stock of the Company's cattle. His example in making water courses encouraged some of the farmers to do the same, with the result that several tracts of useless waste ground were turned into good grazing, with much benefit to their stock.

Within two years of Brooke's arrival the stock of black cattle and sheep had risen considerably, and the money received from sales of cattle, sheep, hogs, fowls, vegetables and fruit to ships had risen from £4,524 to £6,672. The extension of the potato plantations, which also took place during his government, led to a thriving trade with calling ships and brought considerable wealth to the growers, and led to the erection of several handsome dwellings.

It was little wonder then that the Court of Directors, ever generous to those of their servants who served them well, were pleased to increase the Governor's salary to £1,000 a year. Not only this, but at the same time they conferred on him a commission of Lieutenant-Colonel and soon afterwards of Colonel, with the pay which went with that rank.

On the 25th May, 1795, H.M.S. *Sceptre* arrived at Jamestown to convoy the homeward-bound fleet and she brought intelligence that Holland had been overrun by the French and her fleet captured, and that the Dutch would inevitably be compelled to become unwilling allies of France and to go to war with England. A project instantly occurred to the Governor's ever active mind of making an effort to capture the Cape of

Good Hope before this information should reach that Dutch colony. Mr. Pringle, the Agent of the Secret Committee, had lately come to St. Helena from the Cape and he reported that barracks had been prepared there for the reception of some British troops as a reinforcement to the garrison, a circumstance which would well account for the arrival of more British troops on the plea that an immediate attack was apprehended from the French. The same informant said that the garrison at the Cape consisted of about one thousand German mercenaries, and that the Dutch Commander-in-Chief, with the Scotch name of Gordon, was well disposed to the British. He added that in his opinion when the Dutch at the Cape received the news that the French had entered Holland, they would turn out Colonel Gordon (who was suspected by the republican party of being too favourable to the British interest) and put their own man, one Democrats, in command.

Mr. Pringle agreed with the Governor that the project was a sound one, and Captain Essington, of the *Sceptre*, being of the same mind, agreed heartily to co-operate in the undertaking. The proposal was then laid before the Council, and met with their immediate assent, and that of most of the commanders of the Company's ships then at the island. Three hundred picked men were in consequence embarked on board the *Sceptre* and the Company's ships *General Goddard*, *Manship* and a small, fast-sailing vessel, the *Orpheus*, which were lightened of part of their cargoes, and strengthened by additional sailors. A corps of volunteer seamen was selected from the other ships and placed under the command of Captain Price of the *Lord Hawkesbury*, so that with the marines and seamen of the *Sceptre* a force of about six hundred men was collected to act on shore. The military section of this little force was under Governor Brooke, while Captain Essington took command of the naval one. With this armed force on board—with two field guns and two chests of treasure of about £10,000—the fleet weighed anchor and set sail on the 1st of June, in the hope of gaining possession, by stratagem, of the castle at the Cape of Good Hope and holding it until reinforcements should arrive. But on the following morning they fell in with the *Swallow* packet from the Cape and an hour or two after, the *Arniston*, storeship, from England made her appearance. By the latter intelligence was received that the St. Helena expedition was anticipated by a force sent out from England under Sir George Elphinstone and General Sir James Craig. From the *Swallow* it was learned that a valuable home-bound fleet of twenty Dutch East-Indiamen had been on the point of leaving the Cape when the *Swallow* sailed. This news caused a temporary postponement of the Cape expedition, for it was felt that such a golden opportunity for capturing some of the Dutch fleet was not to be missed. Quickly the treasure, the two field guns and the regimental band and everything else not now required, was disembarked, so that every spare warehouse and even the church was filled with stores off the ships, and the H.M.S. *Sceptre, Asia, Busbridge, Manship, General Goddard* and *Swallow* were sent out under the command of Captain Essington to lie in wait for the Dutch fleet.

On the 10th of June the inhabitants of Jamestown were greatly excited when the *Swallow* came into the Road with a Dutch prize, the *Hughley*, to be followed a week later by the rest of the English squadron with seven other large Dutch ships.

These eight East-Indiamen were the only vessels of the Dutch fleet which the English had seen, but as it was well known that they were merely a part of the fleet, the enterprising Governor Brooke immediately despatched the *Echo*, a fast-sailing ship, to England, with information about the remainder so that the Admiralty was able to intercept it and capture several more Dutch ships.

On the 1st of July, the *Sceptre*, with her original convoy and her prizes sailed for England.

The island had scarcely settled down to its ordinary hum-drum life after all these exciting events, when H.M.S. *Sphynx* arrived with despatches from Admiral Sir George Elphinstone and General Craig. Affairs at the Cape were not at all in a promising state. General Craig's little army was held up by the Dutch militia at Muizenberg, and he wrote to say that he had so few troops that "no augmentation could be so inconsiderable as not to be acceptable" and that he had not a single gun nor an artilleryman and begged that a couple of six-pounders and a howitzer with the necessary ammunition and artillerymen might be sent him. The Admiral also begged for immediate assistance and asked Governor Brooke to send him a supply of silver (money). Not a moment was lost in putting on board the *Arniston* ten pieces of field-ordnance, two howitzers, a complete company of artillery and three of infantry, amounting in all to eleven officers, four hundred men, a supply of ammunition and salt provisions, and fifteen thousand pounds in cash.

These two examples of the ability of the Governor of St. Helena to act quickly in an emergency did not pass without recognition and suitable acknowledgment from high quarters. The following letter reached him from the Secretary of War:

Horse-Guards, 30th Oct. 1795.

I have received, and laid before the King, your letters of the 13th of July and 12th of September last, with their enclosures; and it is with peculiar satisfaction that I obey his Majesty's commands in communicating to you, by opportunity of the *Dart* packet, his Majesty's perfect approbation of the zeal and alacrity you have manifested on every occurrence interesting to this country, in the course of the present war, and particularly of your judicious and spirited proceedings since you received the intelligence of the invasion of the United Provinces by the enemy.

The measures taken by you for securing the Dutch East-Indiamen which touched at St. Helena, and the intelligence you have transmitted respecting the remainder of those ships, merit great commendation; and your exertions in forwarding to Admiral Sir George Keith Elphinstone and General Craig, at the Cape, the succours of money, men, ordnance and stores, at a time when a speedy supply of those articles was become so essentially necessary, will, I trust, be attended with the most beneficial consequences to the interest of this kingdom, and of the East-India Company; and I cannot indulge in this pleasing expectation, without feeling that it has been so materially improved by your unremitting vigilance and care to promote that important service.

I have, &c.,

Henry Dundas

Nor was the Honourable Court of Directors backward in expressing their appreciation of their energetic and capable Governor, for they sent him a diamond-hilted sword; which was presented to him at a garrison parade.

Letters reached the Governor also from Admiral Elphinstone thanking him for his prompt and valuable assistance and saying how on the 7th August "we attacked the Dutch camp at the Mysemberg, the Enemy fled immediately." And later on another to say the Cape had surrendered on 16th September "thanks to Gov. Brooke, Capt. Seale and officers and men of the St. Helena corps".

General Craig wrote: "Your St. Helena friends have had their share of our fatigues and hardships, and have acquitted themselves as you would have wished."

What neither of the two Commanders mentioned was that Colonel Gordon, out of disappointment and shame at the English occupation, committed suicide.

Not the least gratifying of the compliments paid to Governor

Brooke must have been the gift to him of a sword of honour from Lord Mornington, the Governor-General of India, and the future Duke of Wellington. The presentation took place on 11th of November, 1799, before the assembled troops and civilians of the island.

With the sword, Lord Mornington's brother brought a letter to Colonel Brooke, which ran as follows:

> Sir, My brother, who carries my despatches to England, will have the honour of delivering this letter to you. He will also, by my direction, present you with a sword taken in the palace of Seringapatam, which I request you to accept as a testimony of my esteem.

With so large a number of troops serving away at the Cape, those who were left to garrison the island had to be doubly on the alert. England being at war with France, the possibility of a raid on St. Helena had to be prepared for. In addition to this there were about three hundred prisoners to guard, including Malays, taken out of the Dutch ships, and there was no suitable place of confinement for them on the island. The militia, however, assisted the depleted garrison, and an unlooked-for addition to their numbers was found amongst the prisoners themselves, for between seventy and eighty of them proved to be Danes, Norwegians and Swedes, who were anxious to change masters, and enlist as soldiers in the Company's service. The Malays also considered their capture by the English as a release from slavery, and readily agreed to take an oath of fidelity and enter the British service. They were accordingly incorporated into two companies and trained to become artillerymen. They very soon proved to be excellent soldiers, and during the two years they remained on the island were conspicuous for their good discipline and peaceful conduct, which may have been partly due to the exceptional way in which they were treated. No European was allowed to strike or chastise a Malay on any pretence whatever; and they were punished by no other authority than the sentence of a court-martial, composed of Malay officers. At the end of two years these Malays were sent to the Company's settlement at Bencoolen and then to Ceylon, and the two companies formed the nucleus of a Malay regiment.

After all these alarms of war, deeds of martial heroism, firing of cannon and general applause, it is pleasant to find in the Records, this simple note:

> March 28—Java Sparrows—Prohibition against catching any for one year. Penalty, if a child, to be whipped, if a grown person, fined.

Fourteen years of anxious toil followed by a severe illness obliged General Brooke to retire from St. Helena and return to his home in Ireland. Upon the 16th of March, 1801, he embarked in the *Highland Chief* and left St. Helena, loved and regretted by all.

WITH the departure of Robert Brooke, St. Helena lost one of the best Governors she ever had. During the period of one year before the new Governor arrived, the Lieutenant-Governor, Colonel Francis Robson, filled the post.

On March 10th, 1802, Colonel Robert Patton landed at Jamestown under a salute of nineteen guns, and was then introduced into the Council Room where the new commission was read by the secretary. The assembly then adjourned to the Grand Parade where the commission was again read in the presence of the garrison by the Town Major, with another salute of nineteen guns. This was followed by a *feu de joie* fired by the troops, and then Colonel Patton entered the Castle under a general salute. This Governor, like the last, had served the Company in Bengal, where he had filled the situation of military secretary successively under General Smith, Governor Cartier and Governor Warren Hastings.

He was a man of many parts, industrious and ingenious. One of his first actions was the establishment of telegraphs, by a simple but inexpensive method of his own invention, an improvement on the old means of signalling and one which greatly added to the security of the island.

He next took in hand the ordnance department. By making certain alterations in the construction of their carriages, the guns on the heights were made to cover many danger spots which with the old type of gun-carriage was not possible.

These alterations allowed the artillery to fire hot or cold shot at any required degree of depression "with a facility and accuracy that has astonished every military character who has lately witnessed the St. Helena artillery practice. Four men were able to work a thirty-two pounder with almost twice the expedition and accuracy that could be formerly effected by seven. Every point where an enemy could possibly effect a landing or ascend the heights was now supplied with these defensive measures, which applied to the interior of the island as well as the coast."[1] If proof were wanted that the new Governor was an industrious man, it would be found in the fact that while carrying out the above improvements and seeing to many other duties, he yet found time to devote himself to authorship, for in 1803 he published his second and best known work, *Principles of Asiatic Monarchies*.

During the rule of Roberts it had become customary to include in every lease granted by the Company, a clause binding the tenant to grow and protect trees on a tenth part of his land. Owing principally to the shortage of labour it had proved impossible to make and keep up fences adequate to protect the trees from cattle, sheep and goats except in the immediate vicinity of the houses, and so the clause had gradually been dropped. As a result of this when Patton arrived on the island he was shocked to see how few trees there were, and so, judging that planting on however small a scale was better than no planting at all, he proposed a new clause in the leases, by which only six trees should be planted per acre, and that they might be planted on whatever part of the occupier's land he liked, which would probably be near his dwelling and therefore best protected. These proposals were fully approved of and confirmed by the Court of Directors.

It is always dangerous to introduce into one country a plant

---

[1] Brooke.

or an animal from another. The world is full of examples which prove this, such as the rabbit in Australia, or the mongoose in Jamaica, to give but two instances. About twenty-five years before Colonel Patton's government the wild English blackberry plant had been introduced, with the idea that it would form good hedges and wind-breaks. The experiment had proved a calamity. Evidently both the soil and the climate were congenial to the blackberry, for by this time it had spread over large tracts of the best pasture land, and was continuing to spread. The authorities and the islanders were alarmed, and the Grand Jury, at the quarter sessions in July, 1806, represented the evil as requiring the immediate attention of the Government. If anything could be done to extirpate the scourge it must be done on a large scale, since individual effort had proved quite useless. The Governor therefore proposed that a part of the Garrison should be allotted to this special duty, commencing where the need was most prevalent, and that each party of soldiers should be regularly relieved by another until the blackberry menace was got rid of. The soldiers were to be paid for this work by the proprietors who were afterwards to keep their land free from this destructive weed. The reason for these wholesale methods was shortage of labour. There were only enough slaves on the island to carry out the ordinary work on the farms, gardens and so on, and not enough to do other work such as fencing and weed destruction.

Another factor was the tendency, as the island became more and more a place of call for ships, for the principal inhabitants to live at Jamestown and enter into trade rather than remain on their farms, where the work was hard and the prospects less good. Almost all the provisions necessary to life were still imported by the Company from Europe and the East Indies and sold cheaply to the inhabitants. Money would always buy provisions, and money was most easily obtained by means of trade, particularly with the passengers on the returning East-Indiamen. Usually St. Helena was the first land they reached after a passage of three months, and many of them appear to have been eager to seize the opportunity to disburden themselves of their wealth. To make this the more easy the prices of European articles were raised to exorbitant heights, and many a St. Helenian made a handsome fortune out of the gullibility of rich Indian nabobs. One result of this was to be seen in the number of handsome residences which went up every year in the town, while the number of dwellings in the country did not alter.

The occupants of these town houses required domestic servants, shopmen, porters, fishermen, hewers of wood and drawers of water, and thus more labour was withdrawn from the farms. Whenever slaves were to be sold, the rich townsman was able to outbid the countryman and the difficulties of the latter were made so great that many, who would have preferred to remain farmers, were induced to leave their farms and migrate to Jamestown and enter into trade.

In 1790 the average price of a good slave was £40; by 1800 it had risen from £60 to £70, and ten years later £120 to £150 was no uncommon price.

The practice begun by Brooke of encouraging soldiers who had served their contract with the Government and were of good character to become settlers was continued by Governor Patton. These men were paid to work for the landholders, and though the expense to the employer of a free white labourer was greater than the estimated annual cost of a slave, yet the difference was more than made up by the greater industry and energy of the European. The matter was well summed up by a contemporary writer in the words: "The labour of a free man, being prompted more by hope than by fear, is universally acknowledged to be more productive than the labour of a slave, whose principal incentive is the dread of punishment."

Although the encouragement given to discharged soldiers
to settle added very much to the numbers of the militia, and
although the landholders benefited by the extra labour, the
benefit did not come up to expectations. The same cause
which brought about the drain of the slaves from the country
to the town, brought the majority of the discharged soldiers
to Jamestown as well, for they found that employment there
under a shopkeeper, a publican or a brewer was easier, more
profitable, and far more congenial than working as a labourer
on a farm. The need of more labourers in the island became
acute and, the obvious source of supply having been cut off
when the law was passed prohibiting the importation of slaves,
Patton began to look about for some alternative, and soon
decided to recommend to the Court of Directors the importation of Chinese labourers and coolies. This was agreed to and
although the first consignment did not arrive until after
Colonel Patton's departure, he had the satisfaction of being the
originator of one of the greatest benefits the Island ever
derived.

Other improvements and reforms to the credit of Robert
Patton were the establishment of a police fund, and a weekly
sitting of the magistrates.

Owing to the great number of dogs in the island, many of
them ownerless and running wild, the dog tax of five shillings
was raised to ten, half of which went to the police fund.
All dogs were ordered to wear collars, and any dog caught
without a collar was to be destroyed. For distinction the
collars of dogs of Government servants carried brass labels,
others tin.

A register was to be kept at the police office of the number
and names of all blacks, whether free or slaves.

On the 20th August, 1802, five months after the arrival of
Patton, Lord Valentia called at St. Helena on his way from
England to India, and went on shore with Mr. Henry Salt, his

secretary and draughtsman. At the landing steps the distinguished visitor was welcomed by Captain Hudson, the Governor's A.D.C., who tendered Colonel Patton's apologies for not offering Lord Valentia a bed at his house on the grounds that his house was too small and his family too large. Accommodation, however, had been arranged for him at the house of Mr. Doveton.

Two days afterwards his Lordship, accompanied by Mr. Salt, set out to walk up to Plantation House in heavy rain. It was, and still is, most unusual to walk from Jamestown up the steep side of Ladder Hill and then along the road which continues to rise steadily until it reaches Plantation. Lord Valentia was a keen though amateur botanist and had he gone on horseback he would not have been able to collect specimens on the way. After a stiff climb of about an hour and a half they arrived "wet and weary" at the Governor's country house. It was still raining, but between the showers the Governor conducted his guests round his gardens, which Lord Valentia considered "interesting from the contrast which their verdure presents to the bleak, barren mountains, and from the mixture of plants of different climates that are assembled together . . . where the oak and the bamboo jostle each other".[1]

The following day they paid a visit to the botanical garden at Jamestown, but although the outing was evidently an enjoyable one, it was not rare plants which made it so.

The fair daughters of the Governor arrived this morning at the Castle drawn in a light carriage by oxen, the only animals adapted to ascend and descend Ladder Hill. They accompanied us to the botanic garden, which, although there is a botanist appointed by the India Company, has no pretensions to that title, as there has not been an attempt to collect even the indigenous plants of the island.

[1] *Voyages and Travels.* George, Viscount Valentia, 1809.

The government botanist was Mr. Porteous, who also kept a boarding-house which stood beside the garden and where a few years later two of the greatest men living were to lodge.

Another day Lord Valentia and Mr. Porteous went on a long botanizing expedition to Sandy Bay Ridge. Already the island was almost denuded of trees, so that the visitor was delighted to find growing in profusion on the upper slopes of the Ridges, gumwood and cabbage trees, numerous specimens of Dicksonia—or tree-fern—some growing to a height of fourteen feet, with leaves five feet long, as well as many other beautiful ferns.

His host, Mr. Doveton, was acting as Deputy-Governor during that official's absence from the island, and living in his official country residence, the old house at Longwood.

Lord Valentia admired the somewhat arid surroundings.

The scenery [he wrote in his journal] is more like England than anything I have seen in the island, and is much admired by the natives for a reason that had no weight with us; it is more level, and was once covered with gumwood trees, but avenues were opened in it, which gave the S.E. wind a free entrance, the consequence was its gradual destruction.

He was interested in agriculture as well as in botany. At the period of his visit hundreds of ships called each year at St. Helena and the farmers were reaping a rich harvest.

"In no part of the world," he wrote, "is farming a more profitable business than in St. Helena", and little wonder, with three crops of potatoes a year, and an acre producing on an average four hundred bushels, which the farmer sold at eight shillings a bushel to the ships.

Evidently in 1802 St. Helena still produced fruit in abundance, for the same traveller states that on every farm there were grown oranges, limes, lemons, figs, grapes, guavas, bananas, peaches, pomegranates, melons, water-melons and pumpkins. Of mangoes, coconuts, pine-apples and strawberries there were very few, and the last a luxury only to be found on the Governor's dinner table.

There was one solitary apple orchard, which yielded the lucky proprietor "not unfrequently five hundred pounds a year".

Lord Valentia's description bears out, as did that of most other visitors, the unreasonably high cost of almost every article of food grown in the island. With the exception of fresh beef which the Company ordered to be sold at fivepence a pound, everything was so dear that only the well-to-do could afford it. These high prices he accounted for by a ring or monopoly formed by the farmers to keep up prices. For example, a turkey cost two guineas, a goose, one guinea, a small duck, eight shillings, a fowl, half a crown to five shillings, potatoes cost eight shillings a bushel, while for one cabbage the charge was eighteen pence.

So powerful was the combine amongst the farmers, that rather than sell their produce at a lower figure than the one agreed amongst them they would leave fruit and vegetables to rot on the ground.

Even fish, which could be caught in unlimited quantities close to the shore, was "immoderately dear". It was little wonder then that most of the inhabitants were obliged to live on salt beef imported by the East India Company, and issued by them at an annual loss of something like £6,000 a year.

News from the outside world reached this isolated little settlement by various means. On the 23rd August, 1803, H.M.S. *Caroline* brought in a Dutch prize and also the news that war between England and France had been declared four months before.

There was great jubilation on the 9th of June the following

year, when the China fleet arrived in triumph homeward bound from Canton. It consisted of sixteen Indiamen and eleven country ships. Off Pulo Aor the fleet had fallen in with a powerful French squadron under Admiral Linois. By one of the boldest pieces of bluff ever conceived, the English Commodore, Sir Nathaniel Dance, signalled his fleet to sail towards the enemy and engage them, with the result that for two hours he enjoyed the extraordinary spectacle of a powerful squadron of ships of war flying before a number of merchantmen. At St. Helena they met a convoy of English ships of the line which escorted them home.

Many distinguished soldiers and civilians were wont to break their journey home and spend a few days at St. Helena. In 1805 Sir Arthur Wellesley, as he then was, arrived in the *Trident*, returning to England after his glorious victory at Assaye. Local tradition has it that he slept his first night on shore, in the tall white house which stands at the lower end of the left hand side of the main street of Jamestown, beside the public garden. If this is so it is a strange coincidence, for exactly ten years later another famous soldier, and Wellington's most dangerous opponent, was to spend his first night in St. Helena under the same roof.

Another famous man arrived in the same year as the future Duke of Wellington, but his claims to fame were of an opposite kind. He was a young man of twenty-four, who had been sent out by the Company in the humble capacity of "schoolmaster and acting botanist".[1] His name was William John Burchell. He remained at the island, teaching the children to read, write and add, and collecting his beloved plants for five years, when he sailed for the Cape, to explore and collect natural history specimens. His name does not occur often in the island records, but there is this entry in the book of consultations, dated the 8th July, 1808:

[1] Dictionary of National Biography.

Mr. Burchill directed to collect a bushel of the most brilliant coloured earths and some of the dung of the Sea Fowls on Egg Island to be sent to England.

According to a more recent authority,[1] young Burchell sailed as a midshipman in the East India Company's ship, *Northumberland*, but before leaving England there was drawn up a deed of partnership between him and William Balcombe of The Briars to trade as merchants and agents at St. Helena. In the log book of the *Northumberland* there is an entry stating that William J. Burchell was left invalided at St. Helena when the ship sailed from there in 1806. Mrs. McKay has been able to gather from several fresh sources considerable information about the botanist's activities while on the island. When not teaching in school or collecting plants, he made sketches, topographical and geological, as well as drawings of flowers, which can be seen at the Kew Herbarium. Many naturalists Dutch and British, used to break their journey home at St. Helena, and young Burchell missed no opportunity to meet and discuss matters of botanical interest with them. He was not interested only in botany, for he made many astronomical observations.

His favourite recreations were music—playing the flute, organ and piano—and dancing. Once he had the good fortune to meet two officers who played the flute and violin. The three musicians started at 10 o'clock in the morning and, stopping only for dinner, played continuously until ten at night, when the violinist broke down from exhaustion, and the two flautists continued playing till midnight. The following day being Sunday, for propriety's sake they refrained from playing till the afternoon, when they resumed and continued the performance until just before midnight.

[1] Mrs. H. M. McKay, "William John Burchell, Scientist." *South African Journal of Science.* Vol. XXXII, 1935.

It was three years after his departure that another distinguished botanist visited St. Helena, Dr. William Roxburgh, the late superintendent of the Company's Calcutta Botanic Garden.

He took a keen interest in the botany and horticulture of the island and recommended that seeds of Cinchona officinalis, from which the drug quinine is extracted, should be brought from South America, and planted, and when strong enough, be shipped to India.

Shortly after the capture of the Cape of Good Hope in 1805 by Sir David Baird and Sir Home Popham the latter sailed from Table Bay on his ill-fated expedition to Buenos Ayres. On May 5th, 1806, he arrived at St. Helena to beg for recruits, for his whole force consisted only of the seventy-first regiment, a detachment of Royal Artillery, some marines and a few extra seamen. With so meagre a force, the smallest contribution would have been very welcome. Home Popham well knew how useful the St. Helena volunteers had been in 1795 when General Sir James Craig attacked the Dutch at the Cape, and he had strong reasons for hoping that similar assistance would be forthcoming on this occasion. Governor Patton, with the recent example of Governor Brooke to go by, agreed, and formed a detachment from the Garrison Light Infantry and Artillery amounting to two hundred and eighty-two men, and placed them under the orders of Popham. Although the expedition failed and met with ignominious defeat, the St. Helena brigade fought bravely and steadily.

Nothing succeeds like success. Governor Brooke had taken a risk and it had turned out well. His reward was public praise and diamond-hilted swords. Governor Patton had done the same, had taken the risk but had lost. No Royal letter of thanks, no swords of honour for him, only a severe reprimand from his masters at London. In vain did the Governor answer their censure by quoting their own secret orders to him: "We hereby direct you to afford every aid in your power consistently with due protection and security of your own Island to H.M. Land and Naval forces under the command of Major-General Sir David Baird and Sir Home Popham *in any operation in which you may be required by them to assist.*" The Court of Directors in their letter of reproof to the Governor did not mince their words nor spare his feelings. It is a long document, containing such expressions as: "rash and illadvised measure and deserving of our most serious reprehension"—"want of energy in every department and lax discipline of the garrison call for our serious consideration of the state of your Island"—"make such alterations in the Government as appears to us to be required"—"we shall direct our attention to the whole of an establishment which we are of opinion requires radical amendment."

Thus it was peculiarly unfortunate for Patton, since the discipline of his garrison had been called into question, that shortly after receiving this rap on the knuckles the brig, *Jolly Tar*, just purchased by the Company for the island's use, and scarcely finished being fitted out, should have been stolen from under the very walls of the Castle on the night of October 11th by some soldiers of the garrison, and carried off. The whole story came out afterwards when Mr. Lees, an officer on board the *Jolly Tar*, arrived back at St. Helena. His account in his own words ran as follows:

On 11 Oct. Mr. Sweete, Chief Officer in command, myself, and eight others were on board the *Jolly Tar*. At 8 p.m. the watch set as usual. At about 11 o'clock Wood the seaman on the watch called out that a boat was alongside. I immediately jumped up and before I got to the gangway I was surrounded by numbers of men with bayonets. Some rushed down the cabin and some down forward to secure the seamen. I was by this time wounded in three different places—head, left arm and neck. Mr. Sweete was most cruelly massacred and was thrown overboard. The cables were cut. Next morning we were out of sight of the Island. The pirates, seventeen in number, were almost all soldiers of the garrison except three Spanish officers who I had seen on shore as I supposed on their Parole of Honour. Eleven days after we fell in with a Portuguese brig and we were put on board and carried to Rio Janeiro. The soldiers were ten of them foreigners enlisted in and belonging to the Garrison. The three officers were Spanish or French passengers from the Cape and were regarded as on parole.

Poor Governor Patton. Everything had gone so happily and so successfully until that unfortunate day when he was persuaded by Sir Home Popham to make a contribution towards his ill-fated expedition to Buenos Ayres.

The next unhappy event was a catastrophe, but one in no kind of way attributable to the Governor.

Early in 1807 a slave ship put in at the Cape of Good Hope, and infected that colony with measles. From Table Bay she sailed with the home-coming East India fleet and in due time arrived at Jamestown. No warning of the impending danger reached the Government until the fleet had anchored, although Captain Leigh of the *Georgiana*, who knew all about the epidemic which was raging at the Cape when he left there, arrived at St. Helena several days before the fleet. Precautions were at once taken to prevent the infection from being brought on shore, but all too late, for it had already been conveyed there in some clothes sent to the wash. This circumstance was not generally known, so that, although in the course of the next few days symptoms of the disease appeared on one or two persons belonging to the fleet, these were promptly sent back to their ships, and the inhabitants were not perturbed.

It was not until some three weeks had passed, and after the fleet had sailed, that the island doctors reported the occurrence of measles in two families.

The alarm at first was not so great as might have been expected, when it is remembered that the disease had never been known in the island before, and that the greater part of the inhabitants and most of the Company's servants, civil and military, were born there, and therefore were totally un-immune. At first the epidemic was of manageable dimensions, and the sick could be nursed and looked after by their friends and relations, but soon it spread, so that whole families, parents, children and servants, were in many cases suffering at the same time from measles in its most virulent form, and there was nobody to tend or feed them. In a short while there was but one subaltern officer fit for duty, and no business was transacted at the public or government offices, the shops were shut and the only workmen employed were carpenters making coffins, and only soldiers could be found to carry the dead to their graves.

Within two months of the outbreak the deaths amounted to fifty-eight whites and one hundred and two blacks, and many more died shortly afterwards.

For a long while before this epidemic of measles the inhabitants had been under the happy belief that some quality in the atmosphere of St. Helena prevented infectious diseases, even smallpox, and they had always refused to entertain the idea of being vaccinated. But the appalling example they had just witnessed made them alter their opinions, for it had given them a shrewd notion of what would happen should smallpox be brought to the island. So when it was heard that vaccine matter had been introduced at the Cape of Good Hope, large numbers of the islanders desired to be inoculated.

To make this possible Governor Patton had six healthy boys selected from the garrison drummers and sent them to the

Cape. There they remained until an opportunity occurred for their return, when two of them were inoculated. From these the infection was communicated, on the passage back, to the others, in succession, and the vaccine was thus brought to St. Helena.

For some time past the Governor's health had been far from good. He had been overworked and worried and of late an old disorder, which he had contracted in India, reappeared, so that in July, 1807, he resigned and embarked for England, and Lieutenant-Colonel Lane, the Lieutenant-Governor, succeeded provisionally to the chair for twelve months.

He was superseded on the 4th July, 1808, by the arrival of Governor Beatson, and Lieutenant-Governor Broughton, who with Mr. W. W. Doveton and Mr. Robert Leech formed the new Government.

Before passing on to recount the story of St. Helena under the governorship of Colonel Beatson, there are one or two incidents relating to Patton which deserve to be recorded.

Extract from Governor Patton's letter, dated "Fareham, Hants, 7th May 1810," to his daughter Maria, wife of Capt. Walker of the 8th or The King's Royal Irish Light Dragoons, stationed in Calcutta.

Robert Patton was always very concerned with the lack of any moral encouragement to the slaves. It had always been customary severely to punish a slave for the slightest wrong-doing, but until this enlightened Governor came to the island it had never occurred to anyone, slave-owner or Government official, to reward or encourage virtue in a slave.

It was Patton who hit upon the novel conceit of rewards or medals as an inducement to good behaviour. Medals so awarded were inscribed, "Honest Faithful Diligent Sober", and if a slave should win one of these coveted prizes in three successive years, he did not, as might have been expected, receive his freedom but only "have his merits completely established". Only one specimen of these medals exists in the island to-day, and is probably the only one in existence in the world. The proud possessor is Mr. Loo Bowers, of Sandy Bay, who is, I believe, a direct descendant of the original slave who received it at the hands of Robert Patton.

The inscription on this unique medal is not the only one in St. Helena to remind us of this amiable Governor or his family. One of the window-panes of the door of Plantation House bears the name of his daughter, scratched with a diamond, "Jenny Patton". She married John Paterson, captain of the ship *Montrose*, and it is pleasant to reflect that the name of the bride is still preserved on the house she left in 1807. She and her sister are also commemorated by the "Sisters' Walk", a wide shady path which their father had cut out of the steep hill side above the Castle garden in Jamestown.

THE mentality of the army officer appears to have changed in the last hundred years. In the late eighteenth and early nineteenth century the military mind seems to have been broader than it is to-day. Perhaps this may be due to specialization, and the twentieth-century army officer is so engrossed in becoming efficient in his own particular branch of his profession that he has no time, or encouragement, to take much interest in other branches or in other pursuits. Whatever the cause, there is no doubt that the officers of the army one hundred and more years ago appear to have been able to turn their hands to many jobs and to have had many interests outside the routine of their profession. Such a one was the new Governor of St. Helena, Colonel Alexander Beatson. His military career began as an ensign in the Madras infantry in 1776. He did well and was appointed to serve as an engineer officer in the war with Hyder Ali, although he appears never to have belonged to the engineers. After that he served in the Guides under Lord Cornwallis, and eight years after that, as a field-officer, was surveyor-general with the army under General Harris which captured Seringapatam in 1799. Beatson was a very efficient soldier, but at heart an agriculturist and an exceedingly able one. Perhaps it was his love of farming and agriculture which prompted the Court of Directors to appoint him to govern St. Helena, and if so, it proved a very wise decision on their part.

Within four days of his arrival in July, 1808, the new

Governor was giving orders which had a bearing on agriculture. He directed Mr. Burchell to collect some dung or
guano of the sea-fowl on Egg Island to be tested for its use as
manure, and also to send to England a bushel of the most
brilliant coloured earths from Sandy Bay to find out if they
would not be useful for the manufacture of pigments for
artists. Specimens of aloe fibre were also despatched to
London for the report of experts as to whether the culture of
aloe would be likely to be profitable. With the fibre went
eighteen casks of kelp and ten of lichens. The agricultural
colonel was in his element. He next ordered to be built on
the west side of the Parade a large granary at a cost of £1,500
—on the site of a cluster of miserable hovels. The burial
ground at Jamestown was found to be in a disgraceful state
"having more the appearance of a common for Dogs than a
burial place for deceased Christians"—words which well
describe some of the shamefully neglected burial grounds at
Jamestown to-day. The new Governor had the graveyard put
into proper order, and it is hoped that the same will soon be
done again by the present Government.

In 1809 Lieutenant W. Innes Pocock, R.N., visited St.
Helena and made various jottings about the island, its inhabitants and customs. He also painted some pictures of the
island; the principal one, an aquatint of St. Helena and Jamestown from the Road is, in the opinion of many, by far and
away the best and most accurate of all the innumerable
drawings and paintings made of the island from this point
of view.

When St. Helena was chosen by the British Government as
the best place to imprison Bonaparte, the London publishers
were ready and eager to buy up any scrap of first-hand description of this little-known island, with, if possible, "Views", and
print them to sell to an eager public. Almost all of the pictures of St. Helena were painted by amateurs, and most of

them are contemptible as works of art. Although Lieutenant Pocock was an amateur he inherited artistic talent from his father, Nicholas Pocock, the well-known marine painter, an inheritance shared by his brother Isaac, who became a successful painter before he turned dramatist.

He gives a very good description of the island, and mentions amongst other buildings at Jamestown, the Freemasons' Lodge and a Theatre. Of the smaller residences in the town he only says that "the inferior habitations are occupied by people who subsist principally by the fleets, and mostly keep wine shops for the accommodation of soldiers and sailors.

"The houses are white-washed, which though extremely offensive to the eyes from its very powerful reflection, gives the town a cleanly appearance."

He describes his tour over the island on foot, for though "horses may be hired, it is impossible to go on horseback out of the direct road and gain the summit of the mountain in the centre of the island, which was the principal motive for undertaking the walk."

Governor Beatson's desire to improve the cultivation of the island was at first held up by the shortage of labour, but in May, 1810, there arrived from Canton the first consignment of Chinese labourers, whose services were found so useful that one hundred and fifty more were applied for. At first the Governor found it very difficult to persuade the farmers that any other methods than those in use might produce better results, for farmers all the world over are the most conservative of beings, and nothing will alter their views unless they see with their own eyes the advantage of deviating from the beaten path. With this object in mind he established a big Company's farm at Longwood and had several fields of ten to twenty acres enclosed and broken up. Fine crops of oats and barley soon made their appearance, and by using the plough he was able to demonstrate that potatoes grew far better than under the older method of pickaxe and spade. To work this farm six skilled farm hands were specially chosen and sent out from England.

The arrival in July, 1811, of the second detachment of coolies enabled the government to spare labourers to work for the farmers, and such was the result that five months after, the names of thirteen planters were mentioned in a proclamation as "amongst those whose exertions had been conspicuous in producing a beneficial change by means of labour they could not before obtain".

The Company's ploughs, ploughmen and teams were willingly lent by the Government to any farmers who wished to employ them, until they were able to provide themselves with ploughs and teams and had trained their slaves as ploughmen.

The terms on which the Chinese were engaged were: a shilling a day for labourers, and one shilling and sixpence for mechanics, besides rations amounting in value to nearly another shilling, their contract with the Company being for three years. Subsequently the engagement was extended to five years, but the numbers which returned to China were more than made up for by the Chinese sailors who had gone to England and who, on returning in vessels which touched at St. Helena, volunteered to remain there as labourers.

The Chinese colony at one time amounted to nearly six hundred and fifty, but afterwards it was reduced to some four hundred.

In conjunction with Colonel Beatson's efforts to promote agriculture and make St. Helena self-supporting in foodstuffs and not dependent on the food imported by the Company and sold to the inhabitants at one-third of their cost price, the Board of Directors ordered the prices of salt beef, flour, biscuits, etc., to be raised. This rise in prices was to apply to the employees of the Company as well as to others, and led to much dissatisfaction, particularly among these employees who claimed a right to buy below cost price as part of their contract with the Company.

What caused far greater discontent and eventually led to very serious trouble was the abolition of the use of spirituous liquor for the garrison. When Beatson arrived at the island and for many years before, the curse of St. Helena had been rum-punch. Strong drink was cheap, and drunkenness was rife amongst the population, and particularly amongst the soldiers, a large percentage of whom were constantly in hospital on this account. Corneille had attempted to curtail the sale of arrack to the soldiers, and a mutiny followed. Since then the soldiers had enjoyed unrestricted indulgence in strong drink, but Governor Beatson determined, at whatever cost, to bring this pernicious state of things to an end. It was not as if there were no alternatives to spirit drinking, for a brewery had been established on the island, and good cheap wines were imported from the Cape of Good Hope. At Beatson's recommendation, the Court of Directors sent an order to Bengal to discontinue any further consignment of rum to St. Helena, rations of Cape wine were issued to the troops at the rate of sixpence per pint and they could buy as much wholesome beer as they wished at sevenpence a quart. The licence to the publicans for retailing spirits was withdrawn and they were encouraged to form themselves into another brewery company by a promise that they should be allowed to import malt and hops in the Company's ships freight free, for a period of two years.

At the time when the retail spirit houses were abolished the garrison numbered 1,250 men, of whom 132 were sick in hospital. Four months afterwards there were only 48 soldiers in hospital. The higher-priced spirits of Europe and the West Indies were only allowed to be imported in limited quantities and then only on paying a duty of twelve shillings per gallon, while the importation of Indian spirits, on account of its cheapness, was absolutely prohibited.

Between the years 1800 and 1808, when Beatson arrived, the net cost of St. Helena to the Company had risen from the sum of £69,000 to £157,300 per annum. The measures of retrenchment introduced in 1808 effected a reduction in expenses from £157,300 per annum to £104,800 in 1812, thus producing a saving to the East India Company of £52,400 odd a year. Naturally these economies, and particularly the withdrawal of the privilege of buying cheap from the Company's store, caused considerable dissatisfaction and from time to time the Governor received anonymous letters, either to warn him that a mutiny was impending or else to threaten him with personal injury if the privileges were not given back. This had been going on for several months when there occurred an unforeseen shortage of the stock of flour, as well as a total want of rice in the public stores. Such shortages were by no means unknown in the small isolated island which depended on stores being sent out in sailing ships, and on former and similar occasions the shortage of flour and bread had been made good by extra rations of potatoes, of which, thanks to the Governor, there was now a plentiful supply, but which the soldiers refused to accept.

The first signs of serious discontent appeared on Sunday morning, the 22nd of December, 1811, when the Governor was handed an anonymous letter which during the night had been slipped under Mr. Doveton's door. It ran:

James's Fort. December 22nd, 1811.
Gentlemen of the Council,
    His it still your intension to percevere in your oppression and tyranney to wards the troops in this garrison, has hitherto you have done; if so, you can expect nothing but an open rebellion.

I am hereby authorized, by the troops of this island, to inform this Council, if they do not immeadatly soply this garrison with liquor and provisions, in the same manner has Governor Brooks did (which regulations you have violated) you shall be made answerable for what may follow, except you make your escape good from this settlement.

It is in your power to prevent the impending vengeance which now hangs over your head's, and save the lives of many poor souls, which will inevitable fall a sacrifice.

This seditious paper was obviously written in a feigned hand, and the spelling and style were evidently intended to conceal the author's identity.

Simultaneously with the reception of this letter, the Governor was informed by the Town Major, C. R. G. Hodson, that he had it on reliable authority that the regiment of infantry was ready to mutiny and planned to seize him and send him away in the *Camperdown*, a cutter belonging to the Company, some of whose crew, it appeared later, were in the conspiracy. The Governor did not lose a moment in preparing for the worst. First of all he ordered the *Camperdown* to sail immediately, and the strong forts at Ladder Hill and High Knoll to be reinforced. He then made arrangements for defending Plantation House, his official country residence, where he intended to defend himself to the last. It was also settled that upon the smallest appearance of disorder the officer at Ladder Hill should fire the general alarm, which would assemble the volunteers or island militia at their rendezvous close by Plantation House. After issuing his orders, the Governor left the Castle at four o'clock in the afternoon, but instead of returning to Plantation House by the Governor's path, or "side-track" by which he usually went, he decided to go up through the town itself so as to let it be seen by the mutineers that he was not afraid of them, and particularly because of two threatening messages, one written on the Church: "A hot dinner and a bloody supper", alluding to the Christmas festival dinner, and another on the Castle gate: "This house let on Christmas day", alluding to his leaving the island by being sent off in the *Camperdown*. When his horses were brought to the Castle gate, he mounted, passed slowly in front of the main guard, who were supposed to be in the intended mutiny, and then rode through the town, stopping occasionally to converse with various friends and acquaintances. About five o'clock he reached Plantation House and sent for the head overseer and asked him some questions regarding the character and dispositions of the artillery and infantrymen stationed there as a working party. Learning that they all were men who could be thoroughly relied upon, he placed Lieutenant David Pritchard in charge of them with orders to serve out muskets and ammunition. The thirty-two men who formed this guard then took up their stations at various places inside the house to await developments.

It was learned later that the mutiny was not planned to break out until the morning of the 25th. It had been settled by the mutineers that when the troops paraded for relieving the guards, the whole regiment, joined by the main guard on duty, should seize their officers, and then march to Plantation House and seize the Governor. Unfortunately for the plotters the measures taken by the Governor caused them to alter their plans, and they commenced operations within five hours of his leaving the Castle. The first news to reach Plantation House came at 7.30 the same evening, when a report was brought in that the mutineers were marching towards Longwood, to gain possession of some field-guns and ammunition. On hearing this the Governor sent a runner to warn Colonel Broughton, the Lieutenant-Governor, who resided at Longwood House, instructing him to oppose the mutineers with some of his field guns. Colonel Broughton at once placed his guns in position, manned by the guard at Longwood; but while the guns were being loaded the mutineers appeared, rushed up and surrounded him and his party and took them prisoner. Before the pre-arranged general alarm was fired, some of the St. Helena volunteer riflemen and artillery had already arrived at Plantation House, which by midnight was garrisoned by one hundred and thirty men. On the ground floor every window and door was guarded by three or four armed men and parties of riflemen lay behind the parapet on the roof. Mrs. Beatson and her children were placed for security in one of the upper rooms.

While these preparations were being taken, parties of loyal artillery and infantry were marching up from Jamestown, led by Major Kinnaird. At midnight these reinforcements passed by Plantation House and took up a commanding position, with field guns, on the roads along which the mutineers would have to march in coming from Longwood. At about one o'clock in the morning two lights and a number of men were reported moving slowly along the side of the hill, two miles east of Plantation House. Major Doveton, Commandant of the Volunteers, immediately despatched two active men of his corps, Bagley and Kennedy, to gain intelligence, but very soon afterwards a black messenger brought news that Colonel Broughton and his party had been taken prisoner. At ten o'clock that night two hundred and fifty men had broken out of the barracks at Jamestown, in spite of the efforts of their officers to restrain them, and marched down the street to the Castle, where they were joined by the main guard. They then forced their way into the armoury and after helping themselves to ammunition, marched in a disorderly manner along the road towards Longwood. Their numbers, though, quickly dwindled as the march proceeded, for many of the soldiers had been intimidated into joining the mutineers and took the first opportunity of slipping away in the darkness, so that by the time the mutineers gained the heights near the Alarm House they numbered only about one hundred and fifty. They had not gone far when they were overtaken by Major Wright, who had followed them on horseback. He rode in amongst them and endeavoured to bring them to a sense of their duty. At first he seemed to be producing some effect, when his voice was suddenly drowned by a cry of "don't listen to him"— "come on" and similar expressions, and an attempt was made to seize hold of him, but he escaped, and with him went some of the stragglers in the rear, whom he led across country to Plantation House. The mutineers, as has already been stated, continued their march to Longwood, where they captured Colonel Broughton and his party.

The rebels informed the Lieutenant-Governor "they did not mean to do him or any other person the smallest injury; all they wanted was the Governor's person, whom they would take and send on board the *Camperdown*" and that he, Colonel Broughton, should be their Governor and go along with them to Plantation House. During this time, Mr. Hall, the conductor of artillery, had contrived to have all the guns spiked except one three-pounder, with which they marched along the road towards Plantation House, placing Colonel Broughton in their centre under the custody of one of the ringleaders.

The loyal militia had been posted with field-guns to defend the road on the Longwood side of Plantation House, and all the passes on the hills were also occupied. The Governor, when he learned from the black messenger that Colonel Broughton and his party were prisoners, was much distressed for his friends. In his report he wrote:

This information gave me at first some uneasiness, on account of the danger to which my friend and colleague would be exposed in the intended attack upon the mutinous troops; but there was no alternative, for however much I value the life of Colonel Broughton, I could not permit considerations of a private nature to interfere with my public duties, nor to deter me from carrying into execution the plans I had formed, which were imperiously necessary for the restoring military subordination and the peace and order of this settlement. At the same time, I considered it proper to make an attempt to rescue his person from impending danger. I therefore wrote a pencil note to Captain Sampson, directing him to advance with thirty chosen men; and with these it was intended to form an ambuscade on the left flank of the mutinous column, and to commence an attack by giving them our fire in such a manner as to avoid Colonel Broughton (who might be distinctly seen by the two lights which the mutineers had imprudently with them), and immediately after to rush upon them with the bayonet. . . .

I had just given these orders, when Major Wright arrived, and informed me that the mutineers had halted within fifty or sixty yards of Major Kinnaird's post, and had sent forward to offer the conditions on which they would surrender.

The negotiations were intentionally protracted until daylight on the 24th, by which time the rebels were able to see the superior force opposed to them so that they unconditionally surrendered, and the attempt to rescue Colonel Broughton became unnecessary.

Of the original two hundred and fifty men who sallied out the previous night from Jamestown but seventy-five remained next morning. The prisoners were put in close confinement at High Knoll fort and the following day, December 25, nine of the ringleaders were tried before a court martial and all of them sentenced to death, and six of the most guilty hanged forthwith on a temporary gallows at High Knoll. On the 26th three more mutineers were court-martialled and convicted.

The awful examples, however, which had already been made, had subdued the spirit of mutiny, and only one more execution was deemed necessary. This was conducted with great solemnity. The whole of the garrison were drawn up on the lower parade in town, the prisoner led along the front, the dead march was played, and immediately after the culprit was hanged. The Town-Major read to the troops an impressive lesson, in the form of a general order, to which the parole *peace* was prefixed.

So ended what might easily have become a terrible tragedy but for the firm handling of the situation by Governor Beatson. It is interesting to read in the Governor's official report on the mutiny:

It is deserving of notice that only *one* sergeant was concerned in the mutiny, and that on this occasion, as well as the alarming one of a similar nature, that occurred in 1783, the blacks to a man, were steady on the side of loyalty.

Incidentally, this sergeant, Lascelles, was sentenced by the court martial to five hundred lashes.

Let us now enquire once more into some of the less important matters which are recorded on the island affairs. It is some while since any of the doings or sayings of the island's clergymen were recorded. The old and bad type of chaplain appears to have died out and we may well sympathise with Parson Jones, over the matter he complained of to the Council.

April 10, 1812. Rev. Mr. Jones complained of a public insult to him at the Easter Vestry where he was elected

"Inspector of the Common Sheep and Goats". Suggests as Inspector that the sheep be taken to their respective owners' farms, and the goats be destroyed, which would prevent his appointment from interfering with more important duties.

Then the Rev. Mr. Jones got in a shrewd thrust with: "Otherwise he had already a very wild herd of goats under his charge, viz.: those whose conduct is here reprobated."

Early in the year 1813 the frigate *Nisus* dropped anchor in the Road. The surgeon on board of her was Lieutenant, afterwards Sir James, Prior, the author of several works, the chief being biographies of Burke and Goldsmith. He published as well, in 1819, a *Voyage along the Eastern Coast of Africa*, etc., which included a description of St. Helena in 1813. A few extracts are not without interest, as they give a vivid and sometimes amusing picture of life at St. Helena at this period.

February 10. At sea.

It is impossible to approach and see this singular island, for the first time, without wondering how the deuce it got there. [The future biographer was then aged about twenty-three.] A vast mass of rock, rising abruptly from nearly the centre of the great Atlantic ocean, jagged and irregular, cut and slashed as it were into pieces by the great hatchet of nature—too large to be passed without examination, and too small, and unfruitful, and badly situated, to be of much use;—seems like a great sign-post of providence that would say of its divine Architect, "My hand has been here."

It is in truth an object that creates surprise, without much satisfaction, its whole exterior being forbidding, and were it not so well known, nobody would suspect it contained inhabitants. . . .

But the charm of novelty erased this impression; we compared it to a good-natured man with a repelling countenance, whose heart, though kind, was veiled under a rough exterior.

The approach to the anchorage leads round Sugar-loaf Point; here ships send their boats on shore to declare their names, destination and country. Batteries now appear in every direction; guns, gates, embrasures, and soldiers continually meet the eye; so that instead of being, as we might suppose, the abode of peace and seclusion, it looks like a depot for the instruments of War.

The lieutenant's opinion of St. Helena was higher when Jamestown came in sight, though he cautiously observed that possibly a sky "serene and cloudless, a tropical sun, moderated by the south-east trade wind, made the prospect better than nature perhaps intended it".

The first view of the town [he went on to admit] is not unpleasing. A line of works, ornamented with tall trees, skirt the beach. Toward the right extremity of this is the landing place . . . through a gate which is closed every night, we entered the town. It is formed by one principal street, of some length, extending directly up the valley, with here and there intersections, tolerably broad, paved, clean and resembling an English village, though more neat and compact. The houses are small and white-washed; they consist principally of shops and lodging-houses, the former retailing the wares of India and Europe at an advanced price, the latter giving a temporary home to the passenger in the India fleets. It also contains a church, a tavern, barracks, and (what would be better in any other situation) a burying-ground. Several batteries and posts surround it on all sides.

It has to be confessed that James Prior bears witness, as did so many other travellers, to the exorbitant prices the St. Helenians charged for what few goods they had to sell.

The India fleets have for many years invariably touched here returning from India, to procure refreshments; but these are so very inconsiderable, considering the expences of the establishment, as to be scarcely worth mentioning. Treading the fields and streets indeed, seeing a new people, wandering over rocks, and imbibing the odours of the fresh earth, all are refreshments to the human frame, jaded by confinement on ship-board during the passage from India; but these are nearly all; for good living is out of the question. The man who should peradventure desire the luxury of a fresh meal, must first reflect on the extravagance he is going to commit; he ought to be made up of pagodas, or have his trunks groaning under the weight of rupees; otherwise he should not land here.

He dare not taste a mutton chop, if indeed such a thing can be had, under a guinea, or refresh his longing and thirsty palate with a bottle of good English porter, under a sum nearly a groat.

Killing a sheep is an event of almost as much consequence in the island, as Bonaparte annihilating an Austrian or Prussian army in Europe; and the slaughter of a bullock nearly equal to the subjection of a kingdom.

Very few of either are to be had. Goats, hogs, and poultry, are more plentiful, but mostly kept by the inhabitants for their own use, seldom or never coming within reach of a poor sailor's pocket, and not always of his officer's.

In fact it is a miserable place; the necessaries of life are scarcely to be procured, and then only at an exorbitant rate.

The refreshments, therefore, afforded to seamen, for

which purpose the island is said to be retained, consist of a few potatoes, cabbages, garden-roots, and the wild water-cresses picked up in the ravines.

The main defects arise as well from nature as the impolitic system and prejudices of the people. According to Colonel Beatson, the present Governor, who has published some pamphlets, and otherwise taken much trouble to point out their true interests, the great error is the neglect of agriculture.

There are no farmers in the island by profession. The majority of the people, being shop-keepers, live in town; and the land being sub-divided between them into small tracts, they occasionally resort thither for amusement, having neither time nor inclination to attend the soil.

But in order to be of some use, these districts have been stocked with goats, which feed and take care of themselves, without trouble to the owners; hence the origin in St. Helena phraseology, of "a goat range", which is advertised for sale, with as much ceremony as a large estate in England.

These creatures wandering at pleasure, destroy not only crops, but young fences, shrubs, plantations of trees, and vegetation of every description, an evil that is little decreased by the infliction of slight penalties. They give no trouble in herding or feeding, and, answering a local convenience, are continued; yet the number of cattle on the whole, is not greater now that it was forty years ago, though the population has more than doubled.

Lieutenant Prior, after making a very close inspection of the agricultural problems of the island and "having seen all the 'live lions' of the town, set off with a friend, mounted on two slow but sure-footed ponies, to view those of the country."

He and his friend climbed up the steep side of Ladder Hill, where a strong battery stood, and then continued past High

Knoll "the worst part of the island" but all of a sudden "a charming valley appeared to the left, decked with gardens and pretty white cottages, the outlines skirted by eminences, a small stream murmuring near the centre and a few sheep browzing."

"The contrast," he admits, "was striking, and only required the aid of a pretty shepherdess, with her crook, to be complete."

After riding for a couple of hours, the two travellers ventured to peep over a precipice, and this is what they saw.

"The eye, pained by looking down, recoils from the awful depth and repulsive aspect, while the hollow roar of the surge against the base, and the shrill cries of the sea-birds striking the ear, seem to suit the churlish sternness and inhospitality of the shores." He noted several possible landing places on the coast "practicable to men who do not care for wet feet; though certainly not suited to the accommodation of a lady stepping out of a boat in a ballroom dress".

The population of the island, if we may credit Prior—and he seems to be an accurate recorder—consisted in January, 1813, of about 3,500 persons, of whom 700 were white, 975 soldiers, 1,400 slaves and the remaining 450 free people of colour.

The garrison, which according to the establishment, should have been 1,400 men, consisted of the St. Helena Regiment and a corps of artillery, all Europeans and paid by the East India Company. But the whole male population were expected to hold themselves in readiness to bear arms in an emergency.

The accusations made against the St. Helenians of their being rapacious is referred to, and explained if not excused, by the anonymous author[1] of a little book published in 1805, *A Description of the Island of St. Helena*.

[1] Francis Duncan, M.D.

It is customary for the passengers of the homeward-bound Indiamen, during their stay here, to live at the houses of the inhabitants. . . . All the inhabitants are ready to accommodate them with board and lodging; the terms of which are generally complained of as being extravagantly high. But it should be remembered, that most articles of provision here are obtained with difficulty; that the inhabitants have but few opportunities of disposing of what little superfluous stock they are possessed of, or of adding to their means of replacing it; and that those whom they entertain can in general afford to pay well for their accommodation.

It seems, therefore, but reasonable, that wealthy strangers, who are treated with the best fare which the place affords, and certainly with much kindness and attention, should contribute adequately to the comfort of their hosts, and the benefit of the settlement. . . .

The arrival of the homeward-bound Indiamen is the greatest event of the year. It fills the whole settlement with alacrity and joy. They quit their gardens, flock to James Town, open their houses for the accommodation of the passengers, and entertain them with plays, dances and concerts.

These gay assemblies are enlivened by the presence of many agreeable and handsome young ladies, natives of the place, who, amid the general festivity, seem to feel a peculiar interest in what is going forward; probably not without some throbbing expectations of being taken from a scene, where they are weary with constantly contemplating the same objects.

Well can we believe, with the author, that "the appearance of so much loveliness and beauty, cast away in a lonesome situation like this, has sometimes raised stronger emotions than those of mere sympathy, in the bosoms of their guests; and the native women of St. Helena have adorned domestic life, and graced the politest circles in India."

After discoursing on the politeness, gentleness and simplicity of the islanders, the author drops these words of warning: "But, however simple they are in some of their notions respecting other countries, they are perfectly well acquainted with their own affairs; and he, who, in dealing with them, expects to find the simplicity of Shepherds and Savages, will be disappointed. In the disposal of the few articles, which their scanty means permits them to sell or barter, they are sufficiently skilful."

The governorship of Alexander Beatson was now drawing to a close, and until he left St. Helena he spent his time and his undoubted talents in the further encouragement of agriculture and in improving the condition of the farmers and the land-owners. Greatly daring, he once again tackled that centuries-old problem of St. Helena, that of the goats. In spite of all the previous laws, protests, advice, threats and rewards, these scourges of green crops, these horned and four-legged locusts, still roamed at large and at will, devouring seedlings, crops and fodder, doing little good and an infinite amount of mischief, and yet the goats remained, as they do still, the curse of the island. If it is permitted to coin a proverb for St. Helena let it be "scratch a goat and you raise a St. Helenian"!

Colonel Beatson, a prolific writer of tracts, wrote an exhaustive treatise on the whole question of the St. Helena goats, from the beginning when the misguided Portuguese explorers set goats at liberty on the new-found island up to the year 1810. This brochure is of great interest historically, and, if only they will read and study it, should be of great value to those who govern St. Helena to-day.

One last thing must be mentioned before we bid farewell to

this most excellent man and Governor. It was not until 1806 that a small printing press was first imported to St. Helena by a few private residents and set up as *The St. Helena Press* under the management of Mr. Saul Solomon. The following year the press was taken over by the Company. With the appointment of Alexander Beatson as Governor in 1808 it is needless to say that the publishing trade began to boom, for he saw in the printing press a heaven-sent medium for disseminating his views on agriculture, and in the *St. Helena Monthly Register*, which began in 1809, he expounded his plans and explained his experiments for the improvement of local agriculture and horticulture, with, as the late Lord Rosebery was to remark a hundred years later, "a minuteness which could scarcely be justified in the case of the Garden of Eden". He published papers on his pet subjects without stint, about goats, land tenure and on a score of other agricultural subjects. Full particulars of this press and of others which followed it are given in Appendix IV, by the kind permission of Mr. G. C. Kitching, the present Secretary of St. Helena. A selection of the more valuable of these articles was published by Beatson under the title "Tracts relative to the Island of St. Helena" with illustrations, at London in 1816.

In September, 1813, Alexander Beatson handed over the governorship to Colonel Mark Wilks and he left for England, to live happily and usefully for another twenty years, as an English country gentleman and farmer, "devoting much attention to experiments in agriculture at Knole Farm near Tunbridge Wells and Henley in Essex". Only one work written by him after his retirement from St. Helena survives; it is a learned little treatise entitled, "A New System of Cultivation without Lime or Dung, or Summer Fallowing, as practised at Knole Farm, Sussex."

His body now lies in the churchyard at Frant in Sussex.

Colonel Mark Wilks arrived at Jamestown on the 22nd

June, 1813, and on the same day Colonel J. Skelton landed, who succeeded Broughton as Lieutenant-Governor.

A native of the Isle of Man, Mark Wilks had had a distinguished career in the East India Company's army in Madras. As it was the wish of the Court of Directors that Beatson should remain Governor until he left the island, Wilks was not sworn in until the 21st August. He had originally been intended for the ministry and so had received a classical education. He was the author of a book of considerable merit, *Historical Sketches of the South of India in an attempt to trace the History of Mysore*, and it was characteristic of this literary governor that one of his first acts was to establish a public library in St. Helena, under his special patronage. Like his predecessor, Wilks was interested in agriculture, which he improved in the colony by introducing better methods of cultivation and by inducing the Company to alter the system of land tenure.

His efforts to economize labour by substituting the plough for the spade, and the more general use of carts and teams in place of slave porters were also successful. In a short while he had enclosed and broken up thirty additional acres at Longwood and formed a plantation of thirty-six acres within a new fence, besides carrying out repairs and improvements of barracks, guardrooms, government houses, hospital and other buildings, and making reservoirs, at the cost of some thirteen thousand pounds.

While all this work was being done and the little colony was living its quiet, ordered and unexciting life, a ship arrived from England on the 15th September, 1815, bringing the glorious news of the Duke of Wellington's decisive victory over Bonaparte, and how two hundred and fourteen pieces of cannon and vast numbers of prisoners had been captured, though the Corsican himself had escaped. A Royal Salute was fired immediately in honour of the great occasion, and a festival was held for the Garrison with an extra allowance of wine for every soldier. All prisoners, both civil and military, were ordered to be released, with the exception of one awaiting his trial for burglary.

Then once more the island went to sleep, to remain in a happy state of somnolence until that never-to-be-forgotten 11th of October, 1815.

On that day His Majesty's Sloop-of-War, *Icarus*, arrived with the astounding piece of news that the greatest man in the world was on his way and would reach Jamestown in a few days' time, to become a resident on the island. Never in all its history had anything happened in St. Helena to cause such universal excitement amongst the inhabitants.

When the first breath-taking surprise was over, some of the wiseacres gave it as their opinion that nothing but trouble would come to the island with "Boney" for a prisoner. Except for the fact that the Emperor of the French was on his way and that the 2nd battalion of the 53rd Regiment was embarked in the same squadron, no news official or otherwise had reached the Governor. The general opinion was that the island would be transferred to the Crown, and many and various conjectures were hazarded as to how the Company's civil and military establishments would be disposed of. The universal feeling among the inhabitants was one of concern whether their popular Governor, who had won the respect and affection of them all would be removed to make way for some new Governor chosen by the Crown. Four days of almost unbearable suspense, and then on the 15th of October arrived H.M.S. *Northumberland*, flying the flag of Rear-Admiral Sir George Cockburn. The Admiral immediately landed and made his way through a vast concourse of people to the Castle. Presently he reappeared accompanied by the Governor, and they were rowed in a boat manned by negroes, dressed in white with red cummerbunds, to the *Northumberland*, for the Governor to pay his official visit of ceremony to Napoleon.

Soon the Admiral and the Governor returned to shore, mounted two horses and rode up through the town.

Eighteen hundred and fifteen, the year which was to prove the most momentous, or at all events the most important historically, in the whole story of St. Helena, opens with particulars in the "records" of an unseemly dispute between two clergymen, the Senior Chaplain, the Rev. Mr. Samuel Jones, and his junior, the Rev. Mr. Richard Boys. The name of Mr. Jones has already occurred in these pages, in the account of his very natural resentment when appointed "Inspector of the Strayed Sheep and Goats". Mr. Jones was a quarrelsome fellow, and soon was at loggerheads with his junior, who was himself a tiresome busybody.

On the 3rd January, 1815, the Council decreed that "the controversy which had arisen between Mr. Boys and the Rev. Mr. Jones is productive of disgraceful effects, and they are ordered to abstain from further personal controversy, or circulation of written or printed letters referring to it, on pain of suspension."

This warning appears to have had little effect, on Mr. Jones at all events, who continued to publish virulent attacks on his junior until the 10th April, when he was suspended from his duties and retired on a pension of five shillings a day, with £150 as compensation for the loss of his house. Mr. Boys was then installed in his place as senior chaplain, and during the next fifteen years was to be a sharp thorn in the sides of the officials and principal inhabitants of St. Helena. In combination with his chaplaincy, Mr. Boys held the post of master of the Head School of the Island, and incumbent of the "Country Church".

Apart from the gossip-provoking quarrels between the two clergymen, life at St. Helena proceeded on its humdrum, peaceful course, undisturbed by the clash of arms or roar of cannons in the war between England and France. The people grew their crops, tended their flocks, visited each others' houses, exchanged local gossip, and when the India fleet came in they all flocked down to Jamestown, to trade, dine, dance, attend concerts and plays; and when the fleet sailed, returned to their normal quiet lives.

And then came the *Northumberland*, bringing Napoleon Bonaparte, and all these quiet, unimportant people were to find themselves living in the most famous, the most discussed and most written about spot in the whole universe.

When Admiral Cockburn and Governor Wilks mounted their horses and rode up into the interior, the object of their journey was to inspect various houses, among them Long- wood, the residence of the Lieutenant-Governor, Colonel Skelton, and to select one for General Bonaparte and his fellow exiles. The Governor considered Longwood to be the most suitable for the purpose, to which Cockburn agreed; but it required to be enlarged and repaired before the distinguished prisoner and his numerous staff could be accommodated there. In the meanwhile Napoleon was to be lodged in Jamestown, at the house of Mr. Henry Porteous, the superintendent of the Company's gardens. It was a large white house, the largest in the town, and the first on the left hand side on entering the street from the lower end.

Unfortunately this historic building was in process of being demolished when the present writer was at James- town in March of the year 1937, to be turned into a motor garage, an inglorious ending to a famous building, and one of the finest still standing in the street, in spite of its having been gutted by a fire lighted by an incendiary in 1865.

From early dawn on the following day, October the 15th, the crowd stood patiently on the wharf in high expectation of seeing the famous captive land, but all in vain. On the 16th, Napoleon's "Grand Marshall," Count Bertrand, came ashore and went up to Longwood to inspect the house and to make the necessary arrangements for the landing next day.

Early on that morning the wharf and landing stages were crowded as never before; every inhabitant on the whole island, white or black, seemed to be there, eager to get a first sight of the illustrious prisoner-of-war. In order to escape such embarrassing manifestation of popularity and curiosity, it was arranged that Bonaparte should not land until after sundown, when it was expected most of the spectators would have returned to their homes, but even then it required a troop of soldiers with fixed bayonets to force a passage for him from the landing steps to Mr. Porteous's house.

From now onwards until the end, no action, not even the most trivial incident, in the daily life of Napoleon was to escape notice and comment, for no man who ever lived had his private life recorded and set down more meticulously than was that of Napoleon during the next six years.

It was common knowledge that Napoleon always went in terror of assassination, and the news soon spread abroad how he had refused to go to bed until a strong bolt had been placed on the door of his bedroom, although it already was fitted with a lock, and how even then his two valets were made to sleep on a mattress on the floor outside the door.

Next morning Sir George Cockburn went with Napoleon and Bertrand to inspect Longwood, a ride of nearly five miles, where they took breakfast with Colonel and Mrs. Skelton. On the return journey Napoleon decided he would not spend another night in the hot and stuffy little town, with the gaping crowds, and suggested to Cockburn that he should stop at The Briars until the alterations to Longwood were completed. The house was already occupied by Mr. and Mrs. Balcombe and their five children, one of them being Betsy, who became such a friend of the Captive and who, thirty years afterwards, published her amusing and valuable recollections.[1]

As The Briars was a small house and only just large enough for the Balcombe family, it was arranged that Napoleon should occupy a small summer-house or pavilion which stood in the grounds some thirty yards from the house. Although it consisted only of one fair-sized room and two garrets, Napoleon preferred to stop there, rather than return to Jamestown for even one night, and so his collapsible iron bedstead, the one he used in his campaigns, was sent for, and with a valet outside his door and soldiers on guard, he spent a fairly comfortable night.

His residence at The Briars lasted two months, during which time he lived on the friendliest relations with the Balcombes, spending the mornings dictating his memoirs to Las Cases, and after dinner strolling in the garden, a wilderness of orange trees, myrtles, vines, pomegranates, white roses, fuchsias, geraniums and many other flowers.

With the arrival of Napoleon began a perfect spate of Proclamations, issued by the Governor and Council, or by Sir George Cockburn.

One of these, dated October 17th, 1815, commenced:

Whereas his Royal Highness the Prince Regent, acting in the name and on behalf of His Majesty, has been pleased to command that General Napoleon Bonaparte and the French persons attending him, should be detained on the island of St. Helena, and the Honourable Court of Directors having been pleased to issue to this Government certain orders consequent on such determination, [and went on to] warn

[1] *Recollections of Napoleon at St. Helena.* By Mrs. Abell. 1844.

all inhabitants and other persons on this island from aiding and abetting . . . the escape of the said General . . . and to interdict most pointedly the holding of any correspondence with him. . . .

Later on the same day another proclamation was issued making it unlawful for any inhabitant to be out of his house between nine at night and daylight the following morning, unless he was in possession of the parole for the night, though it was added:

It is distinctly to be understood by the inhabitants, that this ordinance is in no respect intended to interfere with the customary intercourse of hospitality and that every proper facility will be given to any respectable inhabitant who may intend to return home at a later hour than nine o'clock, by application to the field officer of the day.

With the arrival of Napoleon and his staff came troops, and yet more troops, to guard him. First of all, with the squadron accompanying H.M.S. *Northumberland* came the 53rd Foot Regiment. Later on, the 66th Regiment from India and still later, in 1819, the 20th Foot Regiment. Besides these British regiments there were the H.E.I.C. St. Helena regiments, of artillery and infantry.

This sudden doubling of the population brought with it great prosperity to the island, though at first it caused an acute shortage of food as well as accommodation.

It is not surprising that an island only twenty-eight miles in circumference, which in normal times could often not feed a population of under four thousand, and which lies twelve hundred miles from the nearest continent, could not afford in kind or amount the extra food which the sudden increase of inhabitants required. Long before the arrival of Napoleon and his staff and the troops, fresh beef was so precious as to have restrictions placed upon its consumption, so it may well be understood what a sensation was caused, a few days after he came, when the Emperor's *maître-d'hôtel* demanded four bullocks, in order to make a dish of brains for his master!

This heroic appetite of the Emperor is referred to in the *Roundabout Papers*, where W. M. Thackeray describes a visit he made to St. Helena in 1817, when on a voyage from Calcutta to England.

The novelist was then six years of age, and one incident impressed itself upon his memory.

> My black servant took me a long walk over rocks and hills until we reached a garden, where we saw a man walking. "That is he," said the black man: "that is Bonaparte! He eats three sheep every day, and all the little children he can lay hands on!"

> There are people in the British Dominions besides that poor Calcutta serving-man, with an equal horror of the Corsican ogre.

During the early days of the captivity the matter of supply of food of all sorts was in no wise made easier by the regulations laid down regarding shipping, which were very, and quite needlessly, severe.[1] No ship, other than a Company's or a man-of-war, was allowed to anchor in the Road nor to approach the island, unless in urgent need of fresh water. It sometimes happened that captains emptied their water tanks on drawing close to the island, simply to make an excuse for being permitted to anchor close in-shore. Admiral Sir George Cockburn was taking no risks. Even the fishing boats were not above suspicion as being possible aids to the escape of Napoleon. Only licensed fishermen were allowed to fish at all, and then only in the hours of daylight and close to the shore, so that fish, one of the staple foods of the island, became very

---

[1] See Appendix III.

scarce, the supply irregular, and when obtainable, only to be bought by the well-to-do.

The price of all provisions was raised; not only fresh beef, mutton and pork, but turkeys, geese, fowls and ducks, while potatoes—which formerly were so abundant that the farmers often threw away what they could not sell—fetched from six to eight shillings a bushel.

An example of the meticulous care taken to guard against any attempt to rescue Napoleon is well exemplified in the narrative of Captain Charles H. Barnard,[1] who arrived at St. Helena in the American ship, *Willwood*, on the 23rd August, 1816. The vessel had been severely handled in a storm off the Cape of Good Hope, and called at Jamestown in need of fresh water before continuing her voyage to the United States.

At 4 p.m. we saw a vessel under the land; supposed her to be a lookout vessel; laid off, and after waiting for the daylight, was boarded, at 7 a.m., by his Britannic majesty's brig *Julia*, one of the vessels stationed here to cruise round the island, and in its vicinity, to warn off all vessels except those who were in actual distress.

From our appearance, they did not hesitate to admit that our claim to be considered one of the excepted was well founded.

The lieutenant inquired into the nature and extent of our wants, which were stated to him; they were all composed in one article, viz: water, though strict veracity would not have been violated, had a number of others been included. The officer noted the quantity of water required, and returned to the brig. In a short time, the boat came back with a sealed letter, accompanied by orders for us to stand in towards the anchorage, nearly but not quite abreast the

[1] *The Sea, the Ship and the Sailor*. Marine Research Society, Salem, Massachusetts. 1925.

fort, and there to lay to until the Admiral's boat should board us, when we were to deliver the letter to the boarding officer.

We filled away, and stood in according to instructions, and then laid by for two or three hours, the fleet being in sight. At length we were boarded by a boat from the *Newcastle*, bearing the flag of Rear-Admiral Malcolm: the letter was delivered to the lieutenant. After reading it, he ordered flags to be brought from the boat on board of us, and signals to be made to the *Newcastle*, and repeated by her to the Admiral, who was at his residence on shore, the purport of which was to give notice of the arrival of an American ship in distress for water.

This lieutenant also made a minute of the quantity required, and returned, leaving a midshipman on board to prevent any communication with the shore, and ordered us to remain where we were until further directions.

As we were lying to in an unsheltered situation and exposed to a heavy swell, after waiting a considerable time for further orders, we concluded to run past the fort, and get more under the lee of the land, to be protected from the wind and sea; as we had observed a country ship, from Bengal, under jury-masts, which had experienced the late tremendous gale off the Cape, being dismasted by the lightening, pass the fort, and anchor close in under the island; for we did not apprehend that such a procedure on our part could possibly excite the suspicion that our crippled, dull-sailing ship could, in the face of formidable batteries, and a strong fleet, liberate or attempt the liberation of Napoleon.

If we may be allowed to judge from the events that followed our movements towards the fort, such was the case; for, on our nearing it, a shot was fired ahead of us from the half-moon battery, which caused us to wear ship and stand on the other tack. After keeping off some time, fearing we should fall to leeward, we wore, and again stood towards the fort, which saluted us with another shot, that struck the water just ahead of us: on this we again wore, and observed the admiral's boat coming to us. When alongside, the lieutenant told us to stand in; we then told him the reception the battery had already given us; he said that he would pull in and speak to them.

When we saw that he was near the battery, we made sail, and soon met two men-of-war launches with water, who came alongside, and conveyed the water immediately into the ship's casks.

We were then ordered to make sail, and proceed on our voyage without delay.

The sudden influx of soldiers and sailors also brought about a complete change in the social life of the island. There were high officials, military and civil, and still more important, their wives, some of them ladies of title, to whose houses the ladies of St. Helena vied against each other to be invited: Lady Bingham, Lady Malcolm, Countess Bertrand, Countess de Montholon, Baroness Sturmer and Lady Lowe, to say nothing of a whole bevy of Colonels' and Captains' wives.

There was considerable speculation at first whether St. Helena was to remain in the hands of the Honourable East India Company or be under the British Government during the incarceration of Napoleon. As the responsibility for his safe custody rested with the home Government it was decided that a Governor of their choice should take the place of Colonel Wilks, and on April 14th, 1816, Lieutenant-General Sir Hudson Lowe arrived in H.M.S. *Phæton*.

In their commission to the St. Helena Government the Board of Directors were careful to make it clear that "they could not contemplate without pain the consequent removal of

Colonel Wilks, whose conduct had entitled him to their entire approbation."

The letter from the Court of Directors informing the Council at St. Helena of their agreement with the British Government to make that island his place of internment is dated August 1st, 1815, and runs as follows:

Napoleon Buonaparte having surrendered himself to the Government of this country, His Majesty's Ministers deeply sensible of the high importance of effectually securing the person of a man whose conduct has proved so fatal to the happiness of the world, and judging that the Island of St. Helena is conveniently fitted to answer that purpose have proposed to us that he shall be placed there under a system of Government adapted to serve the end in view, but innovating no further and no longer upon the present constitution of Government and the conduct of its affairs than that end shall require.

We have not failed to express our opinion of Col. Wilkes' merits to H.M. Government, who have also a just sense of his character and talents, and it is from no objection personal to him, or any want of personal consideration for him that they propose another Governor, but because they think the peculiar nature of the service and the confidential communications and details personal as well as written into which they will have to enter with the gentleman who shall fit that office require he should be of the class of General Officers who served in the scene of the late continental events and be sent from this country.

As however the Crown is to defray all the expenses consequent of this new arrangement in the Government of St. Helena, so His Majesty's Ministers have declared their intention of granting Colonel Wilkes a fair compensation for the loss and disappointment to which he will be subjected.

As the officer destined to be the new Governor of St. Helena is not yet arrived from the Continent and it is judged expedient to convey Buonaparte to that Island without delay, Rear-Admiral Sir George Cockburn who commands the squadron appointed to guard him thither, is invested by H.M. Government with the temporary care and custody of him until the new Governor shall arrive.

Dated January 19th, 1816, a copy of the Company's instructions to Sir Hudson Lowe as Governor ran as follows:

The Prince Regent's Ministers having proposed that the Island of St. Helena should be the place of Residence for Buonaparte and that the Comp. would for the sake of the important objects connected with the safe custody of that extraordinary person put the Govt. of the Island during his stay here in the hands of an officer possessing their confidence, the Court of Directors always disposed to make the means of the Comp. available to the public interest, acquiesced in these proposals and the same ministers having further selected and recommended you for the trust, we have appointed you to be Governor.

Naturally the sudden change in the circumstances of the island was attended by a vast additional expenditure, and to adjust this, it was settled that the Company should pay annually a sum equal to the average charge of the three preceding years, and that all beyond that sum should be defrayed by the Crown.

As more troops arrived in the island, the accommodation for them in the barracks at Jamestown was soon insufficient and two large camps were formed, one at Deadwood, opposite Longwood, and another on a level piece of ground, Francis Plain, at the head of James Valley, and above The Briars.

The new Governor soon proved himself to be a man of energy and capability, and had he not continually been harassed by Lord Bathurst, the Secretary for War and Colonies, who was responsible to the British Government for the safe custody of Napoleon, it is possible that the enmity between him and his difficult prisoner might not have ended in calamity.

His enemies—and Hudson Lowe had enemies—English politicians as well as Frenchmen—lost no opportunity of putting him and the residents of Longwood at loggerheads, although history is at last, if reluctantly, granting to him many fine qualities of character and acknowledging the impossible task he was set. During the time he governed St. Helena he was liked and respected by the inhabitants who genuinely regretted it when he left the island.

Even his enemies had to allow him due honour for his successful efforts to abolish slavery in St. Helena.

From the first moment of his arrival Lowe was determined to spare no effort to get rid of this blot on the fair name of St. Helena, though he was too wise to state his views publicly, until he had had time to study local conditions and win the respect of the slave owners. But in August, 1818, an event happened which brought matters to a climax.

Sir George Bingham, the commander of the troops in the island, had just left the Magistrate's Court where he had been presiding when his eye fell upon a poor little slave girl, about fourteen years old, limping down the road with blood dripping from fresh wounds in her arm and back which had obviously been caused by a whip. Sir George, with his well-known kindness of heart and chivalrous disposition, was shocked at the distressing sight, and enquired who had been guilty of such brutality. He was told that the injuries had been inflicted on the girl by her owner, Mr. Charles De Fountain. The Admiral immediately returned to the Court, ordered De Fountain to be brought before him, and inflicted the statutory fine of £2.

Then addressing the public in the Court, he gave vent to his indignation in violent terms, and said he only wished he had it in his power to make the fine £40, and to order the brute, De Fountain, to receive the same treatment he had inflicted on the poor slave.

De Fountain had the effrontery to complain to the Council of the terms in which he had been addressed by Sir George in the hearing of others, but Sir George repeated everything he had said and refused to withdraw or regret one single word he had uttered in anger in the Court House.

The affair made a considerable commotion, and Sir Hudson Lowe immediately gave notice that he would bring up the whole question of slavery at the next Council Meeting.

A few days later he convened a meeting of the inhabitants and addressed them on the subject of slavery, pointing out how public opinion almost everywhere was becoming favourable to the abolition of slavery. He told them that the subject had attracted the serious attention of the Court of Directors, who viewed with regret that the one and only spot under their government where slavery still existed in any shape or form was St. Helena. At the same time, he said, he was quite ready to admit that nowhere in the world did slavery exist in a milder degree than in the island, but exist it did, and would remain in perpetuity if the present system by which every child born of a slave became also a slave. He then spoke of the measure adopted in Ceylon, where it had been declared that all children born of slave parents should, after a fixed period, become free.

He proposed to his listeners that they themselves should copy the example of Ceylon, and in future free all the babies born to slaves, but at the same time, he added, the owners had a perfect right to act otherwise if they wished, and he left the matter entirely to their own deliberation, since he had no wish that any resolution should be arrived at, which did not meet with their full concurrence.

It took less than ten minutes' discussion for the meeting of slave owners to carry by acclamation the general principle of the Governor's suggestion and ask that it should be adopted.

A committee of thirteen was then elected to frame resolutions, which, four days later, were presented to the Governor and Council, with a request that they might be made into a law, which was accordingly complied with. By this law, all children born of a slave woman, from and after Christmas Day, 1818, were to be free, but to be considered as apprentices to the proprietors of the mothers if males, until the age of eighteen years, and if females, until sixteen; and that the masters and mistresses were to enforce the attendance of free-born children at church and the Sunday schools.

Not very long after Sir Hudson Lowe's arrival at St. Helena people began to notice that Bonaparte was seldom seen outside the grounds of Longwood, and had become far more inaccessible to visitors than he was at first. Therefore it was all the more surprising when, on an October day in 1818, he suddenly announced to his staff his intention to visit Sir William Doveton at his house in Sandy Bay, and ordered a cold meal to be prepared to take with him the following day.

The best description of this memorable meal occurs in Forsyth's *History of the Captivity of Napoleon* and is as follows:

We must now describe Napoleon Bonaparte enjoying a picnic, and it has an additional interest from the fact that it was the first he ever paid in the island, and the last time he ever took a meal in the presence of strangers, or anywhere except amongst his own followers in the seclusion of Longwood. About five miles from that place stood the house and grounds of Sir William Doveton, called Mount Pleasant, which at Napoleon's special request, had been recently included within his limits. Sir William was a native of St. Helena, who had been for many years Member of Council there, and having visited England a year or two previously, he had received the honour of knighthood. [This is the gentleman of whom Theodore Hook tells the story that, happening accidentally on his arrival in London, to meet a lady whom he knew in one of the crowded streets, he asked whether they had not better defer their conversation *until the procession had passed*! The natives of St. Helena were called by the English there "Yamstocks" and had the reputation of being very unsophisticated. A lady of the island once inquired whether London was not very dull after the China fleet had sailed.]

On the morning of the 4th of October, as the old gentleman was taking his usual walk before breakfast, he observed several persons on horseback coming towards his house, and, on reconnoitring them with his spyglass, perceived they were the party from Longwood.

Count Montholon dismounted from his horse, and Sir William went to the door to receive him; the Count informed him that the *Emperor* presented his compliments, and requested he might come and rest himself. Sir William replied, that he should be glad to see him, and that any accommodation his house afforded was at General Bonaparte's service.

Montholon then mounted his horse, and, having joined the party, they all entered the lawn. Unfortunately the venerable knight was quite ignorant of the French language, and could only communicate through the medium of Count Bertrand, whose knowledge of English was not as perfect as it might have been. However, Sir William made his compliments in the best manner he could, and, as Bonaparte appeared a good deal fatigued, he requested that he would walk in and rest himself, upon which the ex-Emperor advanced towards the door, and on coming up the steps was assisted by Bertrand's arm.

He sat on the sofa, and entered into conversation with his host, through Bertrand, as interpreter.

Observing Sir William's eldest grand-daughter in the room, he said he supposed she was about ten years old. He was told she was only seven, and he called her to him, placed two of his fingers over her nose, and gave her a piece of liquorice, which he took from a small tortoiseshell box. Sir William Doveton begged Bertrand to inform Bonaparte that he hoped he would stop and breakfast with him; but this the illustrious visitor declined, saying that they had brought their own breakfast, and preferred taking it on the lawn. Sir William endeavoured to dissuade him from this, saying that the house, and whatever accommodation he could afford, was at their service, and he took Bonaparte and Bertrand into the dining-room, where he pointed to a large pot of fresh butter on the breakfast table, saying it was at the service of his guests. Upon this Napoleon smiled, and gently took hold of his host's right ear, as was his custom when he wished to signify his approval. Then they returned to the drawing-room and Bonaparte resumed his seat on the sofa. Soon afterwards one of Sir William's daughters, Mrs. Greentree, came into the room with her youngest child in her arms, and Napoleon rose and pointed to the sofa as a sign that she was to sit there. Two of her little girls had each their noses taken hold of by the affable visitor, and received from him a small piece of liquorice. In the meantime Count Montholon had got a table and laid it on the lawn.

Sir William Doveton sent out a variety of good things, and then the Count came in and announced that breakfast was ready. Their host was requested to go and share their meal, which he did, taking with him, he says, a pint bottle of Mount Pleasant water (alias, orange shrub), made by his daughter, and four liqueur glasses. Bonaparte reserved for

him a chair on his right hand, and desired him to sit there.
After doing justice to some substantial viands, Napoleon
filled a small tumbler of champagne for Sir William and
another for himself, and he afterwards drank a glass of the
shrub. Coffee was then brought, and Napoleon requested
that Mrs. Greentree would come and partake of it. After she
had tasted the coffee, which she found acid and disagreeable,
Bonaparte filled a liqueur glass with shrub and offered it to
her. The party then rose, and Bonaparte handed Mrs.
Greentree into the house, where he took his former seat on
the sofa, with her beside him. In the course of conversation
he put his favourite question to Sir William Doveton, and
asked him, through Count Bertrand, whether he ever got
drunk? To which Sir William replied, rather equivocally,
"I like a glass of wine sometimes." He then turned to Mrs.
Greentree and enquired, "How often does your husband
get drunk?—is he so once a week?" She answered, "No."
"Is he once a fortnight?" She again replied, "No." "Once
a month?" "No, it is some years since I saw him so."
Bonaparte then said "Bah!" and changed the conversation.
After sitting some time he rose and took leave, holding
Bertrand's arm as he went down the steps.

The breakfast (Sir William tells us) consisted of a cold
pie, potted meat, cold turkey, curried fowl, ham or pork,
I could not tell which; coffee, dates, almonds, oranges and
a very fine salad.

According to Sir William, Napoleon was apparently in good
health, in spite of his pale complexion; "his face astonishly
fat, and his body and thighs very round and plump".

Indeed, to use the good knight's own words, which were
more expressive than elegant, "he looked as fat and as round
as a China pig."

This novel picnic is significant as being the last occasion

upon which Napoleon ever went out of the immediate grounds of Longwood, until he was carried in his coffin to his tomb in Sane Valley. Those of the inhabitants who had a fondness for such coincidences, used to point out that Napoleon in his will expressed the wish to be buried "on the borders of the Seine" and no doubt they derived some sort of satisfaction from the similarity of the two names.

While the important people of the island intrigued, spied on each other, made love, quarrelled, went to race meetings at Deadwood, and took part in the social life of the island, one man, with no claim to social position, continued to go his own way, regardless of everybody, following the straight, if narrow, path of duty he had chosen to pursue. This was the Reverend Mr. Richard Boys, the senior chaplain, who was a continual source of trouble to all those, however high and mighty they might be, who were so rash or so unfortunate as to incur his displeasure. He constantly was up in arms, fighting lost causes, defending the underdog, or exposing, as publicly as possible, the backslidings of his flock. Undoubtedly Richard Boys was a very remarkable character, and as the best account of him is that given by Dr. Arnold Chaplin, I have quoted, with his kind permission, freely from the pages of his invaluable and most entertaining work of reference.[1]

It will be remembered that Mr. Boys was installed as senior chaplain after a prolonged and unseemly wrangle with the Rev. Mr. Jones, which ended in the latter being dismissed in April, 1815. In the following April Mr. Boys was again up before the Council, for we find in the Records the entry:

> April 15, 1816. Mr. Boys having refused to take to church the corpse of a deceased person, alleging it being the privilege for the upper classes only; is called for an explanation.

[1] *A St. Helena Who's Who*, by Arnold Chaplin, M.D. Arthur L. Humphreys 1919.

Mr. Boys' explanation was that the island was full of pagan superstitions, that at every funeral a large concourse of people paraded through the streets, that they crowded into the church and passed round the altar, littering the church with myrtle leaves.

On another occasion he received a sharp reprimand from the Council for having publicly insulted a Mr. Blenkins by calling after him in the street: "Blenkins, when is the green bag to be given out?"

Mr. Boys, ever a strict Sabbatarian, complained to the Council on June 11th, 1821, of the violation by the islanders of the Lord's Day. All the satisfaction he received from the Council was that they could see no foundation for his complaint, but thought him to be the "dictator of many of the indecorous and insulting letters to the Government".

It was not only at St. Helena, as Dr. Arnold Chaplin points out, that Mr. Boys fearlessly attacked what he believed to be wrong, for once when on a visit to Rio Janeiro, the British Minister there was obliged to send him away on account of "his indecent behaviour when a Catholic procession was passing by".

Mr. Boys loved above all things to espouse the cause of the downtrodden. Mr. Thomas Breame, the Company's farmer, who was accused, and eventually found to be guilty of, gross irregularities in his accounts, had a champion in Mr. Boys, which brought the latter into further conflict with the Council.

In August, 1820, a lengthy and acrimonious dispute took place between him and the Council over the vexed question of whether he should be paid 7s.6d. or 3s. 6d. for preaching at the Military Camp at Deadwood. The chaplain thought nothing of writing letters of ten to fifteen pages, and the controversy was only ended when the Council wrote:

Your letters only tend to involve the subject by forced or overstrained deductions from what is written to you.

The Council desires that you do not employ the subject as a ground for making any further attacks on the Secretary, nor for collaterally introducing any further matter in your correspondence with them.

The longer Mr. Boys remained at St. Helena the more ruthless and outspoken did he become in his crusade against vice, or what he took to be vice. In so doing he caused great uneasiness to the authorities and particularly to the Governor, Sir Hudson Lowe. The only method of stopping his virulent tongue from wagging was to have him sent back to England, but the Governor dare not do that, for dangerous as his indiscretions might be in St. Helena, it would have been tenfold more so if the outspoken clergyman talked as freely in England, where many enemies of the Government and sympathisers and partisans of Bonaparte would have made much use of the talkative and tactless parson.

Let us turn to the learned Dr. Chaplin:

Enough has now been said to show that the temperament of Mr. Boys was productive of difficulties in his relations with the authorities in St. Helena. But this was not all. In his zeal for the promotion of the spiritual welfare of the community, he was outspoken in his denunciation of evil living wherever found. Now at the time of the captivity the moral tone of St. Helena was low, and drunkenness and moral depravity were to be found in all classes of the island society. In his capacity of spiritual head in the island, Mr. Boys, in the plainest terms inveighed against the moral lapses prevalent, and from his pulpit did not hesitate to single out prominent examples of evil living, and to assail them in his sermons.

The case of Rear-Admiral Plampin was one which excited his righteous anger to a considerable degree. This high official lived in irregular union with a lady who came out with him to St. Helena. Her name is undiscoverable at the present time, for the muster books of the *Conqueror* merely give those not borne on the ship's books under the designation of "Widow's men" . . . The arrival of the Admiral and the lady caused consternation in official circles in St. Helena, and "The Briars", at which they resided, was shunned by Lady Lowe and other dames who formed the high St. Helena society. In a short time Mr. Boys began to make thinly veiled allusions in his sermons to this wickedness in high places. Waxing warmer, he directly preached against Plampin and his mistress, beseeching him to put away from him the accursed woman, and to flee the wrath to come while there was yet time.

The perturbation of Lowe at this turn of events was great, and he was placed in a grave dilemma, for Plampin was a faithful adherent of Lowe in his policy regarding the great captive. He could not afford to lose Plampin, on the other hand he knew full well the commotion Boys would be sure to cause in England were he sent home on account of his chastisement of vice in high places.

From his dispatches to Bathurst, it is evident that Lowe had no sympathy with the moral obliquities of Plampin. He therefore shrank on the one hand from taking action from fear of losing Plampin, and on the other from fear of promoting a scandal in England by the uncurbed tongue of Mr. Boys.

The policy adopted by Lowe in this matter was judicious, for Mr. Boys knew much, and had he been dismissed, the British public at home would have learned that the term "abandoned and profligate Isle" as applied to St. Helena, was no mere empty phrase. Indeed, Lowe's fear that Mr. Boys would make damaging disclosures will be understood when it is stated that as senior chaplain it was his duty to make the official entries in the Parish Registers of all the births taking place in the island. When, as it sometimes happened, Mr. Boys was called upon to record the births of illegitimate children of slave women, begotten of men who were some of the highest and most trusted of Lowe's lieutenants, the chaplain in his righteous indignation did not hesitate to write in bold characters in the registers the titles and high positions of the sires. In these old registers it is amusing to observe the frantic attempts that have been made by means of blots and pen-knife to obliterate the damaging evidence.

But Mr. Boys was determined to write for all time, and the precise titles and positions of the fathers, in spite of the attempted erasures, can still be plainly distinguished. This was probably the real reason for the ostracism of Mr. Boys by the high St. Helena society, and the fear of his outspoken tongue evinced by Sir Hudson Lowe . . . .

There is, however, another and better side of the picture of the activities of Mr. Boys, and in justice to him it must be shewn. It will be found in Robson's *Memoirs of St. Helena*, p. 64, and quoted from a private letter of Lt. G. H. Wood of the 20th Foot. It is as follows:

Mr. Boys was only to be known to be heartily and fully loved; for, for a long time we had been greatly prejudiced against him, by the scandalous reports we were in the habit of hearing from many quarters, and we only regretted that we did not know him before. But, however, we soon became on the strictest terms of brotherly love and intimacy; and he became a Father in Christ to all the young Christians in the Army and Navy; and opened his house and his heart, and all his soul to receive them, and to promote their growth in grace and knowledge, and love, and obedience to the gospel.

All this was blessed abundantly to himself, and he became more spiritual, earnest, and active in every way in the cause of the Lord. We had meetings in his house every week, frequently assembling to the number of twenty; and two days in the week we used to be there to breakfast, and spend the whole day in religious exercises. He would read the Word, and expound, for which he had a most happy talent, then he would pray, then read a chosen sermon, or some good book; then one of us would pray; then all sing a hymn, and pray, and sing alternately till dinner-time; after which, we all walked out together, choosing each his companion, and talked of Christ by the way, until our hearts would often burn within us; then, after dusk, return home to his house to take tea, and spend the remainder of the evening in the same joyous manner. Such scenes and hours can never be forgotten, but must ever be remembered with inexpressible happiness. . . .

On the state of morality existing in St. Helena, the British occupation appears to have had a most salutary effect, and there can be no doubt that the outspoken utterances of Mr. Boys contributed in no small degree to this great improvement. Let, therefore, statistics bear their testimony to the good work of the iconoclastic cleric. Let us inspect the parish registers in Jamestown so far as the illegitimate baptisms taking place between the years 1813–1827.

1813	.	.	198
1814	.	.	101
1815	.	.	58
1816	.	.	46
1817	.	.	53
1818	.	.	39
1819	.	.	50
1820	.	.	17

1821	.	.	16
1822	.	.	6
1823	.	.	3
1824	.	.	4
1825	.	.	7
1826	.	.	17
1827	.	.	33

It was in 1815 that the British occupation commenced, and it was from 1822 to 1825 that the religious revival took place in St. Helena owing to the energy of Mr. Boys, but taken together, these statistics may be regarded as strong evidence that the uncompromising Mr. Boys with all his aggressiveness looked well after his "vineyard" and by no means laboured in vain.

With the death of Napoleon on May 5th, 1821, the six years of the Captivity came to an end and most of the troops and many of the officials were sent away, some to India and some to England. Probably not one of them left with less reluctance than did "The Real Martyr of St. Helena," as Lowe has not inaptly been called. If ever a man had reason to be glad to end a thankless task it must have been the unlucky Lowe, whose duty it had been to act as guardian and jailer of the scheming mischief-makers at Longwood.

The task broke Lowe's career, as it would have broken that of the Archangel Gabriel himself. That Lowe was not the man for the part is now clear to everybody. Although a fine soldier, a good linguist, intelligent, a hard and conscientious worker, and kindly in disposition, he had not a trace of tact and had a "pedantic insistence for trifles" which drove the inmates of Longwood almost to distraction.

On July 25th, 1821, Hudson Lowe and his family sailed for England, and before embarking, the inhabitants presented the departing Governor with an address which shows what respect and even affection he inspired in those who knew him and were governed by him.

The address runs as follows:

Sir,

As your Excellency is upon the eve of resigning your authority on this island, we the undersigned inhabitants cannot be suspected of views of an interested nature in respectfully offering our most sincere and grateful acknowledgement for the consideration, justice, impartiality and moderation which have distinguished your government.

A prominent measure of your Excellency's was a proposal which might have been expected to have been unpopular in a colony where slavery had long been recognized; yet, Sir, it met with the instantaneous and unanimous approbation of the inhabitants; a result which offers no slight proof of our entire confidence in your concern for our welfare.

Under the existence of such ties between the Governor and governed, and your marked discountenance of any rising indication of party spirit, it is easy to account for the tranquility and comfort we have enjoyed during your Excellency's residence among us.

Finding we cannot have the happiness of the continuation of your Excellency's government, we beg you will accept the assurance of our sincere, respectful and affectionate wishes for the health and prosperity of your Excellency, and of every member of your family.

Four years afterwards Hudson Lowe revisited St. Helena for two or three days only, on a voyage home from Ceylon, and was received with enthusiasm by the population. During his brief stay he was entertained by the military, the civilians and the merchants at dinners at the mess and the tavern. In proposing his health, which was toasted repeatedly, the speakers alluded to his justice and impartiality as a Governor, and to his liberality and kindness as a man. Lady Lowe's well-known charity and benevolence were also praised.

While waiting for a new Governor to be sent out to take the place of Hudson Lowe, the first Member of Council, Mr. T. H. Brooke, nephew of the former Governor of that name, was appointed Acting Governor. He is principally remembered as being the author of the *History of the Island of St. Helena*, published first in 1808, and followed by a second and revised edition in 1824. Until instructions arrived from England, Brigadier-General Pine Coffin assumed the supreme military command under the title of Acting Commander-in-Chief, and had exclusive charge of Longwood House and all other buildings and property of the island belonging to the Crown.

During the first year of Mr. Brooke's acting governorship the first and last coinage was issued expressly for the island. It consisted of a bronze half-penny, bearing the inscription, "St. Helena Half-penny 1821" on one side, and the coat of arms of the H.E.I.C. on the other. Some silver coins were also struck but never put into circulation.

The only other "coin" used in the island was a copper half-penny token issued at about the same time by Messrs. Solomon, Dickson & Taylor, still the leading firm in St. Helena.[1] These half-pennies were the only currency, other than the unpopular copper bars, ever issued in St. Helena, and not one of the copper bars is known to be in existence.

On the 11th of March, 1823, the new Governor arrived, Brigadier-General Walker, a distinguished Indian officer from the Bombay Presidency, who, together with Messrs. Brooke and Greentree, formed the new government.

He had no easy problem to tackle, for with the exodus of the French household at Longwood, and most of the naval and

---

[1] £147 worth of these half-penny tokens (70,560) were issued and were in circulation for many years before they came to official notice, when orders were issued for their withdrawal.

military forces who were on the island to guard Napoleon, the inhabitants were suddenly left without their principal supply of livelihood. The troops had spent many thousands of pounds a year which went into the pockets of the inhabitants, and when this supply failed, the islanders soon began to feel the pinch.

Walker did everything he could to encourage agriculture and to induce the islanders to go back to the land to earn their living. To do this he inaugurated agricultural fairs and shows with ploughing matches, at which prizes were given to the best ploughman and team and for the best exhibits of crops and vegetables. The new Governor also interested himself in the improvement, both moral and religious, of the slaves, and they came to be far better and more humanely treated than before. They were compelled by law to attend church once every Sunday, and he revived the humane and wise plan of Governor Patton, of allotting premiums and rewards to deserving slaves. He resuscitated the Benevolent Society instituted by Governor Wilks, which provided the means of education for the children of even the poorest people. The Governor had a great dislike of the popular punishment of whipping, which he considered degrading and demoralizing, and in its place he originated the tread-wheel. That the culprits' labour should not be in vain, the wheel was so constructed as to grind lime, which was used in the composition of cement.

Great strides were made in education. Towards this the Company paid annually the sum of one thousand pounds, besides providing the necessary school buildings, while the Benevolent Society contributed two hundred and fifty pounds a year towards the education of the children of the very poor. By 1823 four hundred children attended at the different Company's schools and those of the Society.

On the 19th December of that year a public examination took place in the presence of His Excellency and Council and many of the leading ladies and gentlemen of the island. It must have been an alarming ordeal for the pupils, though Thomas Brooke found it "a sight of no small interest and gratification, particularly to those whose recollections enabled them to contrast such a scene with the circumstances of former times," and he went on to express the hope that "St. Helena has a fair prospect of acquiring, in some years, a virtuous and industrious *free peasantry*, in lieu of a race of slaves under the lamentable disadvantages which that condition usually entails upon its victims."[1]

The Court of Directors at this time passed a regulation by which the cadets for the St. Helena artillery were required to attend a course of study at the Company's Military Seminary at Addiscombe before receiving their commissions.

An innovation of the Governor's was the founding of the Military Institution, where young officers were able to receive scientific instruction in other than purely military matters. One of the principal subjects was the study of astronomy, combined with the frequent determination of the true time, which latter would be of great use in correcting ships' chronometers. An observatory was built and fitted up on Ladder Hill which, when the Crown took over the Island, was allowed to fall into ruin. The indefatigable Governor also founded an Agricultural and Horticultural Society and, in spite of the failure of previous Governors, succeeded in developing a regular market in Jamestown. A building was erected at the end of the town in the shade of a row of peepul trees and was open for trade every day in the week but Sunday.

He turned old Longwood House, which already was falling to bits, into offices and granaries for the neighbouring farms, and, having procured a threshing machine from England, this was erected in New Longwood, the house which had been built for Napoleon but which he never occupied. This settled

---

[1] *History of the Island of St. Helena*. T. H. Brooke. Second Edition. 1824.

a question which had been a favourite topic in the island ever since the death of Napoleon. Some had been in favour of New Longwood being occupied by the Lieut.-Governor, others that it should be used as a barracks for the troops, or as a house for the senior member of Council, or as a school. Others again recommended its dilapidation and the sale of the materials. The small house where Count and Countess Bertrand had lived was handed over as a dwelling for the Company's farmer, and still is the residence of the farmer of Longwood.

An interesting experiment of Governor Walker's was the introduction of silk-worms. He hoped that this might lead to a new and profitable industry in the island. A supply of these insects was ordered to be sent from India, but they all died on the voyage. Then a Chinese labourer was found who claimed to understand the breeding and care of silk-worms, and he offered to go to China and bring some back. This he was allowed to do, and in due time returned with a supply, and a silk-worm farm was started at The Briars, but it ended in failure.

Every now and again problems came up before the Governor and Council which required the judgment of a very Solomon to settle.

Thus on August 26th, 1824, a recommendation was made by the Vestry that a tax should be levied on all free blacks.

The wise Governor pointed out that they could not possibly recognize any distinction of colour in legislation, and that in any case there were on the island hundreds of individuals about whom it would be no easy matter to decide whether they should be classed as whites or blacks. Further, he added, the law recognized three classes only: the military, governed by articles of war, the slaves governed by a special code, and the rest of the inhabitants, who did not come within either of these two categories.

In 1828 the energetic Colonel Walker left and Mr. Brooke

again took up the reins of office until the arrival of the next Governor, Brigadier-General Dallas.

A most important and useful transaction carried out during his term of office was the construction of a ladder of some 600 steps and 900 feet in length up the steep face of the cliff between Jamestown and Ladder Hill. On either side of the ladder an inclined plane was built, up which could be hauled guano and manure, as well as military stores, and down which could be brought to the town produce from the country. The planes consisted of tramways upon which waggons travelled up and down, operated by simple machinery, worked by a capstan-bar and ropes by mules at the top. The work of building the ladder and planes was carried out under the personal supervision of Lieutenant G. W. Mellis, an artillery officer, and for many years the planes proved a boon to the community, saving both time, labour and expense, but like so many other blessings, were allowed to go to ruin in the bad days which followed when the Company had to hand the island over to the British Government.

The year 1829 is memorable as being the date of the introduction to St. Helena of the Indian mynah bird, which it was hoped would be useful in destroying ticks on cattle and other pests. Apparently they did not thrive at first. J. C. Melliss[1] wrote in 1875 that they had not multiplied to any extent, but a few were still to be found inhabiting the peepul trees in Jamestown, otherwise they were rare.

Later on, in 1885, five mynahs were liberated by Miss Phoebe Moss at her home, The Briars, as well as a number of South African frogs, and to-day both birds and frogs swarm all over the island in suitable localities, the mynahs having become a serious menace to fruit growers, which has also been the case in so many other parts of the world where they have been introduced.

[1] *St. Helena.* By J. C. Melliss. 1875.

Besides constructing the ladder and planes, General Dallas built the barracks in the town and established fire plugs in case of fire—the theatre had recently been burned to the ground. He also sank a well to the depth of eighty-five feet in Rupert's Valley, by which a most valuable supply of water was obtained for that barren waste of dust and rock.

On March 20th, 1830, H.M.S. *Pallas* arrived off Jamestown, on her way home from Calcutta. On board her was a passenger, Captain Mundy, late aide-de-camp to Lord Combermere. He wrote a book[1] about his experiences in India and in it described his short visit of three days to St. Helena.

On first observing the island from a great distance Mundy wrote lyrically, "When I first caught sight of it, it appeared like a single filmy cloud lingering on the edge of the horizon, whose wide expanse was clear of vapours, yet hazy from excessive heat."

But a nearer view caused him to alter his opinion, for "nothing can be more repulsive than the appearance of St. Helena from the sea: . . . it stands abruptly out of the deep, a confused head of bare and craggy rocks, of which the Southern side is, perhaps, the most savage and desolate part."

At 9 o'clock the following morning Lord Combermere and his party landed and were met on the wharf by the Governor, Brigadier-General Dallas, and a salute was fired from the batteries and a guard of honour drawn up in line presented arms while a military band played the National Anthem, so that Mundy "could hardly believe that we were on a little barren rock in the midst of the Atlantic, and so far removed from the civilized parts of the world."

The most interesting portion of Mundy's account is his description of Longwood House, as he found it only nine years after the death of Napoleon:

[1] *Pen and Pencil Sketches, being the Journal of a Tour in India.* 1832.

As we turned through the lodges the old house appeared at the end of an avenue of scrubby and weather-worn trees. It bears the exterior of a respectable farm-house, but is now fast running to decay. On entering a dirty court-yard, and quitting our horses, we were shown by some idlers into a square building, which once contained the bed-room, sitting-room, and bath of the Empereur des Français. The partitions and floorings are now thrown down, and torn up, and the apartment occupied for six years by the hero before whom kings, emperors, and popes had quailed, is now tenanted by cart-horses!

Passing on with a groan, I entered a small chamber, with two windows looking towards the north. Between these windows are the marks of a fixed sofa: on that couch Napoleon died. The apartment is now occupied by a threshing-machine.

Hence we were conducted onwards to a large room, which formerly contained a billiard-table, and whose front looks out upon a little latticed veranda, where the imperial peripatetic—I cannot style him philosopher—enjoyed the luxury of six paces to and fro—his favourite promenade.

The white-washed walls are scored with names of every nation: and the paper on the ceiling has been torn off in strips, as holy relics. Many couplets, chiefly French, extolling and lamenting the departed hero, adorn or disfigure (according to their qualities) the plaster walls. . . .

It is difficult now to judge of what Longwood was when in repair; but I cannot think that it could, in its *best* days, have been worthy of the illustrious occupant, even in his *worst*.

The visitors then remounted their horses and followed the road which passes Halley's Mount and Hutts Gate to the top of the Sane Valley to visit the tomb which contained the mortal remains of the man of immortal memory. And here again they found the same aspect of sadness and corrosion:

The willows are decaying fast, and one of them rests upon the sharp spears of the railing, which are buried in its trunk —as though it were committing suicide for very grief! The foliage of the rest is thinned and disfigured by the frequent depredations of visitors. Fresh cuttings have, however, been planted by the Governor, who intends, moreover, to set cypresses round the outer fence. Madame Bertrand's immortelles have proved, alas! mortal.

The fine, tall, old corporal, who came out from England with the ex-emperor, was full of his praises: "I saw the General often," said the old fellow; "he had an eye in his head like an eagle." . . . After inscribing our names in a book, we drank to Napoleon's immortal memory in his own favourite spring, and mounting our steeds, spurred towards Plantation House.

The visit to the island was soon over, and

after an early dinner at Plantation House, our party took leave of the Governor and his fair daughters—who seem to rejoice in their truly halcyon home—and rode down to the town. The St. Helena regiment, dressed like the Guards, was drawn up, and presented arms; and as we stepped into the Governor's barge, the people on the wharf and on the batteries gave us three cheers. By the time we reached the *Pallas* it was quite dark. At that moment the batteries opened a salute, a rocket going up with every gun, and blue lights burning along the rocks: *Pallas* returned the salute, and blue lights were burnt at all her yard-arms. Nine o'clock, up anchor, made all sail.

Some twenty years previously the Company had sent out to the island a schooner, the *St. Helena*, for the use of the St.

Helena Government. This vessel was now about to become the scene of a shocking tragedy. It began with the arrival in the Road of H.M.S. *Sybille* from the West Coast of Africa. As she had on board several cases of coast fever, pratique was refused, and on the advice of the ship's surgeon, the Commodore decided to sail further south for the benefit of his sick, and he asked that the *St. Helena* might call at Sierra Leone on her passage to England, to deliver his despatches for the Coast Squadron, and orders for them to meet him later on at Ascension Island. His request was complied with and on 31st March, 1830, the schooner set sail, carrying with her as a passenger George B. Waddell, M.D., the Company's assistant surgeon, who was going home for treatment for a disease of the eyes.

Nothing further was heard of the *St. Helena* until June 17th when H.M.S. *Ariadne* dropped anchor at Jamestown from Sierra Leone with the news that the schooner had fallen into the hands of pirates.

The islanders then learned that the *St. Helena* had arrived at Free Town on 2nd May and her crew reported that on 6th April, at 10 a.m., they had been boarded by a felucca under French colours, with a crew of forty to fifty men of various nationalities. The strange ship had ordered Captain Harrison, the commander, to come aboard their vessel and bring with him the ship's papers, which he rashly did. The pirates seized the captain and Dr. Waddell, lashed them back to back, and then threw them overboard to drown, and with swords and knives drove the crew below decks while they plundered the cargo and searched for the ship's money. Seven white and four black members of the crew of the *St. Helena* were killed before the pirates left the schooner to her fate. An hour afterwards the felucca returned and cut away the masts and attempted to scuttle the vessel, but as she did not at once sink, the pirate kept sailing round her, firing shots at her until

6 o'clock, when she made off. The carpenter and five men, who had been in hiding below and were the sole survivors of the crew, returned on deck and managed to sail their ship to Sierra Leone.

The felucca, from the description of her, was well known to the British squadron, and as she could have had no idea that the schooner would escape it was hoped she would proceed towards the coast and so fall into the hands of one of the warships sent to search for her.

This she eventually did and was captured, and turned out to be the *Despegado*, Don Antonio Constanti master, a Spanish craft of fifty tons and one gun, belonging to Barcelona. Needless to say the captain and his fellow pirates met with the fate they deserved.

It was during the government of General Dallas, in the year 1832, that the East India Company finally abolished slavery in the island, purchasing the freedom of the slaves, at that time numbering six hundred and fourteen, for a sum of £28,062 17s., thus putting an end, amongst other abuses, to such atrocious placards as the following:

> At the same time will be let for five years, two women servants, two girls, and a good fisherman.
>
> Also will be sold at the said house, a slave boy aged nine years, and a slave girl aged seven years, with a few articles of furniture.

In 1833 a new industry was launched at St. Helena, a whale fishery. One thousand pounds was subscribed for establishing it, but like so many other innovations initiated to assist an industry of the island, it soon came to nothing.

FOR one hundred and eighty-two years the Honourable East India Company ruled their little colony of St. Helena paternally and generously. The annual expenditure of the Company on the island amounted to between eighty and ninety thousand pounds, in return they received back three or four thousand. The little settlement may be said to have lived in the lap of luxury, for the Company had never stinted the inhabitants, and paid their officials handsome salaries, while they maintained there a garrison of three companies of artillery, called the St. Helena Artillery, a St. Helena Regiment of four companies, in all seven hundred men, exclusive of the corps of militia, and the soldiers' wives and children.

And then came the heavy blow from which this happy, peaceful, flourishing British settlement has never recovered.

In the year 1833 the St. Helenians received the almost crushing intelligence that, by an Act of Parliament dated 28th August, the island was no longer to be ruled by the Honourable East India Company after 22nd April, 1834, but to be transferred to His Majesty's Government. Radical changes took place at once. The garrison was dispersed, some being pensioned and some taking office under the new Government, while most of the civil servants of the Company were summarily dismissed, so that many of them who had been in receipt of a handsome salary were reduced almost in a moment to poverty. Melliss tells how officers of high rank might be

seen twenty years later, digging the soil alongside their own
negro servants in the struggle to support their families.

Conditions for the islanders were by no means improved by
the advent of a new Governor, the first sent out by the British
Government. This was Major-General George Middlemore,
who arrived on 24th February, 1836, and was long remembered by the St. Helenians for his bad manners and his discourtesy. With him he brought a new garrison composed of
His Majesty's 91st Regiment, and as his aide-de-camp his son,
a captain in the same regiment. His first official duty on
landing was formally to take possession of the island in the
name of King William the Fourth, when the red and white
striped flag of the Company was lowered and the Standard of
Great Britain hoisted in its place. His was not an enviable
office, for his orders from the British Government were ruthlessly to cut down expenses. The former Governors of St.
Helena had been in receipt of the substantial salary of £9,000
a year, but Middlemore's was only £2,000. On this it was
impossible to keep up such a large establishment as Plantation
House and its grounds, or to entertain in anything like the
lavish way of the previous Governors.

Almost everybody in the island was suddenly thrown into
a state bordering on penury. For nine years remonstrances
were made against the miserable pensions granted by the
Government, and petitions were laid before the East India
Company begging for grants to their discharged officers, who
had served them so long, and so faithfully, and repeated appeals
to their humanity at last wrung from them a trifling grant of
£740 annually to be divided amongst thirty-three of their late
servants. When an allotment had been made, army captains
who had served twenty-three years received tenpence a day,
or £15 6s. per annum; subalterns of nineteen years' standing
£13 19s. per annum, and the rest were paid in the same ratio.
Nor was this the full extent of the injustice done to the

unfortunate St. Helena establishment. They had been compulsorily removed from situations which they had been led to believe would be permanent, and would form a provision for life, and then found themselves, through no fault of their own, deprived of employment, without which they were unable to support and educate their families, whilst all their appeals to the East India Company ended by being referred to the British Government, who replied to their requests for employment: "We must employ our own servants first, and we have only sufficient employment for them." The Company saved annually £90,000 by relinquishing the island, and yet most ungenerously made no arrangement with the British Government for the provision of their civil and military servants.

To such bitter straits were the inhabitants reduced that in 1838 many whole families as well as about one hundred and ten other persons, consisting principally of young men, emigrated to the Cape of Good Hope. The new Governor made no secret of his dislike of all the old servants of the Company, and seldom, if ever, missed an opportunity of getting rid of them. One of these unfortunates was Major Robert Francis Seale. His history, and the tragic story of the British Government's treatment of the crowning achievement of his life's work, have been traced to their conclusion by Mr. G. C. Kitching, who most generously has allowed me to take advantage of his labours and to give the following particulars of the life and work of Robert Seale.

It is only those who live there who know how exhausting it is to walk about the island of St. Helena, where it has been truly said that to get anywhere at all "one must choose between breaking one's heart going up or one's neck coming down." The value of a large scale map or model, to anyone whose work lies in climbing up and down the steep vallies and mountains would be immense. . . . It is strange that there should be no accurate map of the Island as it was between the years 1815 and 1821, the period of Napoleon's captivity. A beautiful one was made by John Barnes in 1811, but the next was not begun until 1825, and not finished until 1836. Distinguished authorities on the Captivity have laboured at the contemporary documents, and in the published results of their researches one has made a horseman, who plays a vital part in the elaboration of his argument, ride over a 500 ft. precipice and still survive, whilst another attracts Napoleon to a beach with sinister designs, where none exists, and for weeks London audiences delighted in a historical play where the Emperor's shaving water was made to run up 1,700 feet in pipes from Jamestown to Longwood.

Had these eminent authors known that a model was in existence, it is certain they would have visited it, and their admirable works—the results of months of study—would not have been disfigured by small topographical errors.

In 1790 Francis Seale, a subaltern of the St. Helena Regiment, startled local society by abandoning his wife and children and taking to himself Miss Eleanor Alexander, a daughter of an Island family almost as old as his own.

The Governor and Council were deeply shocked, but failing to detect any offence against the "Military Code" by which his conduct might be made the subject of disciplinary action, the only course left to them was to arraign him before the Grand Jury, under what charge is not stated, which in due course ordered him to pay £45 per annum for the maintenance of his family.

The fruit of this irregular union was Robert Francis Seale, born on the 13th of November, 1791. In due course the child was sent to England to "a school near London", and in 1807, at the age of sixteen he was appointed as a junior writer in the Company's service at St. Helena, where he adorned the office of Thomas Henry Brooke, the well-known historian of the Island.

Here Seale proved himself an energetic and high-spirited young officer with a strong scientific bent that soon found expression by an interest in the topography of his Island home.

The authorities of St. Helena, with the infallibility that is inseparable from prolonged residence in small islands, seem always to have assumed that there were only twenty-three practicable landing places at which an enemy might try to attack its rocky coasts; and it was to young Seale that the Government owed the startling information that he had personally landed at over forty-three, from all of which he had reached the interior, often at night.

In 1821 Seale began to think of turning his knowledge to profit and St. Helena having become "Buonaparte's sepulchre", he produced "A Chart of the Coasts of St. Helena and their Elevations", which was presented to the East India Company on the 6th of December, 1823.

His idea, probably, was to whet the appetite of his superiors, because in the same year he disclosed to the Governor and Council a half-completed model of the Island on a scale of one foot to one mile, that he had begun to construct in 1821, and for which he had already been offered four hundred guineas.

This model created a sensation: officially the local authorities were shocked at the secrets of the Island fortress being so easily betrayed to the eyes of prying foreigners, but privately they seem to have been delighted at its artistic merits, and hurriedly instructing Seale to hide it away in the deserts of Deadwood, they advanced him the sum of £50 with which to complete it.

Having reported the matter to the Court of Directors, the

Governor was ordered to express their strong disapproba-
tion of Mr. Seale's conduct, and at the same time to purchase
it for a sum of £500 to be paid to him on the work being
finished.

Seale now set about his task in earnest, and the model was
to show "every fortification, house, road, garden, enclosure,
and division of land", and it was so constructed as "to admit
of separation into four quarters for the purpose of packing".

It was not until February, 1826, that the work was finally
finished, when Seale laid it at the "feet of the Directors",
with a memorial stating that it had taken him three and a
half years to complete, and thirteen years collecting information for the design. The model was shipped to England
in two cases on the 21st of February, 1826, together with
the following covering minute from Governor Walker:

"Mr. R. Seale has finished his Model of St. Helena, and it
is about to be transmitted to England agreeably to the
order of the Hon'ble Court of Directors.

"This has been the labour of many years of Mr. Seale's
life and he appears to have considered it as the foundation
of fame as well as pecuniary emolument. It is more easy to
speak of the Model as a monument of genius and ingenuity
than to appreciate its worth in money. The few men of
science who have had the opportunity of viewing it have
extolled it highly as a work of art, independent of its value
as an accurate representation of this Island. . . . It is the
work of a man of talent and of talent which nature has
bestowed. It exhibits a species of ingenious industry which
excites the curiosity and applause of the Public, but which
unfortunately is seldom adequately rewarded.

"The Hon'ble East India Company have always encouraged their servants who have either displayed natural
or acquired talents and it is to their spirit of liberality that
Mr. Seale can alone look for pecuniary recompense. It will

be an agreeable task in transmitting Mr. Seale's memorial to the Hon'ble Court to point out the extraordinary merits of his work and strongly to recommend it to their further favourable consideration."

For over one hundred years this model of a famous Island has been lost to the public. Darwin is known to have visited it; on more than one occasion it formed the subject for the annual drawing prize at Addiscombe, and a lyrical reference to its merit appeared in the St. Helena Guardian for 1886.

Fortunately, or it has proved unfortunately, its existence did not escape the notice of Dr. Arnold Chaplin, and a paragraph in an old copy of the St. Helena Diocesan Magazine referring to a model of the Island being in a London Museum led to the present enquiries. A letter addressed there elicited the information that it had been transferred to another museum where an emissary was despatched to seek it out. He reported that no one there knew anything about a model of St. Helena nor had they heard of its existence; but after pursuing the subject by correspondence, he was informed there was a model that had been presented as a gift but for ease for transport the removal contractors "had broken it into four pieces which could easily be re-assembled".

A card that accompanied it gave the following description: "Model of the Island of St. Helena. Scale 540 feet to 1 in., or 1/6480. Presented by the Secretary of State for India on the reduction of the late East India Company's College at Addiscombe."

A personal visit to the Museum, sometime later, for the purpose of inspecting the Model, proved fruitless as it had by then "disintegrated".

Further enquiries made by the present writer in the fond

hope that Seale's precious model might after all still be intact in some dim cellar of one of our national museums led to the following surprising information.

It appears that only seven years ago the model was complete and the property of a certain museum in London.

"With a view to displaying some small arms to better advantage", it was agreed (by the trustees), to use the large glass case of the model for this purpose. On removing the model it was found that the wooden base had the worm in it. As it would have cost several pounds to repair it, the model was "disintegrated", which is apparently the official term for "smashed to pieces".

But to return to Mr. Kitching's narrative.

Seale's work of art is, therefore, lost to students and history for ever; and his career, like his model, terminated in misfortune. In 1836, after the transfer of the Island to the Crown, he was appointed as the first Colonial Secretary under the Crown with his Company's pension of £500 and a salary of £400 per annum.

Then he was so unfortunate as to incur the hostility of General Middlemore, the new Governor, who, for some reason other than his habitual bad manners and discourtesy, regarded all the old servants of the Company with a jaundiced eye.

Seale—he was obviously a man of great physical powers —lived and worked hard. He was injudicious in his investments in local properties, and with the change in circumstances arising from the transfer of the Island he became heavily embarrassed by debts and mortgages. Foreclosure followed inability to meet his interest payments, when Middlemore reported him to the Secretary of State for "a defalcation". Never was a more outrageous charge preferred against a public officer; and although the opprobrious expression was afterwards publicly withdrawn, Seale was dismissed his appointment in 1838 and died suddenly the following year "without money to pay for his funeral", leaving a widow and eight children, as well as a crippled son by a former wife, "in a state of penury".

Four years after his death his reputation was vindicated by Middlemore's successor, Hamelin Trelawney, when the Secretary of State was pleased to make a grant to the widow of £100 from the Royal Bounty.

The year 1836 is memorable in the history of St. Helena for events other than the transfer of the island to the Crown.

On the 8th of July that year Charles Darwin landed from the *Beagle*, and needless to say managed in a short stay of six days to make a tolerably exhaustive examination of the geology and flora of the island.

He was particularly struck by the English, or rather Welsh character of the scenery, with its numerous whitewashed cottages and small houses, some buried at the bottom of the deepest valleys and others mounted on the crests of lofty hills. He commented upon the extreme poverty of the lower classes, particularly of the emancipated slaves, most of whom were out of work, due to the dismissal of so many public servants when the island was given up by the East India Company.

"The chief food of the working classes," he noted, "is rice with a little salt meat; as neither of these articles are the products of the island, but must be purchased with money, the low wages tell heavily on the poor people."

Darwin liked the islanders, with their dusky skins and mixture of blood, and their polite manners and gentle voices.

Curiously enough the famous naturalist did not see, or failed to recognize, the wire bird, *Aegialitis sanctæ-helenæ*, as a native, for he does not mention it but stated his belief that all the birds of the island had been introduced within recent years.

Partridges and pheasants he found to be fairly abundant, so that he was not surprised to learn that the island was subject to strict game-laws, though his indignation was roused when he learned of a law which would never have been passed even in such a game-preserving country as England. This was an ordinance which prevented poor people from burning a plant which grew on the coast-rocks—to extract the soda from its ashes—for the reason that if they continued to do so the partridges would have nowhere to build!

The closing paragraph of Darwin's description ends with these words:

> I so much enjoyed my rambles among the rocks and mountains of St. Helena, that I felt almost sorry on the morning of the 14th to descend to the town. Before noon I was on board, and the *Beagle* made sail.[1]

By Order in Council of Her Majesty Queen Victoria, the Supreme Court was established in February, 1839, and in the year following Her Majesty's Government established a Vice-Admiralty Court at the Island for the trial of vessels engaged in the slave trade on the west coast of Africa. Large numbers of these were captured and brought to St. Helena during the following ten years, to be condemned, sold and broken up, while their human cargoes were fed, clothed and kept at the Liberated African Depot at Rupert's Valley, until they were sufficiently recovered from their emaciated condition to bear a voyage to the British West Indies, where a demand existed for their labour. During the time the Depot was in use, over 10,000 liberated Africans were forwarded to those islands or to British Guiana. Until they were re-shipped those who were strong enough to work were employed on various public works, while some remained on the island as servants or labourers in private service.

[1] *A Naturalist's Voyage round the World.* 1860.

A naval squadron was specially employed to hunt down the slave ships that traded between the West African coast and America. Melliss in his book on St. Helena describes how he went on board one of these slave ships which had been brought in to Rupert's Bay.

A visit [he wrote] to a full-freighted slaveship arriving at St. Helena is not easily to be forgotten; a scene so intensified in all that is horrible almost defies description. The vessel, scarcely a hundred tons burthen at most, contains perhaps little short of a thousand souls, which have been closely packed, for many weeks together, in the hottest and most polluted of atmospheres. I went on board one of these ships as she cast anchor off Rupert's Valley in 1861, and the whole deck, as I picked my way from end to end, in order to avoid treading upon them, was thickly strewn with the dead, dying and starved bodies of what seemed to me to be a species of ape which I had never seen before. One's sensations of horror were certainly lessened by the impossibility of realizing that the miserable, helpless objects being picked up from the deck and handed over the ship's side, one by one, living, dying, and dead alike, were really human beings. Their arms and legs were worn down to about the size of a walking-stick.

Many died as they passed from the ship to the boat, and, indeed, the work of unloading had to be proceeded with so quickly that there was no time to separate the dead from the living.

The Liberated African Depot, together with the men-of-war which were employed in cruising for slave ships, brought to the island both money and employment, and did much to alleviate the distress caused by the transference of the island to the Crown. Although no one was aware of it at the time, two disadvantages were to follow the choice of St. Helena for

this splendid work of liberating slaves. One was the introduction of a new race of black people, for hitherto very few
negroes had been brought to the island; the other, a far more
serious one, was the introduction of the White Ant or termite.

In 1840 one of H.M. cruisers brought in a slave ship from
Brazil. She was duly condemned, broken up and the timber
deposited in Jamestown. Nobody suspected her timbers of
being infested with white ants until a quarter of a century had
passed, when definite evidence of their terrible work of
destruction was observable. Long before this, however, the
termites had begun to eat books, furniture, papers and clothes,
with occasionally a beam or two in the houses, but eventually
the town was in ruins and it cost £60,000 at least to reconstruct
it. Starting in the town the invisible army of subterranean
wreckers slowly spread about the country, doing irreparable
damage wherever it went, both to buildings and growing
trees.

It was a melancholy sight five years ago [Melliss wrote
in 1874] to see the town, which had hitherto not been without its claim for admiration, devastated as by an earthquake,
or, as a visitor remarked, a state of siege—the chief church
in ruins, public buildings in a deplorable state of dilapidation, private houses tottering and falling, with great timber
props, butting out into the streets and roadways, meeting
the eye at every turn, and astounding the stranger by a tale
of some awful risk incurred merely when walking along the
pavements; while the Governor in his council-chamber, the
Chief Justice, and the other officials, were accessible only
through a labyrinth of fir-poles and old ship-planking set
on end to prevent ceilings falling on their heads, or, worse
still, whole buildings collapsing around them.

One example showing how quickly these minute fragile
insects do their deadly work, was the reception hall at the

Castle. In 1860 His Royal Highness the Duke of Edinburgh
visited St. Helena and held a levee in it, and the same evening
it was used for a Governor's ball. Six years afterwards the
hall was a complete ruin!

Amongst other valuable property, the termites devoured a
considerable portion of the books in the public library, shewing
a decided preference for theological literature, a preference
which Melliss tried to account for, because such works
generally remained longest untouched on the bookshelves.

The white ants would enter a book by very minute holes,
destroy every atom of the interior, without showing the least
sign of their presence, and then depart, leaving the binding
and gilt or marbled edges of the leaves apparently as perfect
as when new.

In 1840 there occurred at St. Helena one other event of
historical importance.

On the 8th of October in that year the French frigate,
La Belle Poule, accompanied by the corvette *Favourite*, arrived
at the island, with his Royal Highness the Prince de Joinville
and his suite. They had come to St. Helena for the purpose of
removing Napoleon's remains to France.

Included in the party were several former inmates of Longwood, Count Bertrand, with his son Arthur, born on St.
Helena, Baron Gourgaud, Baron Emmanuel Las Cases, Louis
Marchand, Napoleon's first valet, and several domestics who
had remained with their master to the end.

The distinguished visitors were hospitably received by
Governor Middlemore, and it was arranged that the removal
of the coffin to the French frigate should take place on the 15th
of October, the anniversary of the day when the *Northumberland* in 1815 reached St. Helena with her illustrious passenger.

It is significant that the former inmates of Longwood, who
had never ceased to disparage both the scenery and climate of
St. Helena, all found the island very different from their

recollections. From this they concluded, not that their point of view had changed, but that the island itself must have undergone some strange transformation.

The air, they declared, was pleasanter, the scenery brighter and more attractive than it had seeemd to be when they lived in St. Helena in confinement.

But at Longwood itself they all agreed there was indeed a change for the worse. Where had been a garden now stood a windmill, which turned a threshing machine working in the very room in which Napoleon died. There was a hole in the ceiling of the dining-room, through which sacks of wheat could be let down to a machine which stood there.

The exhumation was begun at midnight of the 14th-15th of October, under the direction of Captain Alexander, R.E., when in an unceasing downpour of rain a detachment of British soldiers set to work with pick and shovel.

The coffin was lifted out of the grave and was placed on a hearse, made from a former Governor's carriage, and drawn by four horses to Jamestown. At the head of the procession marched a detachment of the St. Helena militia, followed by one of the 91st Regiment and the band of the militia. Behind these walked the French members of the mission, the officers of the two French ships, the Governor, and other high officials of the island, while the rear of the cortege was formed by a company of the Royal Artillery.

The slow-moving procession did not reach the outskirts of Jamestown until half-past four in the afternoon. Soldiers of the garrison, their arms reversed, lined both sides of the road the whole distance to the quay.

On the quay the Prince de Joinville received the Imperial coffin from the hands of General Middlemore, and thanked him in the name of France for the testimonies of sympathy and respect which the authorities had shown throughout.

The coffin was then lowered on to the deck of a boat from

La Belle Poule, flying a fine silk flag which had been made by three young ladies of the island.

While the boat was making its way from the shore to *La Belle Poule*, the French and British ships in the Road fired salutes. Three days later, the body of the great man and Emperor started on its return journey from the little island in the South Atlantic to find a lasting resting place in France.

Since almost every known scrap of written evidence about the years of the Captivity of Napoleon has been recorded, docketed and published, the discovery in the files of *The St. Helena Herald* of 1854 of a long poem on the subject seems to be worth while printing in full in spite of its being sad doggerel, for it contains much that is interesting.[1] It appeared serially, sometimes in large dollops, sometimes only a verse or two, so that one is led to believe that Joseph Lockwood, the Editor of St. Helena's only periodical, used it as a convenient stop-gap when he was short of copy. On some weeks there would be nothing from Sally Phil, but on others a whole column or more. It begins in the issue of August 1st and continues throughout the year. Evidently there were another verse or two to come, but the poem was brought to an abrupt close by the following which appeared on February 8th, 1855:

NOTICE

Sally Phill will resume her spleen, if Mr. Cash re-commences to use her Name, as she will not allow Mr. Cash with Impunity to reiterate falsehood behind her back.

S. P. . . .

A number of people in the island had cause to be grateful to the memory of Napoleon.

John Young, a pensioner of the Company, who acted as

---

[1] See Appendix V.

guardian of the Tomb, received £40 a year from the French Goverment in 1841; the leesees of Longwood charged 2/- for admission; tea at the Tomb cost 2/6, and here Sally Phil and her husband Jack, both freed slaves, acted as unofficial guides and the former recited her "poem".

In the year 1840 a meteorological observatory was erected at Longwood, at an elevation of 1,760 feet above the level of the sea, under the direction of General Sir Edward Sabine, F.R.S. Observations were conducted there for a period of five years by officers and non-commissioned officers of the Royal Artillery.

In 1842 Middlemore retired and was succeeded by Colonel Hamelin Trelawney, and in the same year the island was garrisoned by a European regiment of five companies raised expressly for the purpose and styled the St. Helena Regiment, which took the place of the usual regiment of the line.

During the governorship of Colonel Trelawney a serious epidemic of measles broke out, which caused many deaths.

The parish church of St. James in Jamestown was considerably altered and repaired and in place of the old square tower, the pointed steeple which is to-day such a well-known landmark from the sea, was built.

By writ of Privy Council a Court of Commissioners was established for the trial of offences on the high seas.

In May, 1846, Governor Trelawney died and was succeeded by Major-General Sir Patrick Ross, who landed in November, 1846. General Ross was interested in agriculture and did much to encourage this and horticulture amongst the islanders by promoting exhibitions of the island's produce.

It was on the 18th February, 1846, that an extraordinary phenomenon took place at Jamestown. For a week or more something strange was anticipated, when the prevalent southeast trade wind dropped and the atmosphere became extremely oppressive. Then in the night the sea suddenly rose higher than had ever been known before and huge waves or "rollers" broke upon the shore, so that at daylight next morning the sea opposite the town was one sheet of white foam and yet there was not a breath of wind. The Road was filled with shipping at the time, including eighteen slavers which were lying at anchor waiting to be broken up. At eleven o'clock the same morning, one of these, the *Decobrador*, was bodily lifted from her anchors and thrown broadside on top of another slaver, the *Cordelia*, and both were swept by the huge seas and deposited high and dry in front of the sea-guard gate. Altogether thirteen vessels were wrecked and smashed into pieces by the time the sea subsided the same evening.

The onset had been so sudden and so unexpected that a number of persons were on board the ships when the "storm" began.

Amongst these were Mr. Seale, a ship-keeper and his wife, who were on board the *Cordelia* and must have perished but for the bravery of an American seaman named Roach, who, taking a rope with him, managed to swim out to the ship, seize Mrs. Seale in his arms and jump overboard with her, and both of them were drawn safely to shore. Mr. Seale, too, was rescued in the same manner by a Lascar.

The cause of this extraordinary occurrence has never been discovered, but the most plausible explanation is that it was the result of a submarine earthquake, although earthquakes as well as thunderstorms and lightning are almost unknown on the island.

In 1850 the foundation stone of the present "Country Church" of St. Paul, otherwise known as the Cathedral, was laid by the Governor. This was one of the results of the visit of the Bishop of Capetown, the Right Reverend Robert Gray, in 1847.

Owing to the rain Sir Patrick Ross was unable to meet his distinguished visitor, the first Bishop ever to set foot upon the

island, but his place was taken by his Aide-de-Camp, Captain
Knipe, who, appreciating the importance of the occasion,
ordered a salute to be fired, an honour the Bishop begged to
be excused.

There were four clergymen then serving on the island, Mr.
Kempthorne, the senior Colonial Chaplain, Mr. Helps,
Military Chaplain, Mr. Bousfield, Assistant Chaplain and a Mr.
Frey, who formerly had been a German missionary in India
and who acted as head-master of the Government Country
School.

Mr. Bousfield's stipend was paid by the Society for the
Propagation of the Gospel. This was not the first occasion
upon which the S.P.G. had come to the aid of St. Helena. In
1704, only three years after the Society was founded, "upon a
motion from the Treasurer", they allowed £5 worth of "small
tracts" to the Reverend Charles Masham, "a minister sent to
St. Helena by the East India Company". A year later Mr.
Masham reported his safe arrival in the island, and also that
the books "were very acceptable to the inhabitants". His
letter still exists in the archives of the S.P.G. and permission
has been kindly granted to print it.[1]

Mr Masham to Mr Hodges.

St Helena Nov: 24, 1705

Sr

I should be doubly in fault should I neglect to write now,
since I did not by the last Fleet, but I was then in a continued hurry from ye time I arrived till ye Fleet sailed, & had
scarce time to write to any one. However I will not slip
this Opportunity of acknowledging with Thanks your past
Favours. I suppose Dr Woodward did inform you that I
got safe hither & I thank God have continued so almost
ever since. I have to ye best of my Judgmt disposed of
most of those books, ye Society were pleased to remitt to

[1] S.P.G. M.S.S. Vol. A2, No. CXXVIII.

my Care they were very acceptable to the Inhabitants, & I hope will prove very useful. Several Children have got that Exposition of the Catechism by heart. I catechise in ye Church one half of the year, preaching at the same time upon some part or other of that. If ye Company shall think fit to transmit any more, or other kind of Books, I'le be sure to dispose of them where I think they may do most Good, & if there be any new Books that may assist my self in the discharge of my Duty, I shall be very thankful for them. I desire my humble Duty to his Grace my Lord AB^p, & to all that worthy & Honble Society. I design to write to his Grace myself by this Fleet. I am

S^r

Your most Obliged humble Servant

Directions are   Cha: Masham

To Mr John Hodges &C.

In 1706 the Society sent him a further supply of tracts as well as a supply of bibles and prayer books.

During his stay at St. Helena the Bishop confirmed about a tenth of the whole population of the island, consecrated the church at Jamestown, together with five burial-grounds, and made arrangements for the transfer of the Church property from the Government to the See of Capetown.

The Bishop's visit to St. Helena must have been anything but a restful holiday, for in addition to the above duties he "held a visitation with a special view to the reformation of some points in which the Church was defective, and the restoration of Church discipline", and reorganized the local Church and Benevolent Societies.

These institutions, with the Government, contributed liberally to the eight island schools, but the state of education the Bishop found to be unsatisfactory, owing to the incompetency of the teachers.

The good Bishop was also exercised that "for the first time during a period of 150 years, division had been introduced into the community by the recent arrival of an advocate of the Anabaptist community", but he was comforted by the fact that "much good had already been brought out of this evil".

At Longwood, the billiard-room in the new house built for Napoleon was being used as a chapel, where "an excellent congregation" attended.

He found time to go aboard a newly captured slave ship at Rupert's Bay. "I never beheld a more piteous sight"—wrote Bishop Gray—"never looked upon a more affecting scene—never before felt so powerful a call to be a Missionary. I did not quit that ship without having resolved more firmly than ever, that I would, with the grace and help of God, commence as speedily as possible to direct Mission work in Southern Africa."

Almost as harrowing to his sensibility was the Bishop's first visit to the slave village or establishment in Rupert's Valley:

If anything were needed to fill the soul with burning indignation against that master-work of Satan, the Slave-trade, it would be a visit to this institution. There were not less than 600 poor souls in it . . . of these more than 300 were in hospital; some affected with dreadful opthalmia; others with severe rheumatism, others with dysentery, the number of deaths in the week being twenty-one.

It soon became evident that the remoteness of the island from Capetown made necessary a resident Bishop, and in 1859 Bishop Gray succeeded in securing its erection into a separate diocese, which included the islands of Ascension and Tristan da Cunha, as well as the British residents of Rio de Janeiro and other towns on the East coast of South America.

The first Bishop of St. Helena, Dr. Piers C. Claughton, landed there on the 30th of October, 1859.

When in 1851 Sir Patrick Ross died he was succeeded by Colonel Thomas Gore Browne.

The new Governor's task was by no means an enviable nor an easy one, for he came with instructions from the home Government to retrench and economize, and in order to do this the civil establishment was yet further reduced.

At this time Jamestown was much over-populated, and being situated in a deep narrow ravine there was no room for it to expand in any direction. To get over this difficulty Governor Gore Browne conceived the idea of establishing a village at Rupert's Valley to relieve the congestion in Jamestown.

As a start or nucleus to this new settlement he had sent out from England a ready-made jail, a sort of model prison, which was erected in the valley, and water was brought there by means of iron pipes leading from The Briars over Rupert's Hill. This building, which was constructed of wood, was burnt to the ground in less than an hour by a prisoner confined in it in 1867.

In December, 1854, Colonel Gore Browne was promoted to the Governorship of New Zealand and until the arrival of Sir Edward Hay Drummond Hay, in October, 1856, the senior military officer, Colonel H. N. Vigors, acted for him.

In the spacious years of the Company, the Governors of St. Helena were carefully selected as men likely to be fitted for the important duty of ruling the island, and they stayed for many years; in two cases, of Governor Hutchinson and Governor Skottowe, for seventeen and eighteen years respectively. But when the island became a colony of the British Empire a quite new type of Governor was chosen and few remained for many years. I cannot do better than quote what was written on the subject of these latter Governors of St.

Helena by Mr. Benjamin Grant, in his valuable little book, printed and published by himself at St. Helena in 1883.[1]

From the time the Island was transferred to the Crown up to 1872, its affairs have been administered by (with a few exceptions) old Major-Generals, worn out Colonels, and pensioned Admirals, whom the British Government delighted to honour, and the Island had to pay £2,000 a year, besides £200 allowances, and supply a splendid house to reside in! They knew nothing of, or were wholly indifferent to, the requirements of the place and its Inhabitants; therefore did naught but receive their salaries and expend the Revenue on what *they* deemed most advisable; while the Inhabitants themselves had no voice in the management of their internal affairs.

And what good has followed to the Island by their administration? In 1871 it found itself burdened with a heavy debt, at a time too when it was verging on a state of bankruptcy! A happy idea suggested itself to the Home Government: they sent out a pensioned Admiral to cut down the expenses, and what did he do? While lessening the expenditure by pensioning young and old servants he caused a great loss to the Island: e.g.—nearly the whole of these pensioners, finding their pensions insufficient to keep them in St. Helena, left its shores, therefore receiving and spending their allowances, (about £1,500), in other lands, thus draining the resources of the Island, and rendering it poor indeed.

A good deal has been said in these pages concerning the clergy of St. Helena, and until the chaplaincy of Mr. Richard Boys there has been little to record in their favour. But about the year 1856 a change for the better occurred in the spiritual welfare of the island. It is not known, as far as the present

[1] *A Few Notes on St. Helena.* St. Helena, 1883.

writer is aware, to what exact denomination Mr. Melliss belonged, but we have reason to believe from the following passage out of his book about St. Helena, that he was a sound member of the Church of England.

Hitherto [he wrote] the Church of England had reigned supreme in the Island, it having been included in the See of Capetown, and subject to periodical visits from that Bishop: but as the Church was represented on the spot only by a colonial chaplain and a garrison chaplain, a very inadequate number of clergymen, Dissent, which was introduced by a Scotch Baptist Minister about the year 1847, soon spread, and became a popular sectarian distinction amongst the native population.

All of which has a curious similarity to the same writer's description of the introduction to the island of the pestilential white ant.

Sir Edward Drummond Hay carried out some of the schemes planned by his predecessor, Gore Browne, amongst them the settlement at Rupert's Valley, and the main drainage works of Jamestown. Of the settlement at Rupert's Valley scarcely a trace is now left. To-day it is a hot, arid waste of stones, under which lurk scorpions, giant centipedes and agile geckos. Only a few houses are left standing and on some of these can be deciphered the words "Hays Town".

He erected new dwellings in one of the worst slums of Jamestown, though there are slums there still which are a disgrace to the ruling powers of St. Helena. He built new Customs houses on the wharf and laid down additional pipes for the supply of water to the ships.

In 1857 the Church of St. John was built, and a few years after, that of St. Matthew at Hutts Gate.

It is as tiresome for the historian as it is for his readers to be compelled to bespatter his pages with dates, but they cannot be avoided.

In 1858, by an ordinance of His Excellency the Governor in Council, and ratified and confirmed by order of the Queen in Council, the land forming the site of the tomb of Napoleon Bonaparte and also the land forming the site of the tenement of Longwood, with the house and appurtenances, were vested in His Majesty Napoleon III and his heirs for ever, as absolute owners thereof in fee simple for ever. To-day and for all time these precious relics of the captivity of Napoleon are part of France, and will never be better nor more reverently cared for than they are by their present custodians, Monsieur and Madame Colin.

Admiral Sir Charles Elliot, at the age of sixty-two, relieved Governor Drummond Hay in 1863 and administered the government for seven years. According to other authorities than Benjamin Grant[1] he won for himself the respect and affection of the islanders by his kindness, courtesy, gentle manners and energy.

Almost his first act was to declare war against the termites or white ants, and he rebuilt nearly the whole of the public buildings in Jamestown, which they had destroyed, with stone, iron and teakwood. During his government the first direct monthly mail by steamships was established, which greatly helped to keep the island in touch with the rest of the world. No Governor, since Alexander Beatson, did so much to encourage the introduction of new and valuable plants as did Sir Charles Elliot.

Amongst others, he imported the Mexican pine, which took well to the climate and soil, the Norfolk Island pine and Bermuda cedars. If only a little trouble was taken and encouragement given, many of these useful trees would be growing in the island to-day.

[1] See p. 322.

Authentic portrait by Wyvill, 1832

By courtesy of The Hon. Ben Bathurst

Imaginary portrait by an unknown French artist, for purposes of propaganda, 1830

SIR HUDSON LOWE

THOMAS H. BROOKE
Secretary to the Governor and Acting-Governor of St. Helena.
Author of *A History of the Island of St. Helena*

BRIGADIER-GENERAL ALEXANDER WALKER
Governor, 1823-1828
From the painting by Sir Henry Raeburn

OLD LONGWOOD
Residence of Napoleon as it is to-day

PEAK
HILL

VE OF
ERNOR
ISCH

JAMESTOWN IN 1794
from a drawing by William Daniell

JAMESTOWN TO-DAY

AND MRS.
IAMS AND
ILY AT
LEY'S LAY

AND MRS.
SEL JOHN
FAMILY
THORN
COTTAGE

FLAX FIBRE
DRYING AT
FAIRYLAND,
SANDY BAY

SAWYERS AT
BAMBOO
HEDGE,
SANDY BAY

It was at this time that the famous botanist, Dr. Hooker, Director of the Royal Gardens at Kew, advised the Government to undertake the culture of the Cinchona plant on the more mountainous parts of the island, for the production of quinine. A skilled gardener was sent out from Kew, and a plantation of ten thousand Cinchona plants soon sprang up on the side of Diana's Peak, and promised the greatest success, and a source of much profit to the island, but most unfortunately, Sir Charles Elliot's successor, Vice-Admiral Patey, being unable to see the advantage of such an undertaking, the plantation was neglected and ultimately abandoned.

To-day, in the only small area of indigenous jungle which remains—thanks to the shortsightedness of several Governors and the stinginess of the British Treasury—plants of Cinchona are still to be found.

When Vice-Admiral Patey succeeded to the Governorship in 1870, he took out to the island in his pocket the pruning knife of retrenchment. It is true that the civil establishment at this time was larger than necessary, but to reduce it without injuring its efficiency called for tact, care and judgment, qualities which were lacking in the Vice-Admiral.

The well-meant endeavours of Governor Patey to lessen expenditure were so unsuccessful that in 1873 he was superseded by Hudson Ralph Janisch, the then Colonial Secretary, the second and the last island-born Governor in the whole history of St. Helena. This honour to the island of his birth was, however, somewhat modified by a considerable reduction in the salary attached to the office.

The new Governor was the son of a German of Hamburg, Georg Wilhelm Janisch, who went out to St. Helena in 1816 as one of the staff of Sir Hudson Lowe, by whom he was employed to make copies of his "Papers". After Lowe's departure from the island he became a ship's chandler, and married

Anne Mira, the only daughter of Major William Seale, by whom he had one surviving son, whom he named, in honour of his old master, Hudson.

H. R. Janisch took a keen interest in the history of St. Helena, and his chief claim to be remembered is his *Extracts from the St. Helena Records and Chronicles of Cape Commanders*, printed and published at Jamestown in 1885.

Copies of the first edition must be very scarce; the present writer, an ardent collector of all to do with St. Helena, has failed to discover a copy. In 1908, Mr. Benjamin Grant printed a second and revised edition, with a preface written by Lieutenant-Colonel H. L. Gallwey, Governor at that time. This small volume, made up of a selection from the old Record Books at the Castle at Jamestown, is a mine of local history and gossip, and has been invaluable to the writer of these pages, as it has been to others who have written about the island's past.

The governorship of Janisch cannot be passed over without some mention of the present state of the island's memorial to his pious memory. It is a tall, handsome obelisk which stands, or totters, in the Baptist Cemetery at Knollcombes. When I saw it in the spring of the year 1937 it appeared to be on the point of falling over, leaning perilously to one side at an alarming angle. More than likely by the time these words are printed, it will have crashed to the ground and will be one more historic relic of St. Helena which has been allowed to fall into ruins. On enquiry I learned that it would cost about thirty pounds to take down and re-erect this monument, and yet so little interest is taken by the authorities or by the St. Helenians themselves to preserve the monuments of their dead or the relics of the past, that nothing was being done, nor was likely to be done, to save this memorial to their island-born Governor, and a man greatly venerated and loved by all during his lifetime.

Cut on one side of the plinth could be deciphered the following inscription:

IN MEMORY

OF

HUDSON RALPH JANISCH C.M.G. F.R.A.S.

DIED MARCH 10th 1884 AGED 59 YEARS.

This memorial is erected by the inhabitants to commemorate the high respect and esteem in which the late Governor was universally held.

"Blessed are the dead which die in the Lord"

Mr. Grant, who wrote so bitterly about many of the Governors, had nothing but good to say concerning Governor Janisch. Possibly the fact that they both were Yamstocks, that is to say, born on the Island, may have predisposed him in his favour.

Referring to Janisch he wrote:

Our present Governor is the right man in the right place; he knows the requirements of his native home, but he has not the funds at his disposal to meet those requirements.

He himself is the worst, and most inadequately, paid Governor in the employ of Great Britain. He is besides Administrator of the Island, a judge of the Supreme Court, yet he receives as salary for such, £900 a year, and provides a residence for himself![1]

[1] *A Few Notes on St. Helena.* St. Helena, 1883.

WHEN in 1858 Old Longwood House and the tomb of Napoleon were made over to the Emperor Napoleon III, three officers with a party of engineers were sent out from France to put them into repair and to restore the house to as nearly as possible the condition it was in when occupied by the Exiles.

One great difficulty was met with when the restorers came to consider the re-papering of the walls, for not a scrap of the original wall-papers remained to give a clue as to their design or colour. Then one day Mr. John C. Melliss, the Commissioner of Crown Property, happened to mention the difficulty to an officer who had just arrived from India on his way home.

Thirty years previously this officer had visited Longwood and had torn off a scrap of paper from the walls of each of the rooms, which he had carefully preserved. These he handed over to the French officers, who sent them to Paris, where new papers, exactly resembling the originals, were manufactured and sent out to St. Helena. Since then several pieces of furniture which belonged to Longwood have been found at Plantation House and elsewhere and have been returned to Longwood, including the famous billiard-table.

If a chart were drawn to show the increase and decrease of prosperity in St. Helena, it would begin in 1673 and rise steadily up and reach its peak in 1821, the year Napoleon died, and before most of the troops and high military officers, civil servants and their families had left the island. It would then begin rapidly to fall, though occasionally the downward curve would be arrested, and even recover a few degrees, as when the West African Squadron used St. Helena for their base during the years that the hunt for slave ships was carried on, although the Liberated African Depot at Rupert's Valley was not finally closed until 1874. In 1864 the squadron left and depression at once resulted and our curve drops suddenly: for the loss of the squadron was not the only disaster which took place in this year of ill-fortune.

The white ants were causing terrible damage, repairs for which the island had to pay out of its already depleted exchequer. So impoverished became the inhabitants that out of this little island about fifteen hundred of the poorest inhabitants emigrated to Natal and the Cape of Good Hope.[1]

An even more serious misfortune was also taking place. Hitherto one of the principal assets had been the large number of passengers who came on shore out of the ships calling on their way home from India.

By now very few of the better-off Anglo-Indians travelled by the Atlantic route, preferring to sail to the Red Sea, cross the isthmus by land, and re-embark on the Mediterranean shore, and so make the journey in a considerably shorter time. Also, owing to the innovation of steamships, many of the larger ships from the east did not call at St. Helena, as they made quicker passages than before, carried greater bulk of water, and with refrigerators and tinned food, were able to do the voyage from India to England without having to stop to replenish their stores on the way.

All these points were mentioned by a Commission which was sent out to the Island to enquire into the causes of the depression.

It is often stated that the death-blow to St. Helena was the

[1] Précis of Information concerning the Island of St. Helena. St. Helena, 1876.

opening of the Suez Canal in 1869. Actually it had already taken place, and the Canal merely was the final stroke from which St. Helena has never recovered.

In 1874 an agricultural experiment was made which, although not at first successful, became eventually the principal, and it might well be said, the only staple industry of the island. In this year one hundred acres were planted with a liliaceous plant, Phormium Tenax, called locally New Zealand flax, a plant originally introduced from New Zealand. The first attempt to extract fibre from the island-grown plants was made, when the Colonial and Foreign Fibre Company set up machinery for the purpose at Jamestown.

The Company, however, soon failed, for two reasons. The price of fibre suddenly fell, and the mill had been erected at Jamestown instead of close to the flax plantations, which meant long and costly transport of every load of fresh-cut leaf to be treated.

In 1907 a Government Mill was started at Longwood under the supervision of New Zealand experts, and since then several others have been built and are working. To-day 3,253 acres of flax are under cultivation, but unfortunately the wages paid to the workmen, both in the fields and in the mills, are so low that this staple industry, which employs 324 mill-hands and should be of the greatest service to the Island, benefits but three or four of the big landowners.

Nor can the present staple export of the fibre of New Zealand flax be regarded as an ideal industry for such a small island. For one thing, land planted with flax yields a harvest only once in every three to five years, so that only when the prices obtained for the fibre are very high—as they were during the Great War—is the land being used to the best advantage.

In 1875 another attempt was made to start a whale-fishing industry. A barque, the *Elizabeth*, was fitted out at Jamestown and manned by island men, many of whom had served on

American whalers. But the enterprise was begun at a bad time, for the South Atlantic whale fishery was then on its last legs and this well-meant attempt to benefit the St. Helenians came to nothing.

Owing to its isolated position in the South Atlantic Ocean, several astronomers have at different times visited St. Helena to make scientific observations.

In 1877 Professor David Gill and his wife were sent by the Royal Astronomical Society on an expedition to Ascension Island to measure the sun's distance and make an observation of the planet Mars, but to get there they had to go first to St. Helena. Mrs. Gill kept a journal which was afterwards published.[1]

The Governor's pony carriage met the astronomers at the landing steps and drove them the short distance to the Castle.

Their first expedition was to the Observatory on Ladder Hill where fifty years before Manuel Johnson—afterwards Radcliffe Observer at Oxford—made his catalogue of six hundred and six southern stars.

Their heavy chronometers were carried up the steep, winding road by some gunners, lent by Captain Oliver, R.A.

Poor innocent astronomers, they were too newly come to St. Helena to know how St. Helena valued her historic monuments.

This is what Mrs. Gill had to say of the famous St. Helena Observatory:

> I say Observatory—alas! it is so no longer. Fallen from its high estate, it is now the artillery mess-room, and in the recesses formed for the shutters of the openings through which Johnson's transit used to peep, they stow wineglasses and decanters, and under the dome they play billiards!
> It may appear ungrateful [she continued] to speak so of

[1] *Six Months in Ascension.* Mrs. Gill. John Murray, 1878.

a change which was productive of so much kindness and hospitality to us; I do not grudge the hospitable St. Helena Mess their mess-room, but I do regret that so fine a site for an Observatory is vacant.

The East India Company spent a large sum of money in building and fitting up this observatory.

Manuel Johnson, 1849

The foundation stone was laid on the 13th September, 1826, under a Royal Salute from a brigade of guns and a *feu de joie* from the St. Helena Regiment. The building was not completed till 1828, and on the 24th January of the same year Manuel Johnson was appointed in charge of the Observatory and began his great work as an astronomer.

"Fortunately," as Mr. Kitching observes,[1] "Johnson was not in St. Helena to receive the insults heaped upon the Observatory when the Island was transferred to the Crown in 1834."

In spite of the important scientific results of Johnson's

[1] *Papers Relating to the History of St. Helena.* 1937.

work there, the Commissioners, who had been sent out to report on the Island, remarked in regard to the Observatory "that they had been unable to learn its establishment had been attended with any important result to science", and that as it cost £300 per annum, they recommended it should be abandoned, and the instruments which were "of a superior description" be sent to London.

All the instruments were sent to Canada but two clocks, two sidereal clocks, the transit instrument, and a chronometer, which were retained for use in the local Time Office.

For seventy-one years the time was given to the shipping; but in 1907 the chronometer began to fail. The Governor of the period, Colonel Gallwey, then asked for a replacement, but was told that all that was required in St. Helena was a sun-dial. At this rebuff the Time Office was abandoned.

Johnson's clocks may still be seen in Plantation House and the Castle, keeping the same admirable time that they kept one hundred years ago. His transit instrument has recently been discovered supporting an ant-eaten bookshelf in the Supreme Court.

His chronometer did not survive the witticisms of Colonial administration and it was therefore sold to a passing French barque which was unable to proceed on her journey without one, for £25.

On the walls of the Observatory there still survives the following inscription:

HAEC SPECULA ASTRONOMICA
CONDITA FUIT   MDCCCXXVI
GUBERNANTE ALEXANDRO WALKER

T. H. BROOKE ⎱ CONSULENTIBUS
T. GREENTREE ⎰
D. KINNAIRD   OP. INSPECT.

Half the roof has fallen in and in a few years it will be a complete ruin.

It is the property of the British Admiralty.

To make up for their disappointment Mr. and Mrs. Gill found a good friend in the Governor, Hudson Janisch. In him they were delighted to discover an enthusiastic amateur in astronomy, and a descendant actually of the great astronomer Encke. And how flattering to the visitors to be told by the Governor, who had never left his native isle, that they were the very first astronomers, professional astronomers, he had ever met.

So kind, so charming and so persuasive was Governor Janisch that the Gills were sorely tempted to make St. Helena their observation station for Mars instead of Ascension. During their short stay on the island they made several excursions on horseback, under the guidance of Captain Oliver. During one of these they stopped for refreshment at the "Rose and Crown" at the high ridge of Hutts Gate, the one and only public house on the island outside of Jamestown.

This useful house of call is now only a small general store where nothing better can be bought to quench a traveller's thirst than gaseous "minerals", and may it be hoped that one of the very first improvements which the new Governor will carry out at St. Helena, will be the re-opening of the "Rose and Crown".

Tom Timm the landlord was overjoyed to see three guests all in one day, and with his dusky face aglow with the heat and the excitement, rushed out, napkin on arm, with the welcome greeting that luncheon was ready.

This was eaten in a long, uncarpeted, unceilinged room, with bunches of stag's-moss hanging from the bare rafters. After lunch, while Tom entertained Mrs. Gill with the local gossip, Captain Oliver and Professor Gill went to Halley's Mount close by to search for the site of the observatory where Halley in 1677 made his catalogue of the southern stars and observed the transit of Mercury.

Much to their joy they found a bit of low wall, duly oriented, and overrun with wild pepper, which had been part of his original observatory.

Mrs. Gill was sorry when the *Edinburgh Castle* was sighted and she and her husband had to leave the lovely island.

No thunderbolts nor lightning shafts, no burning draught nor deadly disease, no savage brute nor noxious reptile, not even a *lawyer*; surely this St. Helena, now melting away in the distance, must be "The Island of the Blessed" so fondly believed in and so earnestly sought for by the ancient mariners.

In the year 1879 news reached the island of the disaster at Isandhlwana where the British under Colonel Durnford were overwhelmed by a force of 10,000 Zulus.

Every man who could be spared from the garrison was immediately embarked on board H.M.S. *Shah* and on February 12th she sailed for Natal with reinforcements.

From its first discovery St. Helena had been accustomed to being a place of confinement for distinguished or ordinary prisoners. The next interesting captive to be brought there was the Zulu chief Dinizulu, son of the great Cetewayo, who arrived with his two uncles and several wives and servants in 1890. The Emperor of the Zulus proved far more amenable to captivity than did the Emperor of the French. He did what he was told, never quarrelled with the authorities, and wandered about the island making friends with all he met. Particularly was he cherished by the Bishop and the clergy, for in the black chief they discovered a willing, even an ardent convert to Christianity, and of his own free will he begged to be baptized. Here an awkward and apparently insurmountable dilemma arose, for Dinizulu practised polygamy, and had several wives. In the end this little difficulty was got over by the official recognition of only *one* of his wives, the others were described as being attendants on some of his, and their, children, and Dinizulu was duly confirmed.

In 1896 all the dusky captives were "cheered and comforted" by a visit from the Bishop of Zululand.

So anxious was he that his own people in Africa should also enjoy the blessing of Christianity, that Dinizulu wrote letters to his mother and to his old followers in Zululand, urging them to place themselves under the instruction of teachers who were to be sent to them by the Bishop of Zululand, and to give them every assistance in establishing a missionary station in their country.

In December, 1897, the converted savage, with his uncles, wives, children and their "attendants", were all sent back to their own country in the steamer *Umbilo*.

Dinizulu had proved himself a perfect prisoner. He learned to read and write English during his incarceration and actually to play the piano, his favourite pieces being hymn tunes.

His uncles were not sociable nor would they adapt themselves to their new surroundings, but set their faces against all the white man's conventions. They refused to sit on chairs, or to use tables or beds, nor would they wear European dress, except when they went for walks, and then only because they were forbidden to go out of doors unless apparelled in European clothing. Dinizulu on the contrary quickly developed a taste for smart clothes and was very particular over the cut and fit of each new suit. When ordering one he would carefully consider the colour and quality of the material before he selected one, and then only after prolonged study of the latest fashion plates.

The despatch of the Zulu exiles brought with it further financial straits to St. Helena, for during the seven years they lived there, they had spent about one thousand pounds annually, and so poor was the community that the loss of this trivial sum was felt acutely.

Scarcely had they left before news came of a further, and
what was likely to be a far greater, influx of prisoners.

The South African War broke out in 1899, and in November
the first submarine cable was landed at St. Helena by the
Eastern Telegraph Company, which connected the island with
Cape Town and was the first stage in the direct England-South
Africa cable which was being laid at that time in view of the
urgent need of additional telegraphic communication. On
the 5th April, 1900, the following proclamation was published
by the Governor:

In a few days the troopship *Milwaukee*, escorted by H.M.S.
Niobe, will arrive with prisoners of war.

No unauthorised persons will be allowed on the wharf
at the time of disembarkation. The police will assist as far
as they can the military, acting under the orders of the
officer commanding the troops, in keeping order. H.E. the
Governor expresses the hope that the inhabitants will treat
the prisoners with that courtesy and consideration which
should be extended to all men who have fought bravely in
what they considered the cause of their country, and will
help in repressing any unseemly demonstration which
individuals may exhibit.

Amongst the first batch of five hundred and fourteen
prisoners were General Cronje and his wife. Instead of being
taken to Deadwood Camp with the others, he and his wife
were allowed to live at Kent Cottage, a modest abode which is
still standing on New Ground, not far from High Knoll Fort.

General Cronje during his incarceration insisted upon
proper respect being paid to his rank, and was offended that
no special guard was placed over him, and demanded that a
mounted guard should be supplied for the purpose.

This request put the Government in something of a predica-
ment, for there were no mounted troops stationed on the

island. However, the Governor, Sterndale, was always willing to do everything in his power to oblige his prisoners and gave orders that some men of the St. Helena Volunteers should be supplied with horses and given lessons in riding.

As not one of these heroes had ever ridden or even mounted a horse in his life, it was not surprising that after only a few lessons in horsemanship they did not become very efficient cavalrymen. As soon as ever they could sit in the saddle without falling off when they trotted or galloped, the troop was sent over to Kent Cottage, to mount guard and to accompany the General whenever he went riding.

No sooner had the mounted guard reported itself than General Cronje decided to go, then and there, with his mounted guard, to inspect the Boer prisoners' camp at Deadwood, a distance of about six miles, up and down steep hills.

The General led the way, at a hand gallop, with his guard following behind.

Arrived at Deadwood the guard dismounted while the General made his inspection.

When he was ready to return to Kent Cottage, he mounted his horse, and was preparing to leave the camp when an awkward situation arose. Not one of the guard was able to mount his horse while holding his rifle in one hand.

The situation must have been particularly humiliating for the guard, as they had as an audience, drawn up in ranks close before them, many hundreds of Boers, every one of whom was an accomplished equestrian.

The situation was quickly developing from comedy into tragedy, or vice-versa, when General Cronje came to the rescue by ordering some of the prisoners to hold the guard's rifles while others assisted them into the saddle.

Amidst hearty cheers the General then left the camp, followed by his mounted guard.

In the months to follow, ship after ship arrived, bringing more prisoners of war to the island.

The Governor, Robert Armitage Sterndale, C.M.G., had, like most of the Governors in the old days of the H.E.I.C. seen all his service in India. He was a good man and a good Governor. He is now best remembered as being the author of the *Mammals of India*.

At this time one of the teachers at the Country School, Miss Emily Louise Warren,[1] on her own initiative, undertook to teach the children of the island the art of pillow-lace making.

With the object of encouraging them she proposed to the Governor that an exhibition should be held of the industrial arts of the island. To this His Excellency readily agreed, and a committee was formed, consisting of himself, the Bishop, the United States Consul and others. To enlarge the scope and interest of the exhibition Miss Warren proposed that the Boer prisoners of war should also be allowed to take part.

This was done, and so numerous were the Boer exhibits that when the show came to be held an extra room had to be provided for these alone.

The prisoners had only improvised tools, such as old table knives made into saws, umbrella ribs into fret-saws, and hammers made of stones, and yet with these and similar make-shift implements they turned out pipes, models of carts, walking-sticks and various articles made out of bones, all of which found a ready sale.

The lace was of several designs, Torchon, Honiton and Point lace. Ever since then lace-making has been a home industry amongst the women of St. Helena, who make a few shillings by selling lace to passengers in the Union-Castle ships which call twice a month. Unfortunately, no one nowadays takes the trouble to help or supervise them, so that they have forgotten most of the designs Miss Warren taught

[1] See Appendix No. VIII.

them, and all make and offer for sale mats, handkerchiefs and lace of exactly the same pattern. Here is an opening for any lady who understands lace-making to help and encourage the St. Helena women to branch out into a larger variety of designs.

In spite of the isolation of St. Helena there were several attempts made by the prisoners to escape, either in fishermen's boats or by swimming off to foreign ships.

Perhaps because of the large prisoner's camp, the old scourge of St. Helena, the rats, became more numerous than ever. The Governor who was, and is still, an authority on the small mammals in India, offered a reward of one penny for every dead rat, and then twopence, and at last, as they became yet more scarce, a reward of threepence a head; a wise measure, as it turned out, for the rat population became greatly reduced and the island was never before so free from these vermin.

In February, 1902, the last batch of prisoners arrived, making a total in all of six thousand, most of whom were in one of the two big camps at Broad Bottom and Deadwood.

Amongst the prisoners were men of most professions or trades: musicians, school-teachers, architects, builders, engineers, carpenters, cabinet-makers, as well as labourers, and many of these obtained work on the island. Some who had been grooms, bakers, shop-assistants and household servants before the war, if well behaved, were allowed to live at the houses of their British employers.

Typhoid, hitherto unknown on the island, broke out before long amongst the prisoners and their British guards, and two monuments to the memory of those Boer prisoners who died during captivity stand in the same Baptist cemetery at Knollcombes which contains the neglected tomb of Governor Janisch. Those of the Boers stand side by side, both conspicuous for being well tended. Needless to say, this reverence for the dead is not undertaken by St. Helena, but at the expense of the Government of the Union of South Africa.

Great rejoicing and festivity took place on the occasion of the coronation of King Edward VII, and a loyal address, illuminated by the versatile Governor, was forwarded to England in a casket made out of the wood of the extinct Native Ebony. It was constructed and elaborately carved by one of the prisoners of war, which probably made this offering of loyalty from the smallest colony of the Empire, unique.

With the conclusion of peace came the repatriation of the prisoners of war and of the British regiments which had guarded them, and once again St. Helena suffered from the termination of a fictitious wave of prosperity.

The popular Governor Sterndale, who was beloved both by the St. Helenians and by the Boer prisoners, left the island in August, 1902, to die shortly afterwards, and was succeeded by an equally able and popular one, Lieutenant-Colonel Henry Gallwey, C.M.G., D.S.O., who was to prove one of the best Governors St. Helena ever had.

The West India Regiment had been ordered to take the place of the regiment stationed at St. Helena during the war, but the inhabitants, having suffered before from the mutinous conduct of this regiment, petitioned against the order. As a result of this, the Colonial Secretary refused to allow them to proceed, and the War Office accordingly decided to send two companies of the South Africa line regiment in their place.

WITH the twentieth century a new and better type of Governor began to be sent out to St. Helena.

The bad practice had come to an end of offering the governorship of the island to some elderly retired army or navy officer, as a pleasant, dignified, easy post to be held for a few years. Instead, keen, ambitious, younger men, who looked forward to some day governing a far bigger and more important colony, were appointed.

In 1903, when Colonel Gallwey landed, he arrived at a difficult period. With the departure of the Boer prisoners of war and their British guards, the revenue of the island had at once dropped, for between them these two brought more than £10,000 a year to St. Helena.

To compensate, in some measure, the loss to the island in fall of revenue with the departure of the soldiery, there occurred a marked fall in the number of prostitutes and gambling saloons in Jamestown.

Colonel Gallwey was an enthusiast on the subjects of forestry and education. Sterndale had employed numbers of prisoners to plant trees, and the new Governor carried on this good work, for the extra need of fuel had laid a heavy toll on the trees of the island.

When he came to make enquiry into the subject of education the Governor discovered how inefficient it was.

There were then nine schools in the island; four Government, two under the control of the "Miss Rebecca Hussey's

Charity", two of the Benevolent Society and one Military, among a population of 3,342.

There was, and to St. Helena's shame, still is, no higher or secondary education, a fact which the Governor considered called for "great need of improvement".[1] Bishop Holmes of St. Helena, in a scathing report on the subject, stated: "The Standard of Education is very low" and that the children were taught to repeat lessons like parrots,[2] and he saw no likelihood of improvement until a much better class of teachers was employed.

The Governor felt so strongly that steps ought to be taken to raise the standard of education in the island—the Hussey School at Hutts Gate having just been closed for want of funds —that he called together a meeting of the ratepayers and asked if they would be willing to raise £115 a year, by a levy of threepence in the pound on the rateable value of property, to assist the Government in improving the facilities of education.

This proposal was rejected by a fairly large majority, though "curiously enough" as the Governor pointed out "the coloured rate-payers were nearly all in favour."

The lack of education shewed itself in many ways. During the Boer prisoners' sojourn, unemployment was almost unknown, though the cost of living had risen considerably. The repatriation of the prisoners and their guards was followed by acute unemployment and distress, and a large number of St. Helenians wished to emigrate to South Africa, but most of them were unable to do so, since they could neither read nor write, two essential qualifications for immigration to Cape Colony.

The high cost of living was largely due to the exorbitant freight charges of the only steamship company to the island, which caused the price of goods brought out by them from

---

[1] Colonial Office. Annual Blue Books.   [2] ibid.

England for the islanders to be twenty-five per cent above their value.   Then, as now, St. Helena suffered from having to rely for all her imports on a shipping company which enjoyed a monopoly, and having no competitors was able to charge whatever prices it chose for carrying passengers or cargo to or from the island.

In 1904 the dwindling revenue was actually up by some £800, but this was entirely due to the world's stamp-collectors who had bought up the whole of the obsolete St. Helena Victorian postage stamps.

The sale of stamps has for years been almost the only steady and profitable industry of the island, and to-day Mr. G. E. Moss, the Postmaster of St. Helena, is in the proud and happy position of being in charge of the one flourishing business of the island.

For many years St. Helena had been noted for her fruit, and particularly her peaches; but a disease appeared in the trees caused by a small insect, the Peach Fly.

To try and eradicate this disease, the Governor and Council passed an ordinance for its extermination by ordering that all trees affected should be cut down. This wise order was not carried out by the poorer classes because "they considered it useless to fight against any visitation caused by the hand of God, for the peach fly must have been sent by the Almighty."

Then came news from Western Australia of a wonderful discovery, that the peach fly *liked* pure kerosene oil, and that they could be exterminated simply by placing bowls of kerosene amongst the peach trees.

The Governor at once had this welcome piece of information printed and circulated amongst the peach growers, but not half-a-dozen of them could be bothered to try it, such was the apathy and indifference of the St. Helenians.

As though conditions were not already bad enough, the Powers then caused consternation by suddenly inflicting a fresh and unlooked for blow to the waning prosperity of the colony.

This was to reduce the garrison of Lancashire Fusiliers by half, a measure which was followed by yet more unemployment, misery and starvation. Perhaps it was with some obscure idea of counteracting this blow that "The Stallion Donkeys Ordinance" was then imposed, with a view to improving the breed of donkeys at St. Helena.

The St. Helena Volunteers (sharpshooters), consisting of three officers and seventy-five men, were also disbanded, and then came orders for the withdrawal of the remainder of the troops, and Governor Gallwey wrote in his annual report: "St. Helena for the first time in her history as a British possession was left without a garrison of any kind. *Sic transit gloria S. Helenæ.*"

Yet more unemployment and want followed. "Begging petitions became the rule of the day," reported Gallwey, though until then no beggars had been known in St. Helena.

Excitement was caused and hopes raised when it was learned that two hundred men were wanted to work in the Transvaal mines. Two hundred men were selected and were all ready to leave by the next ship when a message came cancelling the order. No reason for this was divulged, but it left the poorer population in an ugly and dangerous frame of mind, yet no disturbance or acts of violence followed, which speaks well for the law-abiding inhabitants of that sorely tried little community, with no troops to quell disorders and but some half-a-dozen policemen.

At last, in 1907, a genuine island industry was established. Thirty-two years previously, it will be remembered, the Colonial and Foreign Fibre Company had been formed and for six years had run a mill at Jamestown for stripping and scutching New Zealand flax. In 1881 the Company failed and the mill closed down. Now a new attempt was to be made, this time under the advice and supervision of an expert sent by the New Zealand Government.

One of the mistakes made by the Colonial and Foreign Fibre Company had been to erect its mill down at Jamestown instead of close to the growing grounds. The new mill was built at Longwood and the industry re-started, though Governor Gallwey felt far from optimistic of its prospects, for the year before he had reported to the Government at home:

> The Colony still remains in the unenviable position of being without an industry . . . the islanders themselves are partly to blame owing to their utter helplessness to do much for themselves without material assistance from outside. . . . Their wants are very small, a few days' work occasionally and they are quite content to sit down during the intervals. This unfortunate trait in the St. Helenians' character is really a legacy passed on to them by their forebears who were all too well treated by the old John Company. . . . An equitable and mild climate and the large quantity of fish to be obtained save the situation.

Yet in spite of his gloomy foreboding the growing of New Zealand flax and the manufacture of it into fibre and tow, if it did not at first flourish, increased steadily to become in time the staple industry of the island.

Lace-making, a second industry, and one which had been allowed to die, was also resuscitated in 1907. It began with a grant from the Imperial Treasury of £170 to cover the expense of an expert for six months. Miss Penderel Moody went out to St. Helena and taught the women how to make several patterns of lace and to put the industry on a business-like footing.

The wages earned by the women were a god-send, for the distress amongst the islanders was at this time the greatest in the history of the colony. The hardest hit of all the population were the unmarried mothers with children, who had no bread-winners to provide for them.

In order to furnish employment and yet give work that would be of use to the community, the Governor caused yet more trees to be planted, but reported in 1908 that he feared no good would come of the tree planting until the Government was in a position to *get rid of every goat on the island*. Every goat, he insisted, should be exterminated, and the importation of goats rigidly prohibited. However, no Government has yet had the courage to undertake this wise, if ruthless, measure, so therefore St. Helena is still short of trees, and her good soil is still being washed away into the Atlantic Ocean.

When the colony was in the deepest of social and financial depression came a bolt from the blue, in the unexpected form of the philanthropic Mr. A. Mosely, C.M.G.

Mr. Mosely was rich. He loved St. Helena and he loved the St. Helenians and was determined to help them. He also was a man of ideas. He saw that the blue sea surrounding the island teemed with fish, particularly mackerel, and he decided to set up a factory where the freshly caught fish might be canned for export to other lands, and so bring work and wages to St. Helena. Mr. Mosely spared no expense, he brought out experts to advise him: fish experts, canning experts, every sort of expert who might be of assistance.

On the 26th February, 1909, the canning factory was duly opened at Jamestown. Everyone was ready to play his part in making it a success.

But no one, not even the expensive experts, had reckoned on the unaccountable behaviour of the mackerel. Everything had been thought out and provided for. Mr. Mosely had bought new fishing boats, and fishing gear. Fishermen had been engaged, the factory built, the new machinery was in order, the empty tins in thousands were there in which the mackerel were to be hermetically sealed.

And there were no mackerel! Never before had there been no mackerel. The experts were unable to offer any explanation of this sudden lack of mackerel; only the St. Helenians knew— it was all due to a comet which had unexpectedly crossed the heavens at the time the factory was opened.

For ten months the factory and the canners waited in vain for any mackerel to can, then the factory was shut down, and yet another scheme to help St. Helena had failed.

In 1911 Colonel Gallwey became Sir Henry Galway and Governor of Gambia, and was followed a year later by Major H. E. S. Cordeaux who remained for the long period of eight years.

With the position of Governor of St. Helena goes the rank of Commander-in-Chief, and the military force which Major Cordeaux commanded consisted of a Captain and twelve privates of the Royal Marines: which force is of exactly the same strength and personnel as the present Governor and Commander-in-Chief, Mr. H. G. P. Pilling, C.M.G., has under him.

Although Major Cordeaux ruled over St. Helena during all the years of the Great War, his reign was a peculiarly peaceful one. Few, if any, parts of the British Empire were less shaken by the world's upheaval than St. Helena. The lace-making went peacefully on, employing thirty women as well as twenty embroideresses.

On August 5th, 1914, a telegram had announced that war had been declared against Germany and Austria.

Martial law was at once proclaimed and the defunct St. Helena Volunteer Corps re-established.

In 1915 the Imperial Government undertook the construction of certain military defences and enlarged the wharf, which gave employment to the inhabitants.

Owing to the war, the price of fibre soared. Everyone who was able began to plant and grow New Zealand flax.

To encourage them to do so, grants of small plots of Crown land were made for the further planting of this essential commodity.

Messrs. Solomon & Co. opened a new flax mill at Broad Bottom and Messrs. Deason Brothers another at Hutts Gate. The work went on at all three mills both day and night.

Perhaps it was partly as a result of this boom in flax growing and manufacture—for the St. Helenians appear to have thought of little else—that the Government Lace School closed in 1917, from want, it was reported, of supervision and on the ground of economy.

Meanwhile, stimulated by the fantastic prices paid for it, the St. Helenians grew reckless over their planting of flax, and gave up growing anything else. They made a lot of money, but most of it had to be spent buying, at fancy prices, things to eat which before the flax boom they had grown for themselves.

When the war was over and peace had been declared, the St. Helena Government passed one of those laws or enactments to which all governments are so partial, but which are so uncomprehensible to the unofficial mind. This particular one ran as follows:

Government Notification

By direction of His Excellency the Acting Governor, the Title of the Corps known as the "St. Helena Volunteers Sharpshooters" is hereby altered to "St. Helena Rifles" by which it will be known in future.

By command of His Excellency the Acting Governor.

A. HANDS,
Chief Clerk

The Castle,
St. Helena,
16th March, 1918

In 1920 Governor Cordeaux was promoted to the governorship of the Bahamas and Major H. G. St. G. Morgan administered the government until Mr. Robert F. Peel arrived.

In his final report to the Colonial Office Colonel Cordeaux had cause to refer to the climate of St. Helena, and his remarks are so pregnant with truth that they deserve to be included. They run as follows:

> The popular conception of the weather at St. Helena has suffered from the Napoleonic legend. It appears to be regarded by the general public as a place where heavy rains and high winds are practically constant . . . whereas the climate is probably unequalled in any country in the world.

The only important fact worth while recording as having taken place on the island in the year 1921 is the founding of the Girl Guides, an institution which is still in a most flourishing state, thanks in no small degree to the inspiration of Mrs. Aylen, the wife of the Bishop. There had been a troop, or whatever the term may be, of St. Helena Boy Scouts, but it had fallen into decay; upon the appearance of the Girl Guides, however, in their becoming uniform, the Boy Scouts came to life again, and still form one of the few distractions or organized amusements offered to the boys of the island.

In the year following, the Island of Ascension which hitherto had been administered by the Admiralty became a Dependency of St. Helena. It is now leased to the Eastern Telegraph Company and provides employment for St. Helena men as servants and labourers.

EVER since the prosperous years of the Boer prisoners' internment on the island, the state of the revenue has been the principal item in the annual report of every Governor. To those who study the Blue Books of the Colonial Office, containing full particulars about the different Crown Colonies of the British Empire, an odd fact discloses itself, as far as the reports on St. Helena are concerned. This is that the prosperity or otherwise of this ancient colony appears to rest in the lap, not of the gods, but of the world's philatelists.

In the year 1923 Governor Peel reported a heavy fall in the revenue due, not to drought nor to any failure of the crops, but to the fact that the new issue of Ascension Island postage stamps had not sold as well as had been anticipated, by some two thousand pounds. This the Governor attributed to the abnormally large sales in 1922 of the issue both of St. Helena and Ascension Island stamps. This failure on the part of Ascension Island was all the more regrettable since the Eastern Telegraph Company, which leases the island, gave employment to seventy-five St. Helenians, and so considerably reduced the unemployment in St. Helena.

Six fibre-mills were now working—that of the Government, two of Messrs. Solomon & Co. at Sandy Bay and Broad Bottom Gut, two of Messrs. Deason at Hutts Gate and Woody Ridge, and a new one erected below Francis Plain by Messrs. Thorpe & Sons. Between them these six mills gave direct employment to three hundred people, roughly one in ten of the whole population.

It will be remembered that in 1917 the Government lace school was closed, and the teaching of needlework in the schools and the annual prizes given for needlework had ceased. This had been done on the grounds of economy.

Now, after an interval of six years, the teaching of needlework in the Government schools was resumed and prizes were again offered for its encouragement.

Crime amongst this God-fearing and honest community continued to be almost unknown. What little there was consisted of pilfering vegetables from fields and gardens. Very occasionally a burglary takes place at St. Helena, but in almost every case the hungry criminal makes straight for the larder, and does not touch or steal silver ornaments, coins or other valuables. And who can blame a people, the large majority of whom have seldom quite enough to eat, if they do help themselves occasionally to a few potatoes or turnips which grow in an unfenced field beside a public road?

In the following year, 1924, the revenue was up by by £1,189 14s. 9d., thanks as usual to St. Helena's most profitable source of income, a new issue of postage stamps. This satisfactory state of things, in addition to a grant-in-aid from the Imperial Treasury, made it possible to undertake some much needed and long overdue repairs to Plantation House. The white ants had caused havoc to the wooden structures, and it was decided to purchase some cypress timber, which resists the destructive activities of termites. Unfortunately just when St. Helena had the money to buy this timber, none of it was procurable, so that the repairs had again to be postponed. Perhaps to make up for this disappointment the Government imported two mules from South Africa.

In this year Colonel Peel died, the first Governor to die at his post since H. R. Janisch, in 1884. He will be remembered for the great interest he took in agriculture, for his striking personality, and for the love and confidence in which he was held by the Islanders. The popular Government Medical Officer, the Hon. W. J. J. Arnold, acted as Governor until the end of the year, when Sir Charles Henry Harper, K.B.E., C.M.G., assumed office. In this year Captain Mainwaring of New Longwood House established the first rope and twine factory in the island.

The only legal currency at this period was that of the United Kingdom, but owing to the quantity of South African coin in circulation, and because of the importance of the trade between the Island and South Africa, it was deemed advisable to make the South African coinage legal tender in St. Helena.

At last enough ant-resisting timber was procurable and the repairs were about to be put in hand at Plantation House, when it was learned that H.R.H. The Prince of Wales was to pay a visit to St. Helena in August, and the work was again held up.

Meanwhile Dr. Arnold, the Colonial Surgeon, died, greatly to the sorrow and loss of the inhabitants, for he was a man who had devoted the best years of his life to the colony and on two occasions had acted as Governor. He was loved by all classes of the community, rich and poor. A public subscription was raised to erect a monument to his memory. It now stands in the centre of the parade ground opposite the Castle. An inscription on it styles him "The best friend St. Helena ever had."

The Royal visitor landed at Jamestown on August 3rd from H.M.S. *Repulse*, on his voyage from South Africa to South America. The whole population was down at the wharf to greet him with an address of welcome. H.M.S. *Repulse* was the largest ship ever to visit St. Helena, and crowds of the inhabitants went aboard her to inspect and admire. Each day during the Royal visit the band from the battleship played in the Town Square, "to the delight of a music-loving population".

These stirring events were scarcely over before the islanders, both Government and the people, resumed a burning controversy which had only been temporarily dropped during the Royal visit. The question in dispute was whether or not mechanical transport should be allowed on the island.

Naturally there were two sides to this, as to all important questions. One school maintained that St. Helena had got on very well in the past with horses and donkeys, and in any case they considered their steep, narrow, winding roads unfitted for motor vehicles. Even His Excellency the Governor, who all through this discussion had very properly remained strictly neutral in his utterances, reported to the Colonial Office that, after all, "time is rarely of the essence of any undertaking in St. Helena" and thereby let out a hint of his own private opinion.

The battle raged on until 1928, when in the face of considerable local feeling and opposition, the Motor-Car Ordinance was passed, and it became lawful to import motor vehicles to the Island.

To be ready for the rush of cars, some sixty miles of road were prepared.

The following year, 1929, St. Helena's leading and most enterprising inhabitant, the Hon. H. W. Solomon, O.B.E., imported an Austin Seven, the first motor vehicle to run on the island roads.

To return for a moment to the year 1926. The most interesting part in the annual Blue Book, other than the account of the discussion on motor-cars, is a report written by the then Colonial Treasurer, Mr. H. J. Pink. In it the Treasurer touched upon many aspects of island affairs other than the financial. The average rainfall for the year was nine inches at Jamestown, but thirty-eight and a half at Plantation, only three miles away. He reminded the Minister of State for the Colonies of the very rare occurrence at St. Helena of thunderstorms, and how the last two on record had occurred in 1874 and 1888. He assured him that although St. Helena lay within the tropics, no particular precautions were needed to protect the head from the sun's beams. He strongly recommended St. Helena as a place of residence for people of moderate means, but offered a timely warning that there was little opening for labour or capital. The Treasurer considered that a retired official who was fond of botany, gardening, forestry or fruit growing on a small scale, would be happy living at St. Helena, and we thoroughly endorse Mr. Pink's views. The Treasurer grew quite lyrical in his official report on the island, when he came to describe its general appearance and character. He declared it might well be a part of England, with its English speech, English scenery and English ways. "Life on St. Helena," he continued, "could be passed amid picturesque surroundings in quiet and uneventful fashion similar, one imagines, to life in a retired country district before the advent of railways."

On one of his rural excursions the Colonial Treasurer was enraptured to find growing on a shady bank in the grounds of Plantation, some English primroses in flower.

The Governor, who took a deep interest in the agricultural possibilities of the Island, urged the Home Government to appoint a permanent Horticultural and Agricultural Officer to St. Helena. To support his request he quoted the reports on the Island written by Sir Daniel Morris in 1884 and reprinted in 1906,[1] and that of Mr. Mason in 1921. As a result of this appeal an agricultural officer was sent out and this important post is still maintained.

For the first time in the history of St. Helena a complete

[1] Colonial Reports, Miscellaneous, No. 38. A Report upon the Present Position and Prospects of the Agricultural Resources of the Island of St. Helena. D. Morris.

medical and dental examination was made of all the school children. Their general physical condition proved to be excellent but the condition of their teeth "left much to be desired".

Active warfare against the white ants was now resumed, and within two hundred yards of Government House at Plantation no fewer than sixty nests of these pests were discovered and destroyed, and two hundred trees, infected by termites, were chemically treated.

For the first time the suggestion was mooted of granting old age pensions. It was calculated that if every islander over the age of seventy was given five shillings a week, the cost to the exchequer would amount to £1,500 a year. This modest pittance would have been a god-send, and the benefit both to the poorest inhabitants and their families as well as to the community at large been incalculable. This wise and benevolent suggestion did not materialize. Any proposal of this kind to benefit the St. Helenians has always been opposed on the ground that it would demoralize them, and that it would undermine their self-reliance, arguments which were used, but without effect, when similar schemes for old age pensions and State insurance were first proposed in Great Britain. It was argued by the St. Helena Government—or did the idea originate in London?—that if the old people were given this small dole of five shillings a week to make the last few years of their lives more comfortable, it would discourage thrift, and that the workers themselves should put by a portion of their wages as a nest egg for their old age.

But it has never been explained how a working man, receiving a weekly wage of ten shillings or less, is to pay his rent, clothe and feed a wife and several children, and yet have anything left over to put into the savings bank.

As under the present régime, the land of St. Helena is only for the very few and the comparatively rich, the poorer classes

are unable to grow their own food, and have to rely on purchasing expensive imported food or buying it from one of the
few and fortunate islanders who own a plot or two of their
native land. If, as they ought to be, the St. Helenians were a
race of small-holders, they would, to a very large extent, be
able to grow their own food and not depend, as they do almost
entirely, on the supply of imported polished rice, which is the
cause of the large number of cases in the island of that painful,
insidious, fatal and quite preventable disease, beri-beri.

One of the first matters the newly appointed Horticultural
Officer took in hand was the public garden in Jamestown,
which for many years had become derelict, an eyesore and a
reproach to the Island's capital. In November, 1930, under
his direction, an avenue of Jacaranda trees was planted in
Main Street, and it is to be hoped that the present Horticultural
Officer will receive authority to plant many more trees in the
town where shade is greatly needed. In many of the accounts
of Jamestown in the days of the East India Company, the
number of fine trees is commented on, and the hot, stuffy
little town, shut in as it is, between two tall, rocky cliffs,
on which the sun beats down remorselessly, must have
been a far better place to look at and to live in than it is at
present.

The Government in March, 1930, imported four hives of
bees. Three were placed at Maldivia in James Valley, the
other at The Briars. The bees did well. Not only did they
produce excellent honey, but brought about a very marked
improvement in the cultivated plants in the island, which had
suffered from the want of insects to fertilize them. By the end
of the year several wild swarms were found in different parts
of the Island.

On April 22nd was held the first Arbor Day, when various
trees were planted by the boys of the Town School on a plot
of Government land, leased to Messrs. Solomon and Co., who

"readily released it for this experiment in re-afforestation."
His Excellency the Governor presided at the planting and all
went well, and everybody looked forward to a new era, with a
St. Helena once again clothed in green trees. A few days later
not one sapling survived. The goats had found a weak spot in
the fence surrounding the plantation and had eaten up every one.

In this year an allotment scheme was also started, a few plots
were taken up, but it came to nothing.

It has already been stated that the Island of St. Helena is
governed by the Governor and Council, the Council consisting
of the Government Secretary, the Commander of the troops,
i.e., twelve Royal Marines; and three unofficial members,
chosen by the Governor. The laws which govern St. Helena
are enacted by this body, and whatever views or wishes the
populace may hold on matters however important to themselves, they have no means by which they can voice them, nor
have they a vote or any say whatever in the government of
their own country.

If the Council disagrees with the Governor, he has the
power, by an Order of 1863, to overrule them, and he can pass
what laws or ordinances he wishes, subject to their confirmation by the Home Government.

By the 1863 Order "A copy of the draft of every Ordinance
shall be affixed to a board in front of the Court House for the
inspection of the Public for one month before passing thereof."

It is one of the grievances amongst the more intelligent of
the Islanders that they are not consulted over matters of public
policy, and that there is no member of the Government to
whom they have the right to appeal.

While on the subject of the laws made for the St. Helenians,
it may be stated, without comment, that there is no factory
legislation, nor any legislation to provide compensation in a
case of accident to a mill-worker or other employed person.[1]

[1] See page 373.

If a man loses an arm during his work in a factory, although through no fault or carelessness of his own, the only compensation he can look for is from his friendly society; that is, if he belongs to one.

Discussing the question of franchise in his annual report for 1931, the Governor wrote: "The Island is not large enough to afford scope for any system of local Government as ordinarily understood. There are, however," he continued, "a Poor Relief Board, elected by ratepayers, a Board of Health, of which three members are elected by ratepayers, while the duty of sickness insurance is one that the St. Helenians have for many years taken upon and managed for themselves."

That the St. Helenians, out of their miserable wages, contrive to support societies to assist one another for a few months, in cases of illness, accident or other misfortune, is indeed to their credit, but is no reason why the Government should shelve this responsibility.

The Census held in April, 1931, shewed that the population had risen by 280, from 3,715 to 3,995, and that a considerably larger percentage were then living in the country districts instead of in the town as had been the case ten years before. A good sign if we consider the words of Sir Daniel Morris in 1883: "I look entirely to the soil for the elements to bring prosperity to St. Helena." Similar views to these were held by Mr. Mason, of South Africa, who after an exhaustive enquiry into the problem of St. Helena, decided it "was a country for the small-holder" and observed that in times of depression the country people suffered less than those of Jamestown.

At the time of the Census of St. Helena, one also was taken of the domestic animals. The figures were as follows:

Goats .	.	1,433
Pigs .	.	252
Donkeys	.	1,221

It was also ascertained that sixty per cent of the occupied land was in possession of two owners, and seventy per cent of three, though the writer of the official report was careful to add: "There has not necessarily been any engrossing of the land with sinister intent, but it is the fact that only two or three persons on the Island have capital or enterprise for acquiring land as it comes into the market."

In this long but interesting report of 1931, the question of education is dealt with. Education in the island was still limited to primary education. Of technical education for boys there was practically none, only an odd boy or two receiving appointments under the Public Works Department or the Horticultural Department. As for the girls there was none, although it was hoped "as soon as funds are available" to establish a Domestic Science School. Apparently the necessary funds are still not available.

Once again the question cropped up of old age pensions and government insurance against unemployment and sickness. By the recent Census it was shewn that there were one hundred and two persons over the age of seventy, and to provide these with five shillings a week would cost about £1,300. But again funds were not available, and in any case, were there not the working men's friendly societies, which provided for sickness? The total membership of men in these societies was 1,569.

The oldest is the Mechanics' Society, founded in 1838, supported by a weekly subscription of sixpence; the St. Helena Poor Society, founded in 1847; the Foresters, in 1871; and the St. Helena Workingman's Christian Association, which dates from 1875.

For women, there is the Church Provident Society, 1878, and for children, the Church Benefit Society.

These are the principal societies formed by these poor people to provide some little help for one another in time of sickness and distress. Surely it is not too much to hope that

before long the British Empire, out of its wealth, may see its
way to making life a little less hard for these loyal members of
the community of British peoples.

Nothing is more depressing to read, nor discouraging for
an author or historian to write, than a long dissertation on the
shabbier sides of human life. But a history must be, as far as
is possible, a plain, unvarnished statement of fact, and so we
will give a few extracts from the official Colonial Office Blue
Book of 1932.

We find: "Various projects for building cottages and in-
stalling smallholders postponed until there is an improvement
in the general financial situation."

Comment is made on the great shortage of houses. Over-
crowding amongst the working and agricultural classes had
become serious, *"and is reflected in the high rates of infant mortality*,
with a corresponding high birth rate."

(The italics are mine, as is also the reminder that the climate
of St. Helena is probably the healthiest in the world.)

The writer of this report spoke of the shocking slum
property in Jamestown, and of the wretched hovels of many
of the country dwellers, and of their poverty, and need of land.
This poverty and the ownership of sixty per cent of the good
land being in two men's hands naturally prevent the agricultural worker from building a cottage for himself and so
working on his own land.

The only legislation dealing with overcrowding is a provision in "The Public Health Ordinance 1899," which gives
the Board of Health or any Justice of the Peace power to
decide the number of persons who may live in any house or
room, the minimum space allowed being three hundred cubic
feet for each adult.

In 1932 St. Helena was passing through an unhappy period.
Not only was she suffering from a severe drought, but owing
to the heavy fall in the price of hemp to £15 a ton, all the

nine flax mills in the Island closed down, causing serious un-employment and privation. As a means of relieving the distress, the Government granted a subsidy of £3 15s. a ton on manufactured fibre, and the mills re-opened in November.

It was during this time of financial depression that a new Governor and a new Government Secretary arrived. The new Governor, Sir Stewart Spencer Davis, C.M.G., came with a high reputation in the Colonial Service for finance, having held amongst others, the post of treasurer in the West Indies, Gold Coast, Tanganyika and Palestine. No doubt it was felt by those who selected him for the Governorship, that he would prove the right man to put St. Helena on a sound financial footing.

His task was a difficult one.

Naturally and rightly Sir Spencer Davis's first annual report principally concerned the question of revenue, and he was not long in finding out the root of much of the trouble.

Primarily there was the high cost of living due to the exorbitant rates of freightage charged by the Union-Castle Line. It must be borne in mind that only one line of ships calls at St. Helena, so that there is no competition to keep down freightage or passenger charges.

As the Governor pointed out, these high charges made the cost of importation of fertilizers prohibitive, so that the farmers and agriculturists were not able to manure their land, which it badly needed.

Owing to this, almost every imported commodity, food in-cluded, had gone up in price just when the islanders had even less money to spend than usual. Wages were, for skilled or semi-skilled men, two to three shillings and sixpence a day. The Government wage, for an adult unskilled man, was two shillings a day, or twelve shillings for a forty-five hours week. In the flax mills the wages were even worse, slightly under one shilling and nine pence for a nine hours day. Wages in the mills for women were under one shilling a day. In the rope works men were getting twelve shillings a week and women five.

At this time two hundred and twenty-two persons were being employed at the flax mills.

The wages of domestic servants was ten to forty shillings a month, with board and lodging included, while cooks were paid from thirty to forty shillings a month.

As to food, meat cost one shilling a pound, but fish was very cheap, when available.

Eggs cost 1s. 6d. to 2s. 6d. a dozen according to the season. Fresh butter 3s., imported, 2s. 8d. a pound. Milk, when procurable, fivepence the imperial pint. Rice, the staple diet of the islanders, was 2½d. a pound.

By an ordinance, of 1936, the Governor introduced taxation to St. Helena, by means of Customs duties, with preference for produce of the British Empire and an imposition of increased rates and duties on foreign goods.

Some of these duties hit the poorer inhabitants very hardly, and it is sincerely to be hoped that this ordinance will soon be revised, if not altogether abolished, for the effect of it is to put a heavy financial burden on an impoverished community. If only unnecessary luxuries were taxed no harm would be done, but such necessities as sugar, clothing—old or new—boots and shoes, brooms and brushes, cement, chinaware, coffee, tea, sweetmeats of all kinds, haberdashery, hats, stockings, matches, stationery, soap and toys, to name only a few, are taxed.

And it is not only the tax which the poor of St. Helena have to pay for most of the necessities of life, and for their very few luxuries.

The price of almost every imported article which they purchase out of their miserable wages is increased by high shipping freights, insurance, cost of lighterage from the steamer to the wharf and then by the dock dues, before ever the goods reach the wharf, and before the landing charges have been paid. Even then there is nothing to prevent the shopkeeper asking whatever price he chooses.

Take, for example, cement, which can by no stretch of imagination be described as a luxury. A barrel of cement costing 13s. 11d. when landed on the wharf, is sold at 25s. in the shops.

Worse still is the tax levied on old and worn clothing. To obtain clothes is one of the greatest difficulties the islanders have to contend with.

Not long ago a very poor family was sent a parcel of old clothes by some relations in South Africa. When they called at the post office to collect it, they were informed that they must first pay a tax of several shillings. So destitute were they that they had to borrow the sum demanded from some friends and then only was the parcel delivered to them.[1]

Many of the women at Jamestown make a shilling or two when the ships call by going on board to sell island-made lace or beadwork to the passengers. Sometimes a kind passenger gives one of them an old garment as a present, or in exchange for her lace or bead work. When the woman returns to the wharf she is made to pay an importation duty on this old garment!

One more example will be sufficient to shew the lengths of absurdity and hardship to which this tariff can go.

There is only one person in the island suffering from leprosy. To be thoroughly isolated, he lives all alone at Rupert's Bay, a God-forsaken hot, stony valley next to James Valley. There the wretched creature lives in solitude, and he will continue to live there until death comes and releases him. Some kindly disposed person once gave him a gramophone and a few old records, with which to while away some of his lonely

[1] A recent order, No. 6 of 1937, gives relief in the case of "old and worn clothing or old and worn boots imported by any charitable or religious body approved by the Governor."

hours. Not long ago a lady in England, hearing of the leper, sent out a parcel of old and very worn gramophone records for him. They were small ones, which cost not more than sixpence each when new. On that parcel of records a duty was claimed, and had to be paid, or threepence on each record.

One might go on and on citing similar cases, but it is hoped that these few may urge the St. Helena Government to go seriously into the question of these new tariffs and consider whether they cannot be modified, so as to give the poor complete relief from any taxation whatever except on acknowledged and unnecessary luxuries.

In a letter recently written to me by a gentleman living in St. Helena who has the welfare of the island's poor very much at heart, occur the following passages:

> The poor St. Helenian is, as you know, in a bad way, for there is not sufficient work to go round, and he has no protection except the local government whose hands are tied by the Treasury and its parrot cry—"You must increase your revenue and decrease your expenditure."
>
> I am not versed in economics [the writer continues] but it seems a queer way to improve the revenue by putting on a general tariff and at the same time reducing the spending capacity of the mass of the population. As practically every penny is spent on English goods brought out on English ships, I cannot see what advantage it is to England to keep the Island in penury and its people in a state of semi-starvation.

Sir Charles Harper consistently refused to reduce the labourer's half-crown a day or to impose a general tariff which must inevitably increase the cost of living. He was succeeded temporarily, for administrative purposes, by Major Lucas, who reduced the Government workmen to two shillings and threepence a day.

Sir Spencer Davis, it is understood, arrived with special instructions. He imposed the tariff and he further reduced the wage to two shillings a day, concerning which an under-secretary stated in Parliament that the labourer was perfectly satisfied.

They are only satisfied on the strength of the fallacy that "silence gives consent," for they are afraid to speak.

This Customs Ordinance No. 5 of 1936 is a very close-meshed net, and little escapes it.

There are exceptions, though, which allow certain articles to be imported to this tropic isle free of all duty, such as ice, articles for the use of His Majesty's Navy, Army and Air Force and the Colonial Government, and articles for the personal use of the twelve Royal Marines who guard the island from foreign invasion. Artificial limbs and crutches are, quite rightly, exempt from paying tax or duty, and so are tombstones, vermin traps, false teeth, wine for public worship in churches, empty bottles, and uniforms for the Salvation Army.

But the new tariff must be judged by results, and these are disclosed when we examine the revenue report of the following year.

The revenue was up by £5,926!

Due to the new taxes? No: due to St. Helena's old friends and benefactors, the postage stamp collectors. 1934 was the hundredth anniversary of the transference of the island from the East India Company to the Crown, and to celebrate the occasion, though what benefit St. Helena ever reaped from the change of ownership is by no means clear, a special set of commemorative stamps had been issued. And they sold like hot cakes and brought to the exchequer the tidy sum of £7,876, to which Ascension Island contributed £2,566.

In the beginning of this year work of reconstruction was

begun on parts of Longwood, which were not completed at the time the building was made over to the French Government in 1858. The work was carried out by the Société des Amis de Sainte-Hélène.

Certain articles of furniture at Plantation House, including the billiard table, which had belonged to Longwood, were returned to their original home and thus formed the nucleus of a museum.

Like his predecessor, Governor Davis called attention to the serious shortage of houses in both Jamestown and the country and to the dilapidated condition of many of the cottages—"which, with the steadily increasing population was causing serious over-crowding with its attendant evils."

Nothing appears to have been done to rectify this serious state of affairs.

The price of fibre dropped lower still, to £11 a ton, the lowest price on record.

Only one person in the whole island now undertook to supply local needs in meat and dairy produce.

Another enquiry was set in hand to ascertain what proportion of the inhabitants owned land and in what amounts. Here is the result:

Under 10 acres				414 holdings	
Over 10 and under		50 acres	57	,,	
,, 50 ,,	,,	100 ,,	9	,,	
,, 100 ,,	,,	500 ,,	7	,,	
,, 500 ,,	,,	1,000 ,,	2	,,	
,, ,,		1,000 ,,	nil		

On the 5th May the reconstruction of Old Longwood House was completed, and this and the inauguration of the Longwood Museum was celebrated by a reception given by Monsieur and Madame Colin, the French Consular Agent and his wife.

It may truly be said that Old Longwood and the Castle at

Jamestown are the only two historic buildings in St. Helena which are well and reverently taken care of.

This brings to an end the summary of information which may be, and has been gleaned from the official reports of the Governors of St. Helena.

On the 23rd October, 1937, the retiring Governor, Sir Spencer Davis, C.M.G., delivered his farewell address to the assembled inhabitants of St. Helena.

It was a lengthy address for such an occasion, and enumerated the many improvements which had taken place during His Excellency's Governorship.

Naturally the financial position came under review, and it will not be out of place to quote the words of the Governor who was the instigator of the Customs Ordinance, (No.5), of 1936, which was to bring financial prosperity to an insolvent colony by the magic wand of a general and preferential tariff.

My address to you would hardly be complete without a brief statement of the financial position of the Colony. At the beginning of my administration the accounts shewed a deficit of £7,219, but in consequence of the receipt of a grant-in-aid from His Majesty's Treasury the balance at the 1st January, 1933 (two months after my arrival) was converted to a surplus of £1,143. At the 31st of August last—the latest date upon which the accounts have been compiled —the surplus balance had grown to £25,265.

This very satisfactory position has been brought about solely from adventitious revenue derived from sales of St. Helena and Ascension stamps, in particular the Coronation stamps of Their Majesties King George VI and Queen Elizabeth. To some extent also the normal revenue was augmented by proceeds from sales of the St. Helena Centenary stamps, which were issued in the year 1934, and from the sales of the Ascension pictorial stamps which were issued in 1935. As the author—and to some extent the designer—of the last mentioned two special issues, the improved financial position is of special satisfaction to me.

It is beyond question that St. Helena is overshadowed by the memory of the great Napoleon. Longwood is, and for many more years will be, a place of pilgrimage, as well as a personal source of income to many. In fact, Napoleon and postage stamps are two of the principal items of revenue to the Colony. The stamps issued in 1935 by St. Helena and Ascension to commemorate the Silver Jubilee of King George V brought in a sum of about £10,000, though this windfall was appropriated by the Treasury in London, and only a part of it reached St. Helena, and then only to replace the usual grant-in-aid.

If to the world at large St. Helena has a double interest—Napoleonic and philatelic—there is, however, no connection between the two. Neither Napoleon nor the places made famous by his exile appear on any of the St. Helena stamps. To many it seemed that an opportunity was missed in 1935, as well as in 1934, when numerous pictorial stamps were issued and not one of them recalled Napoleon's connection with St. Helena. Such a postage stamp would have been welcomed by the pilgrims to Longwood, both for their stamp-albums or as something of local interest to put on their letters to their friends.

One of the stamps of the 1934 issue had a reminder of Napoleon's jailer, Sir Hudson Lowe, in a picture of Plantation House. Would it not have been well balanced by another showing Longwood Barn, where the Emperor was lodged?

In two years' time—1940—will occur the centenary of the exhumation and removal of Napoleon's remains from St. Helena to France.

Will this unique opportunity be missed of issuing a small

commemorative set of three postage stamps? I suggest a portrait of the Emperor, a view of Longwood and another of the Tomb.

It would be a compliment, if belated, on the part of the British Government, to the memory of St. Helena's most distinguished resident.

Ever since the Crown took over St. Helena from the East India Company she has been Nobody's Child. At first the island was grouped by the Colonial Office in the "West Indies", later on to be transferred to "Ceylon". Her next foster-parents were an oddly matched couple, known as the "Mediterranean and the Pacific Isles". Within the last few months St. Helena has once again changed parents and been adopted by "West Africa".

For purposes of administration St. Helena is grouped with Ascension Island[1]—700 miles North—and for religious instruction both are included with Tristan da Cunha—1,500 miles south—in the diocese of the Bishop of St. Helena.

When the British Government chose St. Helena as the place of captivity for Napoleon it was running no risk of his escape, and took possession of and garrisoned both Ascension and Tristan da Cunha, to obviate any danger of these islands being used as bases for attempted rescue by sympathizers of the Emperor.

As a result of persistent publicity in the Press people know far more about the island of Tristan da Cunha than they do about St. Helena—if we leave out Napoleon's connection with it. St. Helena has a longer and more romantic history, and also her need of assistance is far greater and more pressing than that of Tristan da Cunha. This is proved by the fact that whereas in St. Helena there are hundreds of people who, to better their condition, are willing—however sadly—to emigrate

[1] On the 12th January, 1938, the islands of Tristan da Cunha, Gough, Nightingale and Inaccessible were declared Dependencies of the Island of St. Helena.

to foreign countries, but are unable to do so, the Tristan islanders have, time and again, refused to leave, although offered free passages to South Africa and given the promise of work and land when they arrived there.

CHAPTER XIV
THE LAST

THIS book was to have come to a close with the previous chapter, but on reading it again the writer felt he had made the grave mistake of ending on a note of depression. He feared that what he had divulged concerning the condition of poverty, want and unemployment so prevalent at St. Helena, might have left his readers with the impression that the inhabitants of that small and remote island were sad or unhappy.

Far from it; they appear to be a happy, smiling people, who have suffered privation for so long that they have become accustomed to it. Their wants are few, they dwell in a lovely land, the climate is unrivalled. They are a brave people, but their courage is not that of the dull, obtuse rustic. On the contrary, they are as a race highly intelligent. It is possible at St. Helena for an educated visitor to carry on a rational conversation with the most humble cottager, peasants of a class with which it would be impossible to do so in rural England.

After all, they have much to be thankful for. Who, in this world gone mad, has not some time or other allowed his fancy to picture some delectable land, some fair tropic isle, to which he could retire, where peace and quiet reigned, where there were no newspapers, no loud-speakers, no income-tax, no lidos, no by-pass roads, no noisy crowds, no glaring posters on hoardings, no dog-races, no cinemas; and where the sun shone on most days of the year?

These are some of the blessings which the St. Helenians enjoy and which go a long way to alleviate the drawbacks.

St. Helena is the Cinderella, or shall we say the poor forgotten orphan, of the British Empire.

Once upon a time she was the pampered darling of the Honourable East India Company. Given just a little help, a little encouragement and a fair share of their own land to cultivate, and a voice in the government of their native island, the St. Helenians would be the happiest and most contented race in the world.

I am an optimist about St. Helena. I believe a real change for the better is on its way. St. Helena has been forgotten now for so many years, but those in whose hands her fate lies are beginning to show that they are determined that a new era of prosperity shall come to her. In July, 1937, an Ordinance (No. 7, 1937) was enacted by the late Governor relating to the supervision of factories. True, it does not go very far, but it is an important step in the right direction. It is understood that the matter of an enactment of workmen's compensation is now under consideration and there appears to be good reason for hoping that laws will soon be passed to give some compensation to an employee who receives an injury while at his work.

When the new era of prosperity comes into being, what form will it take?

There are two, or perhaps three, possibilities. It may be agriculture, or perhaps St. Helena is destined to become a health and holiday-resort, or, once again an important stepping stone between England and the East.

Let us first consider the reasons for the last presumption.

The whole political situation of the world is changing. In some ways it is coming to resemble that of the sixteenth century. It is not a wild extravagance to foresee that in time of war the Mediterranean and the Suez Canal might be closed to British ships, in which case the old sea route of the East, round the Cape of Good Hope, might regain its importance, and St. Helena would become once again a vital half-way house between Europe and Asia.

In the days of the East India Company, St. Helena was the most strongly fortified spot in the world. To-day if you sail round the island in a whale boat—a circumnavigation no traveller should fail to make—fort after fort, battery, bastion and gun emplacement are to be seen. In ruins now, and in any case completely out of date.

The island may become an important place of call for aeroplanes, and those flying to and from the East may call at St. Helena for "refreshment", as did the old East-Indiamen, only the new ships of the air will stop to take in petrol and oil, instead of fresh water and beef.

As to the other two roads to prosperity, one of them is the possibility of catering for visitors, whether healthy or in search of health.

The equitable climate has often been remarked upon ever since man first placed foot upon the island.

The country itself is exquisite. Steep hills, green valleys, winding roads and shady bridle paths to walk or ride along. Lovely flowers which have been introduced in the past from all quarters of the globe and have escaped from the gardens and run riot. There is no malaria nor any other insect-borne disease, nor any fear of sunstroke. All that is needed are houses or hotels where visitors might stay. Given these and also a reasonable charge for the passage to and from St. Helena, and people who can be happy without what are styled "organized amusements" would flock there, bringing with them money which would circulate throughout the island, and give employment to large numbers of the islanders.

The third measure which I believe would bring prosperity is agriculture, or to be precise, horticulture.

Almost anything will grow and flourish on St. Helena if given the least encouragement. In the old days the island was world-famous for its groves of lemons, oranges, pomegranates and other fruit trees. They used to grow in profusion in valleys which are now dry and arid stony wastes. In one or two of the valleys a few coconuts, dates, mangoes and bananas and other tropical fruits are to be found. At Maldivia by Jamestown there still grow a few banana trees which produce short, thick, yellow fruit, delicious and scented, unrecognizable as belonging to the same family as the tasteless and enormous plantains which pass for bananas in England.

Some excellent coffee is grown in Sandy Bay; with a little enterprise and trouble enough coffee could be grown there to supply the whole island, yet coffee is imported.

Amongst the colonial exhibits at the London Exhibition held in 1851 a parcel of coffee grown on St. Helena won a first prize.

Six years earlier some coffee berries shipped to England fetched one penny per pound more in the open market than did coffee of any other description.

For an island so small as St. Helena is, it would be out of the question to attempt to compete in the world's supply of such commodities as sugar, coffee, tobacco or bananas, even if the freights for exportation were less exorbitant. The salvation of St. Helena lies in growing for export small, select crops of special produce. But first of all she should grow far more for her own consumption. All sorts of fruit, vegetables and salads could be grown by small-holders, to supply their own needs and those of their countrymen. Oranges are actually imported from South Africa and are expensive luxuries, and yet years ago hundreds of orange trees grew and bore fruit in the island and would do so again if properly planted and tended. There is no reason why all sorts of fruit should not be grown, as well as oranges and lemons, such as apples, granadillas, pears, plums, peaches and nectarines.

If St. Helena were populated by a race like the Maltese, every sheltered valley would be a vegetable garden or an orchard, and those hardworking gardeners would have terraced the steep hillsides to grow their vegetables and crops.

But even the Maltese could not do this if most of the best land belonged to two proprietors.

Tobacco has been grown experimentally in the past, and according to Sir Daniel Morris there is no reason why enough should not be grown for home consumption.

Bee-keeping should be encouraged. There are only a few hives on the island, but these produce excellent honey.

As to exports, the only present staple one is the New Zealand flax, but this is far from being an ideal crop. It can be harvested only once in every three to five years, and then is only profitable when the price of flax is high.

Labour in St. Helena is both plentiful and cheap, and no doubt the most suitable crops would be those that yield a harvest at least once a year.

Investigations carried out in recent years by Mr. Toms, the Agricultural and Forestry officer of the island, have proved the possibility of establishing a small export of new potatoes to England in the latter months of the year, and he has shown that the small white haricot bean used for canning grows well.

Other products for export now being investigated are Pyrethrum, Geranium oil, Chenopodium oil, and Wattle bark, but the one that holds out greatest hope of ultimate success is the cultivation for export of the bulbs of the exquisite St. Helena lily, *Lilium longiflorum var.*

These are now being exported each year so as to arrive in England in the spring. They can then at once be planted in the garden or in pots and in the following August they will begin to flower and continue to flower for several weeks. In fact, by planting the bulbs in relays a supply of flowers can be maintained until Christmas. Amongst the advantages which the St. Helena lilies have over similar lilies imported from Japan is their freedom from disease and that they need not be retarded or forced to produce flowers in the autumn, and therefore are far bigger and healthier. At present these lily bulbs are grown in the cottage gardens, but it is hoped, now that the demand for them appears to justify it, to grow them on a far larger scale.

Of course none of these projects can succeed until a fair proportion of the land fit for cultivation is allotted to the working classes to form small-holdings.

It seems strange to anyone who has been there how little people know about St. Helena and how few have stayed there. Except for a very occasional visitor who remains on the island for a while, the great majority who know it, do so only from going ashore for a few hours from one of the steamers which ply between England and Cape Colony.

The arrival of these bi-monthly ships is the one great event in the quiet life of the islanders, for not only do they bring the mails from home or South Africa, but they also bring visitors. It is reckoned by the St. Helenians that the passengers from one of these vessels spend on an average about £200 during the few hours they are on shore, and this comparatively small sum is a welcome windfall. The money goes to the boatmen who row the passengers to the shore, to the drivers and owners of the few motor-cars which take visitors up to Longwood and other parts of the island, and to the poor women who make lace, mats and necklaces of native seeds, and baskets of aloe fibre, to sell to the passengers, for they have no other market for their produce.

Sometimes a steamer does not arrive until nightfall when it is too late for the passengers to go ashore, and their disappointment is shared, though for other reasons, by the islanders.

Some captains of liners have the reputation for calling in the morning to enable their passengers to have six full hours in which to explore the island—these are known locally as "Good Captains".

Others seem to make it a practice to anchor at night, and these are styled "Bad Captains".

Most of these transient visitors appear to imagine that the only "sight" worth while is Old Longwood House and they hire a car, go there, stopping on the way to glance at the empty Tomb, and then return to Jamestown. By doing so they make a grave mistake. To the majority the mention of St. Helena suggests Napoleon Bonaparte and little or nothing else. True that Longwood, in the pious and efficient care of Monsieur and Madame Colin, is something which cannot fail to impress and inspire, but Longwood is by no means the only object worth while visiting, though to leave St. Helena without seeing Longwood would be like leaving Egypt without seeing the Pyramids.

The majority of passengers who land at Jamestown for a few hours on shore, after purchasing stamps at the post-office, are hurried in motor-cars to visit the Tomb and then the abode of the great man and Emperor, but very few of them go a few miles farther and see one of the wonders of the world. This is Sandy Bay on the south or windward coast, a place of indescribable beauty. It is half of an extinct volcano, the other half having fallen into the blue sea below. This vast arena appears suddenly, without warning. The unsuspecting traveller leaves the road and walks a short distance across a high plateau, which reminds him of the Wiltshire Downs, and there laid out at his feet is a fantastic and almost incredible abyss.

Here and there are little green hills looking like a child's toy, with little white toy houses perched on their summits. These homesteads have such enchanting names as Mount Pleasant, Fairyland, Lemon Grove, Rose Cottage, Green Hill, Bamboo Hedge, Distant Cottage and Virgin Hall.

Farther down below all vegetation ceases, and there is nothing else but a disordered confusion of bare rocks and earth, of every colour of the rainbow. The place names down there are of a different sort, such as The Gates of Chaos, The Devil's Garden, Lot, Lot's Wife and Broad Gut.

High above the amazed spectator and to his left runs the Ridge, the highest part of the island, with its three summits; Diana's Peak, the tallest, 2,697 feet, Cuckold's Point and Mount Actaeon. The upper part of this ridge is still clothed by the primeval forest of the island, at least by what little of it has been spared by the greedy goats and more recently by the even greedier growers of New Zealand flax. This last trace of the indigenous forest is very interesting botanically and very beautiful. At one time the whole island was covered by similar forest, but now it has all disappeared except this last vestige. On both the steep sides of the Ridge the ruthless and rapacious flax growers have hacked down and grubbed up wild olive, tree ferns, cabbage trees, lobelia, and everything else which God planted there, in order to grow their flax, which would grow just as well in many other parts of the island.

Let us hope that at this eleventh hour the Government of St. Helena will forbid, once and forever, a single tree, shrub or fern to be destroyed in this wanton manner.

The Ridge should be inviolate. It should be in the safe

keeping of the island for all time, and not one square foot of it should belong to a private individual or company.

Another reason, if one were needed, for not being content only to visit Longwood, is that the scenery of St. Helena is so varied, and it is only on a long drive that half of its beauties can be seen and appreciated. The lower parts of the island are mostly stony and arid, with little vegetation save aloes and cacti; higher up, however, all is a brilliant green. Green valleys, down which burble little streams, and green hills. Here and there are pine and fir trees which call to mind hilly places in the Balearic Islands or Corsica. Higher still are turfy uplands; while higher yet runs the forest-clad Ridge, crowned by Diana's Peak.

In the middle zone flowers bloom the year round. Garden flowers and flowering shrubs have, from time to time, been introduced from all quarters of the globe and have run riot. Purple and mauve buddleia is a weed, flaming hibiscus and blue plumbago form shady hedges in the winding lanes. Incongruities abound; a flowering honeysuckle clambering over a banana tree, or English gorse or bramble growing cheek-by-jowl with tree ferns and olives. Flowers of every shade and colour are to be seen, only the native island ones have no colour; they are all white.

It is a sad moment when the time comes to say farewell to the kind, hospitable people of St. Helena, whether they be well-to-do or poor, white or brown.

After much shaking of hands and many last good-byes, you leap down on to the poop of a whale-boat which has been skilfully manœuvred close in to the landing steps on the crest of a passing wave, clutch the upright post to save yourself a drenching, and clamber down into the well.

The men soon pull the heavy seaworthy boat to the waiting liner. You climb aboard—a bell rings—"all for the shore"—a blast from the steamer's fog-horn and the journey home has begun.

ST. HELENA

Gradually the grim, towering, brown cliffs glide away; the Barn, Flagstaff and High Knoll grow smaller. In a few hours there is nothing else to be seen but an immensity of blue sea, and St. Helena has become a memory—a very precious memory.

I

LAWS AND ORDERS CONSTITUTED FOR THE SLAVES BY THE WHITE INHABITANTS OF ST. HELENA, WITH THE APPROBATION OF THE GOVERNOR AND COUNCIL

FRAMED EITHER IN GOVERNOR FIELD'S TIME OR IN THE EARLY PART OF BLACKMORE'S GOVERNMENT, BETWEEN 1674 AND 1678

THAT no Black or Blacks upon any pretence whatever shall wander from his master's plantation upon Sundays without a lawful occasion granted by their said masters or mistresses, either by writing or some other token that shall be known by the neighbourhood, upon the penalty of ten lashes on his naked body for the first offence, fifteen for the second, twenty for the third, and so for every offence thereafter committed; but if the master of the said slave or slaves should refuse to comply with this said order, the person who shall have taken the said slave or slaves acting contrary to this order, shall be obliged to complain to the Governor and Council whom we desire to fine him or them that shall so offend at discretion. That negro, or negroes,

For pilfering and stealing that shall be known to steal the value of eighteen pence, shall have twenty lashes on their naked body, inflicted by the master or masters of such slave or slaves in the presence of the person so offended; but, if the theft should amount to three shillings, the lashes aforesaid are to be increased to thirty; and if six shillings to sixty, and the party so prejudiced shall receive the value of the thing so stolen in specie, or in money from the owner of the said slave or slaves; and if the theft amounts to above six shillings and under thirty shillings, the offender shall be seized and brought to the Fort, where he shall immediately receive fifty lashes on his naked body, and secured; two days after that he shall receive thirty lashes, and two days after that twenty more; and the master of the black shall pay the value stolen as aforesaid.

Absentees and runaways Those that absent their master's service three days and three nights shall be punished according to the last foregoing article and the master make satisfaction for what they have stolen as aforesaid.

For breaking open houses For the first offence of this kind, the master or masters shall make satisfaction for what is stolen and repair all damages done by the slave or slaves; so soon as taken he shall be brought to the Fort, and immediately receive on his naked body one hundred lashes, then secured; four days after that thirty; six days after that twenty more, and branded in the forehead with the letter R. For the second offence of this kind he shall be punished as aforesaid and wear for one year a chain and clogg of thirty pounds weight; and for the third offence, satisfaction shall be made as aforesaid to the loser or losers, and the slave or slaves shall suffer death, at the discretion of the Governor and Council.

In relation to striking or assaulting any white person In case any male slave from the age of sixteen years and upwards shall presume and attempt to strike or assault any white person whatsoever correcting him or otherwise, for any cause whatsoever, shall for the said offence or offences (though without weapon or dangerous instrument) undergo and suffer the punishment of castration; and in case any such slave or slaves shall chance to die under the punishment aforesaid or before he be well, then the country and public shall bear the loss and make good the value of the said black, according to an appraisement made by the Governor and Council for the time being; further, but in case the said slave or slaves should die through neglect of the master or owner, then, upon proof thereof, the said master or owner to bear their own loss of the said slave or slaves and the whole charge of everything relating thereto; and if the said slave live, the master to be at all charges.

In relation to those that shall give saucy language, resist or oppose or strike any white person That if any negro slave, male or female, shall presume to resist any white person whatsoever in the taking or pursuit of them upon any lawful occasion, the slave or slaves so offending and resisting as aforesaid for the first offence shall be immediately conveyed to the Great Fort and secured till they have undergone double punishment according to the constitution of runaway negroes, and branded in the forehead with the letter R; and for a second offence in this nature, the said slave or slaves so offending shall suffer the same punishment as is adjudged and ordered in the case of striking; but if a female, to be severely whipped and both ears to be cut off, and branded in the forehead and both cheeks. And in case any slaves, male or female, shall presume to strike any white person whatsoever with any weapon, they shall suffer death, except those white persons who demean and debase themselves in conversing corresponding and gaming with the blacks, as if they were equals, which we judge shall have no more benefit of those laws than blacks themselves.

And in case any negro slave shall presume to give saucy or impertinent language or answer to any white person (except those white persons aforesaid) shall, upon complaint thereof to the master or owners of the said slave, be severely whipt in the presence of the party offended, to his satisfaction; and if the said master or owner of the said slave shall refuse or neglect to punish the said slave so offending, then the party offended may complain to the Governor; and so cause the said slave to be apprehended and conveyed to the Fort, and punished according to the nature of the offence.

Against one black bartering with another That no negro slave shall truck, barter or exchange anything, without the foreknowledge and consent of the owners of the said negroes, both the sellers and buyers, deliverers and receivers of any commodity whatsoever to the value of one shilling, upon the penalty of twenty lashes or more, if it should exceed that value according to the judgement of the Governor and Council, severely to be inflicted on them at the Flagstaff, upon the complaint of any one aggrieved by such a clandestine way of one negro dealing with another.

Against any white person trucking or bartering with blacks. That no white person whatsoever shall truck, barter or exchange any commodity whatsoever with any negro or negroes, to sell to them nor buy of them any sort of commodity, without the foreknowledge and consent of the owners of the said negro or negroes upon the penalty of being adjudged accessory to felony, and so consequently liable to a fourfold restitution to the owners of the said negro or negroes, besides a fine to the Lords Proprietors; nor no negro shall alienate any commodity or thing whatsoever to any white person whatsoever, without the leave and consent of the said negroes' master or mistress before had, upon the penalty of severe correction according to the judgement of the Governor and Council.

No blacks to prescribe physic to each other. That no negro whatsoever shall prescribe or administer any physic or medicine whatsoever to any negro or negroes without the consent of his or their master or mistress of that negro unto whom he shall prescribe or administer any physic or medicine upon the penalty of severe correction, according to the judgement of the Governor and Council; neither shall any negro whatsoever take or receive any physic or medicine or follow the rules or prescriptions of any pretended black doctor whatsoever, without acquainting their master or mistress therewith, upon the penalty of the like pain and punishment as the black doctor who pretends to physic is liable to.

In 1792 laws for the better government of slaves were issued.

These were embodied in forty-two articles, ordering slaves to be diligent and obedient, and to demean themselves as faithful servants. These laws certainly much improved the condition of the blacks.

They ordained:

That masters and mistresses shall treat their slaves with kindness and protection, with good and wholesome provision, and in sickness necessary medicines, care and attention.

That masters and mistresses are to be allowed to correct slaves moderately for wilful neglect or turbulence or abusive language; the punishment not to exceed twelve lashes with a cat-of-nine-tails.

That for faults and crimes of greater enormity than above, they should be carried before the justices of the peace and punished by their orders.

That if masters and mistresses inflicted heavier punishment than was authorized for the offence, or punish without reasonable cause, that they should be considered as guilty of assault as if the offence had been committed against a free person.

That in case the proprietors of slaves did not supply them with proper clothing, medicine, etc., it shall be lawful for the slaves to make complaint to the justices of peace, the Governor to be one, and if necessary, the proprietors to be fined.

All slaves except those employed as household servants, shall be allowed Sunday to themselves, and not be required to work thereon for their masters.

And that household slaves also shall be spared from labour on Sundays as much as may reasonably be consistent, and to be allowed alternately one Sunday in two for themselves.

And that no slaves shall be allowed to collect or carry wood on a Sunday, either for their masters or mistresses or for themselves, on pain of being punished by the order of two justices of the peace.

II

PROPOSITIONS AND ADDRESS TO THE GOVERNOR AND COUNCIL

14*th* June, 1709

ARMS.

1stly.—They desire the chief families may have arms in their houses.

ASSEMBLIES.

2ndly.—In their friendly meetings and merry-makings, it may not be deemed as riots; and that upon any time, by order of the Governor, they will separate, if ever it should enter into his thoughts such meeting is for any evil intention; which they say God forbid it should.

ALARMS.

3rdly.—They desire they may not be corporally punished, in case any neglect their duty; but to be punished in their purses.

BLACKS.

4thly.—They humbly desire, that when their blacks are run away from them, they may not be obliged to pay fourfold for what they steale, but only to make sattisfaction for the thing stole to the person injured.

MARKETT-HOUSE.

5thly.—They desire, if there be a markett-house built, they mayn't be obliged to bring their goods out of the country to a publick markett.

BEEFE.

6thly.—They desire to have free liberty to sell beefe to shipps.

DOGGS.

7thly.—They desire that themselves may not be obliged to lead their doggs in a string; but are willing their servants shall do it.

CATTLE.

8thly.—They desire the toll of cattle may be taken off that they sell to one another, which is two shillings per head; for that the trouble of giving such accounts is more burdensome to them than the thing itself.

DITTO.

9thly.—They desire that the trouble they are put to, when they kill any cattle, in carrying the hide, hornes, and ears, to persons that has bin appointed for that purpose, may be redrest.

FENCING LAND.

10thly.—They desire they may not be obliged to fence in their land at all, it being a new thing they never heard of before.

JURYS.

11thly.—They desire all other matters may be tried by jurys, besides life, limb, and land, as the plaintiffe shall think fitt.

WHOLESALE.

12thly.—They desire that the liquors, &c. called Wholesale, being three gallons, may be reduced to one gallon arrack, four pound sugar, and one or two pounds of tobacco; and this be deemed a whole sale.

LIQUORS RETAYLED.

13thly.—They desire that we would establish a certain rate upon liquors retayled by the punch-houses.

CAUSES.

14thly.—They desire to be tryed by the civill law, and not by martiall law.

SHIPPS.

15thly.—They desire the liberty that they always had to go on board of any ship when in the Road, asking the Government first.

TAXES.

16thly.—They desire to be eased something in the tax of paying ten shillings every year for each black they have.

GAME.

17thly.—They desire that each chief of family that has guns allowed them, may, for their diversion, have liberty to go a shooting.

GREAT WOOD.

18thly.—They desire liberty to make use of the Great Wood and Common; otherwise they will be ruined.

LESSEES.

19thly.—They desire lessees may vote for parish officers; and also serve in their turns.

And all these grievances they humbly begg may be redrest, as by their ADDRESS, in the following manner:

ISLAND OF ST. HELENA:

That whereas your Worship and Council was pleased, on the 16th day of Aprill last past, to summons thirty-six of the principal inhabitants to the church in the country, and there to hear the laws read over, which was accordingly done: And forasmuch as we were a long time kept in the dark, and knew nothing of it; the inhabitants so summoned did, by a consent, choose twelve of us to inspect into them, and to make our remarks, upon the promise of your Worship and Councill, that in case of any grievance which appeared reasonable, that your Worship and Councill would be pleased to make address to the Lords Proprietors for redress.

And this day we do with submission present the same to your Worship and Councill, with our remarks thereon, and hope you will find them reasonable. And, in the mean time, we shall be obedient to those laws and orders delivered to the churchwardens on the 26th of April last past.

And whereas your Worship and Councill having represented to us the necessity we are in, for the good of ourselves and successors, to use means for the preservation of wood, which grows very scarce, and will inevitably be, at last, the undoing of the island and the inhabitants of it, if due care is not taken for the maintaining of wood in planting the same; Wee, making serious reflections on this account, come to this conclusion; viz.

That every planter possessed of twenty acres of land, shall be obliged to enclose one acre, and plant it with wood, and so proportionably for more or less; and to take that care that no cattle or hoggs shall come to graze on the said land, that the said wood so growing may not be spoiled. And also, that every planter shall, from the time of this resolution, be obliged to fence the said piece of land in three years time. This is to be understood of those planters that have no wood growing on their land, to take in any more land for the same purpose.

After having made inspection into all the laws concerning this island which your Worship and Councill have bin pleased to communicate to us, to the end where we saw any thing that was not agreeablè to peace, and against the common interest of the island, to make our remarks thereon, and to give our reasons for it, which we have done accordingly: We hope, if your Worship and Councill find anything in those remarks and reasons that are not consonant with reason, will not attribute it to us, as done on purpose to infringe some of the properties that rightly belong to the Honourable Company and the Government of this place; but are willing to submit ourselves to anything that reasonably shall be established by your Worship and Councill; and that every one of us will comply with the utmost of our power, for we all know we must submit ourselves to our superiors, not only for wrath, but conscience sake also. And we hope that every one of us and all together, will do our utmost endeavours to do anything for the preservation of this island, and the good of the Honourable Company; and that we promise that we will not be remiss in our military dutys; but when occasion shall present, wee will not be frugal of our blood, but ready to spil every drop of it for the preservation of the island, our wives and families, against any enemy that shall come here to invade us. And finally we give your Worship and Councill our humble thanks for having bin pleased to communicate to us the aforesaid laws and constitutions for our perusal, that we might the better be enabled to know our duty (a thing which was never done before), but have always bin kept in ignorance of the same.

We have no more to say to your Worship and Councill; but wishing you all the health imaginable in your government, and we a quiet and peaceable living under it, which we beseech Almighty God to grant to you and us, we remain

Your Worship and Councill's
most humble
and obedient servants,

HENRY COALS,
JOHN NICHOLS,
THOS. SWALLOW,
ROBT. ADDIS,
MATT. BAZETT,
JAMES GREENTREE,
HENRY FRANCIS,
RICHARD GURLING,
ORLANDO BAGLEY,
CHARLES STEWARD,
JOHN COLES,
RICHARD SWALLOW.

To each of the foregoing articles the Governor and Council annexed their answers: and the committee, on the part of the inhabitants, subjoined a declaration, expressive of their satisfaction to most of the Council's resolutions, as follows: first,

ARMES.

As to armes, the Governor will give them his warrant in the following manner to such chiefs of families:

Forasmuch as the principal inhabitants of this island have solicited to have armes in their houses, which they think very necessary to them (which the law prohibits), but the Governor and Councill have dispensed with it;

Wherefore this does give leave and licence to you, Mr. A. B. for such necessary armes as you think convenient; which armes you are to deliver up at any time when required by order of the Governor for the time being;

And you have further power to seize any armes from any person that has not my licence; which armes shall be your's to dispose of as you think fitt, giving me notice of the person; and for so doing this shall be your warrant.

Given under my hand, at the United Castle, in James's Valley.

JOHN ROBERTS.

They then ordered that the following declaration be issued:

ST. HELENA.

These are to give notice to all persons inhabiting the said island, that none do presume to possess, keep, or carry, any armes, without leave and licence first obtained from the Governor, under hand and scale, upon penalty of twenty shillings to the Honourable Company, and having the same seized and taken from them by any person licenced thereunto, for their owne use, and to receive such corporal punishment as the Governor and Councill shall think fitt; and that no licenced person do lend, or permitt any person to make use of their armes, upon the penalty of having their licence and armes forfeited.

Signed per order of the Governor and
    Councill, per me,

JOHN ALEXANDER.
They are sattisfied.

ASSEMBLYS.

2ndly.—God forbid that any merry meetings and innocent diversions should be deemed riots; it's not the intent of the law.

Sattisfied.

ALARMS.

3rdly.—You shall not suffer corporal punishment for not coming to alarms; except it be in time of warr.

Sattisfied.

BLACKS.

4thly.—We shall dispense with that law of fourfold, and desire the Lords Proprietors to repeal it.

Sattisfied.

MARKETTS.

5thly.—As this law is not penall, we cannot see how it can be a grievance; and altho' marketts have never bin used, and not beneficial to the inhabitants, it is no rule it ever should, so in your favour we shall write to our Masters about it.

393

BEEFE.

6thly.—You desire free liberty to sell beefe. We shall write to our Masters in your favour about it.

DOGGS.

7thly.—You desire not to lead your doggs yourselves, but your servants.

We shall dispense with it.

Sattisfied.

CATTLE TOLLED.

8thly.—You desire the toll of cattle may be taken off, for that it creates you a great deal of trouble.

It is necessary that we should know how you sell your cattle to one another, because of our Common, that it may both prejudice you and us too by not knowing it.

CATTLE.

9thly.—You desire that the trouble you are put to, when you kill any cattle, in carrying the hide, hornes, and ears, to persons appointed, may be redrest.

We designe to make this trouble easier to you; but the law is of so great use to this island in generall: as for example, a man kills a beast, and sends for his next neighbour, he being a reputed man, and warranted by the Governor to have armes in his house; he shews him the mark of his beast that he has killed: That shall be a testimony sufficient, without going any further. Now the usefullness of it: A man loses a beast, and getts a warrant to search suspected houses, in which houses, if they find any beefe, if he cannot being his testimony that he killed it at such a time, by such substantial men as aforesaid, or where he had the same, such person ought to be convicted.

And we believe if it went as far as hoggs, goats, and sheep, it would be much to your benefit, for (if we are rightly informed) that several suspected persons eat more flesh than we think in reason and conscience they are able to do if they come by it honestly.

Sattisfied.

And ordered that a new statute be penned accordingly, and sent home by this shipping to the Honourable Lords Proprietors, for their concurrance; and that it take force from the publication.

LANDS.

10thly.—You desire you may not be obliged to fence in your lands at all; it being a new thing you never heard of before.

This law has bin made above twenty-seven years ago, and no doubt but it hath bin published, for it is what you hold your lands by. And we must say, by this law, that what land is not fenced in, is, by course, the Lords Proprietors: We have no other way to know which is your land and which is theirs. However, because you say you have bin so long kept in the dark, by not knowing any thing of it, we shall, for this time, neglect our duty in making seizures, and will intercede with the Lords Proprietors that the time appointed for enclosing may begin anew from the 25th of March last. In the mean time friendly advise you to enclose as fast as you can, least we should be checkt for this our neglect of duty, and receive orders from them to make seizures.

CAUSES BY JURYS.

11thly.—You desire all other matters may be tryed by jurys besides life, limb, and lands, as the plaintiffe shall think fitt.

No Governor and Councill will trouble themselves to give sentence upon intricate matters, and that may be of great importance, as you urge by giving a definitive sentence, tho' never so just, seldom pleases both partys, which creates an odium to the Governor and Councill, when the same thing may be judged by yourselves. As the Governor is Judge of that court, he ought to be a judge what shall be tryed by jurys, and what he himself will try in Councill; otherwise, a litigious man that hath wealth, and a cause depending with a poor man, altho' a trifling one, shall come and demand to be tryed by a jury, which will create the poor man such a charge that he will rather sit down in his wrong.

The Governor would willingly put you in mind, that he hath refused to try severall causes in Councill, as some of you know.

And, indeed, to take all this matter right, we look upon it as a burden our Masters has laid upon us to ease you.

> Sattisfied that the Governor shall be judge of what shall be tryed in Councill, and what in Court, except life, limb, and land.

LIQUOR.

12thly.—You desire that the liquor called wholesale, being three gallons, may be reduced to one gallon arrack, four pounds sugar, and one or two pound of tobacco, be deemed wholesale.

We cannot see what occasion there is to deem any thing wholesale less than what is expressed in the law, without prejudice and wrong to those who pay for licences. And you all know very well that you may have what small quantity you please out of the stores, even to a pound, or quart, of any thing.

Sattisfied.

DITTO, RETAYLED.

13thly.—You desire that we would establish certain rates upon liquor retayled by the punch-houses.

ORDERED,

That the following declaration be issued out:

These are to give notice to all lycencees, or retaylers of strong liquors, that a bowle of punch, made with one pint of arrack, with sugar and lemon answerable, be, from the day of the date hereof, sold at two shillings per bowle, and no more, while arrack is at six shillings per gallon: and if any one presumes to exact more, shall, upon information thereof given to the Governor and Councill, forfeit their license, and double the value. Which pint of arrack aforesaid is to be put into such sizeable bowle as will not be too strong, nor yet too weak, but palatable and pleasant for the buyer. But if any lycensee or retayler of liquor shall think this not a sufficient proffitt, they may deliver up their licences, paying proportionable for the time they have had it, after the rate of four pounds per annum; which all such retaylers are to do within eight days from the date hereof.

Sattisfied.

MARTIALL LAW.

14thly.—You desire to be tryed by civill law, and not by martiall law.

We shall write to our Masters about it; we think it is but reason that the planters should be tryed by the civill law, except it be in time of war and action, or, that we hope never to see, rebellion, cowardice, neglect of duty which may be the ruine of the island,

and severall other misdemeanors, in time of action, which cannot be judged by the civil law; and we likewise design in our court martiall to choose such of the worthy people of this island to be of it.   Sattisfied.

GOING ON BOARD SHIPS.

15thly.—You desire the liberty that you always had of going on board any ship or ships in the Road, asking the Governor's leave.

It is what our Masters say was never done at the Cape, or, as we know of, done in any other Dutch factory in India; however, if there be any urgent occasion, the Governor, at that time, will not deny them leave.   Sattisfied.

BLACK'S TAX.

16thly.—You desire to be eased something in the tax of ten shillings every year for each black you have.

There is no nation under the hopes of Heaven, nay, we are apt to believe, if there be any wild people, they contribute to their own safety in some measure. And if any man will look into our mother-country, England, we shall there find the four shillings in the pound tax alone gives the Queen, every fifth year, their whole estate, besides taxes of window lights, parrish dutys, and Parsons tythes, and sundry other taxes, which every Englishman knows that he that has five hundred pound per annum never gets in above three hundred pound, and very well if that. And now that the Honourable Company has, for six years last past, paid for fortifications, by employing the blacks and artificers of this island, about fifteen hundred pound a year, besides the constant charge of the garrison, &c. for your preservation. We shall only now give you our Masters' reasons; but must tell you we little expected, at this time of day, such an article from you; which, indeed, as we find, by a medium of six years last past, amounts but to fifty-eight pounds per annum: a great mite to such a vast charge.

The reason of which order is, as the Negroes increase upon the island, it will be necessary for the Honourable Company proportionably to increase the garrison and soldiers, for the security of the inhabitants, as well as the island.

397

ST. HELENA

17thly.—You desire that each chief of a family that have guns allowed you may have liberty to go a shooting for your diversion.

You must keep within the law of the preservation of game. But if any person should desire any further privilege, they are not to presume to do it without leave first had of the Governor, which is left to his pleasure to give or let alone.

Sattisfied.

GREAT WOOD.

18thly.—You desire leave of the Great Wood and Common.

Provided you will agree to make a law to plant one acre of wood in every ten acres of land you possess; otherwise you shall have no benefit of our Wood or Common, as our published order.

Agreed to and Sattisfied.

LESSEES.

19thly.—You desire lessees may vote for election of parrish officers, and serve in their turns.

We shall dispense with that, and write to the Lords Proprietors to repeal that law, and hope they will comply.

Sattisfied.

III

HIS EXCELLENCY THE GOVERNOR'S LICENCE FOR THE RETURN OF THE BRIG PERSEVERANCE TO THIS ISLAND

BY His Excellency Lieut.-General Sir Hudson Lowe K.C.B. Governor and Commander in Chief of the Island of St. Helena.

Licence is hereby granted unto the British Brig Perseverance John Amber Master to return to the Island of St. Helena for one voyage subject however to the following regulations and conditions.

1st That the Master of the aforesaid Brig shall not take on board any passengers nor other persons beyond the usual crew a list of which crew shall be published to the Colonial Office in Cape Town (without the permission of his Excellency the Governor) previous to the sailing of the brig on her intended voyage, in order that a copy thereof being given to the Post Office, a proper officer therefrom may muster the said crew and search the brig to ascertain whether any other persons have been secreted on board, the last thing previous to the departure of the said Brig.

2nd That the said Master receive from the Post Office a certificate of such muster and deliver the same to the Commander of any of His Majesty's vessels arriving off the island of St. Helena that may board him previous to his arrival at the anchorage of St. Helena.

3rd That no shipper of goods on board the said Brig be permitted to send a supercargo under any pretext whatever to St. Helena.

4th That sealed copies of the Brig's Manifest be taken from the Custom House at the Cape of Good Hope certified by the Collector and Comptroller of the customs to be delivered unopened to the authorities at St. Helena.

5th That no communication whatever shall take place between

the Brig and the shore at St. Helena unless under the special authority of His Excellency the Governors.

6th That neither the said Master nor any other person in the said brig shall receive any letter or packet except such as shall be made up or delivered at the Post Office, or the office of the Secretary to Government or the Deputy Adjutant General at St. Helena or at the Cape of Good Hope from the Governor of that Colony, the Post Office, the Collector or Comptroller of His Majesty's Customs or from the agent of the East India Company there.

7th That the owner of the brig do enter into engagement with this Government by Bond with effecient securities in the sum of fifteen hundred pounds sterling to be forfeited and paid by him should the aforesaid articles be in any way infringed.

> Given under my Hand and Seal at the Island of St. Helena this third day of December One Thousand eight hundred and eighteen.
>
> H. Lowe.

By Order of His Excellency
the Governor.

> Mr. H. Brooke.
> Sec. to Government.

> The above Licence is hereby renewed for another

voyage.

> By order of His Excellency the Governor.
> Mr. H. Brooke.
> Sec. to Government.

St. Helena.
26th March, 1819.

> The above licence is hereby renewed for another

voyage.

> By order of His Excellency the Governor.
> Mr. H. Brooke.
> Sec. to Government.

St. Helena.
21 October 1819.

IV

THE ST. HELENA PRINTING-PRESSES

Reprinted from Notes and Queries, *December* 5, 1936

BOOKS and pamphlets printed in St. Helena are something of a curiosity. It was not until 1806, or close upon 150 years after the Island had been first occupied by the British, that a small press was imported by a few private residents and set up as *The St. Helena Press*, under the management of Mr. Saul Solomon, whose family have contributed so much to South African and local history. The business was taken over later by the East India Company, but during the years 1807–1813 it produced a number of interesting publications. An early specimen of its work, the *Government Gazette, Published by Authority*, No. 5, June 20, 1807, is preserved in the public records at Jamestown, no other copies are available locally, and as the paper does not appear again, and then in another form, until 1845, it would be interesting to know what happened to it and whether it was published during the intervening thirty-eight years.

With the appointment of Alexander Beatson as Governor in 1808, the publishing trade began to boom. He seized on the press as the means of disseminating his views on agricultural development; and in the *St. Helena Monthly Register*, which began publication in 1809, he described his plans and explained his experiments with, as the late Lord Rosebery was to remark a hundred years later, "a minuteness which could scarcely be justified in the case of the Garden of Eden". Twelve copies of this curious little journal, about 8 in. × 4½ in., were sent regularly to East India House, but so far only one compilation has been found, and that incomplete. Other publications during Beatson's period of office were "Papers relating to the Devastation committed by Goats on the Island of St. Helena". By Authority. 1810; a compilation of laws relating specially to land, "Abstract of the Laws and Ordinances relating to Land and Tenures and the Moral and Agricultural Improvement of the Island of St. Helena". By Authority c. 1810; the laws of the little settlement under the title "Abstract of the Laws and Regulations established by the Honourable Court of Directors or by the Governor and Council of the Island of St. Helena". By Authority. 1813; and more papers on goats and sheep. "Island of St. Helena. Proceedings of the Governor and Council regarding Lands, Tenures, Goats and Sheep". 1813.

The *Register* was, of course, a quasi-official newspaper; but soon after the appointment of the Rev. Richard Boys to the junior chaplaincy in 1812, it seems to have got into trouble. "Objectionable remarks" appeared in its columns, with the result that any future material about which there was any doubt, was required to be submitted to the Government Secretary before publication. Dr. Baildon, the Company's Medical Superintendent, who acted as editor, was so outraged by this order that he wrote an angry memorial to the Court of Directors protesting at the reflection on "his literary attainments and general respectability of character" which, as Mark Wilks observed later, "would be invaluable in any community". His protest was unavailing and Boys was appointed to his place. Island life became perceptibly brighter when he and the Rev. Mr. Jones began to print and circulate abusive letters to each other; but the squabble that ended in the latter being retired to the post of tutor to the Balcombe children on a pension of 5s. per day, supplemented by the Emperor's sympathy, put a stop to private publishing in St. Helena for very many years.

With the departure of Beatson, the *Register* ceased publication, and, with the exception of the printing of the first "Report of the St. Helena Benevolent Society", 1814, the press was confined during the captivity to turning out official notices, Acts of Parliament, regulations, menacing proclamations, etc., until at the last scene of all, it printed the catalogues of the dead Emperor's household effects.

The next seven years saw the issue of the *Proceedings* of the St. Helena Agricultural and Horticultural Society 1824 to 1831, and a very uncommon item, a *Flora St. Helenica*, 1825. New type also seems to have been received about this time; and in 1828 a new compilation of laws was published entitled "Bye Laws of the Island of St. Helena and Regulations for the Civil, Judicial, Medical, and

Marine Departments", 1828, of which a further edition with supplements was issued in 1834. An addition to the equipment of the press of this period was a "Lithographic Press" which was used to reproduce Manuel Johnson's famous catalogue of the stars in the southern hemisphere before it was transmitted to East India House for publication in London in 1835. Another publication, by the "Government Printing Office" was the *St. Helena Calendar and Directory*, printed in 1832, 1833, and 1834, when the Island was transferred to the Crown.

The printing office, happily, survived the shock of a change which revolutionised St. Helena; but to the printer it meant only a change in the design of the coat-of-arms at the head of his public notices and proclamations, the solid brass block used for those of the East India Company still being preserved in the present printing-office.

The exhumation of Napoleon's remains in 1840 provided the opportunity for a major publication, *Narrative of the Proceedings connected with the Exhumation and Removal of the Remains of the late Emperor Napoleon*, by a Resident, 1840, rightly attributed to W. G. Janisch, and crudely illustrated with sketches by Sergeant Patterson of the 91st, lithographed on the old press. In 1842 there was issued the first of what was to prove a long series, of *The St. Helena Almanack and Annual Register*, which was to continue in publication for upwards of forty-five years; and in 1845 the *St. Helena Gazette, Published by Authority*, reappeared in its new form. This paper set out to be something more than an official newspaper, and it provided extracts from the London newspapers, descriptions of local events of interest, obituary notices, and such like. The *Gazette*, and the *Almanacks* with their valuable introductions, tables of remarkable events, and lists of officers, constitute one of the most important sources of information on the history of the Island after its transfer to the Crown.

The history of modern printing in the Island dates from the year 1851, when George Gibb, who was allowed to undertake private work, printed and published "A Guide to St. Helena Descriptive and Historical with a Visit to Longwood and Napoleon's Tomb", by Joseph Lockwood, 1851; and in the same year the first "free" press was imported and established. Its introduction was hailed with a joy that was almost delirious; Magna Carta cannot have had a more jubilant reception; public opinion was no longer to be suppressed; and the liberty of the Press, the birthright of mankind, was also to provide a remedy for all the Island's economic ills.

These transports were somewhat moderated by financial considerations and the gloomy reflection that to ensure success, the local Government must become the new venture's largest subscriber. The Governor obligingly closed down the *Gazette* and presented the new paper with a small income as payment for the advertisement of official notifications, etc. Assured of this steady support, the *St. Helena Advocate and Weekly Journal of News* began publication on 8 May, 1851. It soon got into trouble for intemperate criticism of its chief subscriber, who retaliated, not unnaturally, by withdrawing the official advertisements and publishing them in a new official paper, the *St. Helena Chronicle*, printed, but not "By Authority", at the Government Printing Office, the first number appearing in March, 1852. The withdrawal of official support killed the *Advocate* and it was replaced in 1853 by the *St. Helena Herald*.

In the course of the past ninety years St. Helena has been served by two able journalists, the first of whom, Joseph Lockwood, was the editor, in practice if not in name, of both the *Advocate* and the *Herald*. He was a curious character with a marked historical sense, and held the appointment of Clerk of Works, when he was responsible for the building of the present Cathedral Church. He contributed an excellent account of the exhumation to the *United Service Journal;* his *"Guide*, etc.", is much sought after; and he adorned the columns of the *Advocate* with valuable material when he printed "Andrew Darling's Account of the Funeral of Napoleon", which was reprinted by the *Times Literary Supplement* in 1915. Another very uncommon pamphlet published at this time, for which Lockwood may have been responsible, was "Longwood Old House, A Brief Sketch of its past history and present state in connection with the late Emperor Napoleon, Anonymous, 1855", which seems to have been written with the object of calling the attention of the French to the neglect prevailing in the house in which the Emperor died, and recommending that a marble column be erected in its place. Subsequently he used his position with the *Herald* to ventilate his views on the abilities of his superior officer, action which earned him the distinction of a new edition of the regulations relating to the subject of officers contributing to the Press.

The *Herald* was superseded by another weekly, the *Record*, in

1860, and in 1861 the *Guardian* appeared; from henceforth all papers published in the Island were to be weeklies. The editor of the *Guardian*, Benjamin Grant, was the most successful of a long line of St. Helena printers and journalists. His paper, always admirably conducted, had a place to fill in the Island's social life; and it continued its circulation, under the editorship of his son, until comparatively recent times. Grant was fully alive to the interest taken in St. Helena's historical associations, to which he made more than one valuable contribution, and scientists are under an obligation to him for printing and publishing *The Geology of St. Helena*, J. R. Oliver, 1869, which still remains one of the standard works on the subject. Competitors to the *Guardian* were not slow in appearing, and the *Advertiser*, 1865, the *Spectator*, 1866, and the *Star*, also 1866, all had short but hectic lives, but for the next twenty years the *Guardian* Press was to have the field to itself and, with the exception of some official material published by the Government Press, it had a monopoly of private printing. Rare pamphlets from the official Press were "First Report of the Committee of Enquiry on the Ravages of White Ants", 1864; "Scraps from Records", H. R. Janisch, 1872, and a "Précis of Information concerning the Island of St. Helena prepared by the Governor and Colonel Commanding the Troops", 1876; whilst the *Guardian* was responsible for printing and publishing the "Report of the St. Helena Industrial Exhibition 1874".

"A Few Notes on St. Helena", "A Descriptive Guide to St. Helena", and "Some Remarks on St. Helena as a Health Resort", all written and printed by Grant, were published in 1883, followed by *Extracts from the Records of St. Helena*, H. R. Janisch, in 1885, some of which had been published in the *Gazette* and the early newspapers.

With the appointment of an active personality as Governor in 1887, political feeling in the Island began to run high, when there was a lamentable lapse into vulgarity on the part of the local printers. Rival political factions borrowed their type and produced two disreputable sheets, the *Bug* and the *Mosquito*, both illustrated with "jellygraph" cartoons of prominent notables. Politics also gave birth to new weeklies, the *Times*, 1889; the *Monthly Critic* and *Flashlight*, 1891; the *St. Helenian*, 1895, and the *Observer*, all disappearing when the particular crisis to which they referred was over. In 1889 it was announced that St. Helena would be abandoned as a military post, whereupon the Guardian Press produced *The Citadel of the South Atlantic*, being a reprint of letters from various persons urging the claims of the Island to be regarded as the great fortress of the South Atlantic.

The Boer War saw the appearance of a foreign edition of what was really the *Guardian*, the *Krijsgevangene* published in Afrikaans for the use of the Boer prisoners then on the island; and in 1908 Grant's son published a new edition of *Extracts from Records*.

The *Guardian* ceased publication soon after the close of the European War, when private printing and publishing passed into the care of the Church magazines which had begun with the *St. Helena Church News* in 1888. This was followed by the *Parish Magazine*, 1889, the *Diocesan Magazine*, 1901, and the *Jamestown Monthly*, 1912, which is still in circulation under the title of the *St. Helena Magazine*, 1933.

Collectors and students will, no doubt, be able to add to the books and pamphlets that have been described; and there are, of course, many official reports, etc., that have not been mentioned, whilst little has been said of the problems that arise in the management of a printing-press in St. Helena or of the services of the Government Press. There is no printer who has not learnt his craft in the Island, and none has seen a modern power or roller press. At one period their art, which passes from generation to generation, was in danger of being lost to the Island; but owing to the labours of the late Canon Porter, who taught the apprentices himself, it was kept alive with much benefit to the small community. His example has been followed by the present Vicar of Jamestown; and printing in St. Helena has never reached a higher standard than that which can be read to-day in the *St. Helena Magazine*, and some of the official publications such as the *Government Gazette* (which was re-issued in its present form in 1871) or the *St. Helena Highway Code*, 1935.

G. C. KITCHING

SALLY PHIL'S POEM

Extract from The St. Helena Herald, 1854

VISITORS to Napoleon's tomb have for their cicerone, a
remarkable woman who has many an interesting tale to tell
both regarding Napoleon and herself. A friend who thinks
it a pity that the old woman's yarns should not receive a much
larger circulation than they have hitherto had, has kindly furnished
the public with the following lines. (Ed.)

Sally Phils Tale at the Tomb of Napoleon on the Arrival there of a Visitor

GOOD morning good Captain, and how do you do?
And I hope your dear lady is very well too,
And another good thing, I really must say,
We all are quite glad, this is a fine day.
You seem to be tired, so Captain sit down,
Your ride is quite long, to this place from the town,
Then here is a comfortable, nice painted stool,
Right under the willow, to sit in the cool.
I hope now you'll listen to Sally Phils tale,
Which is not like the teapot that held a great whale,
And if you have patience, I'll relate off by heart,
Some curious things, about great Buonaparte.
But before I shall do so, I'll speak of myself,
Or else I do think, I'll be put on the shelf.
I once was a slave, and without any light,
I was owned by a Master—good Colonel Wright,
I work'd very hard—carried loads on my head,
Felt always fatigued, on going to bed.
And after hard work, in slavery's chains,
I gave to my master much money in gains,
At last became free, and on my own hands,

ST. HELENA

For Buonaparte broke here—dread slavery's bands.
So breathing Free air, in a different orbit,
Went into the service, of good Mistress Torbett,
Whose husband did own, this land which is good,
When Buonaparte died out there, at Long Wood.
She kept a nice house, below the next fence,
Where refreshments she gave, for two and sixpence,
But now she is gone from under the hill,
And her place is now taken, by me—Sally Phil.
And now I shall tell you of other great things,
About the great man, who was king of the kings.
In October fifteen, he came to this place,
As then he had clos'd his political race.
He died at Longwood, in the good month of May,
And if I am right, 'twas on the third day,
And just at the moment, of setting of sun,
For the year was one thousand, eight twenty-one.
At his house at Long Wood, he was laid out in state,
Where he lay to be view'd both early and late,
For two full good days, his corpse could be seen,
By Inhabitants—all—both rich, poor, and mean.
Four coffins were made, with care and great pains,
To safely secure Boney's precious remains,
And now my good Captain, I wish you to learn,
That his stomach was placed, in a new silver urn,
His heart by the Surgeons, in slices was cut,
Which between silver soup plates, were carefully put,
And these were fill'd up, with the very best sort
Of rum from Jamaica, in town, could be bought,
The edges were solder'd, and strongly secured,
And immediately after, the rum was in pour'd
Both these with some coins, were also encased,
And his hat 'twixt his legs, was carefully placed,
When his coffins, of tin, mahogany and lead,
Were soon closed up, with the hero then dead.
Procession now formed—and proceeded to go,
By command of the Governor—Sir Hudson Lowe,
Who with Admiral Plampin, Montholon and Bertrand
Follow'd next to the hearse, in front of the band.
Then Madame Bertrand, her children and priest,
Which with servants and others were greatly increased.
Now Soldiers, Militia, Inhabitants all,
Including the four who held up the pall,
Amounted to three thousand persons at least,

ST. HELENA

The sight, my good Captain, was quite a great feast.
Procession now mov'd, along the high ground,
Which was led by sweet music, of most solemn sound,
One hour then brought it, to 'top of the road,
From whence could be seen, the hero's abode.
Soon orders were given, for procession to halt,
When twelve Soldiers bore him, away to his vault,
And this being done, the workmen were sent,
To build up the grave, with Roman cement.
And large slabs of stone, and thick bars of iron,
To fasten well down, this once daring Lion—
When people dispersed, and went to their home,
A Lieutenant's guard was placed o'er the Tomb.
The Catholic Priest consecrated the grave,
As the then resting place, of Napoleon the brave,
Holy water he sprinkled, and made latin prayers,
Which to learn them, would take me, twelve dozen of years.
When all this was done, and the Coffin lower's down,
The Priest then soon changed, his curious gown,
Field pieces were fir'd—from each three loud rounds,
Which through the near vallies, sent forth their strong sounds.
Minute guns also added, their thund'ring reports,
Which were carefully fir'd, from off all the forts,
Where colors, half masted, were also display'd,
And the Shipping and Consulates, like respect paid.
The Tomb has been watch'd while Bonny lay there,
His remains did not go, 'till the twenty-fifth year,
When the French Prince de Joinville, came here on the wing,
With orders he had, from his father the King.—
To exhume the brave hero, from where he did lay,
And with the "Belle Poule" to take him away,
So off he then went, after twenty-five years,
And ever since then, I have shed floods of tears.
And now my good Captain, I farther must say,
When down in the tomb, they Bonny did lay,
In a chamber they put him, just eight feet one deep,
Into which not a soul, could ever once peep,
Six feet and one inch, is the breadth of the grave,
And with thick Portland stone, they the bottom did pave,
When his body was laid, by the Catholic Priest,
His head was plac'd west, and the feet to the east.
And now I would have you, to well understand,
Some flowers were planted, by Madam Bertrand,
And these I assure you, were call'd if you please,

ST. HELENA

In French *Flower de Luce* and in English *Hearts ease*.
Now Sally has told you, a very long tale,
At this place which she named, *Napoleon Vale*,
Then let my man Jack, a clean tumbler bring,
Fill'd with clear water, from dear Bonnys spring,
And here my good Captain, is a box full of willow,
And one of the sprigs, to put under your pillow,
And as we have lately, had sev'ral fine showers,
I'm enabled to give you, some sweet smelling flowers.
Then with gold my kind Captain, I hope you'll endorse,
The patience of Jack, who is holding your horse,
And when you are gone, I assure you, you will,
Be remember'd with thanks—by—Poor Sally Phil.
And another nice thing, I will tell about oil,
Which to think of, has oftentimes made my blood boil,
Some sweet oil he wanted, to eat with his beans,
So he sent Cipriani, who went to *Tom Green's*,
When six dozen quarts, were order'd and sent,
But the same through the hands of Sir Hudson Lowe went,
When tasted in town, was pronounced very good,
But not so when up, at the house at Long Wood,
For Bonny, decided, the oil was no go,
As it came under notice, of Sir Hudson Lowe,
The oil was repack'd and sent back as bad,
Which made poor Tom Green, look foolish and sad;
But Green, not so *green*, in this trap to be caught,
Two pint bottles made, out of every quart,
And soon he made known, he had lately bought,
A beautiful oil, of a much better sort,
And if they would buy,—to Longwood it should go,
And quite unbeknown, to Sir Hudson Lowe.
The answer was "yes"—it was off in a trice,
And away it was smuggled, at twice the first price.
The oil now arriv'd—and safe at Long Wood,
Being so smuggled up, was pronounced very good.
And now let me tell you,—when Bonny did land,
The yards of his ship, were crowded and mann'd
'Twas the *seventy-four* called the *Northumberland*.
And one of the suite, was Doctor O'Meara,
To give his attendance, upon the great hero,
His honor was pledged, not to speak nor yet write,
Anything politic, to induce Bonny's flight
Lascassas—Bertrand—Gourgoud—Montholon,
Madam Bertrand, and Lascassas's son,

ST. HELENA

With valets and cooks, all in number complete,
Made up the whole lot, of Napoleons suite.
The Admiral—General—with Bonny in tears,
On a tuesday they landed, at the lower stairs,
And for him there was got, the best house in Town,
'Twas hir'd and paid for, at charge of the crown,
Fifty five pounds per week, was the price it is said,
To Porteous the owner, the Government paid:
Bonny slept at this house, for only one night,
As the following morning, just at broad day light,
He and the Admiral, went off without food,
On their horses to have a good look at Long Wood:
Which when they had seen, and returning to town,
They both on the Briars, chanc'd to look down;
When Buonaparte said, he prefer'd to go there,
Than pass thro' the crowd, who at him would stare.
The owner was there, the good Mr. Balcombe,
Who told Buonaparte, he was certainly welcome,
To have both his houses, and gardens and fruit,
And also his furniture, and servants to boot.
But another strange thing good Captain I'll state,
You will hardly believe, when it I relate.
In the very same room where Napoleon repos'd,
Wellington, when Wellesley, often times dozed;
And to this I must add, when Buonaparte died,
Some sailors stood very close, by the tombs side,
Who had on their hats, "Ship Waterloo" painted,
When seen, it so struck me, I thought I had fainted.
And another thing also, I beg to remark,
The *Waterloo* ship, and *Belle Alliance* bark,
At anchor in safety, they both of them lay,
Quite close to the Flag Ship, in Saint James's Bay,
When Bonny in state, at Longwood did lay.
And to render the tomb, most perfect and snug,
They had from a platform, some stones which they dug.
And more circumstances, now I must let you know,
About Buonaparte, and Sir Hudson Lowe;
At Longwood a Captain, was put to look out,
To see what Napoleon, was alway about;
He was ordered to see, Bonny every day twice,
A duty it was, I should say far from nice:
At Longwood the signals, were plac'd on a pole,
And pass'd to the Governor, through the post at High Knoll,
The purport of which, was the Governor to tell,

411

That Buonaparte was, both safe and quite well.
Another great fact, I would wish you to know,
About our good Governor, Sir Hudson Lowe;
The Government order'd him, to take great care,
To lay out no more, than *twelve thousand* a year,
As ev'ry expenditure, that sum shall meet,
For Bonny himself, and also his suite:
Napoleon however, soon took a great huff,
Complained that the money was not near enough;
But Sir Hudson replied, that altho' he felt sore,
And altho' very sorry, he could not give more,
As his orders were such, he must strictly obey,
And could not, and dare not, one shilling more pay.
Then—Bonny and suite, poor Sir Hudson did vex,
And they did all they could, this man to perplex,
Multiplied all their wants, in many a score,
And said they must have, *six thousand pounds* more.
Sir Hudson not wishing, to have any fight,
Replied—to his Government, he would then write,
And hoping a favorable, answer would come,
He ordered the payment of this good round sum.
He stated—if Government, then should refuse it,
That he, good Sir Hudson himself must then lose it:
Months hardly had gone, when Bonny again,
Recommenced to put, poor Sir Hudson in pain.
And stating that now, as his purse was quite bare,
Demanding a further, *six thousand* a year;
This astonish'd Sir Hudson, and made him feel sad,
So he said that he thought, it was really too bad.
However—he said, he could no more advance.
Not if Bonny was even, the Emperor of France:
And altho' his refusal, was thought odd or funny,
The prisoner now, must use all *his own* money.
Yes—to this Bonny said, and felt quite content,
If Sir Hudson would only, give up his consent:
Consent now was had, and Napoleon then told,
That a firm in the town, would advance him the gold:
On condition however, which Bonny must know
That his bills on the backs, must be signed "Hudson Lowe."
So then every month, there were *five hundred pounds*,
Paid over to Bonny, in gold and half crowns,
They seem'd then contented, to all outward signs,
But imprisonment rankled, in all of their minds.
A Chinaman who, was employ'd at Longwood,

ST. HELENA

To carry from town, a part of the food,
Was like in his person, perhaps not in heart,
Exactly the counterpart, of Buonaparte.
Both his face and his mouth, and his nose and his eyes,
As well as his frame, and his walk and his size.
He was much like the Emperor—resembled him so,
That when it was known, to Sir Hudson Lowe,
He sent forth his orders, the very same day,
Commanding the Chinaman, quickly away.
Sir Hudson now thought he ought fairly suppose,
That the pris'ner might use the Chinaman's clothes,
To get off the Island, in such a disguise,
And therefore thus acted—in which he was wise.
One anecdote more, to your notice I'll bring,
When Bonny came down to visit the spring,
He got under shelter, of all these nice trees,
Where he felt himself cool by the fan of the breeze.
A book now he open'd, and in it did peep,
And in a short time, he fell fast asleep,
Then Madame Bertrand, who was on Bonny's right,
Was sensibly struck, at this novel sight,
And whilst looking at him, to her it did seem,
That Bonny was then, no doubt in a dream.
One hour soon pass'd, and the charm was then broke,
The sleeper refresh'd,—and then he awoke.
He dream'd that his Josephine, to him so dear,
Had died, and her body, was buried just near,
And hence he express'd, that it was his desire,
That one sacred thing he would strongly require,
Which was if at Longwood, or elsewhere he died,
He might there be buried, at Josephine's side.
When the New House was finished and fill'd with nice things,
Needful and useful, for this mighty of kings,
Then, so soon as Napoleon, was offer'd the keys,
Now, that was the time he Sir Hudson did teaze.
Bertrand sent them back, on the very same day,
With a message from Buonaparte, which went to say,
That the house was *not* finish'd,—it wanted some gutters,
And also the windows, they all wanted shutters.
So then all the Carpenters, poor, good, and best,
Sir Hudson immediately put in request,
And to work they all went, and took the best pains,
To finish the job, with their saws, nails, and planes.
The timber they used, was fir, oak and teak,

And the whole was completed within a short week,
The keys now sent back, which Bonny soon learn'd
Were by his directions, most quickly return'd,
With Sir Hudson the messenger had a long talk,
Who said, gravel they wanted, on every walk,
Then Sir Hudson employ'd, all the carts and the drays,
And he gravel'd the walks, in three or four days,
But just as the last load, came over the hill,
Poor Bonny was taken, most awfully ill,
Alarm now was felt, and the news quickly spread,
And in fourteen days time, poor Bonny was dead.
And now I will tell you, about an earthquake,
For it made all the houses, and furniture shake;
Eighteen Hundred & Seventeen, on Sunday night,
Poor Sally and others, were put in a fright.
The month was July, and the clock half-past nine,
When I was out walking, with friends on the Line;
The shock was most sudden, and frighten'd us all,
And I ran away screeching, and had a bad fall;
Recovered and up, I did very soon meet,
Dear Mrs. Fernandez, then out in the street,
The moment she saw me, she ran face to face,
And before I could turn I felt her embrace.
In hugging me up, she gave me a squeeze,
So I fainted and fell, right down on my knees;
The weight of this lady, was full twenty stone,
She was nearly all fat, with scarce any bone.
In her fright she exclaimed, she expected to be,
In five minutes more, in the depths of the sea.
At Longwood Napoleon, had just gone to bed,
And he scarce on his pillow, had laid down his head,
When Marshand sprang in,—to the Emperor said,
An Earthquake there was!—and he felt as tho' dead.
Bonny just turn'd his head, and at him did peep.
And with thundering voice, cried out *Bah* like a sheep.
And getting his bed clothes, right up in a heap,
He turn'd himself over, and fell fast asleep;
For Earthquakes you know, Buonaparte did not care,
As he felt many shocks, for many a year.
One thing more of Bonny, I now must relate,
When up at Longwood he was lying in state,
Which was—when the corpse, was fully prepared,
And the hero was shav'd, of his last growing beard,
The stomach remov'd—and also the heart,

ST. HELENA

Of the great and renown'd N. Buonaparte.
His uniform coat, was of deep bottle green,
And the cloth was the finest, that ever was seen;
On his shoulders two epaulets, made a display,
But remember this was, on the fifth day of May.
His waistcoat was made, of the best kerseymere,
The color of which was uncommonly rare;
His boots very long; and quite large in their size,
And they reach'd past his knees, quite up to his thighs,
His sword of Marengo,—being awful in taste,
On his left hand by Bertrand, was carefully placed,
A crucifix made, out of silver did rest,
In a most striking manner with care on his breast.
His cock'd hat was put, on the crown of his head.
Which made him look martial, altho' he was dead,
He lay on the bedstead, he used in his wars,
The curtain thrown back, being made of fine gauze.
At the head of the corpse, stood his General Bertrand,
And at foot Montholon, also took up his stand;
At the altar there was, the old priest at his prayers,
At which there were burning, Roman candles in pairs.
And General Gourgaud did take up his stand,
Quite close to the elbow, of General Bertrand.
The ceilings and walls, of the room were all clad,
With finest black cloth, which made things look sad,
The floor of the room, was twenty feet square,
And the height of the same, twelve feet in the clear.
In forties the people, then pass'd to the door,
And ranged themselves standing, erect on the floor.
Remaining five minutes—on Bonny they gazed,
And many there were, who appear'd quite amaz'd,
When these forty had then felt themselves gratified,
Then forty more viewers, changed place by *his* side.
By these well plan'd means, all had a good sight,
The high and the low,—the black and the white.
When first at the corpse, I had had a fair peep,
Bonny looked as if, he was quite fast asleep,
And altho' he laid there, with all certainty dead,
He appeared to us all, that he had just gone to bed.
His face was as smooth, as bright polish'd glass,
And his hands were as small, as a fifteen year lass;
Neither wrinkle nor furrow, to me did appear,
On his forehead or cheeks—for all these were quite clear.
His skin to my mind, did really look sallow,

It approached in color, to a pale looking yellow.
And further kind Captain, I think I am right,
When I say he was five feet, five inches in height;
A cast of his face, good Sir Hudson did take,
With plaster of Paris, which with care they did bake.
And then came the scissors, to cut off his hair,
Ah! that was the act, that started the tear;
Then his locks were dispersed, with scrupulous care,
His last living hours, were watch'd night and day,
For attention was paid, to hear what he'd say;
Of his son and the army, he often did speak,
But very soon was he taken, most fearfully weak.
His last effort made, was as if inspired,
And without groan or struggle, he quickly expir'd;
It was just at this time, some papers were found,
In a roll—and the same, were with twine tightly bound,
They into the fire, were thrown in a hurry,
But the person who did it, was in such a flurry,
That they flew past the fire, to back of the grate,
Which obtain'd for them all, quite a different fate.
The sheets tho' much scorch'd were most easily read,
And they all appertain'd, to the hero then dead;
This circumstance over, the Island soon spread,
And the writer well known, at least so 'twas said.
Reports got abroad, that Sir Hudson did say,
That if at this Island, he longer did stay,
He would send this nice person, most quickly away,
Who in England, the penalty of law he should pay,
But by some means or other, the thing was past over,
Which prevented his seeing, the white cliffs of Dover.
I also good Captain, to you must unfold,
The account which to others, has often been told,
About Bonny's remains, when the same were exhumed,
To be buried in France, as his nation had doom'd.
The persons who had, all this matter to do,
Were—for the French King, the Count de Chambo,
And on part of the English, the chief Engineer,
For these two great persons, Commissioners were.
After each to the other his power did show,
To the job the Commissioners, and workmen did go;
With pick axe and shovels, they dug all the night,
But reached not the coffin, 'till next morning's light.
The men work'd quite hard, and did labor and toil,
And they had to remove, many tons of the soil;

ST. HELENA

At the Masonry work, their backs were quite bent,
The stones being bedded, in Roman cement.
The first things remov'd, were the slabs and the rail,
Then commenc'd they to dig, but at at this they did fail.
Which obliged them to open the Tomb at the side,
And they made excavation, extremely wide,
The chamber now enter'd,—the coffin was seen,
Which appear'd quite uninjured—was smooth and quite clean,
Their labors with every, success being crown'd,
The coffin was lifted, to top of the ground.
The Commissioners order'd, it then to be sent,
Away a few yards, into a nice tent,
Where the Catholic Priest, with his book and his prayers,
Stood by with Bertrand, and Gourgoud in tears.
A guard of Militia, surrounded the tent,
Into which but a very few persons were sent;
Of the guard Captain Kennedy, had the command,
And he sentries placed, round the Tomb in a band.
The Doctor then near to the corpse took his stand.
And held a sharp auger, most firm in his hand:
I peep'd in the tent, and there I espied,
That he bored a large hole, in the Coffins right side.
To let all the foul air, escape if it could,
Thro' the Coffins which were, made of Tin, Lead, and Wood,
When these were unsolder'd, and nicely unscrewed,
Then Bonny's remains, were scrupulously view'd,
The Doctor quite thoughtful, and anxious and calm,
Sprinkled chemical liquid, to check any harm,
The piece of white satin, which lay on his face,
They tried to remove, right away from its place,
But sticking so close, it adher'd to the bone.
So the Commissioners said, it was best let alone,
On boring the auger, thro' coffin and clothes,
It unfortunately broke, the bridge of his nose:
Quite mouldy appear'd, both his hat and his clothes.
And from holes in his boots, you could see all his toes.
But when Buonapart's hand, was exposed and made bare,
Most contented and satisfied, all did appear,
When the corpse was identified,—carefully view'd,
The Coffins were solder'd, and as before screw'd,
Except the one outside—in pieces was broken,
And pass'd all around, as a most solemn token.
These things being done, with quickest of haste,
Then in the Sarcofagus, the coffins were placed.

Sarcofagus closed—lock'd up and secur'd
To the French then poor Bonny, was once more restor'd?
The key was then given, to Count de Chabo,
To unlock this box holding, John Bull's former foe;
Then a hearse with four horses, in harness was brought,
With a Pall brought from France, of a curious sort—
Purple Velvet 'twas made of, and sprinkled with bees,
And an N in each corner, work'd in gold if you please;
There were on it, gold eagles, and crowns to amaze,
Which with tassels and ermine, shone out in a blaze.
Twenty-five thousand francs, for this Pall it was said,
In France by the King, for this purpose was paid,
In the front of the Hearse, was the priest Coquero,
Then next came two Choristers, dress'd in robes, but who
Carried Censer and Crucifix—in strange-like style,
Which astonish'd most persons, in this our small isle.
The horses by grooms, in deep mourning were led,
In black harness to drag, down the hero then dead;
Gourgaud and Lascases, and Monsieur Marchand,
Bore up this rich Pall, with General Bertrand.
Then came Bonny's servants, in mourning quite deep,
And for their great Master, they sadly did weep;
Next follow'd in order the Count de Chabo,
With three Naval Captains, who walk'd two and two.
Then Arthur Bertrand, and the Surgeon, who were
All the time on their march, with their heads very bare,
Next follow'd Inhabitants, and Officers too,
Who with Strangers and others, were not a few.
Behind were the Regiment—Militia before,
And in rear of the whole—General Middlemore;
Who on foot paced the roads, up and down the steep hill,
Notwithstanding he then, felt himself very ill.
The drums and the fifes, solemn music did play,
Before the procession, down all the long way;
The procession arriv'd in the town very late,
Before it did go, thro' the principal gate;
Which when both the Hearse, and the people had past,
Was quickly closed up, and made firm and fast.
To prevent the great crowd, from causing disorder,
And this was according, to Government order,
The Troops and Militia, formed a street very wide,
Who faced the procession, on the right and left side.
At last the procession, got down to the Crane,
Which for two or three hours, had been in the rain;

When good Prince de Joinville, and all his large suite,
At the wharf the said Governor, there then did meet,
Who close to the Hearse, he took up his stand,
And paid his respects, with hat in his hand;
Then deliver'd the hero, in form the most solemn,
Which fully to tell you, would fill a large volume.
Whilst procession was passing, just after the Hearse,
The arms of the Soldiers, were held in reverse;
Both at the commencement, and whilst it did last,
All the flags in the place, were display'd at half mast.
And all from the forts, and shipping were fired,
Salutes without number, which were much admired:
Sarcophagus now, was plac'd safely in slings,
And into the Launch, lower'd the might of kings;
The Band of the Prince, played music most rare,
Overwhelming it was, for any to hear.
The moment the body, was in the Launch lower'd,
Then the guns of the frigate, three salvoes they pour'd;
The Sun in the West at that moment went down,
Which was with delight, view'd by all in the town.
The flash from the cannon, produced such a light,
Through the masts, yards, and rigging, most pleasing to sight,
The Launch held French officers, fifteen in all,
And amongst them were those, who were bearing the pall;
The pullers who row'd, were in number two scores,
And with greatest precision, they feather'd their oars;
All the boats from the *Belle Poule*, and *Favourite* also,
When placed in their stations, commenc'd then to row.
Each oar together, they did lift and did dip,
And the boats kept due distance, from shore to the ship;
The boats now alongside, and corpse safe on board,
Then the guns from the frigate, a second time roar'd.
And now came the time for the priest and his prayers,
For most of the people, were melted in tears.
They held a high mass, for most of that night,
Which with light of their candles, was quite a great sight;
They had in the ship, a nice *Chapel ardent*,
Into which Bonny's corpse, was safely sent.
The size of this Chapel, I think was quite near,
To the best of my memory twenty feet square,
Impressed ever since, has it been on my mind,
That the Chapel was with, the best black velvet lin'd.
And 'twas sprinkled all over with nice silver bees,
And tassels and cords, of like sort if you please,

There were three or four pyramids, made out of tin,
Which had many sockets, to put candles in;
A gilt ball of wood, from the desk was suspended,
Which they told us on board, was meant and intended,
As an emblem of justice, to honor the dead,
And therefore was placed, right over his head.
I carefully look'd and nigh at one side,
An altar and crucifix—soon I espied;
An N for Napoleon, in gold was inlay'd;
On top of Sarcophagus, when it was made.
Days and nights on the deck, they had prayer and some masses,
For the quiet repose, of Buonapartes ashes;
No doubt all these things, did afford a great feast,
To Padre Cockero, the Catholic Priest.
The yards of the Frigate, were crossed like an X,
And the masses and prayers, were held on the decks;
Holy water was sprinkled, in every direction,
The same being done, with much circumspection.
All the time they display'd, all their colors half masted,
Just as long as the whole of the ceremonies lasted,
When the Frigate *Belle Poule*, left the shores of her France,
Towards this good Island, she was slow to advance,
This was done by the Prince, as it fully appears,
To make Bonny's tarry, just twenty-five years.
Alive dead, and buried, the prisoner had been,
As you know he arrived here, in *one, eight, fifteen*,
A matter of history, this thing was to be,
As it just made one fourth, of a long century.
Two beautiful flags, they display'd in the boat,
Which from shore to ship, in the air they did float,
On the top of the staffs, black crepe was there placed,
In a curious manner, and also with taste.
In advance of the Barge, was the Princes' fine band,
And then all the *Belle Poule's*, long yards were full man'd,
On the Barges right bows, the boats number'd four,
And on the port side, there were three large boats more,
From the *Belle Poule's* mast head, right down to the water,
Scores of flags were display'd over stern, bows and quarter.

In 1875 Sally Phil's poem was reprinted as a quarto-size pamphlet
by the *Guardian*, at the expense, it is believed, of an aged merchant,
Mr. C. A. Carrol, who had been a young man when Napoleon died.
The only copy known to exist is, at present, in the collection of
Dr. Paul Wilkinson.

ST. HELENA

The title-page is as follows:

An Account of the late Emperor Napoleon the First
At Saint Helena.
From his Arrival there in 1815,
To his Death & Burial in 1821
also
The Exhumation of his Remains
for Conveyance hence to France in 1840.

By an Old Inhabitant.
Saint Helena 1st. January 1875.

———

Copy-right secured.

———

VI

GOVERNORS OF ST. HELENA

FROM the first possession by the English East India Company, 1657, with the dates on which they assumed the Government.

John Dutton	1657
Robert Stringer	1661
Richard Swallow (Acting) . . .	1670
Richard Coney	1671
—— Bennett (Acting) . . .	1672
Anthony Beale	1672

The Island was captured by the Dutch on the 1st January, 1673, and "Dyke" is supposed to have been the name of the Dutch officer who held the Government until Munden re-took it on the 7th May the same year.

Sir Richard Munden	1673
Captain Richard Kedgwin, Keigwin or Kelinge	1673
Captain Gregory Field	1674
Major John Blackmore . . .	1678
Captain Joshua Johnston . . .	1690
Captain Richard Keeling . . .	1693
Captain Stephen Poirier . . .	1697
Captain Thomas Goodwin (Acting) . .	1707
Captain John Roberts . . .	1708
Captain Benjamin Boucher . . .	1711
Captain Matthew Bazett (Acting) . .	1714
Captain Isaac Pyke	1714
Edward Johnson, Esq. . . .	1719
Edward Byfield, Esq. (Acting) . .	1723
Captain John Smith	1723
Edward Byfield, Esq. (A second time) .	1727
Captain Isaac Pyke (,, ,, ,,) .	1731
John Goodwin, Esq. . . .	1738

Duke Crispe, Esq. (Acting) 1740
Captain Robert Jenkins 1740
Major Thomas Lambert 1742
George G. Powell, Esq. (Acting) . . . 1742
Colonel David Dunbar 1744
Charles Hutchinson, Esq. 1747
John Skottowe, Esq. 1764
Daniel Corneille, Esq. 1782
Colonel Robert Brooke 1787
Lieutenant-Colonel Francis Robson (Acting) . 1801
Colonel Robert Patton 1802
Lieutenant-Colonel William Lane (Acting) . 1807
Major-General Alexander Beatson . . . 1808
Colonel Mark Wilks 1813
Lieutenant-Colonel Sir Hudson Lowe, K.C.B. . 1816
Thomas Henry Brooke, Esq. (Acting) . . 1821
Brigadier-General Alexander Walker . . 1823
Thomas Henry Brooke, Esq. (second time, Acting) 1828
Brigadier-General Charles Dallas . . . 1828

Island taken over by the Crown from the H.E.I. Company.

Major-General George Middlemore, C.B. . 1836
Colonel Hamelin Trelawney . . . 1842
Lieutenant-Colonel G. C. Fraser (Acting) . 1846
Lieutenant-Colonel J. Ross (Acting) . 1846
Major-General Sir Patrick Ross, G.C.M.G.,
K.C.B. 1846
Lieutenant-Colonel Clarke (Acting) . . 1850
Colonel Sir Thomas Gore Brown, K.C.M.G.,
C.B. 1851
Colonel H. N. Vigors (Acting) . . . 1854
Sir E. H. Drummond Hay, Kt. . . . 1856
Admiral Sir Charles Elliott, K.C.B. . . 1863
Hudson Ralph Janisch, Esq. (Acting) . . 1870
Vice-Admiral C. G. E. Patey . . . 1870
Hudson Ralph Janisch, Esq. C.M.G. . . 1873
Lieutenant-Colonel Grant Blunt, R.E. (Acting) 1884
W. Gray Wilson, Esq. (Acting) . . . 1887
R. L. Antrobus, Esq. (Acting) . . . 1889
W. Grey Wilson, Esq., C.M.G. . . . 1890
Robert Armitage Sterndale, C.M.G. . . 1897
Lieutenant-Colonel Julian Penrhyn Evans (Acting) 1901
Colonel Price, C.M.G. (Acting) . . . 1902
Lieutenant-Colonel Gallwey, C.M.G., D.S.O. . 1902

ST. HELENA

Henry J. Bovell, Esq. (Acting) . . .	1910
Dr. W. J. J. Arnold (Acting) . . .	1911
Major H. E. S. Cordeaux	1912
Colonel Robert F. Peel	1920
Dr. W. J. J. Arnold (Acting) . . .	1924
Sir Charles Henry Harper, K.B.E., C.M.G. .	1925
Sir Steuart Spencer Davis, C.M.G. . .	1932
Geoffrey C. Kitching, Esq., O.B.E. (Acting) .	1937
H. G. P. Pilling, Esq., C.M.G. . . .	1938

VII
LIST OF BIRDS

THE land birds of St. Helena are, with one exception, of little interest to the ornithologist, for they all have been introduced to the island from other countries.

The exception is the Wire-bird, *Aegialitis sanctae-helenae*, which is the only indigenous bird and the only land bird which was already resident on St. Helena when the island was discovered. Several early travellers described it, which has been noted in the earlier pages of this volume.

The wire-bird is far from being rare and is to be found in uncultivated and stony parts of the island. In shape and habits it much resembles our ring-plover, *Charadrius hiaticula*, but appears to have longer legs.

The following are the names of the birds introduced to St. Helena:

Averdevat, *Estrelda astrid*, from South Africa. One of the commonest birds in the island, wandering from place to place in flocks.

Java Sparrow, *Padda oryzivora*, from Java. Also common in a few localities.

Cardinal, *Euplictes madagascariensis*, from Madagascar.

Canary, *Serinus flaviventris*. As plentiful as the averdevats.

Mynah, *Gracula religiosa*, from India. Introduced in 1829 to keep the cattle free of ticks. The good they do to the cattle is more than countered by the damage they do to the fruit. By 1871 they had almost disappeared but are now only too common.

Rock Dove, *Columba livia*, from Europe. A few live in the cliffs.

Ground Dove, *Geopelia tranquilla*, from New South Wales. These are frequently seen and heard.

Partridge, *Caccabis chukar*, from the Persian Gulf. Cavendish in 1588 reported "great store" of these birds. They still occur in coveys in the more remote parts of the island.

Ring-necked Pheasant, *Phasianus torquatus*, from China. Mentioned by Cavendish in 1588. Are still quite common.

An owl, introduced from South Africa a few years ago. A pair bred in 1937 in the grounds of Plantation House.

Amongst the birds which were introduced, and were once common but are now extinct are the Turkey, *Meleagris gallopavo*, from Mexico, the Guinea Fowl, *Numida meleagris*, from West Africa, a bird which was common when Melliss wrote about it in 1875, and the Peafowl which were killed off about 1820, because of the destruction they did to the crops.

Many other foreign birds were liberated from time to time, with a view to acclimatisation, but without success.

According to Melliss the American mocking bird was introduced some seventy years ago, and in 1852 thrushes, blackbirds, larks and starlings were let loose, but did not establish themselves, nor did Cape pheasants and francolins, which Melliss himself imported. A few years later, Mr. George Moss turned loose a number of English larks at The Briars, but they all disappeared.

Melliss imported and liberated, providentially without success, a "carefully selected lot of English birds, comprising twenty-six London sparrows, five green linnets, seven blackbirds and six thrushes". These were set free at Plantation House, but the sparrows immediately migrated to the houses and more inhabited parts near the town, where they soon increased in number. Melliss's excuse, and one was certainly needed, for introducing the ubiquitous London sparrow to St. Helena was that it was hoped they might assist in destroying the white ants. When, in 1871, Melliss left the island, the sparrows already had greatly increased, and "the other birds also were fairly established, and the song of the thrush was not uncommon in the country woods at early dawn".

Why these birds which at first appeared to flourish and multiply should have died out has not been explained.

Until not long ago the St. Helenians did quite a brisk trade in catching wild birds to sell to the sailors and passengers on calling ships, and the more attractive-looking birds, as the averdevats, the orange cardinals and the yellow, sweet-singing canaries, were in danger of becoming extinct. Then a law was passed making it illegal to trap or sell wild birds, and these species have become abundant again.

Of sea-birds there are eight species, other than rare or infrequent wanderers:

Right-whale-bird, *Procellaria glacialoides*.
Mother Carey's Chicken, *Thalassidroma melanogaster*.
Booby, *Sula*.
Man-of-War Bird, *Tachypetes aquilus*.
Tropic-bird, *Phaeton æthereus*.
Egg-bird, *Sterna fuliginosa*.
White-bird, *Gygis candida*.
Noddy-Tern, *Anous stolidus*.

In a short description of St. Helena which occurs in Ogilby's *Apuca*, published in 1670, these Noddy terns or Meaws are spoken of as follows:

> On the Cliff-Islands, at the South side of this, are thousands of grey and black Meaws, or Sea Pies, and also white and colour'd Birds, some with long, and some with short Necks, who lay their Eggs on the Rocks; and so unaccustomed to fear, that they suffer themselves to be taken up with the Hand, and gaze at their Surprizers, till knock'd on the head with sticks.

There are no snakes nor lizards on the island; but numbers of geckoes, which do not frequent the houses and verandas as in India and the East, but appear to spend their lives hiding beneath flat stones down in the sweltering valleys.

There is one tortoise which lives in the grounds of Plantation House. It is of colossal size and is said to be the only living link in the world with Napoleon Bonaparte. It is supposed to have come originally with two others from Mauritius. One of the three died in 1877 and its shell may be seen at the London Natural History museum in the Cromwell Road.

The second fell over a cliff in 1918, broke its shell and died. The survivor continues to pursue its sombre, dignified life in the grounds of Plantation House. When caressed, that is to say, prodded or smacked, it emits alarming hissing noises, but is in reality of a friendly disposition.

According to Professor H. F. Gadow in the *Encyclopedia Britannica*, this specimen was brought to St. Helena more than one hundred and thirty years ago, but even Professor Gadow could hazard no opinion of its age, which island tradition puts down as two hundred years. Mr. H. W. Parker, of the British Museum, has identified the St. Helena giant tortoise as *T. elephantina*, a species from the Seychelle Islands.

Of native frogs and toads there are none, but there is one frog, *Rana Grayi*, Gray's frog, of South Africa, which abounds in every rivulet and pool above the altitude of about one thousand feet. They love to squat in the cool shade of the big leaves of the water yams and emit their rasping song. These frogs owe their existence in St. Helena to a Miss Phoebe Moss, member of a distinguished St. Helena family, who brought some live specimens from Cape Colony in 1885, and liberated them at The Briars.

VIII

THE HISTORIANS OF ST. HELENA

THERE have been three histories written of St. Helena, by Brooke, Melliss and Jackson.

The first by T. H. Brooke, Secretary to the Government and twice Acting Governor of St. Helena in 1821 and 1828, was published in 1808, and was followed by a second edition in 1824, which included an account of Napoleon's captivity.

The second by J. C. Melliss, who was Colonial Surveyor, a post which his father had held before him, was published in 1875, and is more concerned with the geology, fauna, flora and meteorology of the island than with its history. Out of a total of four hundred and eight pages, only forty-five deal with the last subject. It is well illustrated by coloured plates.

The third historian of St. Helena was E. L. Jackson, whose *St. Helena: The Historic Island* was published in 1903. It is a work full of useful information but sadly in need of "editing". It lacks an index. It is profusely illustrated by photographs, far too many being of groups of British soldiers who guarded the Boer prisoners. Undue space is allotted to this subject in the text. All the same, it is a useful work of reference.

The author was a woman remarkable for her energy and her gift for organization.

St. Helena stands to-day in sore need of such another helper.

A prominent resident of the island has kindly written for me the following short biography of Mrs. Jackson.

Emily Louise Jackson, née Warren, was the fourth of a family of thirteen. Both her parents were school teachers. She came out under three-year contract to the Colonial Government as Head-Mistress of the Girls' School and would seem to have been an asset to a rather dull community. She sang well and was a born organizer. She introduced Maypole dances and children's plays such as

"The Rose Queen", etc., amongst school children, who were found easily taught, born dancers, and delighted with the costumes made of cheap muslins, etc.

With these she began giving entertainments and raising large sums for local charities. With variation, no one tired of them and occasionally too she gave an adult concert when a ship was in port.

On completion of her contract she married Thos. Jackson, a Durham man, Chemist and Dentist—a childless marriage.

In one of her visits home to Devon she conceived the idea of starting a lace industry for natives similar to those in Malta, Madeira, and Madagascar, and remained in England some eight months learning Honiton, Torchon and Bucks.

Returning, she found an able assistant in Mrs. McArthur, wife of the Police Sergeant, and the art began slowly to spread. The workers were again quick to learn and very clean.

On another trip she met a Mrs. Porter, wife of H.B.M. Consul to Madagascar and she aided with prickings of Madagascar, Indian and Chinese lace. This work Mrs. Jackson thought too beautiful to be done in cheap cottons and insisted on reproducing in Knox's Kilbirnie Thread with life-long wear.

Classes so increased and lace-making so improved that it became necessary to make some teachers out of the earlier pupils, thus establishing country classes.

Colonel Gallwey, then Governor, became very interested in Mrs. Jackson's work and got into touch with the Home Government for a grant. This was delayed a year or two, however. Mrs. Jackson in the meanwhile started a Boys' Industrial Institute on self-made funds, got a gift of a small lathe and had boys taught to make bobbins for the girls, at a nominal value. Other boys she taught to make fillets for the girls to work upon.

The Home Government then came in and sent a Miss Penderel Moody, a lace expert, who arrived with a weaving loom, but nothing came of it. It was hand-lace that caught on and the making of worked squares for teacloths, etc.

Miss Moody's arrival, however, polished up the workers and militated against the sale of bad work by beginners, and compelled all work to pass through a scrutiny channel before leaving the island, thus finishing off and commercialising what was undoubtedly Mrs. Jackson's original idea.

Of her early pupils Miss Pritchard of Cambrian House survives and still handles the best work in lace, teacloths, seed, aloe and bead work. Mrs. Jackson died in Capetown in 1923, surviving her husband by five years.

As an organiser she had few equals, and her enthusiasm was such that many found themselves as artistes in concerts, etc., before they knew it.

Shy ones fled at her approach, feeling discretion the better part of valour.

She wheedled me once into a quartette, and after that a series of glees such as "Oh who will o'er the downs so free" and others.

But as a money-raiser for local charities she excelled, thought nothing impossible. In three concerts she raised money for a Broadwood piano for public performances under a committee.

I think she exemplified the term "live-wire".

IX

A MOTOR DRIVE AT ST. HELENA

SUGGESTED route for a motor excursion for a visitor landing at St. Helena for a few hours only.

Starting from the Wharf, and passing through the Main Street of the little town of Jamestown, he will take the following route:

Side Path, The Briars, Alarm Gun, Devil's Punch Bowl, The Tomb, Longwood, Hutts Gate, Halley's Mount, Bates's, Cabbage Tree Road, Stitch's Ridge, Sandy Bay Ridge, Carson's Gate, Bate's Branch, Plantation—inner road—Ladder Hill, China Lane and so back to the Wharf, a drive of about eighteen miles, and one never to be regretted nor forgotten.

BIBLIOGRAPHY

THE following is a list of some of the books, etc., used during the compilation of this volume.

The only attempt hitherto made to form a complete St. Helena Bibliography is that of Mr. G. C. Kitching, of which only twenty copies were printed by Mr. W. E. Henry, the Government Printer at the Castle, Jamestown, in 1937.

Abell, Mrs.: *Recollections of Napoleon at St. Helena,* 1844.

Anderson, A.: *History of Commerce,* 1787.

Anderson. F. C.: *History of the Connection with India and St. Helena of the Family of Findlay Anderson,* 1927.

Anon: *Das kleine Paradiess gezeiget an St. Helenen-Insul,* 1673.

Anon: *Account of the Island of St. Helena,* n.d. [1815].

Anon: *A Few Thoughts for the Stranger and the Resident in St. Helena,* 1868.

Anon: *Most Wonderful Account of a Voyage to the Moon from St. Helena by a Flight of Geese,* 1801.

Anon: *Beschreibung der Insel St. Helena,* 1816.

Anon: *Views of St. Helena,* n.d. [1815].

Barlow's Journal, transcribed by Basil Lubbock, 1934.

Barnes, Capt. J.: *A Tour through the Island of St. Helena,* 1817.

Bazett, M.: *The Bazett Family.*

Beatson, A.: *Tracts relative to the Island of St. Helena,* 1816.

Beazley, C. R.: *An English Garner,* 1903.

Beekman, Capt.: *A Voyage to Borneo,* 1718.

Bellasis, G. H.: *Views of Saint Helena,* 1815.

The Book of Duarte Barbosa, Hakluyt Society.

Boxer, Capt. C. R.: *Uma Desconhecida Victoria Naval Portuguesa no Seculo XVII,* Boletim da agencia geral das Colonias, No. 52 Lisbon, 1929.

Brooke, Col. R.: *An Address submitted to the consideration of the Proprietors of East India Stock.*

Brooke, T. H.: *A History of the Island of St. Helena,* Second Edition, 1824.

Bruce, J.: Annals of the Hon. East-India Company, 1810.

Busteed, H. E.: *Echoes from Old Calcutta,* 1908.

Bye Laws of the Island of St. Helena, St. Helena, 1829.

Chaplin, A.: *A St. Helena Who's Who,* Second Edition, 1919.
                Thomas Shortt, 1914.

Churchill's Collection of Voyages and Travels, 1704.

Clifford, H., in *Blackwood's Edinburgh Magazine,* February, 1903.

Colonial Reports, St. Helena.

Dampier's Voyages, Edited by John Masefield, 1906.

Darwin, Charles: *Voyage of H.M.S. "Beagle",* 1905.

Davis, Sir S. S.: *A Farewell Address,* St. Helena, 1937.
                Mileage of Roads, St. Helena, 1937.

Dictionary of National Biography, 1921–1937.

Downing, Clement: *A Compendious History of the Indian Wars,* 1737.

Duncan, Francis, M.D.: *A Description of the Island of St. Helena,* 1805.

Fay, Mrs. Eliza: *Original Letters from India* (1779–1815), Edited by E. M. Forster, 1925.

Forbes, Prof. E.:*Notes on the Extinct Land-Shells of St. Helena,* Quarterly Journal of the Geological Society of London, Vol. VIII, 1852.

Forsyth, W.: *History of the Captivity of Napoleon at St. Helena,* 1853.

Foster, W.: *Acquisition of St. Helena,* English Historical Review, No. 135, 1919.

Fowler, T. E.: *Views of St. Helena,* St. Helena, 1863.

Fryer, J.: *A New Account of East India and Persia,* 1698.

Gentleman, A: *A Brief Account of the Island of Santa Helena,* 1815.

Gill, Mrs. David: *Six Months in Ascension,* 1878.

Gibbons, Stanley: *Catalogue of Stamps of the British Empire,* 1937.

Gould, R. T.: *Case for the Sea-Serpent,* 1930.

Grant, B.: *A Few Notes on St. Helena and Descriptive Guide,* St. Helena, 1883.

Gray, Rev. R.: *Cape of Good Hope: Journals of Two Visitations,* 1849.

Hakluyt, R.: *Principal Navigations and Discoveries*, Glasgow, 1903.

Hall, Capt. Basil: *Voyage to Java, China, and the Great Loo-Choo Island*, 1840.

Hamilton, A.: *A New Account of the East Indies*, 1930.

Hannay, D.: *Short History of the Royal Navy* (1217–1688), 1898.

Hare, Rosalie: *Voyage of the "Caroline"*, edited by Ida Lee, 1927.

Hickey, W.: *Memoirs* (1749–1775), 1919.

History of the British Possessions in the Indian and Atlantic Oceans, Book IV, St. Helena and Ascension Islands, 1837.

Ingram, B. S.: *Three Sea Journals of Stuart Times*, 1936.

Jackson, E. L.: *St. Helena: the Historic Island*, 1903.

Jameson, J. F.: *Privateering and Piracy in the Colonial Period*, New York, 1923.

Janisch, G. W.: *Three letters written by Georg Wilhelm Janisch*, 1816–1843, St. Helena.

Janisch, H. R.: *Extracts from the St. Helena Records*, St. Helena, 1908.

Kerr, J.: *Views of the Island of Saint Helena*, n.d. [1822].

Kerr, Robert: *Voyages and Travels*, Edinburgh, 1824.

Kitching, G. C.: *A Model of St. Helena*, 1937.
                Notes on Napoleon's Captivity and other papers relating to the History of St. Helena, 1937.
                "The St. Helena Printing-Presses," *Notes and Queries*, December 5, 1936.
                A St. Helena Bibliography, St. Helena, 1937.
                Corrections in the History of St. Helena, Colonial Office Archives, 1934.

Kitson, Sir A.: *Geological Notes on St. Helena*, Colonial Office, 1931.

Knox, Robert: *Historical Relation of Ceylon*, Glasgow, 1911.

Lancaster, Sir James: *Voyages*, Hakluyt Society.

Le Chev. H***y G*****t: *Notice Topographique, Historique, Statistique et Militaire sur L'isle Sainte-Hélène*, Paris, 1815.

Lee, Ida: *Captain Bligh's second voyage to the South Sea*, 1920.

Linnean Society, Proceedings of, Session 147; 1934–35, p. 11.
     Zoological Notes:
         Birds, N. B. Kinnear.
         Sea Elephant, F. C. Fraser, 1935.

Linschoten, J. H. van: *Voyage to the East Indies*, Hakluyt Society.

Luard, Lt.-Col. John: A Series of Views in India, Part X, St. Helena, 1838.

Lubbock, Basil: *The Blackwall Frigates*, 1922.

Macdonald, John: *Travels, 1745–1779, Memoirs of an eighteenth-century footman*, 1927.

M'Leod, J.: *Voyage of H.M.S. "Alcest"*, 1818.

Manwaring, G. E.: *My Friend the Admiral* [James Burney], 1931.

Markham, C. B.: *Life of John Davis*, 1889.

Marten, R. M.: *The British Colonies*, Vol. IV, n.d. [1855].

Melliss, J. C.: *St. Helena*, 1875.
    St. Helena, Royal Colonial Institute Proceedings, Vol. 38.

Melliss, G. W.: *Views of St. Helena*, 1857.

Mundy, Capt.: *Pen and Pencil Sketches in India*, 1832.

Mundy, Peter: *Travels*, Hakluyt Society.

Nicol, John—Mariner: *Life and Adventures*, 1937.
Notes and Queries.

Oliver, P.: *Voyages made by the Sieur D.B., 1669–1672.* For the Hakluyt Society, 1897.

Osorio da Fonseca, J.: *Narrative of the Voyage of Joao Da Nova in 1502,* translated by J. Gibbs, 1752.

Ovington, F.: *A Voyage to Surat*, 1696.

Palmer, W. C.: *History of St. Helena and the Route to the Indies* (1659–1702), 1924.

Phil, S.: *Sally Phil's Tale at the Tomb of Napoleon*, Saint Helena, 1875.

Pillans, D.: *The Real Martyr of St. Helena*, 1913.

Pocock, Lieut. W. I.: *Five Views of the Island of St. Helena*, 1815.

Précis of Information concerning the Island of St. Helena, Janisch and Warren, St. Helena, 1876.

Prior, J.: *Voyage along the Eastern Coast of Africa . . . to St. Helena*, 1819.

Purchas, Samuel: *Purchas his Pilgrimies*, Glasgow, 1905.

Pyke, Isaac: "Twice Governor of St. Helena," reprinted from *Notes and Queries*, 1937.

Pyrard, F.: *Voyage to the East Indies*, Hakluyt Society.

Relation of the Re-taking of the Island of St. Helena, and Three Dutch East-India Ships, 1673.

Rennefort, S. de: *Histoire des Indes Orientales*, Paris, 1688.

Robson, T.: *St. Helena Memoirs*, 1827.

Sainsbury, E. B.: *Court Minutes of the East India Company*, 1664–1667, Oxford, 1925.

St. Helena, The Home Friend, No. 41, 1853.

St. Helena Advertiser, St. Helena, 1865.

St. Helena Almanack and Annual Register, St. Helena, 1881–2.

St. Helena Chronicle, St. Helena, 1852–53.

St. Helena Gazette, St. Helena, 1845–49.

St. Helena Guardian, St. Helena, 1861–83.

St. Helena Herald, St. Helena, 1853–60.

St. Helena Magazine, St. Helena, 1922–1937.

St. Helena Record, St. Helena, 1860–61.

St. Helena Records of Consultations, The Castle, Jamestown.

Seale, R. F.: *Geognosy of the Island St. Helena*, 1834.

Seaton, R. C., *Napoleon's Captivity in Relation to Sir Hudson Lowe*, 1903.

Seller, J.: *A Sea Atlas*, 1682.

Snow, Capt. E.: *The Sea, the Ship and the Sailor*, Marine Record Society, Salem, 1925.

Stack, F. R. and Ward, Mrs.: *Souvenir of the Emperor Napoleon*, 1851.

"Susannicus": A Description of St. Helena, *Gentleman's Magazine*. 1759.

Tavernier, J. B.: *Six Voyages*, Paris, 1676.

Temple, R. C.: *Tragedy of the "Worcester"*, 1704–1705, 1930.

Theal, G. McC.: *Chronicles of Cape Commanders*, Cape Town, 1882.

Tomlin's Geography, 1835

Two Hundred Years of the S.P.G. (1701–1900), 1901.

Valentia, Lord: *Voyages and Travels*, 1809.

Vernon, B. J.: *Early recollections of Jamaica . . . trifles from St. Helena*, 1848.

Walker, General G. W. W.: *Some Account of Philip Patton, Merchant and Baillie of Anstruther, and His Descendants*, n.d.

ST. HELENA

Wallace, Alfred Russel: *Island Life*, 1880.
Warren, E. J.: *Souvenir of St. Helena*, 1937.
Wathen, J.: *Series of Views of the Island of St. Helena*, 1824.
Wollaston, T. V.: *Coleoptera Sanctæ-Helenæ*, 1875.

Young, Norwood: *Napoleon in Exile: St. Helena*, 1915.

INDEX

A. naō Sᵗᵃ Maria
Souta Capitayna

A. naō